HERE'S
THE
DEAL

HERE'S THE DEAL

The Making and Breaking of a Great American City

ROSS MILLER

 NORTHWESTERN UNIVERSITY PRESS
EVANSTON, ILLINOIS

Northwestern University Press
Evanston, Illinois 60208-4210

Northwestern University Press edition published 2003.
Copyright © 1996 by Ross Miller. Introduction copyright
© 2003 by Ross Miller. First published 1996 by Alfred A.
Knopf. All rights reserved.

Printed in the United States of America

10 9 8 7 6 5 4 3 2 1

ISBN 0-8101-2037-2

Library of Congress Cataloging-in-Publication data are
available from the Library of Congress.

The paper used in this publication meets the minimum
requirements of the American National Standard for Information Sciences—Permanence of Paper for Printed Library
Materials, ANSI Z39.48-1992.

For Philip Roth

"My lord do hear me! A piece of land worth four hundred shekels of silver—what is that between you and me? Go and bury your dead." Abraham accepted Ephron's terms. Abraham paid out to Ephron the money that he had named in the hearing of the Hittites—four hundred shekels of silver at the going merchant's rate.

—Abraham negotiating his wife Sarah's grave site
with Ephron the Hittite

Do you know that the price of land has gone up, especially around the city. . . . So the candidates are competing; they're battling to buy up whatever they hear is for sale, and thereby, they're causing more things to be put up for sale. Anyway, if you're sick of your Italian estate, this is the time for selling, Hercules!

—Pliny, A.D. 23–79

A man may not sell above the current price, i.e., such a price as is usual in the time and place, and as another (who knows the worth of the commodity) would give for it, if he had occasion to use it; as that is called current money, which every man will take.

—John Cotton's first principle of proper trading for Christians,
from Governor John Winthrop's *Journal*, 1639

I don't permit lawyers to lean on that thing [lectern]. That was put there by the government, designed by Mies van der Rohe, and I want you to use it for that purpose.

—Judge Julius Hoffman to attorney William Kunstler, 1970

The experts are all saying that our big cities have become ungovernable. What the hell do the experts know?

—Mayor Richard J. Daley, 1971

Such information about corruption, if you had grown up in Chicago, was easy to accept. It even satisfied a certain need. It harmonized with one's Chicago view of society. Naivete was something you couldn't afford.

—Saul Bellow, 1975

CONTENTS

ACKNOWLEDGMENTS

This book was written with generous support from the Graham Foundation for Advanced Study in the Fine Arts, the National Endowment for the Humanities, and the University of Connecticut Research Foundation.

My years in Chicago were made more productive by many people who gave tirelessly of their time and experience. Many sat for long, detailed interviews: Michael Anania, Howard Arvey, Mark Bauman, Paul Beitler, Saul Bellow, Miles Berger, Abel Berland, William Brubaker, John Buck, Wayne Cable, Robert Christiansen, Sonia Cook, William Cowhey, Peter Cunningham, Ivan Dee, Tim Devlin, David Downey, Thomas Foran, Bertrand Goldberg, Geoffrey Goldberg, Bruce Graham, Kenneth Grenier, Jack Guthman, Dennis Harder, Henry Henderson, Lewis Hill, Elizabeth Hollander, Marshall Holleb, Paul Jay, Walker Johnson, Mathew Keller, Eugene Kennedy, Neil King, Thomas Klutznick, Frank Kreusi, Christopher Kuehnle, Francis Lehayne, Lawrence Levy, John Loeb, Carter Manny Jr., Judith McBrien, Vincent McBrien, James McDonough, James McKevitt, Leo Melamed, Vince Michael, Gail Missner, David Mosena, Lawrence Okrent, Chuck Olin, Ann Paden, Keith Palmer, Van Pell, Alexander Polikoff, Alan Prince, George Ranney Jr., Roy Roberts, Richard Ross, William Ryan, Tim Samuelson, George Sax, Samuel Sax, Earl Shapiro, Charles Shaw, Leonard Sherman, Jared Shlaes, Noah Shlaes, Michael Silver, Richard Solomon, Richard Stein, Gardner Stern, Richard Stern, Gene Stunard, Bob Thall, John Vinci, Bernard Weissbourd, Robert Wilmouth, Robert Wislow, Carol Wyant, Samuel Zell.

I was given unusual access to large private and public archives, including the Burnham and Ryerson Libraries at the Art Institute of Chicago; the Chicago Public Library; Municipal Reference Library; Newberry Library; University of Chicago Libraries; Public Building Commission; Skidmore, Owings and Merrill library; University of Connecticut Interlibrary Loan; and Yale University libraries. The current staff of the city of Chicago Department of Planning and Development was especially helpful. I am particularly appreciative of Gregory Longhini and former Commissioner Valerie Jarrett's efforts in opening their department's North Loop files to me. The Realty Club made me feel welcome and something of an honorary member. Aimée Houghton and Andrea Stern were two excellent research assistants. And I am especially appreciative of the assistance of Eric Purchase, who brought a keen critical intelligence to the project.

There are several key individuals in Chicago to whom I feel deeply indebted: C. John Anderson, Thomas Beeby, Rhona Hoffman, Helmut Jahn, Stuart Nathan, John Sweeney, Stanley Tigerman, Michael Tobin, and John Zukowsky.

For two years in Chicago I was scholar-in-residence at the Chicago Institute for Architecture and Urbanism and for six months its program director. I was invited there by the director, Janet Abrams, who generously supported my work and involved me in the general program of the institute. Harold Schiff, chairman of the institute's distinguished board of directors, provided invaluable backing for this book.

INTRODUCTION TO THE 2003 EDITION

BLOCK 37 REVISITED

A decade after I first thought to write Here's the Deal, *Block 37 is still confounding those who thought to master her. While urban renewal has many precipitating causes, the events of September 11, 2001, have demonstrated for another generation that cities will never be immune to sudden catastrophe. A small piece of any big American city considered meticulously can uncover the fundamentally human activity of destruction and renewal.*

Ironworkers and excavators, trained to build, took less than a year to demolish the 100-million-ton "pile" that was once the World Trade Center. With the rubble painstakingly sifted, cleared, and hauled away, Ground Zero revealed little of the 2,801 lives lost on September 11, 2001. Yet even as the catastrophe recedes into history, New Yorkers continue to experience anew the disaster's unfolding consequences. What was a lurid murder scene and graveyard is now just the site of a colossal redevelopment project.

Once America's third-largest central business district (after Midtown and the Chicago Loop), Lower Manhattan, since the attacks, has lost 83,000 jobs and 13 million square feet of office space. The losses do not appear to be temporary. No major company has relocated downtown despite generous tax breaks and grants. On Ground Zero's first anniversary, New York City comptroller William Thompson estimated that the affected square mile of Manhattan had already lost close to $3 billion in taxes and nearly $500 million in unreimbursed expenses. He cautioned that the total economic cost might actually be as high as $95 billion. And yet this is only a down payment on what will surely be the costliest urban disaster in U.S. history.

With so many conflicting constituencies—victims' families, retailers, corporations, and real estate developers—actively involved, there are bound to be expensive delays. One tenant, Cantor Fitzgerald, which lost 658 employees on 9/11, is challenging the federal compensation fund responsible for settling legal claims resulting from the Trade Center collapse. Nothing substantive relating to the rebuilding has been firmly established. Even ownership of the seventy-foot hole at Ground Zero remains unresolved. Two months before the attacks, Larry A. Silverstein leased the complex from the Port Authority of New York and New Jersey for $3.2 billion and therefore has the right to rebuild what was there. After several hastily conceived large tower schemes were met with nearly universal rebuke the call went out worldwide to architects and planners to come up with something better. Three hundred firms applied to the Lower Manhattan Development Corporation (LMDC) for a role in redesigning Mr. Silverstein's property. On September 26, 2002, seven teams of designers, representing twenty-seven architecture and design firms, were chosen by the LMDC to help reconcile all the legitimate competing interests. In mid-December the participants in this "Innovative Design Study" unveiled the results of their eight-week-long charette on the stage of the newly restored Winter Garden at the World Financial Center, which itself had suffered extensive damage from the September 11 attacks. In March 2003, Studio Daniel Libeskind was picked as the finalist. It remains to be seen if any of Libeskind's ideas will ever be built. How much of the site will never be developed at all? How much space will be devoted to a memorial? How much to commercial buildings? Will any of Daniel Libeskind's notions of memorial architecture stand up to Larry Silverstein's more mundane requirements of restoring over 10 million square feet of "Class A" commercial space?

The ways in which this land is finally used will have serious repercussions for generations. It is more than a design problem or a discussion of public mourning. For instance, if a permanent multiblock memorial is built to commemorate the lives lost at the World Trade Center, the massive economic losses will be unrecoverable. Naturally at odds with each other, public and private interests have already joined the battle over Lower Manhattan's "hallowed ground." These conflicts are nothing new. Fighting over valuable land—its ownership and use—is as fundamental to the making of America as the Constitution and the Civil War.

A year and a half ago, ten young men transformed jetliners into smart bombs and brought to bear the force of two small earthquakes on an area no bigger than a small American town. New York City's side-by-side main streets— 125 feet apart—each reached a quarter of a mile into the air. Together the twin buildings contained more than 200 acres stacked one atop the other. On the average workday the towers could easily accommodate 50,000 people. The Twin Towers were perfect targets for anyone wishing to do maximum harm.

When before in history had so many people been fitted so densely into such a small, vulnerable area? It required human genius to recognize such a diabolical opportunity and uncommon planning to execute such slaughter. The World Trade Center carnage was neither a natural disaster nor the unpredictable, undefendable "act of God" that its Islamist perpetrators claimed. Nor were the events of 9/11 and their aftermath without precedent. Like the Hiroshima A-bomb, Dresden firestorm, and London Blitz, the World Trade Tower attacks were premeditated acts of man.

THE PATTERN: DESTRUCTION AND RENEWAL

New York was attacked with extraordinary ferocity on September 11, but the city is no stranger to organized violence. During the Revolutionary War, on September 20, 1776, a few weeks after the Battle of Brooklyn, the British burned to the ground the three- and four-story structures built wall to wall on the World Trade Center site. In the nineteenth century the area was repopulated with hotels, stables, boardinghouses, wholesale dealers, cigar makers, grocers, and other such commercial establishments. The neighborhood continued to develop without the benefit of planning decades beyond the 1930s, when New York City began to be reengineered on the scale of Peter the Great's St. Petersburg and Baron Georges-Eugène Haussmann's Paris. Yet this significant portion of Lower Manhattan was not able to resist autocratic urban renewal forever.

During the second half of the last century, entire residential neighborhoods and business districts in Manhattan and the boroughs were razed to make way for "improvements" such as roads and public housing. The initial instrument for New York's construction mania was a once sleepy public works agency called the Triborough Bridge and Tunnel Authority, revamped in 1933 by Robert Moses, a young technocrat whose earlier planning experience had been limited to the city's obscure Bureau of Municipal Research and the Long Island State Park Commission. But Moses was a quick learner. For three decades under his leadership, the Triborough Authority spearheaded the country's most active urban renewal program. With the power to issue municipal bonds, collect tolls at its bridges and tunnels, and enter into redevelopment deals with other public and private entities, the Triborough Bridge Authority by the 1950s was richer than most countries.

Moses's shrewd consolidation of power and his knack for public financing made him the envy of a rival bureaucracy and sometime partner, the Port

Authority of New York. In the 1960s, just as Robert Moses started to face successful organized opposition to his slum clearance and massive road-building projects, including a crosstown expressway that would have annihilated Greenwich Village, the Port Authority belatedly got into the business of bulldozing whole neighborhoods.

The Port Authority's executive director, Austin J. Tobin, concluded that large-scale commercial development—one of the few areas of urban growth that Moses disdained—was the sort of grand project that could make the Port Authority financially whole and ensure him his own legacy as a city builder. Both Governor Nelson Rockefeller and his brother David, chairman of the Chase Manhattan Bank headquartered downtown in a new steel-and-glass International Style skyscraper, a few short blocks from the World Trade Center site, encouraged Tobin to plunge into the high-stakes office building market. The business community had hopes of reviving the entire square mile around the New York Stock Exchange and investment banks. To this end, the governor got a bill passed in the state legislature that gave Tobin's agency the authority to develop the property, with David Rockefeller's Downtown Lower Manhattan Association providing necessary private collateral. At the time, Manhattan housed 128 of the Fortune 500's largest corporate headquarters, but even those businesses that remained in the New York metropolitan area had started to move north to newer buildings in Midtown or farther out to the Connecticut and New Jersey suburbs. In the early 1960s, Manhattan's historic downtown, like Chicago's Loop and other major central business districts, was in danger of becoming obsolete.

The Port Authority already owned some of the land it needed for what would become the World Trade Center and confiscated the rest through eminent domain. Before the "taking," the neighborhood on Manhattan Island's narrow southern tip had degenerated into a mix of bars, clothing outlets, and one-of-a-kind businesses like violin bow makers and rare-book dealers. Known in its prerenewal final decades as Radio Row, the area was principally a low-rent home to electronics shops and their suppliers. To the Port Authority planners there was not a single structure worth saving. Scores of old buildings on Radio Row were condemned and quickly demolished to make way for acres of inviting new commercial space.

In 1962, the architect Minoru Yamasaki was hired to design and supervise the construction of a seven-building complex containing 10 million square feet. The first building was opened in 1970, followed by the "Twin Towers" and plaza six years later. Public streets that for centuries connected the city grid at its southern end were permanently eliminated and removed from the maps. When completed, two 110-story flat-topped boxes were the world's tallest buildings: tollbooths on the tip of Manhattan taxing the international gateway to America. But Moses's admiring rivals miscalculated. For most of the Towers' tragically aborted life, only government agencies and businesses lured initially by steeply discounted rents were willing to set up shop there. The complex took a decade to post even a modest profit. Like the Cross Bronx Expressway (1948–63), which evicted 1,500 families in East Tremont and Morris Heights, and the aborted Westside Expressway, which would have walled off Manhattan from the Hudson, the World Trade Towers were monuments to bureaucratic violence. Built to make money into perpetuity for a "super government" entity that had completed its original New Deal mandate conceived by FDR's urban planners decades earlier, the World Trade Center was a gargantuan expression of bad urban planning, not the sainted architecture that only through loss has it become.

Because cold-blooded murderers leveled New York's second downtown, considering Ground Zero within the context of other urban disasters is difficult. Yet as long as the rhetoric of patriotism and heroism dominate Ground Zero, remaking the area intelligently will prove impossible. Serious proposals to rebuild defiantly exactly what was destroyed or replace every inch of lost office space are only the worst examples. New York's situation is not unprecedented.

All American cities have had at least some experience with this expensive process of deconstruction: the unbuilding of postwar urban renewal. Expressways in San Francisco constructed after the Second World War with generous federal highway grants have been demolished and carted away to reconnect the city to its waterfront. Providence removed the massive concrete decking that had turned a picturesque river into a parking lot. The still-unfinished "Big Dig" has taken more than fifteen years and $14.6 billion to recover twenty blocks of Boston's historic downtown by demolishing the city's Central Artery, a crumbling two-mile elevated roadway (completed with great fanfare in 1959), and rerouting it underground. After the Second World War, mayors whose cities were spared natural destruction simulated catastrophe with bulldozers and TNT, simply for the intoxicating imperative to rebuild.

THE FEDERAL BULLDOZER COMES TO CHICAGO

In the winter of 1989, when I began writing *Here's the Deal*, the city of Chicago was nearing the end of a long campaign to modernize its downtown. The one man who had concocted this monumental effort was long dead, and the city increasingly mendicant, relying upon the unregulated private real estate market to sustain its growth. A short review of the history will clarify the plot.

The plan to make Chicago over was concocted during the Great Depression when Richard J. Daley was working as an accountant for a meat packer in the old stockyards and volunteering his services to the local alderman after hours. Daley rose quickly within the Democratic political organization. At the time he was elected in 1955 for the first of his six consecutive terms as mayor, not one new building had been built in Chicago in more than thirty years. The Loop—the city's central business district—looked to be in a terminal state of decay. To remedy the situation, Mayor Daley married the bureaucratic ruthlessness of Robert Moses with FDR's capacity for leading the rich in directions they didn't want to go.

Just like Robert Moses, Daley learned a modern form of municipal governance through observing Roosevelt's stewardship of the New Deal. Political and financial institutions had failed after the Crash of 1929. In recognizing that there needed to be a new way of doing business, the president, acting as the nation's ward boss, recruited big-city mayors to oversee the rebuilding projects that would help spend the country out of the Depression. The Triborough Authority in New York City was just one of the new public agencies that spearheaded the national recovery.

Federal money was fed to local agencies for new highways, parks, bridges, beaches—highly visible, high-quality public works. These costly improvements were made to pay for themselves through tolls and increased economic activity. When Richard J. Daley first came into office, a Republican, Dwight D. Eisenhower, was in the White House. The Depression was long over, and the U.S. victory in World War II had ushered in a period of sustained prosperity. But there was no New Deal–type program specifically for America's neglected downtowns. Republicans focused their efforts on the suburbs by building roads and making single-family-home ownership affordable through the Federal Housing Act (1949). Federal money was indirectly available to the cities in the form of large interstate highway grants and public housing allotments, but it tended to be administered far away in Washington and by rural politicians hostile to big-city Democrats of the Daley ilk. Daley wanted to make it appear as if he were delegating executive responsibility. He needed a bureaucratic frame for his boundless ambition, something like the WPA or CCC—impressive-sounding New Deal–era acronyms—that he would run absolutely himself.

Like other skilled Democratic mayors of his day, Daley garnered generous interstate highway funds meant to unite America geographically. The mayor agreed to run multilane roads right through Chicago but only if he could decide exactly where they'd be built. In the late 1950s and early 1960s, Richard J. Daley paved over the neighborhoods of his political rivals and took all the public housing money he could get his hands on to build hundreds of high-rise towers and army-style barracks to collect the city's poor in a seven-mile corridor south of the Loop. But until well into his unprecedented third four-year term, the mayor of Chicago wasn't willing to use the federal bulldozer on the downtown. Until Daley had forged useful alliances with people who could help pay for the expensive rebuilding, he exempted his city center from the sort of urban renewal that was ripping apart American cities from New Haven to Los Angeles.

Keeping the cranes and heavy earthmoving equipment safely away from State and Dearborn Streets and busy tearing up poor neighborhoods was all part of the plan. By quarantining the poor (mostly African American) in public housing and busting up old ethnic enclaves with interstate highways, Daley was not only expediently helping himself but was also pushing forward what he commonly called the "Republican interests." These were the same people whose banks (there was no branch banking in Illinois), insurance businesses, hotels, department stores, corporations, and title companies monopolized the Loop. Without publicly embarrassing them, Daley let it be known that in return for taking care of the corporations' social problems and providing modern highways to transport executives from the suburbs downtown to work, he would ask for a hand in the rebuilding. To this end, Daley appointed major figures from commerce and industry to the Central Area Committee (CAC), an idea that he had come up with right after the war, when he was still an apprentice to Martin Kennelly, the last businessman mayor of Chicago.

The CAC was formally organized in 1956, a decade before the public had any idea that the mayor had extensive plans to revitalize the central business area. Daley handpicked William E. Hartmann to devise an executable master plan. Hartmann was an architect and a partner at Skidmore, Owings and Merrill—a firm just beginning to design and engineer new buildings in Chicago. While Daley organized the businessmen, Hartmann chose the best of the local architecture and engineering community, including Ludwig Mies van der Rohe, the world's most celebrated modern architect, who had a practice in town.

The mayor presided over the Public Building Commission (PBC), his own personal New Deal. With a $100-million credit line provided by local banks like Continental and Northern Trust (collateralized with generous federal urban renewal grants deposited by the city for safekeeping), Daley initiated the long process of condemning property and rebuilding the Loop. He started with a block on Dearborn Street situated between City Hall and Block 37, where, with more than $100 million in PBC bonds (issued in 1959), he built a new state and municipal courts building.

Completed in 1965, the Civic Center was meant to demonstrate that

Chicago's reengineering of its downtown would be of uncompromising artistic quality and that Richard J. Daley's public works would never be second rate. To underscore the uncommon quality of Daley-brand urban renewal, Pablo Picasso donated a monumental public sculpture for the Civic Center's empty plaza. The buildings the mayor initiated were built to be the equal of the Chrysler, Empire State, and Seagram Buildings in New York. His Civic Center (renamed the Richard J. Daley Center after his death) was designed by Chicago architects with international reputations. Teamed with Mies van der Rohe's Federal Center (1961–71), a few blocks south on Dearborn Street, the Civic Center confirmed Mayor Daley as the world's most unlikely patron of modern architecture. And he happily held on to the role of America's master builder until the early 1970s, when all the "Great Society" money siphoned off to the downtown had finally run out.

By the time Block 37 was finally trussed with scaffolding and awaiting demolition in late 1989, it was the last small piece of Daley's original downtown urban renewal puzzle still left out of place. Almost thirteen years to the day, Mayor Richard J. Daley had died on the job of a heart attack. Gone with him to the grave was the unlearnable set of attributes that made him uniquely qualified to run a large urban bureaucracy and discipline Chicago's rich corporate community into joining forces for the public good. The politicians and businessmen who inherited Daley's half-finished initiatives to remake the city were in the dark about how to complete them. Both the public and private sectors reverted to type. What had started as a vast public/private civic partnership to rebuild Chicago ended up as a tawdry land grab and just another bungled urban-planning effort.

So as New York begins to deal with the four-square-block crater at Ground Zero, where is the city of Chicago after more than a decade of trying to rebuild only one parcel of land one-fifth its size? Situated in the heart of America's Second City, Chicago's Block 37 once had its own impressive cast of internationally celebrated architects and engineers, political promises, and corporate allegiances. Yet Block 37 remains an embarrassing hole in the ground. What has happened or, more to the point, what has not happened since we last paid close attention to this block?

BLOCK 37: WHAT HAS HAPPENED SINCE WE LAST LOOKED

On June 20, 2001, Planning Commissioner Alicia Berg announced that the city of Chicago was going to develop this key downtown property on its own. Vacant since 1985, demolished and graded down to bare earth in 1990,

Block 37, bounded by State, Dearborn, Washington, and Randolph Streets, has long been progress's orphan. One of the city's original 141 three-acre sections, the block has been subdivided, bought and sold, burned to the ground in the Great Fire of 1871, bankrupted in the Depression, speculated upon after the Second World War, and targeted for urban renewal in the 1960s. For half a century, two Mayor Daleys have been frustrated by a piece of land that has resisted all their efforts at improvement. On the day Commissioner Berg made her announcement, Block 37 had already cost the city more than $60 million in direct public expenses and many times that in tax shortfalls. FJV (a joint venture comprising three development firms of unequal size), which had confidently contracted to develop the land parcel in 1989, had lost on its own account well over $100 million in expenses and carrying costs. Nearly a quarter of a billion dollars in all has already been squandered on a still-empty block.

When Ms. Berg made the city's long-awaited announcement, she effectively fired the remaining partners of FJV, who had tried everything but in the end had failed to develop a publicly subsidized 2-million-square-foot mixed-use retail-and-office complex for the private real estate market. Although hardly a surprise, why had the city acted so decisively after so many years of drift and indecision? The timing of the commissioner's action was particularly puzzling because FJV's fortunes seemed only recently to be changing for the better. A year earlier, Mayor Daley had reluctantly agreed to a radically "scaled-down" version of the original Helmut Jahn–designed twin-tower retail atrium plan. The beleaguered developers hired a new, less flamboyant architectural firm, lured Lord & Taylor to be an anchor commercial tenant, and got the Marriott chain to build hotel suites in a new residential condominium tower. The developers valued the revised deal at $251 million and were asking the city for an additional $40 million in tax breaks to supplement the millions in public funds already invested in the stalled development. But even with these new subsidies and concessions, FJV failed to deliver. Private financing for the plan evaporated. The architecture looked as bad as the ugliest taxpayer on the block before it was officially declared "blighted" in the 1970s. In one last desperate attempt sure to offend the mayor, FJV offered to build a four-story retail box that would sit in the three-acre site like a fallen soufflé. Abandoning their promise of future condominiums and a big hotel, the developers, in one last mad act, demanded $37 million in public funds simply to break ground. Away on vacation in Ireland, Mayor Richard M. Daley told his aides that he was "very disappointed" with the way things were going. He was determined that finally the city should take over the project that his father as mayor had initiated nearly half a century earlier.

But the mayor had a big problem. *The city no longer owned Block 37.* The city's original 1989 redevelopment deal, which sold three-quarters of the land (gained through condemnation) for a little over $12 million, made no provision for taking the property back. In fact, FJV had an airtight contract to hold on to the 220,000-square-foot block even if it never managed to build anything. If the city wanted the land back, the redevelopment agreement stipulated that it must pay the owners at inflated 1989 prices. In that final year of the last real estate boom, comparable parcels south of the Chicago River were selling for more than $500 a square foot. So instead of quickly getting the block back on the tax rolls and starting to generate the fortune predicted when it was bulldozed, Mayor Daley had to start negotiating again with Neil Bluhm and Judd Malkin, the two lead developers whom his commissioner of planning had unceremoniously fired. The city agreed to pay FJV a minimum of $32.5 million—virtually the last of all the public money available for downtown development—in addition to the original $40 million it paid for the same land in the 1980s. In little more than a decade, Chicago bought Block 37 twice. And paid too much both times. To have any hope of getting it developed, the city would have to give the land away to yet another developer and keep paying millions in various fees to the private sector.

Commissioner Berg is only the most recent in a long line of government officials charged with developing these last stubborn acres of the Loop. Another year had passed between Ms. Berg's announcement that the city would take back the land to the moment Chicago once again secured clear title to Block 37. In the intervening period the city had managed to find another developer to pick up the pieces from FJV. On March 23, 2002, ten firms responded to the Department of Planning's "request for qualifications." A mix of local and out-of-town developers vied for the opportunity to take a crack at finishing off the North Loop. They would in effect be given the land for free. All the city required in return was that the next developers of Block 37 be "qualified" to do the job and willing to act in a timely manner. No more costly delays. The planning department announced that it had rehired Robert Wislow, the chairman of U.S. Equities, to advise the city on negotiations. A private developer and close friend of the mayor, Wislow was there to prevent the sort of fiasco that fatally crippled the city's last redevelopment deal with FJV. Commissioner Berg thought everything was now in place to finish the job. She declared, "From this list we will choose an experienced development team with the skills, resources, and commitment needed to successfully develop this important downtown site."

With the particularly difficult development history of Block 37, the lucky winner of this latest land lottery would need more than just "experience" and "commitment." In JMB Realty the city had what once was the country's most successful developer of regional malls and manager of urban commercial complexes like Chicago's Water Tower Place and 900 North Michigan Avenue. By the summer of 2002, when the city was confidently reciting its Burnhamesque anthem of making "no little plans," JMB's real estate empire had been downsized by many millions of square feet and billions of dollars. Block 37 was just the last drop in a flood of losses for JMB. Their main partner in FJV, the once-mighty Metropolitan Structures, which had had a big part in building postwar Chicago and reestablishing the city's preeminence in modern architecture, was long bankrupt. Larry Levy, who got JMB and Met Structures to finance his first real estate purchases on the block in return for a small piece of the redevelopment deal, had been thrown overboard a decade before when the project first started to fail. JMB was the last standing when the city decided to start all over again.

On June 21, 2002, the city anointed the Mills Corporation the "master developer for 108 N. State Redevelopment Project." The new State Street designation was intended to discourage any negative associations with Block 37. Yet a simple name change could not obscure the fact that the city was giving away a key piece of its downtown, a black hole into which nearly a quarter of a billion dollars of public and private money had disappeared forever. With an impressive-looking record of developing profitable "retail centers" in eleven states and two current projects in Canada and Europe, Mills Corporation, based in Arlington, Virginia, is a smaller, out-of-town version of what homegrown JMB once was. Why should they have better luck?

It is true that Mills's CEO, Laurence Siegel, has a knack for the rhetoric of contemporary city building. But so did all the others. Quoted in the city's press release (June 21, 2002), Mr. Siegel said, "We are excited to have this opportunity to partner with Chicago to create a dynamic and visionary new icon in the heart of the city. Working shoulder-to-shoulder with the City of Chicago, we will develop a global destination worthy of Chicago's history and pride." Mills Corporation is not short on ambition. It is building Xanadu in Madrid, Spain, a shopping and entertainment extravaganza that includes nightclubs, restaurants, and year-round skiing on an artificial Alp. An architect has not yet been chosen to realize a Chicago Xanadu, but Steve Jacobsen, Mills's executive vice president for development, was "hopeful by the end of [2002], we'll be able to have a fairly definitive vision."

A Chicago taxpayer well might ask what beyond the rhetoric of progress, remembrance, and improvement will this new $64 million "partnership" with the city amount to? The previous government/private business partnership came to little more than thirteen years of costly inaction. What has changed in the way cities and private developers do business, from State Street to Ground Zero, that will guarantee success this time around?

AN UNCERTAIN FUTURE

The accumulated costs of having Block 37 mothballed while awaiting renewal are nearly equal to the quarter-billion-dollar budget for acquiring and developing the entire seven-block area in the North Loop Redevelopment District during the late 1980s and 1990s. Although the site between Marshall Field's flagship department store and the Daley Center remains empty while the other "blighted" blocks have been rebuilt, it is a mistake to think of Block 37 as the only failure. Hundreds of millions in publicly subsidized corporate skyscrapers were in foreclosure within months of the national real estate crash of 1990. The majority of these new corporate towers were returned to the banks that underwrote their construction and resold to vulture capital funds like the one run by Samuel Zell, an early speculator on Block 37, for about thirty cents on the dollar. The Chicago and Oriental Theaters also proved to be serious financial liabilities during a decade when the Loop was increasingly losing market share to the city's new downtown across the river. A prosperous alternative to the historic central business district, the mile-long shopping district along North Michigan Avenue has all the civic and architectural virtues of a suburban mall. Notwithstanding its aggressive mediocrity, North Michigan Avenue is playing Midtown to the Loop's faltering Lower Manhattan. To reverse the decades-long downward trend of the Loop, Mayor Daley and the Mills Corporation tried but inevitably failed to clone London's one-of-a-kind Harrods Department Store at 108 North State Street—the prestige address on Block 37 right across the street from Marshall Field's.

The nation's largest banks and pension funds long ago wrote off billions in bad real estate deals that were prompted by the city of Chicago's bold demolition of its historic downtown. These losses to pensioners and limited real estate partners were buried many quarters ago in the fine print of annual reports. The North Loop skyscrapers, apartments, and cultural venues in the immediate neighborhood of barren Block 37 can now be pawned off as good investments, like a ten-year-old car with its odometer turned back to zero. But they weren't profitable in the least for the public and private investors who paid for them. Even today, with all the old investors long out of the buildings, the North Loop's future is hardly secure. Block 37 missed the boom of the 1990s that caused big users of office space headquartered in the Loop, like Arthur Andersen, to go bankrupt. Other large corporations, financial organizations, and law firms able to afford premium skyscraper rents in Chicago are currently experiencing layoffs and reorganizations. Now as the block seems to be finally at the point of development, Chicago appears to be facing another national real estate downturn.

State Street's retail vacancy rate is currently at 13.9 percent—about the same average as "blighted" old Block 37 when it still had buildings on it. Downtown commercial rents continue to fall on both sides of mile-long State Street. With more than 2.8 million square feet of available space, Chicago's historic retail corridor (revitalized by the return of Sears, Roebuck and Co. after an absence of eighteen years and a city subsidy of $13.5 million) is equal in size to a large regional mall. Yet more than 100,000 square feet of recently built or renovated real estate on the street are vacant, including the Toys "R" Us, Carter Jewelers, and Syms Corporation stores. These are hardly auspicious signs for an expensive, publicly subsidized, and privately capitalized urban redevelopment project on 108 North State, already more than $200 million in the red. No marketing-inspired renaming of an infamous piece of real estate will change that implacable fact. Playing out for our own time the age-old story of urban destruction and rebuilding, the ongoing saga of Chicago's Block 37 told in all its compelling factuality in *Here's the Deal* provides a way to view the larger drama of modern political and economic ambition that goes on mostly unreported every day.

March 2003

NOTE TO THE READER

Here's the Deal centers on a single city block in the middle of Chicago that brought together politicians, developers, and financiers, all looking for a way to capture its wealth. The history of Block 37 (as it has been known since 1830) is a perfect lens through which to expose the deals by which American moneymakers and powerbrokers operate—to examine in its gigantic intricacy the great American moneymaking machine about which most Americans, strangely enough, know nothing.

The subject of this story is the central activity of our society—the accumulation of capital, the creation of value. The story concentrates on fewer than ten key actors and less than three acres. The action takes place over almost four decades, during which millions and millions of dollars were squandered—and many millions were made—putting at risk nothing less than the authority of the country's most powerful municipal government.

All over America during the 1980s, mayors desperate for operating capital handed over their cities to developers who treated large city blocks like playing cards. Skyscrapers, built on credit, were used to raise millions and then traded before the debt came due. On Chicago's Block 37, the skyscrapers were never built, demonstrating the dire consequences of intertwining business and politics. Block 37 is currently a gold-plated hole in the ground, a dead and bleak vacancy at the heart of a great American city.

To follow in detail the frenetic action surrounding the monumental transactions that produced this hole in the ground will require the reader to penetrate a vocabulary that at first may seem as foreign as Russian or Chinese. In fact, the terms "acquisition fee," "balloon payment," "down zone," "fee simple," "flip," "land-bank," "quick-take," "rent-gap," and "write-down" are American to the core. As is this story of the extraordinary collusion of opportunity that makes our system still pay out billions even when it appears not to be working.

Those deals that *do* work are the most glamorous, of course, but the stunning particularity of their details is lost forever in the euphoria of success. It is the deals that fail that live on forever in the brilliant complexity of what went wrong.

January 1996

HERE'S THE DEAL

1 LORD OF THE LOOP

Richard J. Daley, six-term mayor of the city of Chicago, rose early every morning to survey his domain. The five-mile trip to City Hall was a chance to see firsthand how he was doing. A new fire station, lights for a schoolyard basketball court, a nice spring planting of trees, were all palpable signs of progress. Daley was right in the middle of things, calculating: adding each success and subtracting every nagging imperfection. His commissioner of Streets and Sanitation would hear before noon about the broken streetlight on Cermak and State, the plugged gutter at Wabash and Harrison, even the paper swirling in the wind outside the mayor's bungalow at 3536 South Lowe. Every new building was his triumph, every errant gum wrapper a personal affront. Before arriving at the office, he had many a time ordered his driver to stop so that he could get out and set right an overturned garbage can.

Problems he could see, go and fix, were his pleasure. Attending to those areas of governance that rewarded his direct involvement, and avoiding the rest, Daley produced results. He practiced human accounting: a ledger he kept himself that froze in place Chicago's violent competing interests from the day he first took office. The ins stayed in, the outs out. You were either on "good paper" with the mayor or out of business, permanently; Chicago was so neatly divided, in his mind, between the parts he controlled and those he didn't. Right up until the end, when the mayor died on the job December 20, 1976, it was hard to believe that Chicago, like every other older American city, was suffering steady decay. So efficiently had Daley hidden the city's problems behind a façade of efficient leadership that it took two strokes in 1974 and a prolonged hospitalization in his last full term for the public to see that this madly personal system was truly breaking apart. Not until that late date, almost twenty years into his long reign, did the courts successfully attack the city's shameful segregated housing and public schools, its apartheid unions, dismantle the machine's extensive patronage system, and put many a Democratic regular in jail. Until then, Daley's Chicago was a gray Oz with one man fully in control. Under the mayor's spell, the city of Chicago was paradoxically open and closed at the same time. In his own person, he captured the city's mixture of rough and plain dealing, direct and roundabout. No use in trying to reconcile opposites. "The manifest Mayor Daley was incoherent and sometimes vulgar. There was another Mayor Daley, who was infinitely knowledgeable and subtle," longtime Chicago resident Saul Bellow concluded. "Both of these Daleys were real."[1]

It's hard to know exactly when Daley first got the idea to run a permanent campaign against his own downtown. But it's likely the thought came to him on one of those sunrise inspections. He looked out the window of his black Cadillac and saw, as for the first time, an unremarkable, standard three-acre Chicago block. In sixty years' worth of trips downtown, the mayor had never bothered much with the life on blocks like 37. They were always in the background, a second stage, removed from where the important action of the city took place. Traders, bankers, and corporate attorneys were on LaSalle Street; respectable businessmen operated out of new skyscrapers; Block 37 was a remnant of the past: the commercial equivalent of the residential firetraps Daley was already busy knocking down.[2]

He invited his commissioner of Streets and Sanitation to take a look with him. Commissioner James McDonough remembers it was a warm day in the fall of 1967. As the mayor's car turned off State, going down Randolph on its way back to the Hall, it passed right by Block 37. Daley was so agitated by what he saw that he mistook McDonough for Joseph Fitzgerald, his commissioner of buildings. The mayor said, "I want those buildings down, they're a disgrace." Daley had nothing more to say on the ride back. Later, McDonough phoned Fitzgerald and told him he had just agreed to take "these buildings down on State Street." What could he do, he told Fitzgerald. "He got me confused with you and I decided to take down the buildings." Block 37 was now officially an overturned garbage can the mayor had vowed to set right. He thought it would be just that easy.

Block 37, a piece of real estate older than the city itself, came in time to represent everything Daley hated. Two-bit lawyers romanced judges in the dark booths at Mayors Row on Dearborn Street; pool hustlers eyed their marks on Randolph; coin dealers fenced gold on Washington, and zoot-suit

Mayor Richard J. Daley with William E. Hartmann of Skidmore, Owings and Merrill
(1967)

clothiers were the retail mainstay of this part of State Street. What wasn't
there to hate? Nothing abstract about blight when you saw it at this scale.
A great city with a rotten core mocked all the accomplishments of a lifetime in politics. This block and at least ten others in the Loop—Chicago's
highly concentrated version of Manhattan Island—calibrated decay down
to an intimate personal scale.

   In his first terms, Daley had reduced the intimidating bigness of postwar
governance until everything was measured against him. He had successfully segmented and cordoned off the creeping pathology of daily urban
life, unavoidable elsewhere, until it was nearly invisible. So complete was
the veil that the mayor was surprised himself when blight inevitably metas-
tasized from the historically poor outlying neighborhoods to the city's prosperous center. When he saw the ruin of Block 37—mocking him only fifty
brisk paces from where he worked—he took the crumbling pantomime as
a threat to his power, and instructed his law department to find some way
to do something about it.

Unmistakable by the mid-1960s, the downtown's deterioration was well
under way when Daley first took office in 1955. It had been accelerated in
Chicago as in other places by the replacement after the Second World War

of a predominantly stable white and middle-class population with one increasingly dependent, black, and brown. The well-to-do were leaving—first to live and then to work in the suburbs—and the poor relentlessly kept arriving. In 1960, Chicago's population was 3,550,000; it would decline 5.2 percent by 1970 (3,369,000), while the metropolitan area increased its size 12.2 percent, from 6,220,000 to 6,977,000. Between 1960 and 1970, Chicago's white population lost more than 470,000, and the black gained 288,000. New arrivals settled in the destitute West Side ghetto rather than the more stable Black Belt, running directly south of the Loop; their concentrated presence near Skid Row on West Madison Street made their plight impossible to ignore.

The postwar economic boom, underwritten by low-interest GI mortgages and FHA loans, was in most respects antiurban. Generous housing subsidies scattered new one-family homes within an expanding commuter belt on property that had been fertile farmland for more than a century. Cheap gasoline, affordable cars, and a quickly multiplying interstate highway system allowed people to travel farther out from the old cities. The central business district (CBD)—the downtown's dense commercial core—assumed a crushing financial burden as taxpayers were increasingly replaced by tax consumers.[3] The downward trend appeared irreversible.

Daley could understand why people were leaving. The streets were dirty, buildings old. Only a small proportion of the city's fine stock of architecture was properly air-conditioned; most buildings were still coal heated and belching dark clouds into the dense Loop. Downtown air was a foul mixture of methane and the gaggingly sweet odor of processed flesh blowing northeast from the packing plants. In the 1950s, Ross Beatty, a commercial real estate broker, headed Operation Clean-Up for the mayor. "Buildings from the Chicago River to Michigan Ave., from N. Wacker Ave. to Congress St., will have their faces sandblasted," Beatty told the newspapers in 1959. He added, "New flagpoles will sprout like beanstalks."

The Chicago Beatty wished to make over was the same gritty place that Nelson Algren and Carl Sandburg had romanticized. Postwar Chicago had become America's representative American city. Algren admired the corruption, singling out for special praise Chicago's "driving vigor" and "reckless energy." On assignment for the *New Yorker*, A. J. Liebling, more like Rudyard Kipling and Lincoln Steffens, earlier visitors who couldn't get out of town fast enough, dismissed the Loop as "a boundless agglutination of streets, dramshops, and low buildings without urban character." The city reminded the journalist of "Times Square and Radio City set down in the middle of a vast Canarsie."[4]

Just assuming office, Daley could have done without Liebling's patron-

Block 37, corner of Dearborn and Washington (1957)

izing tone, his invidious comparisons, but took his point. His highbrow generalizing was more useful politically than all of Sandburg's "broad shoulders" praise and Algren's paeans to junkies and bums. Daley and his brand of machine politicians recognized that no American city could survive the image of a begrimed, predominantly working-class, industrial haven. Chicagoans had watched helplessly as Buffalo's, Cleveland's, and Detroit's commercial centers were cored out, their middle class pared away. Could their city be next?

Before he could effect real change, Daley decided that, at least, Chicago would be made to look different—more like a little Manhattan than a Detroit. Early in his first term, the mayor instructed his city planning head to "get some flowers around the buildings." Then he authorized the privately administered Central Area Committee (CAC) in 1956 and recruited William E. Hartmann, a principal architect at Skidmore, Owings and Merrill (SOM) and former head of the Chicago Plan Commission, to come up with a permanent plan to fix the downtown. The Central Area Plan was two years in the making, but the committee from its inception revealed an activist mayor willing to take charge. Those key executives who ran the utilities, big department stores, and hotels—fixed enterprises tied to the central city—had been unable to prevent their core market from leaching out inexorably to the suburbs. In Daley, they had a politician whose self-interest appeared remarkably similar to theirs. He was a guy with whom they could do business.

The mayor began his campaign of revival by directing the Central Area Committee to make recommendations for a sprawling two-and-one-half-square-mile area—from North Avenue to Roosevelt Road, Lake Michigan to Halsted Street. He added that he was particularly interested in one sector of the "central area"—the few blocks around where he worked. In 1958, the CAC recommended that a new civic center should be built on land barely one hundred feet away from City Hall, where essential property could be "acquired with a minimum displacement of essential elements . . . [to] stimulate rehabilitation and new construction in nearby properties."[5] If he had a model of antiprogress in Block 37, the Civic Center represented progress itself. Organizing, financing, and building this great public skyscraper was the mayor's opening counteroffensive against "blight"—the word that had come to express for him all the physical and moral decay of the city.

The Civic Center (rededicated as the Richard J. Daley Center after the mayor's death in 1976) was meant to demonstrate that blight could be cured with modern high-rise architecture. Daley intended to do more than clean up the city. He planned to remake it completely. The whole Loop— the city's core thirty-five square blocks, its Fifth Avenue, rue St. Honoré, and Piccadilly Circus—was his target. First, he would concentrate on the property he already controlled or could get his hands on through eminent domain, the constitutional provision that permits governments to take private property for a clear public purpose. A new civic center qualified, but Daley would have to find another rationale to take private property like Block 37. There were just so many courts and city offices even he could build.

Daley could attempt such an ambitious program of monument building only because, in more than fifty years in politics, he had mastered the intricacies of government. He so completely controlled the budget and administration of basic city services that complicated labor negotiations were concluded with a "handshake," and fractious quarrels between party loyalists were settled after one visit to his inner office.[6] The mayor was a seductive autocrat who imposed cyclical performance reviews on bureaucrats and encouraged the normally hostile county governments in the greater metropolitan area to be "public partners," at the very time he was drawing more and more power to himself.[7] He substituted revenue bonds for direct taxation as a source of capital to ensure that the banks and financial markets, not the voter back in the neighborhoods, would pay for the city's growth.[8] To help him account for every dime, he instituted five-year budgets and long-term planning. Each one of these dry administrative moves consolidated more authority until his influence reached beyond simple governance and out to every aspect of life in the city.

His goal above all was to stimulate the development of commercial property so that the city could feed off higher assessments and his constituents work at better jobs. Good government to him was a simple matter of quid pro quo, including the complicated process of urban renewal, which he would do himself with other people's money. Power in Daley's Chicago was personal, not bureaucratic. If you worked for the city as a meter maid, a commissioner, or an unpaid adviser on a blue-ribbon civic committee, you were directly responsible to the mayor. He reviewed your employment authorization, interviewed you, and remembered your first name. Daley was a practical fellow who lived all his adult life in the same knickknack-packed bungalow and arrived at the office the same time every morning. He was the only politician in Chicago who mattered; he gave you one shot, no appeal. "If Daley said march the troops into Lake Michigan, you put on your bathing suit," said Judge Abner Mikva of the U.S. Court of Appeals.

He also knew how to move slowly. Well before he built anything in the Loop, Daley learned the ins and outs of the redevelopment process by building public housing. In less than a decade, he had so successfully applied the Federal Housing Acts of 1949 and 1955 to his own purposes that Chicago soon had the country's highest concentration of public housing, effectively compacting and quarantining poverty away from the downtown.[9] By the mid-1960s, the Chicago Housing Authority (CHA) owned or managed 103 developments, home to more than 140,000 people. After condemning and demolishing miles of slums, Daley immediately built a denser, high-rise "second ghetto" in exactly the same place. He bulldozed once-vital neighborhoods to accommodate the new wide roads and tower housing and replaced them with nothing. Gone with the rats, firetraps, and cold-water flats was any semblance of a normal social fabric of streets, stores, and churches. According to students of the period, this radical re-assignment of land use was all part of a conscious deal to retain downtown business support in advance of redeveloping the central area. Public housing was the *"vital link* permitting private business to begin the postwar reconstruction of Chicago."[10]

So Daley never viewed the city's public housing as an architectural or social calamity. Using his influence, he transformed high-minded national social reform into a practical local economic arrangement. By removing, relocating, and concentrating the city's poorest citizens, public housing became a highly profitable, parasitical system that ran on constant mechanical breakdowns and accelerated decay.[11] Every union worker, mostly white, had a reliable high-paying job; local vendors of elevator cable, plumbing fixtures, and dry wall had standing orders. It was a classic big-city arrangement. No one already in the system was left out. In return for African Americans getting this instantly dilapidated housing right in their old neighborhoods, black politicians, loyal to the organization, had a concentrated voting bloc. A precinct worker could canvass thousands of voters in one place. Earl Bush, the mayor's longtime press secretary, called this realistic balance of benefits a good example of a "pure deal."

After successfully decanting the poor, Daley was emboldened to take urban renewal further into the heart of the city than anyone had dared try. His targets changed. No longer were they the derelict or abandoned parts of the downtown but those very blocks already functioning with considerable business activity, particularly at street level.[12] He singled out blocks like 37 not because they had failed economically, but paradoxically because they were succeeding too well. The downtown's retail clientele was composed increasingly of those who used to shop the thriving ghetto retail strips, such as Forty-seventh Street with its stores and fine nightlife. But the main street had been "improved" to the extent that it no longer functioned as a legitimate commercial zone. And those who patronized the South Side shops had no choice but to travel to the Loop.

Back when Daley first took power, Chicago was experiencing a jarring change from a manufacturing to a service economy, a postindustrial transformation bound to affect, in time, all older American cities.[13] While he never regarded the filtering of blacks back into the downtown to be a direct result of his own brutal attempt at containment, he did astutely identify another one of its sources: the breakdown of the larger metropolitan economy. Specifically, Chicago's stockyards, packing plants, steel mills, and tool-and-die shops had steadily been losing their market share to Omaha

Randolph Street (1971)

and Kansas City, and to the rebuilt cities of Japan. By the seventies these critical industries offering entry into the city's larger economy would be completely gone. Industrial and commercial Chicago—dominating an area with a five-hundred-mile radius, once responsible for a third of the nation's total economy—was shrinking back fast to the boundaries of its original square mile.

Chicago was rapidly ceding manufacturing and office jobs to suburbs that were purposely just outside commuting range of the working poor. Over the years, the city had lost its unique geographic advantages, the stuff of legends that made her in the nineteenth century the Queen of the Northwest Territory. As airports out at the edge replaced railroads and shipping nearer the core, Chicago was asked to compete on more equal terms with every other city in the world for its share of the giant corporations and financial institutions that meant the difference between continued progress and economic ruin. Daley's real estate advisers alerted him to the fact that the only workable urban renewal was full-scale commercial redevelopment. Rebuilding should no longer be social, like slum clearance with all its human problems, but property led, specifically by office towers able to accommodate high-paying service jobs and almost limitless fee-generating transactions. He concluded that skyscrapers could be the steel mills of tomorrow. The very commercial architecture

Chicago had pioneered might hold the key to its economic survival. These new towers would fit very nicely in the Loop. Once he had decided on this form of "urban renewal," the rest was politics. Disguise a large-scale land-trading operation with a higher public purpose—that was the challenge.

To sustain his emotional involvement in the dry world of real estate, Daley the politician instinctively recognized the need for an opponent, someone to hate. To this end, progress became identified in his mind with the new skyscraper city, and failure with the poor, mostly black folk "taking over" the downtown. The city's campaign against blight combined the assault on old and dilapidated buildings with an intolerance of the marginal and unconventional. Eradicating blight was for him patriotic—something of a crusade.

For Daley, city building was never simply a show of power or an opportunity for businesses to expand and profit; civic improvement required a grand rationale, a regulating piety. American striving for someone of his generation had a decidedly theological cast. Along with the catechism and basic instructional texts, every eighth grader read an impressively illustrated book, *Wacker's Manual of the Plan of Chicago*. Written in 1911 by Walter Dwight Moody, celebrated author of *Men Who Sell Things* (1907), the *Wacker Manual* exhorted Chicago's twentieth-century architectural ambition. So popular, Moody followed it with a later volume, *The Plan of Chicago in 1925*.

Hired by the Chicago Plan Commission to popularize planning ideas argued academically in Daniel Burnham and Edward Bennett's *Plan of Chicago* (1909), Moody was charged with making 1.5 million Chicagoans "plan conscious." The commission subsidized the publication and advertising. In addition to getting the Chicago Board of Education to adopt a thirty-four-cent hardcover copy of the manual as a required text, Moody prepared a condensed primer and made it available to the city's 165,000 property owners and to any tenant who paid twenty-five dollars or more in rent. Moody's *Chicago's Greatest Issue: An Official Plan* was a best-seller.[14]

The 1909 Chicago Plan, conceived and underwritten by the Commercial Club, a collection of the city's richest businessmen, was an exclusively private initiative to bring international capital back to Chicago without having to burn down the city again. The plan shunned skyscrapers—the city's indigenous architecture—in favor of multiple square miles of buildings with a unified cornice line and a relentless classical formality. The result would look more like a swollen version of Haussmann's Paris than any modern American city. But the Commercial Club recognized at the outset that the ambitious plan was then "beyond the financial ability of the community." It could be considered only as an idea; in the future it might have a chance of being underwritten by the public, as had the internationally successful World's Columbian Exposition a generation earlier, in 1893.

Thus by the 1960s the idea of a completely remade metropolis was already a half-century-old countermyth to the fast-decaying real city on view outside Mayor Daley's City Hall window. Much the way the contemporaneous Horatio Alger novels trumpeted the American dream as fact, the 1909 Chicago Plan conjured an economic alchemy of rising real estate values and higher taxes for the troubled city. The Plan's authors concluded that, "The very growth of the city, creating as it does *wealth greater than mines can produce,* gives a basis of bond issues in excess of the utmost cost involved in carrying out this plan."[15] The neoclassical architectural result was less important than the underlying act of faith, of reimagining the old city completely transformed. Like all his schoolmates, Daley was programmed from childhood to see El Dorado right in the stinking flats west of the Chicago River, a civic center with a dome larger than St. Peter's, built on the rubble of the old neighborhood at Congress and Halsted, within sight of his boyhood home.

The future mayor learned that "Chicago is destined to become the center of the modern world."[16] Richard Daley, beloved child and dutiful student, who went to church every day and studied his *Wacker Manual,* was inspired. He read and reread Moody's gospel with its incongruous illustrations of Mount Lycabettus in modern Athens, Siena, and the Temple of Vesta in Rome, juxtaposed with images of Chicago. Chicago, the holy land, ancient Rome, all stirred together in a polemical soup that would provide him intellectual sustenance for a lifetime in politics. Mayor Daley volunteered that Walter D. Moody's *Wacker's Manual of the Plan of Chicago* was his favorite book.

For thirty years, he had risen patiently from job to job, from party hack to positions with power, until he was finally at the top. A good listener, controlled, and unexpectedly quiet in company, he was always unusually effective with people. Men naturally sought his approval, carefully measured out and dispensed erratically in miserly portions. Hardworking, mostly Catholic boys from good families, willing to take orders, these were the young people he favored. He didn't understand the others.

Daley had grown up "Back of the Yards" on the Near South Side, in an insular Irish neighborhood called Bridgeport. There Chicago's leaders were trained—a political Sandhurst and West Point that prepared officers to lead the city's vast patronage army of nearly forty thousand troops at its height.[17] Richard Daley was a sophisticated operator who never lost the distinctive malaprop stammer of the neighborhood. But right from the beginning he allowed himself a few luxuries to set himself apart. As soon as he could afford them, the jowly young man sported dark conservative suits and expensive shoes, giving him the outer look of a banker. As party leader, he shopped at Pucci's, a custom tailor on Michigan Avenue, where he received private fittings and was given the sort of attention befitting a head of state. An only son, rare in a neighborhood of large, immigrant families, Richard Daley had a doting family's huge ambition focused all on him.

He was an obsessive detailer, an accountant with a law degree, earned after hours at DePaul University. As a young man in the 1920s, he balanced the books at Dolan and Ludeman, a stockyard commission house, during the day and worked for the local Democratic club at night, helping the alderman process the weekly patronage checks. His meticulous work as an Eleventh Ward precinct worker brought him to the attention of the city-wide organization. He soon had a job downtown as a clerk in City Hall, on the fast track to higher office.

Daley later served in the Illinois House of Representatives and Senate, rising to minority leader down in Springfield, where he represented the interests of Chicago mayor Edward J. Kelly, an old-style machine boss. He quickly developed a reputation as a reliable ally who had an unusual way with numbers and could keep his mouth shut. In 1937, after making the switch from the lower to the upper house, he was appointed chief deputy county controller, a sensitive political position that afforded intimate knowledge of the patronage lists. He quickly committed them to memory.

In 1946, he ran for Cook County sheriff in the only election he ever lost. But by 1949 he had fully recovered, taking over as county controller and, only four years later, chairman of the Cook County Central Committee: boss of the country's best organized big-city machine. Amassing power without anyone really paying much attention, he got the last of his formal political education when Governor Adlai Stevenson brought him into his cabinet as revenue director.

By the time he was inaugurated mayor, April 20, 1955, and added the position of head of the government to the equally powerful one of leader of the party, he needed no help with budgets or managing money. He could do it all alone under the new guidelines proposed by the Illinois Home Rule Commission that provided the city with wider taxing jurisdiction—a useful increase in power engineered a few years earlier when he was still only head of the party. Once formally in office, Daley started immediately working on consolidating the city's bureaucracy—controlling the purse.

He quickly got a law passed that gave him and not the city council the power to prepare the budget. Daley worked it so he personally controlled every dollar that came into City Hall.

The third Irish-Catholic mayor in a row, he wanted to distinguish himself from his ineffectual predecessor, Martin Kennelly, and the notoriously corrupt Edward Kelly. His ticket was to "convert programs into action," to make the bureaucracy work for him. He started immediately with those things he knew he could easily control. Streets and Sanitation and the Department of Public Works were his infantry. Garbage was collected, streetlights repaired, potholes filled, alleys lighted so the people back in the wards knew that he was busy at work. From a purely political angle these were "shrewdly chosen" civic projects. Critics of municipal politics, Edward C. Banfield and James Q. Wilson, argued the value of highly capitalized public works. "They were highly visible; they benefitted the county as well as the city; for the most part they were noncontroversial; they did not require much increase in taxes; and they created many moderately paying jobs that politicians could dispense as patronage."[18]

By the end of his second term, in 1963, Daley had secured the perimeter of the downtown with multilane highways as forbidding as moats. With the poor safely cordoned off in housing projects, and the wealthy suburbanites having a fast in-and-out on the expressways, Daley turned all his attention to the center, where his larger ambitions could take shape. Commencing with the new civic center—a large office and court facility—he took on the entire blighted downtown.[19]

Richard Daley, in his seventh decade, began moving on a concentrated process of renewal, directing development exactly where he wanted it: to one big downtown site after another. Lacking anything that would pass for an architectural vision of the city, he enlisted architects in the same way that, as party chieftain, he convinced someone to run for office. He approached the regulation-bound, red-taped business of development as just another sclerotic city department requiring his direct intervention. He expedited the normal sluglike pace of the planning process until things started moving smoothly. To the architects who waited like everyone else on the soggy couch outside his office, he was always encouraging but vague. They presented him with expensive models, full-size mock-ups of the space, long-winded explanations, and he always replied, "Great, now make it nice."

Daley viewed architecture as a boundless resource to be exploited like water or air. But the mayor knew how fickle development could be in prac-

tice. He was old enough to have seen firsthand how factories, grain elevators, and oil refineries had industrialized the shores of Lake Michigan and
the banks of the Chicago River and how private developers, without much
concern for the city, later colonized the Loop's interior streets with office
buildings. He knew that some areas of the city had prospered as others
went into permanent decline. Development always followed the money. As
mayor he would try something different.

In making underused commercial property available to private development, he wanted nothing less than to control the direction of capital, making it pour into only the buildings he wanted, so *he* and not the market
would determine the lucrative rebuilding process. The city would be a true
partner, directing the investment of private money with the same total control Daley had demonstrated over the millions in federal War on Poverty
funding.[20] If the plan worked, Chicago would be able to luxuriate into the
millennium with dependable sources of revenue while other cities continued to fail.

As Daley envisioned it, businessmen who were used to bullying conventional politicians would pay to redevelop Chicago for him. He already knew
how to target his favorite projects as well as any of his contemporaries:
Boston's Edward J. Logue, New Haven's Richard Lee, or Robert Moses of
the New York Port Authority.[21] But unlike his reckless colleagues, Daley
kept urban renewal money clear of the downtown until he was certain it
was completely under his control. Although this caution never kept him
from claiming a huge share of available funds. During the peak of Great
Society spending (1966–70) for the cities, Chicago's piece of the pie added
up to a 169 percent increase in federal intergovernmental aid. Since Daley
wasn't mired in extensive downtown renewal projects, the extra revenue
was a pure windfall. During his fourth term, he increased city expenditures
by 40 percent and didn't have to raise taxes.[22]

All through the 1960s with the federal government paying two-thirds of
redevelopment costs and accepting credits for the rest, it was tempting to
play the urban renewal game right in the center of the city. But Daley had
seen how ambitious plans had ripped out the heart of cities with nothing
much to show for it. He'd been to other downtowns "improved" by urban
renewal, empty except for uncompleted highways going nowhere, the steel
rebars sticking out of the cracked concrete like cheap dental work.

No years of construction barricades, job actions, and disgruntled taxpayers,
Daley's style of downtown renewal was, he thought, different. Because as
with everything else he would not overreach; he started slowly and delib-

erately with only one project. With the cooperation of the city's biggest banks, employing the best architects, Chicago, after a fifty-year wait, built the Richard J. Daley Center on a prime site in the Loop.[23] The monumental civic skyscraper demonstrated that the Daley administration would cooperate in getting land into the hands of developers—in this case a public authority—and wanted development to proceed all at once, one whole block at a time. By taking small lots and combining them to build one great building, Daley indicated that he was ready to trade land, not for shapeless development at the city's edge but for skyscrapers, as large as they could be built, right in the middle of a municipality of 3 million people. He showed that he wouldn't stand aside as land was slowly traded parcel by parcel on old blocks like 37 that hadn't seen a new building since 1930.

Right from the beginning, Daley was encouraged by some of the city's most conservative businessmen. David Kennedy, head of Continental, the city's largest bank, and a number of his banking colleagues were some of the mayor's "good Republicans." Between 1951 and 1971, Chicago spent more than $1.5 billion, in public and private funds, on urban renewal. Daley's bankers, led by Kennedy, helped the mayor pass $195 million in bond issues for necessary capital improvements such as sewers and rapid-transit tracks. This cooperation translated almost directly at the polls when Daley used a share of the money to have the Department of Streets and Sanitation illuminate (fifty-one thousand lights) every alley (2,300 miles) in all fifty wards, so that every voter had something real to show for the mayor's political dexterity downtown.

Purring "Do it for me," Daley took all the credit when "his" Republicans provided the float—daily reserves of cash—necessary to keep city government operating smoothly. Given his unprecedented influence with big business, Daley was certain that Chicago wouldn't become a doughnut like Newark or Detroit. There would be no untimely fits and starts that left his city with its center hollowed out. Development, once it was initiated, would proceed quickly with no delays—just as it had in the building of the Daley Center (completed in 1965), where the mayor had reformed the way business was traditionally done.

He bypassed the entrenched ward-based political alliances and dispensed a new sort of patronage on downtown businesses, which, he realized, were threatened as much as he by the accelerating suburban exodus.[24] Added to the captive banks—compelled to remain downtown by an antiquated Illinois law prohibiting branch banking—were hotels, theaters, tourist industries, and utilities. Daley recruited them all as part of a new "nonpartisan" constituency, controlled directly from City Hall through two inventions: the Public Building Commission (PBC, 1955) and Central Area

Chicago Civic
Center (Richard J.
Daley Center)
(1967)

Committee (1956).[25] A sham planning apparatus represented by the city's largest private employers was used to validate policies Daley had already decided.

The Daley Center's radical civic architecture lacked any of the classical detail the mayor personally preferred as an expression of authority. But this strange little man had successfully "developed" a steel-and-glass tower—a customized public version of the world's best private office buildings. The project proved how land held in private hands for more than a century could be given back to the people. To emphasize the mayor's largesse, 65 percent of the entire site remained open space. From the architects' use of Cor-Ten steel that oxidized to a russet brown, to the eagle span of the sweeping bays, the spandrels broad as railroad bridges, the eighteen-foot floor-to-floor heights, the Daley Center, thirty years later, still remains America's most assertively modern public building.[26]

An up-to-date steel-and-glass high-rise instantly conferred high status on public employees used to laboring in rotting buildings and hand-me-down offices. The choice of form was critical. For a brief time the city's tallest tower, the Daley Center gave instant parity to the public sector, the same cracked-linoleum, leaky-pipe realm in which the mayor himself worked. That his government was important enough to be housed in a fine skyscraper that put one in mind of the Seagram Building on New York's Park Avenue was just the sort of signal he wanted to communicate to the private markets that he would need to complete the long job of redeveloping the Loop.

The building of the civic center combined his ready mastery of organization with his new interest in development—the first product of the Public Building Commission, a public authority or shadow government, invented by Daley during his first days as mayor.[27] The mayor presided as chairman over an eleven-person board, comprising businessmen and political strongmen, with broad powers that included the right of condemnation and the authority to issue tax-exempt bonds, without state referendum, to fund its operations.[28] These were self-liquidating financial instruments—long-term investments paid off through rents collected from government tenants. Those receiving the greatest benefits from a public improvement would pay for it directly. In return the city got an "improved" block, a glamorous building and an ordered way of doing business.

The PBC consolidated control, under the mayor's direction, of six local governments, including the Chicago Park District, the board of education, and the Metropolitan Sanitary District (formed in 1889 to administer construction of the Chicago Sanitary and Ship Canal), that were formerly local baronies.[29] Amortizing debt, in the form of monthly rent payments, wherever possible through its users, segregating it from the general operating budget, and dealing almost exclusively with local banks, professionals, and contractors who directly benefited from these transactions, the mayor was able to preserve the city's excellent bond rating.[30]

As chairman of the Public Building Commission, Daley had an independent source of funding and a handpicked group of downtown business leaders eager to please.[31] To make sure that there would be no mistaking the hierarchy of this power pyramid, the mayor engineered the election of Ira Bach, the head of the city's newly established Department of Planning (1957), as PBC secretary and made sure that three of the city's top architectural firms would cooperate, not compete, to build the Daley Center.[32]

From a long list of qualified practitioners, the PBC assembled the architects. The architects, always encouraged to think they were guiding the process, were viewed pragmatically by Daley's crew, who thought them essential to the new daisy chain of connections to the big corporate money. As other blocks were inevitably developed without public buildings—as the whole operation was privatized—it would prove invaluable to have architects dependent and well-schooled in the Daley system.

The civic center work was divided carefully. Naess and Murphy—which had successfully completed several difficult public works projects—was responsible for design. Chicago's successful blue-blood firm, Skidmore, Owings and Merrill, provided additional engineering services and planning expertise. To round out the team, the PBC included the firm of Loebl, Schlossman and Bennett, whose responsibilities were vague enough to indicate that it was on board just for the sake of ethnic balance.

The new building rose on a site that had been the home of a fine old restaurant, Henrici's, and some active businesses, including the headquarters of David Rockola, who ran a jukebox and arcade business out of a jumble of buildings across from City Hall.[33] The sprawling Rockola empire was replaced with a bare plaza, fountains, and a public sculpture that completed the transformation of low- into highbrow. A block that once had an active street life was permanently replaced by a "deblighted" version that encouraged none.

The transformation went one step further as William Hartmann, Skidmore's front man, spent weeks in France successfully convincing Pablo Picasso to design a monumental sculpture for the former Rockola-Henrici site.[34] Richard Daley, who didn't know a cubist from a T square, trusted Hartmann, a longtime friend of the artist. Built as solidly as the mayor, SOM's managing partner spoke to him authoritatively about what Picasso meant to modern art. But all Daley needed to hear was that the proposed sculpture was "good for Chicago," the only sort of recommendation that finally mattered. Just in case he was interested, the mayor volunteered his opinion to Hartmann that he personally favored a realistic statue for the great space in front of the courts, something like Blind Justice holding a set of scales. The architect closed the deal.

Picasso designed the work, waiving his fee as a gesture to his friend. The "Communist" artist was delighted that the world's two most famous gangster cities—Chicago and Marseille—had each commissioned from him a public sculpture. At the big public unveiling on August 14, 1967, the mayor looked up at the hulking steel abstraction and told Hartmann he thought he saw an angel spreading his wings.

What had begun, only a decade earlier, as a low-budget beautification campaign was by the midsixties a full-fledged renewal effort. For just as the

Block 37 as backdrop to new Civic Center Plaza (1967)

city of Chicago was making over a critical block near the top of Dearborn Street, the federal government improved it from the bottom. Down on Jackson Street a deteriorating building, housing all the federal courts and offices, was demolished to make way for a new government center. Until the city got involved, the proposed replacement, crowding the entire block, was not much of an improvement over the classical pile it replaced. But when it was finally built, with its own public plaza, the hundred-million-dollar project was nicely incorporated into the mayor's larger plan to rehabilitate the street.

The General Services Administration's (GSA) original idea was for a seventy-five-story skyscraper that would have dwarfed the Daley Center. That concept was abandoned in favor of a more parklike, open scheme after the Chicago Plan Commission convinced the GSA that housing federal courts and offices in the tallest building in town was a little aggressive, too much like the Soviets in Eastern Europe. In response to the criticism, Ludwig Mies van der Rohe—then the world's greatest living modernist architect and a Chicago resident—produced a campus-style ensemble (1959–75) of two high-rise buildings, one a courthouse, and the other an office, each oriented to the other in the manner of his celebrated residential work. So in the end, the federal government had commissioned a monument to propriety and proportion, anchoring Dearborn Street on one end of the Loop, as the Daley Center did on the other.

A bright red Calder stabile dressed the Federal Center's plaza. This giant work by an American artist further reinforced the impression that under Daley all governments were acting as one. With their tasteful placement of high art on open space, these exemplary public buildings in the center of town was bait for independent developers. Luring them to ante up their own towers, to cash in early on the area's obvious change in fortune, Daley carefully set his nets. One big one, Arthur Rubloff, was his first catch.

Across Washington Street, on a site facing the civic center, Rubloff, a local developer, retained SOM to design the city's first speculative office building.[35] Without any public subsidy, he built the Brunswick Building (1965) at considerable risk. Rubloff had not fully leased the space before he started construction on the exposed-frame, thirty-seven-story concrete tower. The Brunswick Building, with a large plaza of its own, left more open space than required by the liberal zoning code, thus increasing the gamble. Leaving rentable space fallow was Rubloff's acknowledgment that he might make the new civic style of tower and plaza work for him. A nod to Daley that he understood the new rules of the game.

His gamble quickly paid off. Once completed, Rubloff's building leased up at much higher rents than the land had ever produced before.[36] Another private developer soon followed that success with another large concrete building, designed by C. F. Murphy Associates (Naess and Murphy's successor firm), at Dearborn and Wacker. The fifteen-story headquarters of Blue Cross–Blue Shield (1968) supported the mayor's contention that architects who worked for the PBC would obtain an unimpeachable public reference.[37] All the architectural firms involved with the Daley Center were in short order busy at work for private developers.

Daley had reason to be confident. It had only taken four high-quality public buildings (one city funded, three federally) to spark a massive private renewal of the entire downtown. Immediately after Rubloff committed to build the Brunswick, the First National Bank began planning a sixty-story, nearly 2-million-square-foot headquarters. This meant that one of Chicago's largest employers was not only remaining in place but dramatically multiplying the size of its downtown operations.

Completed in 1969, the new bank building had followed a decade of indecision and uncertainty about the future of Chicago's failing core. The bank's lengthy deliberations confirm the mayor's sense of the high cost of urban blight, and the long-term consequences for the downtown. A close look at the First National's correspondence with its main real estate adviser provides a window on the process from the private side, revealing the deep anxiety of at least one business about to reinvest millions in the center of Chicago.[38]

Interested in expanding his aging South Loop location, bank president Homer J. Livingston commissioned appraiser Gilbert H. Scribner to look for alternate sites. Scribner's observations in a series of confidential letters support the notion that Daley's attempts to raise the value of downtown real estate were followed closely by the entrenched private sector—what the old-time organization men called "Republican interests"—at the time of the civic center and Federal Building improvements.

Scribner's first appraisal concluded that the bank should consider improving its current site, noting that "there are few solid blocks obtainable."[39] Just a few months later, the bank's indecision—whether to search for a new location or expand its current facilities—had progressed to the point where Scribner was concerned that land values were being adversely affected. Too many people already knew the bank was "looking for property." The appraiser advised Livingston, "I don't know whether your architects talk too much or whether it has gotten out through other sources, but I think an effort ought to be made to keep this more or less quiet."[40] Public knowledge of the bank's interest in downtown land would help speculators bid up the price, a good thing only if the bank stayed at its current location, but disastrous if new lots had to be bought at premium prices.

On July 10, 1961, Scribner wrote to Gaylord A. Freeman Jr., the new president of the bank, advising him to stay put. Announced improvements for the area, including the federal and local projects, had already driven land values up.[41] Specifically the land around the bank—equally distant from the Federal and civic centers—had improved sufficiently to justify a large new investment at an enormous increase in scale. The rise in property values in the Dearborn corridor had the real estate pros thinking exactly the way Daley wanted. Entrepreneurs like Arthur Rubloff and a huge private employer, like the First National Bank, were thinking big, on the scale of the block rather than the lot.

With Scribner's encouragement the bank invested an additional $4.4 million to control the land under the parts of the block they didn't currently own. With the old First National Bank Building appraised at $10 million, these new pieces gave them all but one small sliver on which they could build as much as a 4-million-square-foot tower, more than three civic centers, on their own 128,000 square feet of land.

The change in scale amounted to a remarkable change in attitudes.

Scribner, representing the normally conservative real estate establishment, had for decades warned the bank's executives about the fall of downtown property values. He was now a bull, advising Freeman to build privately on the same gargantuan size as the city's new public buildings.

In the past, the bank had moved cautiously. Limited to single-location banking, the First National had always sought modest ways to expand its operations. Through a 1953 ordinance the bank had received permission to "construct and maintain [for a period of 20 years] a four (4) level bridge structure over the east-and-west public alley" that connected the bank building to back offices in the Hotel Chicagoan and Hamilton Hotel. This was legal bridge banking, not illegal branch banking, a Rube Goldberg solution to the need for new space. Until Daley took office, there seemed no practical way to get control of the entire site.

Daley understood that he had leverage with the bank. He knew that it could only grow within the limits of the block and that its expansion plans came down to one final piece of land that the city owned. Specifically, the bank needed an alley. Since it was exclusive property of the city, no one had ever thought to make it available until Daley simply agreed to sell it to Freeman for a modest $77,500, a minor expense for a $120 million project.[42] The deal was done quickly, over the phone, directly with the mayor. No committees, no reports, no lengthy deliberations, no glossy plans. A setup. Gaylord Freeman told Robert Wilmouth, then a young First National vice-president, to call Daley on the mayor's personal line. The mayor, whom Wilmouth had never met, answered "Hi Bob" and directed him to an insurance firm in Evanston, a near-in northern suburb that at one time or another employed two of Daley's sons. All the necessary paperwork for transferring ownership from the city to the bank was done without anyone outside the circle of the deal knowing about it. The First National Bank was half finished before the building department even required a permit to begin construction.

Bank executives didn't hesitate to exploit their opportunity. At the exact geographic center of the Loop the First National Bank put up what was at the time the most distinctive building on the city's skyline.[43] C. F. Murphy Associates and Perkins and Will Partnership did their own version of the newly established formula of a large tower on a generous plaza. The architects provided a seamless link between public and private ventures: the same firms designed both. With its own work of art by another acknowledged master, Marc Chagall, the First National Bank was favorably compared to the great public buildings in the Dearborn corridor. The construction of a profitable 2-million-square-foot skyscraper, so tall and wide that it did not have to consume even one-half of its permitted zoning envelope—the volume for which an architect could design—advertised Chicago internationally as a good place in which to invest and build.[44] A private "Civic Center" right in the middle of the renewed street: just where the mayor wanted it. Then everything went to hell.

• • •

Late into the 1960s when other cities were already ripped apart, Daley kept order, always finding a way to make a deal, turning dissent into consensus. But 1967 was to be the last of the good years. Then all the anarchy, poverty, and racial unrest he had, he thought, isolated permanently out in the neighborhoods boomeranged back into the Loop.

In the year leading up to the disastrous convention week (August 24–29, 1968) Richard Daley broke every rule he had learned in a half century of political education. He had unaccountably lost sight, amid his mastery of the physical environment, that the social problems long hidden from view still remained. He had become complacent, thinking that his brand of old-fashioned ward politics still worked while his more progressive contemporaries were mired in labor protests and racial unrest. Chicago was relatively calm during a summer of rioting in twenty-three cities, including Detroit, Newark, and Houston.[45] As the mayor was fond of repeating, Chicago had no riots because the city had only fine neighborhoods, no ghettos.

Right to the end, Daley kept having his own way. One great triumph after another. In 1967, less than three weeks after forty-three people were killed in the Detroit riot, Daley was presiding at the dedication of the Picasso sculpture in front of the Civic Center. Fifteen thousand people attended the ceremony. Archbishop Cody, Lieutenant Governor Shapiro, the poet Gwendolyn Brooks, and the mayor, among other dignitaries, sat during the festivities with their backs to tumbledown Block 37—the mayor's next project. President Lyndon Johnson and Pablo Picasso sent telegrams; the archbishop invoked a benediction; Ms. Brooks recited a poem written for the occasion. Dwarfed next to Hartmann, the mayor held the line to the plastic wrappings covering the statue, ripping like a spinnaker in the plaza updrafts. In the previous year, more office space was completed in 4 new buildings than was vacant in the 160 older buildings comprising the majority in the downtown inventory. A great new civic building, a public ceremony, more than 2 million square feet of office space coming on line that year alone, and the Democratic National Convention due in town the following year—Daley felt invincible.[46]

The Democratic Party's coming to town was like a small world's fair. Daley welcomed the opportunity to show off the rebuilt city. But early on,

even in the planning stages, he had a problem. The city's modern convention facility had burned down on January 16, 1967.[47] A new facility wouldn't
be ready in time to host the Democrats. So rather than giving Daley the
pleasure of showing off his brand-new downtown and beautiful lakefront,
the convention had to be held at the Chicago Amphitheater, on the
grounds of the old Union Stock Yards. Fate would deliver the world to the
very part of the city Daley most wanted to forget. Roads in direct proxim-
ity to the amphitheater were encrusted with a century-thick slime, a
ghastly gelatin of bone and gristle. A sheen of dark-brown oxidized blood
coated the asphalt, most noticeably near the large storm drains. The wonderful architecture of Daley's rebuilt downtown would be ignored as delegates and journalists were transported back into the tough old industrial
city where the mayor had last worked as a kid. He made an effort to clean
up the area cosmetically along the convention route by erecting miles of
redwood fencing to hide the empty lots and abandoned buildings.

In August, the convention was upon him, and it was worse than he had
imagined. The Democrats arrived trailed by thousands of demonstrators,
from the Black Panthers to a group of prankster provocateurs from New
York calling themselves yippies. The mayor never got the joke. All he saw
were hordes of "outside agitators," out on the streets spoiling his plans.
During the convention the police threw these uninvited visitors to his city
through plate-glass windows on Michigan Avenue. Officers mounted on
horses ran down women. There were hundreds of beatings—most, it
proved later, totally unprovoked—on credentialed journalists. The
Chicago police had, in late August, effectively brought the April terror of
West Madison Street, where fatal rioting had followed the 1968 assassina-
tion of Martin Luther King, right to Michigan Avenue.[48]

The week's hysteria was capped off on August 28 by the battle at the corner of Balbo Drive and Michigan Avenue. There had been violent episodes
before on all the side streets leading to the Loop, but the televised confrontation in front of the Conrad Hilton, where most of the delegates were
staying, is the one that remains most clearly in mind, nearly thirty years
after the fact: cops swinging batons, cracking heads, cursing at bleeding
kids, pushing demonstrators back into the ornate hotel lobby, fogged in a
cloud of tear gas. All the while Daley and his oldest son, Richard Michael,
were back on the convention floor, acting as if nothing out of the ordinary
was happening in their downtown.

Apologists for the mayor have offered explanations for Daley's catastrophic lapse of self-control. There is mention of how he was personally
offended by the demonstrators ragtag antics, the sort celebrated the following summer at Woodstock. Encircled by thousands of police in blue riot

helmets, young people, camping out in Lincoln Park, had been pho-tographed frolicking naked, smoking dope, fornicating, carrying "Fuck the Draft" signs. The police department's Red Squad even concocted some as-sassination plots that the mayor later trotted out to help excuse his hyster-ical reaction to the convention-week activities. He took seriously the threats to dose the city's water supply with LSD. The mayor watched the television coverage of Abbie Hoffman and his pals walking around with a pig, dressed up as the yippies' candidate for president. At every chance they got, kids screamed out an obscenity, called the cops pigs. The mayor couldn't keep his eyes off the tube. And it got him thinking. Daley privately told his aides that he didn't like the fact that the good young men of Bridge-port who had already come back from Vietnam were looking a little wrecked, a little like the kids sleeping out in the parks, and suddenly not as enthusiastic about a lifetime job at "Streets and San."

So at the same time his police force was enforcing the law lawlessly, Daley let go. In the process, he started acting more like the hippies he de-spised and not a bit like the choirboy he had tried all his life to imperson-ate. On the floor of the convention, only a few hundred yards from where cattle used to be slaughtered, his precinct workers hassled reporters for their credentials. A high school marching band drowned out speeches crit-ical of the mayor, as Daley turned off the microphones placed among hos-tile delegations, such as Colorado and Wisconsin. (He had a switch for this very purpose back in the city council chambers, where he never really needed it.)

Listening to delegates, such as Abraham Ribicoff of Connecticut, lec-turing him about the carnage on his streets, having to hear references to his "Gestapo tactics," just made him crazy. It was as if the air of permissiveness out there finally reached the mayor. A man under a lifetime of impulse-denying control had been given a taste of liberation himself. Instead of the prudent, defusing sort of response he used every day, Daley took a holiday from inhibition. He appeared to be lost in his own world, drowning in the moment. Among his cronies, crowded together at the front of the hall, the mayor suddenly felt free to do whatever he wanted. At first, he just started bellowing out from the floor, enjoying every bit of it. He was Khrushchev beating the heel of his shoe on the table at the UN, Castro giving six-hour harangues; Richard J. Daley was having the time of his life. And then Ribi-coff goes and spoils it all.

It was one thing to get criticism from the press; he never paid any at-tention to it. But it was quite another matter to hear a canny politician, from a state smaller than Chicago, criticize him in public. Egged on by his council floor leader Alderman Thomas Keane and supported by his oldest son, the mayor forgot that he was at the center of the media extravaganza and just yelled out what he was thinking, no more, no less.

But Daley wasn't in the safe back room of the Tavern Club or at breakfast at the Bismarck, where anyone who overheard such a rare, spontaneous outburst of candor would immediately know enough not to remember it. No, he was now out in the open, as in a bad dream, marooned naked in the middle of a crowd. Hearing Ribicoff's pious concern for the kids out in the street was enough to push Daley over the edge. Senator Ribicoff, who had been "kissing his ass" for two days, trying to cut a deal for George McGovern, was pointing at him from the podium. To Daley, Ribicoff looked like Moses, or was it more like Charlton Heston playing Moses, laying down the law in *his* town. Daley snapped. He yelled out at Moses, "Fuck you, you Jew son of a bitch, you lousy mother-fucker, go home."[49]

After 1968, the mayor started taking off time from work. His aides said he was suffering from fatigue. He also began committing political mistakes of the sort he would never have tolerated in a subordinate. Perhaps the fall began, in an innocent enough way, when the mayor of Chicago "sold" the public alley to the First National Bank: emboldening him to think of all the land in the Loop as his own. With this one small exercise of power, reallocating on his own authority the tiniest unit of valuable public land for exclusive commercial purposes, he had crossed the line. His outbursts after the April riots, when he had issued a "shoot to kill" order, and his antics at the convention had made him a public joke. The Democrats finished him off when they denied him credentials to the 1972 national convention in Miami. It was the first one he had missed in more than fifty years in politics.

A man dedicated to self-control and jealous of his own dignity, Daley had brought himself down. Out of control, a parody of the steady leader he was all his life, he never recovered. In his last two terms, the balance of power shifted permanently from the public to the private sector. After the events of 1968, the mayor could never recapture the aura of invincibility required to lead his urban renewal campaign. The green-eyeshade sort of accounting that he had dutifully mastered was suddenly inadequate to handle the size and velocity of capital demanded by the new real estate deals; it was no longer the world in which he had once computed spreadsheets in his head. There were to be new lords of the Loop. Nonetheless, Daley struggled to retain the initiative on redeveloping the downtown, never fully realizing that it was already beyond him. Recklessly, he was to try one last desperate gambit.

. . .

A Republican, Richard Nixon, was in the White House; the country was moving toward a less bureaucratic approach to funding cities, and the great funding bonanzas of the Great Society programs were now beyond the reach of traditional forms of local control. As Daley had predicted more than a decade earlier, corporate reinvestment was the key. Before, redevelopment had been simply a matter of coaxing huge amounts of federal aid from a sympathetic Congress—politician to politician. Now it was purely big business. Since he had already begun playing that game with the local architects, bankers, and developers, he wasn't ready to give up quite yet.

With the completion, in 1969, of the First National Bank Building, there were eight new downtown buildings, adding 4,607,723 square feet of office space. This doubled the total of the best previous year, 1965, when the Brunswick Building opened along with three other office towers (2,230,000 square feet).[50] Only New York was building at a faster clip.[51]

Daley wasn't prepared to wait out the complicated process of development as entrepreneurs methodically bought one parcel at a time. He knew that the private markets didn't need him for that. But if he could somehow get the authority to acquire underperforming commercial lots and assemble them back into complete blocks, then he could once again make himself essential to the development process. Buying wholesale by the acre and not by the lot, he could then be an exclusive middleman, reordering the downtown at will. He wouldn't "develop" anything himself; he would simply make land—long obstructed by small-time owners—available for development. If acres of property, thought permanently out of reach, suddenly came on the market, money from aggressive private investors would naturally follow.

But he still needed a legal way to get the land away from the old owners, who, the city would argue, had allowed their property to deteriorate and warp the entire environment of the Loop. Many downtown parcels were so derelict that the buildings had no assessed value and were taxed as raw land. Given this widespread state of neglect, the politicians assumed they could purchase the land at between forty dollars and a hundred dollars a square foot and instantly resell it to developers on a no-write-down basis.[52] The difference between the depressed present value and the expected future value of the redeveloped property was discount enough to attract buyers.

A beautiful plan in theory: sleek skyscrapers, on big consolidated blocks, would rise in place of the woeful structures that were there. Improved, attractive, large properties, with their higher tax assessments,

North Loop with new Civic Center (late 1960s)

paying out a bundle to operate, would make everybody appear to be a winner. The city and county would get a wider, more reliable income stream from commercial property taxes; in turn, the big developers would get to play with land they never thought they would have a chance to own. Loaves and fishes; something out of nothing. Everyone would get their big piece. But if this miracle was ever to take place, Daley needed to extend his authority.[53]

The idea for taking commercial property was, in the beginning, little more than a dream of James Downs. Downs, chairman of his own local think tank, the Real Estate Research Corporation, wanted the mayor to explore the possibility of declaring all small, commercial Loop properties blighted land. Once the designation was made, Downs reasoned, the city could find a way to assume title through its power of eminent domain. Small lots, some as narrow as twenty feet, encumbered back to the fire with multiple ownership, long-term leases, liens, and mortgages, could then be wiped out and reconfigured into one simple unblemished rectangle. The result would be a new, enlarged footprint that could easily accommodate block-filling real estate projects of the sort then favored exclusively by suburban developers.

Blighted architecture was potentially worth a fortune in increased property and sales tax revenues, even if the city had to give the land away to private developers. Once the old buildings were gone, the objective would be to connect the dots between all the small parcels and turn them over unfractured to those with their own private funding. For the politician able to pull it off came the ultimate power, making something out of nothing.

Under the Fifth and Fourteenth Amendments to the American Constitution, the use of the power of eminent domain was strictly limited to areas that posed clear health hazards or were needed for defense of the city. The radical step of "taking" private property was never intended to be used on underperforming commercial land. Nevertheless, Richard Daley instructed two young attorneys, Thomas Foran and Earl Neal, to find a way to condemn out—find a legal rationale to demolish—Block 37 among other eyesores in the Loop. The process they initiated on a whim took at least ten years to complete. It was not until 1977 that the Illinois state legislature allowed the city, once it had demonstrated a condition of blight, to take downtown land from its rightful owners and resell it for a new public purpose. But from the day Foran and Neal took their first walk from City Hall over to Block 37, Daley acted as if he firmly had the condemnation power in his hands.

A century after the Chicago Fire, Daley abstracted, in effect legislated, a machine-made disaster to get his hands on capital.[54] The bulldozer was his fire and flood, his "devastation of battle," requiring wholesale rebuilding.[55] Blight no longer needed to be physical—the way a residential slum was dangerous, obviously down and out—but could be functional, still profitable but at a level dramatically below some arbitrary norm. Consequently, the "public purpose" of transforming the downtown was deliberately left vague to encourage private developers, wary of public regulations. Daley's new renewal effort rested on inventing a way "which permitted government or government corporations to take private land found to be blighted . . . in order that the land could be reassembled and redeveloped, by private purchasers as well as governments."[56]

Slums in this new format became ingenious abstractions, almost a state of mind, applicable to any land Daley chose. Foran and Neal knew their brief. Daley expected his law department to formulate some precedent to level the downtown, a workable fiction to acquire the land, to prove in some way that the center of Chicago was infected with business slums. Earl Neal remembers the first time it really registered what was on Block 37: "We left the office and walked over to State Street. And looked at all of the buildings. And he [Foran] said the mayor has a concept that this Loop should be cleaned out and redeveloped and he was wondering whether or not there was a legal method whereby we could acquire land like we do urban renewal."[57]

From these vague beginnings Daley succeeded in stigmatizing the Loop. Once downtown land values were driven down to zero and the North Loop qualified as a slum, the mayor figured he, in time, would find a way to buy it back for resale. The marginal businesses could be eradicated and, in their place, the international businessmen would move in. Looking back, Earl Neal confesses that "economic blight wasn't there."[58] But at the time, the young attorney and his boss did their job all too well. Even before they finished their review, with the threat of condemnation hanging over every downtown landlord, the Loop changed: empty and lurid at night and an eyesore during the day. Blight imagined became blight in fact.

Now Daley had to get the new money flooding downtown.[59] For this he would need more than the law department. To get anything going in Chicago's inbred development community, the mayor required an experienced real estate man with a line to out-of-town capital. That's why he bothered reacquainting himself with Arthur Rubloff, who, with the Brunswick Building, had already made a great success across the street from City Hall. In their infrequent face-to-face encounters, Rubloff would do all the talking as Daley sat silently puffed up behind his desk, encouraging the businessman, as he would any other petitioner for civic favor, to mistake his affable quiet for agreement. One of Daley's commissioners remembers, "Three people went in to see him for the same purpose. All three came out smiling and happy. Obviously they all thought they won. And only one could. He had that ability to say no without saying no."[60] When reporters finally got exasperated with the mayor's delphic dodges, his press secretary instructed them, "Don't write what he says, write what he means."[61]

Daley signed no papers and made no commitments in his meetings with Rubloff, just nodded knowingly. But as much as Daley was playing Rubloff, he was being played in turn. As Rubloff understood it, their "deal" to rehabilitate the vast northern half of the Loop was shaping up quite nicely. Rubloff would do the planning, attract the financing, and the city would only have to provide the land. The old developer told anyone who would listen that Daley was "extremely enthusiastic about furthering my plan; he wanted me to get going immediately."[62]

.   .   .

All the same, between 1968 and 1972, neither the city nor Rubloff had a real plan for what eventually was designated, in 1973, the North Loop Redevelopment Project. Through intermediaries, principally his urban renewal chief, Lewis W. Hill, and Miles L. Berger, a young appraiser and property tax consultant, the mayor tried to get something going. He was already overcommitted to condemning the property, and he wanted the money to be there when he got title to the land. If he could only get the measure of control over these businessmen that he had over the patronage workers.

For starters, the mayor used Berger, whom he had appointed to the Plan Commission in 1965, to find a way to let Rubloff know that the Department of Planning had begun some important "back office planning" for the North Loop. Rubloff later claimed that he had even been shown some early architectural plans by someone in the department.[63] But the city was essentially stalling; Daley, in a completely new arena, was still not sure what he wanted to do next.

Some months after the 1968 convention, the city's urban renewal department, aware of Foran and Neal's efforts, had gone one small step forward with the city's inchoate North Loop plan. Lewis Hill suggested that Robert Christiansen, executive director of the PBC, make some preliminary inquiries of his own as to the current status of the desired land. The results of Christiansen's foray into the existing web of downtown ownership were not immediately encouraging. He reported back to Hill that he quickly found himself "blocked by land interests" critical of the commission's right to condemn land. These interests included two PBC members who happened, between them, to own nearly one-quarter of Block 37 and had ties to the block directly to the north. Christiansen remembers, "We got the shit kicked out of us."[64] The city's initial sally into the world of commercial real estate revealed that it was not unusual to have landowners with significant private holdings and prominent public positions.

For example, the interests of PBC commissioners Colonel Henry Crown and Samuel Sax were submerged in several blind land trusts, intended never to be made public. Crown, who was once landlord of the Empire State Building and had control of a good deal of downtown Chicago land, owned the United Artists Theater and was an investor in the Roosevelt Theater, both on Block 37. Sax's family owned the Exchange National Bank and had nearly thirty thousand square feet on State and Randolph. Neither man wanted his property condemned.

They had come on their own to Daley's conclusion that their land was blighted and tried once to redevelop it themselves. In December 1963, the two families met secretly to talk about it. The meeting didn't last long be-

Crown and Sax family properties (Block 37, State Street, 1977)

cause the Crowns wanted to sell to a developer and realize a quick profit, and the Saxes wanted to raise a hotel and office complex, using a part of the new 1-million-square-foot development for their bank. This collision of two business cultures, speculator and user, prevented anything from happening on the block at that time but served notice that any reuse of this property would have to include them both. The hidden Crown-Sax alignment suggests that Daley, himself, was initially quite naïve about the intricacies of downtown landownership.

If only in this regard, Arthur Rubloff would have been an invaluable resource to the mayor. As a broker Rubloff had been involved in many transactions on Block 37. He knew exactly who owned the land and recognized that only the city could get the Crowns and Saxes out, and him in.[65]

So eminent domain was the last card the city held. As the 1960s ended, Rubloff was encouraged to believe that the city was still thinking of putting a library on Block 37, directly to the east of the successful Daley Center. Even as Daley was inexorably turning to the private markets, his preference was to keep urban renewal somehow under formal public control. This is why Rubloff continued to expect that the city, in the end, would issue PBC bonds for a central library. These public funds for as many as two blocks—36 and 37—would help collateralize the initial investment in his North Loop project. But any public financial participation was scuttled

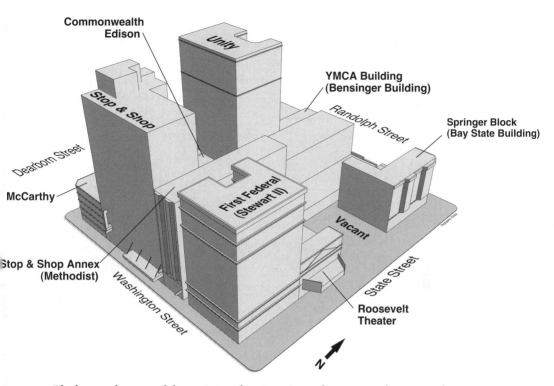

Block 37 at the time of the city's initial interest in condemnation. The Roosevelt Theater on State Street and the United Artists Theater on Dearborn (out of sight here, it was next to the Unity and Bensinger Buildings) were two key properties controlled by members of the Public Building Commission.

from the start, though no one in City Hall bothered telling Arthur Rubloff. Hopes of public money helped keep the developer motivated and on a short leash.

In fact, a genuine redevelopment effort would be well under way before anyone found out for certain that the city had never had any real plans to ante up public money. But that was long after the false promise of public under-writing and the promiscuous use of the condemnation authority had already propelled the city imprudently into the private real estate market. Even though Daley figured he was merely setting up Arthur Rubloff, leaking "secrets" meant exclusively for him, he never considered that Rubloff needed little motivation to convince him that it was right and proper to demolish a fifth of the old downtown.[66] Rubloff was never under Daley's control.

.   .   .

Rubloff would outlive the mayor, who never recovered from the losses of 1968. With the cutoff of federal aid, deregulation of the banks, and increased influence of the financial markets, the position of big-city mayor, in Daley's final years, became more ceremonial than real. Daley, who had set into motion a chain of events aimed at strengthening the city's financial position, had irrevocably entangled the city in the cataclysmic rise and fall of its real estate market.

But this was before the power that he had so assiduously concentrated in his office was squandered forever. Daley thought he had found a way to get private developers interested in risking fortunes in land arbitrarily declared blighted and next to worthless. And downtown land would prove, for a short time, to be as valuable as oil or gold, but in ways he could never have imagined or put under his control. Daley nearly succeeded in reconstituting the city's Department of Planning, and its Plan and Public Building Commissions, in concert with the old Republican interests downtown, in a new agency under his exclusive direction that had no public accountability. In the end, however, the process of urban redevelopment would prove to be uncontrollable even for him.

He never took any of the warning signs, but continued accumulating power that he wouldn't live long enough to use. Large-scale urban renewal, of the sort the mayor had long savored for himself, would be left to others, both inside government and out, to misuse and treat as their own private franchise.[67] Yet, in his Lear-like last years in office, Daley was planning greater changes, with greater audacity, than the public improvements visible to all in his successful rebuilding of Dearborn Street.

The five mayors who followed him, including his son, would all, to some degree or another, have to respond to the outsized shape and form of the old man's ideas for the center of town. What in the following years became known bureaucratically as the North Loop Redevelopment Project— seven completely builtup, privately owned downtown blocks including 37—was in the beginning little more than a story told cautiously to intimates within the tightly controlled environment of Daley's City Hall. How the story finally got out, how it was used, how it came to be told and retold to bring billions into the downtown, makes for the unlikely saga of down-and-out Block 37.

II THE
GREAT
GAME

To Afghani horsemen, the great game is *buzkashi,* a ferocious sport using a goat's carcass for a ball; in big cities the game is played without horses, and the carcass is land. On the high Asian plains the winner is the one who grabs the carrion, slings the trophy over his saddle, and rides away. In the city, score is kept and figured in square feet: who owns the most buildings; who brokers, manages, or leases the most usable floor area; who makes the most money. These are just some of the ways *buzkashi* was played in town during the last boom. Alexander Burnes, an English visitor to Kabul, remarked, "The rapidity with which the goat sometimes changes masters is very laughable, but the poor animal is occasionally torn to pieces in the scuffle."[1] Sir Alex took to calling the odd spectacle, in which the contested object was destroyed in the playing, the laughable game.

This ancient sport is relatively new to Chicago. Until recently, land was rarely traded, much less bandied about. Real property was kept for centuries in the same family, leased out long term, and it was thought bad form to treat land simply as one more commodity. Sometimes it was swapped, but always in secret, protected by an old Illinois law that still keeps landtrust ownership blind. A self-regulating code of behavior, an instinctive etiquette, developed that made land trading quiet and seemingly uncompetitive. Most of the large nineteenth-century fortunes, founded in manufacturing or cash businesses that were once themselves crassly entrepreneurial in nature, eventually found their way to scarce downtown land. Like the buying of fine art, a well-managed Class A office building made moneymaking appear more a proper gentleman's calling. Even the coddled children of successful businessmen, who had never seen firsthand the gritty process of making money, quickly learned that commercial real estate was the ultimate asset.

Yet even before the big private and public syndications, the 115 percent financings, sixty-story skyscrapers built recklessly with no preleased space, real estate investment trusts (REITs), tranches, and all the other Wall Street formulas created to securitize land in the last two decades, there was still the great game. Its early rules were written not by a coupon clipper, but by outsiders who knew urban real estate the way Afghani riders know their horse.

As the 1970s began, waiting for some rich uncle to save them, those responsible for planning in the city of Chicago had outwitted themselves. The city—searching for private investment to renew its downtown—was about to participate in one of the largest giveaways in American history. Unable to devise a decent redevelopment plan, the Daley administration allowed the private markets to sneak in and capture its most valuable resource, downtown land. All the city had accomplished in more than a decade of indecision was to drive Loop real estate values down to the very bottom, where speculators could pick off priceless property—a whole block at a time—and do with it whatever they wanted. In the end, there were no plans, few controls, and hardly any civic improvements required for the best located land in town.

Incredibly, the Loop had been *redlined*. Redlining is the now-illegal practice of controlled real estate panic, perfected after the Second World War in the city's outer wards. Financial institutions in neighborhoods identified as ripe for racial change—areas where whites are rapidly exiting and nonwhites are filtering in—started refusing mortgages and insurance. Exploiting this situation were realtors who encouraged the remaining white families to sell their homes directly to real estate holding companies. These firms quickly resold these properties, at a large profit, to minorities eager to move in.

A redlined downtown was the justification for a broad public taking of core Loop land. This began in the late 1960s, ironically, right at the moment the area was being given a second life by working- and middle-class blacks. Theatrical producer Ira Rogers, who only a few years earlier had been spit on in the Loop, was gradually beginning to feel accepted downtown. He expressed his feelings to a local reporter: "Until recently, the Loop has been an ivory tower place. . . . Black people felt unwelcome for so long, that now that they have a little money and feel comfortable in the Loop, they're just damn glad to be there."[2]

Urban renewal's savaging of neighborhood commerce had proved an unexpected boon to State Street merchants. Black shoppers suddenly were

Corner of State and Washington Streets (early 1970s)

the new backbone of State Street retail and what remained of the entertainment district—a positive ecological shift that occurred at precisely the moment the city readied to bulldoze the downtown.

But rather than improve the city's infrastructure, the mayor by his persistent negative rhetoric accelerated its deterioration, particularly that of the Loop's first-run motion-picture theaters. Instead of running features with wide audience appeal, the theaters provided a steady diet of black-exploitation and action films. The Plitt Theatres in the North Loop proved a useful target for Daley. But what the mayor must have surely known was that Henry Plitt and his new real estate partner, Thomas Klutznick, were simply servicing the down market that the mayor had helped create.

In place of serious redevelopment, which takes a long time, the city was experiencing an instant boomeranging of the poor into the Loop, particularly after hours. Lured to the arcades and movies clustered around Randolph Street, as many a white neighborhood or suburban kid had been before them, these young people in Superfly shirts and pointy shoes gave form to Daley's menacing rhetoric. Merchants who before could not hope to peddle their wares on State Street were now thriving in the shells of es-

Woods Theater (Randolph and Dearborn Streets, across from Block 37) in the 1970s

tablished businesses frightened out by the new clientele and persistent rumors of impending demolition.

Not content to reap the economic benefits of this natural development, the mayor was committed to replacing the existing building stock with something at least ten times the size—a scale of commercial renewal never before attempted. Daley was caught in a terrifying paradox. A natural booster and cheerleader for the city, Richard Daley felt he had to continue bad-mouthing the downtown.

He already had one false start to his credit: the Madison-Canal project. The city's first downtown initiative came two decades after masters of the game like Robert Moses had, in the 1950s, skillfully diverted hundreds of millions in federal aid and learned how to stimulate private development.

Moses's biographer, Robert Caro, writes, "For the first time in America, government was given the right to seize an individual's private property not for its own use but for reassignment to another individual for *his* use and profit." Moses saw immediately how a billion dollars appropriated in 1949 (federal housing legislation) was only "seed money" for far "greater plantings of cash."[3]

Still, Daley waited until August 1968 to invite proposals from private developers to renew the Main Stem, the city's Skid Row just west of the central business district. The Main Stem had the country's greatest concentration of hoboes, mostly alcoholic single men, under-

Charles Swibel (1970s)

employed or clean out of work.[4] The Department of Urban Renewal quickly cobbled together a six-page plan it named Madison-Canal after the two major cross streets in the district. The land was sold for thirty dollars a square foot to a development company headed by Charles Swibel, whom Daley had appointed in 1962 to head the Chicago Housing Authority. This was an act of mutual convenience. Swibel's private real estate operation already held mortgages on the majority of the property in the zone.[5] Expedient politics, but hardly a model of professional planning.

As a teenager Swibel had escaped the Nazis in Poland and landed in Chicago, where Ellis Marks, who owned a string of West Side flophouses, put him to work attending to his nomadic clientele. The single-room-occupancy hotels (SROs) and older lodging houses with their five-by-seven-foot sheet-metal cubicles and chicken-wire ceilings, renting for sixty to ninety cents a flop (one night's stay), were the foundation of a sophisticated and profitable company town.

Money on Skid Row was recycled efficiently from the down-and-out into the hands of landlords and store owners. Taverns kept the men in alcohol while providing them a permanent address to receive their relief and disability checks; loan sharks fronted the men cash at 50 percent interest for three days; "Buy and Sell Anything" shops offered a market for stolen goods; junkyards took scavenged metal by the pound.[6] With a darting swipe of his paw, Charles Swibel learned to pluck the money flowing down Madison Street. These were the same ursine skills he would perfect over the next twenty years as chairman of the Chicago Housing Authority. Exploiting the cash flow of a closed system like the Main Stem taught him how to leech millions from the CHA, and to do it much more efficiently. Swibel brilliantly removed the middleman, the alcoholic with a check to cash, and started playing with the billions the CHA received over the years in federal housing grants. Charles Swibel, who resurfaces several times in this tale, was the enduring counterexample for any serious, professional developer. But there was no better deal maker.

Swibel continued playing both sides of the line separating public and private development. He was chairman of the patronage-rich CHA and a public servant when he bid on Madison-Canal, the last of the crudely "inside" redevelopment deals. One of Swibel's original partners at Madison-Canal was Kemmons Wilson, who had developed Holiday Inn from a single motel into a billion-dollar enterprise. Wilson and Swibel proposed to build two tall office buildings on two blocks of Madison Street between Clinton and Des Plaines. But once Swibel got clear title to the land, nothing got built. Kemmons Wilson left Chicago, and Charles Swibel had acres of cheap cleared land, compliments of the city.[7]

In 1976, the federal government built a new General Services Administration (Social Security) headquarters on the condemned land between Des Plaines and Jefferson. Swibel sold the land to the GSA for a profit. This went directly against the terms of the original redevelopment agreement, which stipulated that only Swibel had the right to develop the property and specifically prohibited him from selling to others for profit. But no one in the city or federal government called him on this violation; they continued to let him land-bank—locking in a low price and waiting on development. With the general inflation of real estate through most of the 1970s, the former slum land doubled several times in value.

Retaining title to the land, but assiduously failing to keep up the taxes between 1974 to 1980, Swibel just waited for someone to come and buy him out. An out-of-town executive who had to do business with him left, swearing, "I won't have any part of it, now or ever. There are just too many buckets of honey to get stuck in if you don't play their games in Chicago."[8] When Swibel was asked by a friend why, rich as he was, he still grabbed for more, Swibel answered with a question, "What else can I do?"

Anticipating an imminent sale of his Madison-Canal blocks in April 1981, Swibel paid Cook County more than $1 million in back taxes and penalties, making the unusual request that Judge Reginald J. Holzer put the cashier's checks in escrow pending an appeal. Holzer was a sitting judge in chancery court with jurisdiction over foreclosures and other potentially lucrative matters concerning real estate. It came out later in Operation Greylord that Holzer was an especially useful choice for a referee. An elaborate federal sting, Greylord put nine judges and thirty-nine attorneys in jail and provided a rare view of how cozy business and politics can get in Chicago. In 1986, Judge Holzer was sentenced to eighteen years in prison on charges including extortion, racketeering, bribery, and mail fraud. "He turned his official position into a cash station" was the prosecuting attorney's summation of the jurist's view of the law.[9]

Yet, Swibel continued on, in the 1970s, after Daley and the brief successor administration of Michael Bilandic (1976–79). Swibel remarkably resurfaced as Mayor Byrne's chief real estate adviser at precisely the time his urban renewal problems were becoming widely known and just as his two-decade tenure at CHA was coming to an end. A final United States Department of Housing and Urban Development (HUD) audit revealed that Chairman Swibel was, among other things, running the CHA with twenty separate checking accounts. As of January 1, 1982, his agency had accumulated a $38.56 million deficit despite generous subsidies in the form of administrative loans. HUD belatedly charged that Swibel had wasted millions in "questionable purchasing practices," had been provided a $50 million personal line of credit from Continental Bank after parking unspent authority funds in low-interest accounts there, and was using the collateral from these deposits to work out favorable terms for his personal real estate deals. The audit, along with editorial pressure from the local press, forced Mayor Byrne to "reluctantly" remove him as CHA head in 1982.[10]

Swibel, who continued as an unpaid mayoral aide, kept "developing." In 1983, he completed transfer of the Madison-Canal land to McHugh Levin, in partnership with Dan Shannon Associates, who developed an ill-fated, four-tower, mixed-use residential project that by the end of the decade would cost federal and local governments nearly $200 million in defaulted mortgages, loans, and subsidies.[11] The free spending and easy concessions at Presidential Towers, through the 1980s, would provide an eerie counterpoint to the struggle to build in the North Loop, where money somehow proved much harder to come by.

When Mayor Daley first began looking seriously at the North Loop and the area south of Congress Parkway (South Loop), where a "new town"—a semiautonomous city within a city—was proposed for some abandoned railroad property, he at last started backing off from his persistent attack on blight. But he had simply been too good at running the place down. Addressing the State Street Council, a key business group, he insisted, "I'm not afraid to come down to the Loop to shop—with or without bodyguards. In fact, the Loop is the safest part of the whole city—people shouldn't be afraid of coming down here."[12] His reassurances were too late. Land was already in the hands of speculators. After the condemned movie theaters were sold at a huge profit, Thomas Klutznick admitted buying them "for the sole purpose of trying to control these pieces of property, which were all beautifully located in the downtown."[13]

Think of the land under the Empire State Building, Eiffel Tower, Houses of Parliament, suddenly made available at auction. That's the goat the city of Chicago threw out onto the field. There was no getting it back.

Mayor Daley and Charles Swibel were not the only ones in Chicago interested in controlling downtown land. Calling himself Mr. Real Estate, Arthur Rubloff was prepared to spend, he said, up to a billion dollars to transform the seediest part of the North Loop into a paradise of department stores, specialty shops, apartments, theaters, and even an opera house—connected above- and underground by skyways and tunnels. The teeming streets, he declared, were obsolete, ugly relics of the past. Once demolished and cleared, Block 37 would be a perfect site for a new city hall or public library. These North Loop blocks were an agglomeration of litter; not one building was worth saving. If the developer had his way, everything would soon be bulldozed and replaced by a "fabulous idea."

Rubloff had no interest in competing with Swibel in his sleazy part of town. He had bigger plans. From a government report prepared by William Slayton, commissioner of the Federal Renewal Administration of the Housing and Home Finance Agency, the developer learned that between 1950 and 1963 there had been 1,300 urban renewal projects nationwide; 129,000 structures had been demolished on 21,970 newly acquired acres. At the time of Madison-Canal, Rubloff was tracking these mouthwatering statistics, wondering how he might benefit from what the old men at the Realty Club called upzoning. Just as Chicago was finally preparing its downtown for renewal, according to Slayton's calculations land values in the worst parts of towns all over America had increased 427 percent simply in anticipation of redevelopment.[14] Rubloff did the rest of the arithmetic in his head. He had seen the rise in values himself at Carl Sandburg Village, a Near North Side slum-clearance project, completed in the 1960s. There he had joined Albert Robin, the primary developer of a large residential project along Clark Street between North Avenue and Division Street. Rubloff's high bid of $9.17 a square foot won his group the right to build six twenty-nine-story rental towers, two ten-story cooperative buildings, and seventy townhouses. He was allowed to add higher-income units later by simply ignoring the original urban renewal agreement. Ira Bach praised Rubloff's efforts, calling Sandburg Village "the first instance we had seen of spontaneous urban renewal."[15]

But Sandburg needed some political help to keep it in the black. Begun in 1962, the project only proved financially workable as long as Rubloff could keep the taxes low. When the compliant county assessor P. J. "Parky" Cullerton left office in 1974, Rubloff and his partners lost their advantage and were "forced" to sell, albeit at a considerable profit. But Rubloff thought residential urban renewal projects were small change, almost public works, his margin was so low. If he wanted to give money away, he'd build a wing of the Art Institute of Chicago and make sure he got his name on it.

He concluded that without being able to build first-class office buildings as dense as the zoning would allow, there really was no point in dealing with politicians. Arthur Rubloff hadn't spent six decades schlepping around the city in order to waste his time breathing the planning department's foul air. He told anybody who would listen that "he didn't need the city and its lousy politics."[16] Unless, of course, it could really pay off. Getting State and Dearborn Streets at Main Stem prices and then riding the gain, that was something different. Then he could retire to Palm Beach with the rest of his cronies.

· · ·

Arthur Rubloff always had a love for big projects. Right after the Second World War, he fashioned out of a decaying industrial area in north Kansas City a five-square-mile self-contained municipality. In the late forties, he renamed Chicago's North Michigan Avenue the Magnificent Mile, where he conveniently already owned a little land, claiming full credit for an idea that went back to 1910. He followed that, in 1952, with Evergreen Plaza, one of the country's first regional shopping malls. Patiently assembling more than a hundred tiny parcels of land on Chicago's Southwest Side for Evergreen, he had created something he called "astonishing," out of nothing. In the 1950s, Rubloff became so adept a promoter that he could raise land values simply by advertising his interest in an area. With his promotion of North Michigan Avenue, along with Fort Dearborn—150 acres just west of North Michigan Avenue—and Sandburg Village, all ambitious projects extending the downtown to the north side of the Chicago River, Arthur Rubloff solidified his reputation as a real estate prime mover, someone able to get things done. His advertising signs were all over town. He made himself unavoidable, an inevitability.

· · ·

One of Arthur Rubloff's ubiquitous downtown real estate signs (1970s)

With his one good eye, natty suits, gray bowler, and walking stick, Rubloff had taken to visiting City Hall the way a plaid-suited dandy goes to the racetrack. Leaning on the infield fence, smoking a cigarette with an Elmira filter, he liked to think himself an expert handicapper. Staying close to the action, a tout could pick up useful information.

A political junkie, Rubloff wormed his way onto the tenth floor of City Hall, the Department of Planning, greeting the secretaries with a "Hi, call me Art" sort of familiarity and leaving small thank-you gifts for the bureaucrats he romanced for information. Daley received him semiannually in his outer office, knowing Rubloff was always on the scent for new city projects. So what if he got the bum's rush. From Rubloff's point of view it was worth the aggravation to get a firsthand impression of what the mayor was thinking a little earlier than the next guy. He wanted to be in position to "help the city," the way Charlie Swibel and his buddies were giving Daley a hand over at Madison-Canal, but without ever stepping over the thin line that separated smart dealing from political fixing.

In the last years of the 1960s, when Rubloff began talking privately about doing something about Block 37 and the rest of the North Loop, he made it sound as if he had the authority, directly from the mayor's office. No other respectable businessman had ever bothered with the area before, except to pick properties off on a building-by-building basis. Their haphazard efforts at rebuilding had resulted in a gap-toothed downtown. Century-old lofts were wedged in like doorstops next to steel-and-glass towers. With one landlord investing a fortune to improve his property, there was no incentive for his neighbor to do anything with his. For spending nothing—cultivating a commercial slum—the landlord received an enormous passive benefit from the neighboring improvement.

Uneven development was a new lamp shade in an old living room and made no economic sense. The real estate market left to its own sluggish pace had produced too many small owners on prominent blocks. So Rubloff didn't wait for the troops to rally around him. He simply climbed the trench. In his own mind, he was merely imitating the way Daley, in building Daley Center, had treated long-unproductive real estate. Rubloff retained the city's best architects to draw plans and build elaborate models of the downtown. These "visions" he would show to people in his office as if he himself were heading the Department of Planning. No one in the city bothered to correct this impression.

For Rubloff and the city had two big problems they couldn't solve individually. When Rubloff let the word leak out in 1970 that he was ready to improve the center of the city, an improbable alignment of ambition was formed. Neither he nor the government yet had any capital of their own to invest in the redevelopment area, nor did either party own any of the land. An odd, uncelebrated marriage of self-interest took place. City Hall and the Brunswick Building, diagonally across the street, where Rubloff worked, were two nodes of power in the city during the 1970s. No referendum was ever held, no agreement was ever signed, but somehow Arthur Rubloff was given the strong impression that he was Mayor Daley's North Loop Haussmann, his private Robert Moses.

For almost a decade, this private developer claimed he had the authority to reshape the center of America's second-largest city, and no one in the city ever successfully contradicted him. The Rubloff-Daley North Loop Redevelopment Project was the last time in America a big-city mayor and someone representing rich international interests would meet as equals. In the 1970s, with municipal governments in steep decline and the private sector on the ascendancy, Arthur Rubloff—already well past retirement age—got himself in position to appropriate no less than one-fifth of Chicago's downtown for his own purposes. Appreciating how he nearly pulled off this coup requires a detailed understanding of the intricate tango of manipulation and influence peddling that has reshaped American cities in the last twenty years. Richard Daley and Arthur Rubloff, frequent adversaries who shared no deep trust, were astonished to discover that they were locked in each other's arms, each one trying to lead; neither could go forward without the other.

Arthur Rubloff said he was born in 1902. But he lied about his age, one of many tiny vanities that got fixed in place during his long lifetime. He was most likely two or three years older than he claimed, an inch shorter, and a lot richer.

He was the oldest son of Russian-Jewish immigrants who had settled in a series of small towns near Duluth, in Minnesota's Mesabi Iron Range. The American Siberia, where Solomon Rubloff owned a small variety store that supported his wife, three sons, and two daughters, was a gulag of company towns owned by United States Steel. The iron mines and lumber mills employed immigrants who worked hard and saved money so that their children might one day reinvent themselves. A rugged, single-purpose, boomtown mentality stayed with Arthur Rubloff all his life.

As for the place itself, the young man couldn't get out fast enough. In towns where adults did hard work with their hands, Rubloff used his head. He cornered the town's newspaper business, delivering the *Duluth Herald, Chicago Evening News,* and the *Police Gazette.* For extra money he set pins at Chisholm's Neilly Hotel and set traps for rabbits that he sold to the trade for meat.

Barely out of grammar school, he shipped out for eighteen months as a cabin boy on a Great Lakes freighter, only to jump ship in Buffalo after he discovered a shipmate had grabbed his life savings—$165 hidden in his mattress. Arriving with only a paper suitcase, Rubloff settled for a time in Cincinnati, a destination chosen at random off the big map in the Buffalo railroad station. There he found occasional work: sweeping out buildings and working as a drapery boy. Going to sea, dogging odd jobs, he had done all his awkward growing up away from any witnesses. By any measure, he had become a great success. At this early date, tall tale and fact were already confused with his own life.[17]

In 1918, he joined his family in Chicago. When Solomon Rubloff saw his son again after five years' absence, the boy had grown into a six-foot-two man with an eye on a new profession: real estate broker. Solomon Rubloff was so impressed; he hired him right on the spot. The elder Rubloff required cheap loft space for his new ladies' garment business. He needed someone he could trust to negotiate for him in this unfamiliar city.

This wasn't a bad assignment for someone who was only recently knocking around Chicago looking for work. Arthur eventually secured unspecified employment with a cloak-and-suit business on Thirty-fifth Street, considerably south of the main manufacturing area. Still in his teens, he began his real estate career by accident. His employer unexpectedly asked him to scout out some space on Market Street, an area west of Wells Street at the lip of the downtown, called the Wholesale District, where Chicago's garment industry was concentrated. The Jews called it the ghetto.

Near Maxwell Street, the Roosevelt Road retail area, and the meat and produce markets, the Wholesale District was also the center of the Jewish real estate business. At its northern limit, in the shadow of the old Chicago Mercantile Exchange on Washington and Wells, mostly Jewish traders bid contracts in butter and eggs, second-line commodities cast off from the high-class Board of Trade on LaSalle Street. Until the Depression, the entire district—right on the Loop's edge—was effectively segregated from downtown. Jews dealt commercial real estate, like butter and eggs, predominantly in the ghetto and never in the Loop. Rubloff's experience of trying to rent out loft space on South Wabash, he recalled years later, was a "nightmare." Not so, brokering in the Wholesale District, where he got work with a knowledgeable old-timer, Alfred Miltonberg, who taught him the business. Rubloff was a productive salesman, but he and Miltonberg soon fell out when the boss insisted on taking over a lucrative transaction with one of the firm's oldest clients that Rubloff had aggressively initiated and was about to consummate. Unwilling to give Miltonberg his usual cut, Rubloff raised the asking price almost 20 percent and took the property to another client, unattached to the firm. He completed the deal, on his own terms, within twenty-four hours.

Through this early brush with authority, Rubloff discerned a powerful network of bright professionals who would be of great help to him as his business interests expanded. Hugo Sonnenschein, the lawyer he retained to negotiate his full share of the commission, got him a job in 1921 with Robert White and Company, with whom he remained until the stock market crash. The deal with White, a 50 percent split on all commissions originating with him, allowed the young broker to get rich and established the pattern for the way he would run his own business. White's company was simply a shell, a way to charge off expenses, for land trading.

When, in 1930, the business began to fail, Rubloff made a list of the city's top-nine Loop real estate firms. But he found that though he was already generating a hundred thousand dollars a year in fees, even during the early years of the Depression, he couldn't get hired. Abel Berland, a Rubloff executive for almost fifty years, explains the problem: "Real estate was a very WASP industry at that time. Not only was the land controlled by New England families and Old Chicago families, but there were very few or any Jews in downtown real estate. Only a handful were so employed and they were employed in the Wholesale District, where Arthur had gotten his start because they were dealing primarily with Jewish merchants and Jewish manufacturers. A little real estate ghetto. Otherwise it was *Judenrein*, and he could not get a job anywhere."[18] Jews were supposed to confine their brokering to the Wholesale District and the neighborhoods in which they lived. As with architecture, banking, property law, and title insurance, the rich downtown commercial real estate business was an effective, tightly controlled monopoly. Arthur Rubloff was about to change all that.

He saw that one way to get into the bigger arena was by doing small favors for the same elite that had denied him entry. The group included Graham, Anderson, Probst and White, a prominent architectural firm, where Rubloff knew a young man on the make, not so different from himself. The firm's specialty was huge, beautifully adorned office blocks, such as the Wrigley Building and Lyric Opera. Rubloff's contact at the firm was Ernest Graham's personal secretary, Charles F. Murphy, who later headed the firm under his own name.[19] Murphy was from the Eleventh Ward, the breeding ground for Chicago's long string of Irish mayors. In return for Rubloff's excellent service to his firm—including tips as to who owned land and was likely to need an architect—Murphy was to provide Rubloff a permanent way out of the business backwaters.

Waiting to move up, the future developer kept an eye on the downtown, learning about the bigger game and working the streets he could. Since deals were leaner in the Wholesale District, Rubloff just did more of them. He had become accustomed to a style of living during the 1920s that, through good and bad times, he never altered. An understudy of his own future prosperity, Rubloff always lived beyond his means, devouring the city's *Social Register* and local blue-blood publications such as *Clubfellow* and *Town Topics* and trying to get the knack of conducting business on a grand scale. He was relentlessly preparing himself for the "big one," a project that would make his name. In the *Social Register*, a thin blue volume that ranked Chicago's first families along with the churches and clubs to which they belonged, Rubloff learned how successful people kept score.

He was cobbling together a credible version of a gentleman from society columns and national magazines like *Vanity Fair*, in which he kept up with international celebrities, such as the dashing Morgan banker Thomas Lamont. But he couldn't hope to perfect a manner anchored in ancient pedigrees and small differences. A society matron of the day explains: "The manner habitual must be self-possessed; there must be an air of well-being and success. Graciousness in readily adjusted degrees, which at one degree warms and at another cools the recipient, is indispensable. An air of complete self-confidence, of easy assurance, with an occasional glint of *hauteur,* is requisite to social success."[20] Harder than patting his head and rubbing his belly at the same time; Rubloff would never get the social game quite right.

All the same, he forged ahead, purchasing his shirts at Sulka's and mailing them back to New York to be laundered at the establishment where Lamont and the other swells sent theirs. He had gold buttons on his fly, emerald studs and links on his shirts; he ordered three dozen suits at a time from Oxxford, the Chicago manufacturer of fine tailored clothing, until he alone was their biggest customer, bigger than Nieman-Marcus. On his frequent trips to Europe he would purchase a dozen assorted sizes of the rosette Stella Solidarieta Italiana—a lost aristocratic order—that he would wear as boutonnieres in the lapel of his coats. He collected clocks to remind himself not to waste time, had his underwear and socks ironed, sent his urine semiannually to the National Bureau of Analysis to assure proper kidney function.

No detail of his personal well-being escaped his staff's attention. He owned a dozen vicuña overcoats, three dozen ties, six gray bowlers from Herbert Johnson Hatters of New Bond Street, London. After only a few months of wear, they were automatically replaced. To make his exquisite taste known to others, he would write letters to business associates, particularly architects whom he controlled in a dependent relationship, to ask small favors. He once messengered over one of his old "sport moccasins" to William Hartmann, to take with him to the French Riviera. Years earlier, Rubloff had bought several pairs but hadn't had the opportunity to replace them. This was business, not fashion—a brilliant improvisation of power. Always dangling another big Chicago project, he knew he had Hartmann mesmerized, under a spell. "This slipper fits me perfectly, except it is a little narrow across the instep, so I would suggest you ask for size 9½ and see that it is the same length. I want the identical style, made by the same people—and if I can't get the same style, then I don't want any," Rubloff instructed. "If you are lucky and can find them, I would like three pair of white, one pair black and one pr. brown," specifying that he wanted them airmailed and marked "Unsolicited Gift," to avoid paying duty. It gave him pleasure to think that Hartmann, key member of the Central Area Committee and partner in the world's most successful architectural firm, was carrying *his* dirty shoe in and out of Europe's grand hotels.[21]

A lover of any artwork he could hold in his hand, Rubloff collected ivory by the shelf at Gump's in San Francisco and fine glass paperweights, stopping only after he had cornered the market. "He bought everything by the joblot," a longtime employee recalled.[22] When the developer agreed to give millions to the Art Institute, he included the paperweights, stipulating that they be exhibited prominently in the corridor that connected the new galleries with the old museum. Until he died and the glass was hauled down to a remote basement gallery, Rubloff's collection would be seen inadvertently by more people than Seurat's *Grande Jatte*.

A magazine Englishman, Arthur Rubloff kept three horses, although he cared little for riding, and an apartment at the Churchill Hotel, which he couldn't afford. For years he owned a mansion in Wisconsin built for the Florsheim family, which he boasted was "just a little something for weekends and holidays." Situated on a chain of seventeen lakes, the 560-acre estate was large enough to require its own fire department and separate houses for two sets of caretakers. A thirteen-car garage, greenhouses, sixty-stall stable, game preserve, and cow barn were maintained at the ready for his rare visits to the country.

More than all the toys that came with success, Rubloff craved work. Then all the ingratiating details of making it in business—all the tiny slights and miserable indignities of selling himself—paid off. His professional friend Charles Murphy gave him an opportunity to break into the closed system of downtown real estate. It was 1930, and the Depression had already shut down many of his more formidable competitors. Murphy explained to Rubloff that his boss, Ernest Graham, might have a "little job" for him. Fifty years later, Rubloff recalled the conversation: "I hurriedly secured an interview [with Graham]. They [Graham, Anderson, Probst] had recently completed the Merchandise Mart on Northwestern Railroad air rights [the legal title to build above the tracks] for Marshall Field and Company. . . . The Mart was the largest building in the world with 4,250,000 square feet of space, but most of the space was vacant. Management had assumed many leases to secure tenants and was now obliged to pay the rent on the unexpired leases it had assumed."[23] Graham needed a real estate agent tough enough to evict the "freeloaders" and replace them with the few people in town still doing any business.

The Mart's architect had convinced James Simpson, Marshall Field's chairman of the board, to hire the broker. Simpson complained that he hated the idea of having to use Rubloff for what he considered the gentleman's business of letting first-class space. A former partner of Daniel H. Burnham and a gentleman himself, Graham countered that in disastrous times business required salesmen and not gentlemen. The little job Murphy steered Rubloff's way would prove to be a franchise. From 1930 to 1934, he was Moses leading the Jews from the wholesale ghetto to the empty Merchandise Mart.

Rubloff succeeded in getting sixty-six cents on the dollar for the worthless leases Field's had taken back after the crash and made himself so indispensable that the initially reluctant Simpson later offered the broker management of the whole operation. Rubloff politely declined Simpson's offer, stayed in business for himself, and watched the $38 million Merchandise Mart go bankrupt and into the hands of another aggressive entrepreneur, Joseph P. Kennedy, future ambassador to the Court of St. James, for only $300,000 down.

As the Depression wore on, all the established Chicago monopolies that had kept Rubloff on the wrong side of Wells Street began to crack, one by one.[24] Working first from rented space on Adams Street and then from a building he owned, 100 West Monroe, Rubloff became a fixture in the Loop. By 1945 he employed 250 people. Pretty much on his own terms, he was downtown for good. But lacking his competitors' old school ties, Rubloff knew he needed a more aggressive formula to attract business, something better than the real estate gentry's conservative strategy of buy and hold—owning a building for decades and living off the rent. Rubloff liked to handle little pieces of many large properties, preferably held by his friends, that he could trade on his own schedule. There was too much potential liability in buying and developing himself. He would rather get in and out of transactions as quickly as possible.

Rubloff's flamboyant style was unique. Other outsiders, mostly Russian Jews, had found a way in earlier, but they played in the shadows, showing off only on their own turf, like A. N. Pritzker, son of Nicholas, who had come to Chicago's West Side from Kiev at the turn of the century, built up a powerful law firm, Pritzker and Pritzker, made money, but never quite made the social grade in America. The final passage for every Eastern European Jew was from the ghetto to the Standard Club, bastion of the earlier arrivals, the German Jews. Decked out like a cruise ship and solid as a bank vault, the Standard Club is only a brisk walk from the Board of Trade and fine professional offices on LaSalle Street. The club represented in its sheer architectural heft the greenhorn's wildest fantasies of success, including the exclusion of others. The Standard Club distanced the daily ceremony of spending money from the gladiatorial spectacle of accumulating it. A tie and jacket are still required in the dining room, and doing business there is discouraged.

Old man Pritzker did deals in his own corner, used the gym and pool as an outer office, signed his name on a wet napkin in the steam room as a makeshift IOU. A. N. had made it from the ghettos of the West Side to the Standard Club, but still hadn't lost entirely the style that had made the family fortune. It took one more American generation to complete the transition.

The Pritzker children were educated in the Ivy League, and they dominated the society pages; so too the Crowns. Also products of the poor immigrant neighborhoods, Colonel Henry Crown and his brother muscled a sand-and-gravel business, Material Service, into a monopoly. Real estate was simply the inevitable by-product of all their other dealing. Cash rich from transactional businesses and pouring concrete, these families needed safe, long-term investments. In time, the Pritzkers and Crowns owned, financed, and leased acres of Chicago real estate, submerging it in the blind trusts that were originally invented to keep all but the elite out of big downtown land deals, keeping their "assets polished," as Nicholas Pritzker liked to say, and always out of sight.

Already established immigrants called this intuitive adaptation to the rough and tumble of business "discovering America." A newly minted American and night-school lawyer, Nicholas Pritzker boiled down complicated constitutional property protections to a simple rubric, "Never sell your land—lease it."

Each of his direct descendants, secretive as a Skull and Bonesman and publicly discreet as an Episcopalian cleric, has worked the system brilliantly. Only when it surfaced that the Pritzkers owned the Hyatt Hotels, and the Crowns a huge piece of the Hilton chain, was the public vaguely aware of these closely held real estate empires. Anchored in Chicago real estate and business, the Pritzkers and Crowns control family fortunes in the billions; their extraordinary wealth has international reach. In the late 1970s, the Pritzkers endowed the annual Pritzker Prize, the "Nobel in Architecture," thus artfully combining philanthropy with self-promotion in the august manner of the Fords and Rockefellers.

Although, in the end, Arthur Rubloff would give his entire fortune to charity, he was never confused with a Carnegie or an Astor, American moneymakers who were able to shed their reptilian skin. He was at best amphibian, grand in pretension but not fully evolved. Rubloff was never really welcomed at the Standard Club, nor really for that matter at the Covenant Club on Dearborn, where the members went for a steam and played cards, freed from work forever by piles of loot made in less easily disguised businesses.

Rubloff was the link between entrepreneurial cash businesses and large-scale commercial real estate projects. He brought Abraham Pritzker as an early investor into Evergreen Plaza and sold the Crowns 300 West Washington, the site of the Chicago Mercantile Exchange until the 1970s. Worried about holding real estate in the 1929 crash, the traders who ran the exchange sold the building to Henry Crown at a fraction of its worth. Even in the worst years of the Depression, the annual rent exceeded the purchase price. These were the sorts of cunning deals upon which the broker solidified his reputation. But the Pritzkers were never comfortable with Rubloff and in the early 1950s pulled their money out of the lucrative Evergreen development. The Crowns continued doing business with him only a little longer, although right after the war, Rubloff used his connections to one of his mentors, New York's William Zeckendorf Sr., to conceal Henry Crown's financing of the United Artists Theater on Block 37.

Rubloff was invariably useful, but neither family ever considered him a peer.[25] Never content to play off center stage, too overt, always making a big fuss over his own role, he was "mean as acid," even one of his closest associates recall, when he didn't get his way. He never deferred, refusing even to share credit for a small leasing deal with his brother Burt. The Pritzkers dealt with Rubloff the way the LaSalle Street law firms dealt with Nicholas Pritzker when he first proudly hung up his night-school shingle. These paragons of American success kept their distance from Rubloff, who still had the stink of the ghetto under his bowler and Savile Row suits. After all, the Crowns owned the Empire State Building, General Dynamics, a mountain in Aspen; and the Pritzkers lorded over vast timberland, farmland, shopping centers, and luxury hotels; Rubloff was a throwback, a Piltdown ancestor. With Rubloff in the picture, the Crowns and Pritzkers thought themselves permanent contrast-gainers.

Social acceptability, of course, carries its own liabilities. Never really "clubbable," a polite term to designate one's social acceptability, Rubloff was free to do what he wanted. His wildest improvisation was to insinuate high-stakes real estate dealing into municipal government, not simply for residential slum clearance but for high-margin commercial development involving hundreds of acres. Before there was any notion of economic slums (derelict commercial property), before a single politician had identified a crisis requiring government remediation, Rubloff saw a business opportunity in the faltering American downtown. This was his genius, his greatest invention. In a 1959 address to Chicago's Building Managers Association he imagined something he called "the central business district slum," exactly the language that would be used twenty years later to justify demolishing nearly seven blocks supporting fifty buildings in the North Loop. "The eradication of commercial slums in our central business district will not come about by itself," he began. Private interests lacked the authority to assemble enough land, and government lacked the financial resources to rehabilitate the failing downtowns.[26] Rubloff had the foresight to position himself right in the middle, between myopic businessmen and paralyzed governmental agencies.

Since the late 1940s, when Rubloff first became involved with a group of businessmen calling themselves the Greater North Michigan Avenue Association, he had been interested in reviving the city commercially by replacing unproductive property with new businesses. He was frustrated that government at all levels lacked the authority to condemn and later transfer to private developers all but severely derelict residential land. And even then cities were required to demonstrate that the subject property met severe legal requirements. There had to be an imminent fire or health hazard and a plan to relocate residents before land could be taken by eminent domain.

The Chicago Land Clearance Commission, created under the Illinois Blighted Areas Redevelopment Act of 1947, was the municipal corporation with those specific powers of condemnation and the government agency that Rubloff initially attempted to leverage. Operating funds provided in 1947 by state grants and city bond issues amounted to $25 million. These were in effect supplements to the federal government's commitment to provide two-thirds of a qualifying project's net cost. The net cost was calculated as the difference between the city's real costs for condemnation and demolition, and resale, at deep discount, to private developers. Rubloff understood immediately that the slum clearance program was a developer's land markdown program. Writing down actual costs to stimulate development was a fine social program, but not for him if the redeveloped area wouldn't support a huge growth in business. There was little profit in rebuilding residential slums.[27] Rubloff concentrated his energies on purchasing huge blocks of as-yet unavailable written-down or discounted commercial land, which he knew he could make pay.[28]

Without a way of redeveloping failed or blighted commercial property in the center of the great city, the stalemate that Daley had recognized between the men with access to capital and the bureaucrats in City Hall would continue. This inaction guaranteed that development would bypass the traditional commercial center of the metropolitan area and leach out permanently to the suburbs. Rubloff warned, "The road blocks must be cleared before the task itself can be performed. They must be cleared by the combined initiative and efforts of all of us who are concerned with the problem—in private business and industry and in national, state and local agencies of government."[29]

Huge real estate projects, not arranged behind the scenes or brokered in back rooms, but planned, announced, and executed publicly as if they were the result of years of solemn deliberation: this was Rubloff's big idea. It set him apart from the contemporary real estate elite of his own background, who barely deigned to take a meal with him. Private capital aligned with city politics until the two were indistinguishable: this was how Arthur Rubloff changed real estate forever. Transforming the business from a polite parlor game to a free-for-all was his complicated legacy.

Daley admired go-getters; they reminded him of himself. But he figured he never would need one like Rubloff again. Sure, during the time he was slowly coming up through the ward organization it never hurt to have a street-smart businessman in his corner. But not now, when he had the big-five bank presidents and CEOs outside his fifth-floor office, waiting on *him*. Nor did he like the idea of having to go outside the safe group of Republican businessmen who had made his job so easy during the successful redevelopment of Dearborn Street. Daley thought he was at last free of the Rubloffs, characters who always had an angle.

Dealing with Rubloff was always risky. Daley knew that he would fight him for recognition. No compliant, invisible man, Rubloff stood out. The developer drew too much attention to himself. All strut, forward leaning with determination when he got out of one of his three Rolls-Royces. His vanity Illinois plate number was 49, only one number less in status than Chicago's cardinal. His chauffeur, in full British Empire livery, matching the colors of the car, drove Rubloff everywhere, even to City Hall, one-half block away. Rubloff so loved making entrances. If Arthur Rubloff saw a kid, he would give him a buck, John D. Rockefeller style. He called it "a buck for luck." This wanton display of power in front of children was just the sort of spectacle that made the mayor queasy. Even the dumbest precinct worker knew that if you really had clout—as every variety of political influence was called in Chicago—it was best kept under wraps until you really needed to whack somebody.

For his part, Rubloff didn't relish flattering this little Irishman even if he was mayor. Squirrel faced, with prominent black-frame glasses, Rubloff towered over Daley. "Mutt and Jeff," one couldn't help thinking when they were pictured together in the newspaper. But he knew everyone had to pay court to Daley. And there was lots to admire about him. He wasn't on the take; he did all the right things to distance himself from the sleaze in City Hall; he was smart; he never got too far out in front of an issue. He was a builder of all the usual stuff, plus miles of public housing, hospitals, a convention center, and a downtown campus for the University of Illinois. Rubloff agreed with the majority of the business community that Chicago had never seen a more effective, reform-minded politician. Rubloff readily conceded that the rebuilt Dearborn corridor—skyscrapers designed by the world's best architects—was an enduring measure of his power: Daley's pyramids. He gave him full credit for that. For the rest of his ambitious building program Daley would have to turn to professionals, like him. That's where Rubloff figured he had the upper hand.

Already in his eighth decade, in the 1970s, and not in the best of health, Daley needed a way to finish cleaning up the downtown. But the mayor had a problem that went well beyond financing a billion-dollar scheme. With the exception of some public garages built during Kennelly's two terms (1947–55), the city owned none of the area, and with Richard Nixon elected on a pledge to end Great Society spending on the cities, Chicago would soon be out of money.

After the disastrous convention and the November presidential election, Daley began carefully sounding out developers. This was about the time Lewis Hill and Miles Berger first began to test Rubloff's interest in the North Loop. Berger was doubly useful to Daley. Not only was he a member of the Chicago Plan Commission, the agency responsible for all land-use decisions, but he also had deep roots in the larger real estate culture. Beginning as property tax advisers in the 1920s, Berger's family had built the sort of business that naturally brought them into contact with the new breed of commercial real estate traders that the mayor required to redevelop State Street and its immediate environs.

Mayor Daley's promotion of the son of a deal-making businessman was the sort of backdoor influence with an important voting block he had always favored. In this quiet way, methodically, on a street-by-street basis, the mayor had dramatically added to the organization's core Irish and black wards. Although not a politician himself, Berger's father, Albert, had solid ties to the West Side Democrats, the base from which Alderman Jacob Arvey had risen to power after the Depression. Arvey was Chicago's most prominent Jewish politician, a former chairman of the Cook County Democratic Party and onetime mayoral hopeful.[30] On July 21, 1953, when Daley became chairman of the Cook County Central Committee, it was Colonel Arvey whom he replaced. Given this turbulent history of inter-ethnic rivalry, Daley needed a young man like Berger as a way back to the Jewish business community, still stewing throughout the sixties over its leader's sudden fall from power.

Miles Berger was the perfect recruit: loyal as any guy from Bridgeport who owed the mayor his job and eager for a chance to be so close to power. And whether Berger knew it or not at the time, he was also being initiated into the city's way of doing business—the pure deal—as near as the mayor ever came to sharing power. The pure deal—the highly ritualized quid pro quo of power sharing—worked not on muscle, like some of the old politics, but purely on mutual advantage, as it had down in the housing projects.

This is how pure dealing worked in Chicago. Businessmen, usually successful in some area of real estate, would be offered one or several pro bono advisory positions in their field of expertise, and the city got the services of talented professionals who would never have stepped inside the grim underpaid catacombs of City Hall. They provided the mayor their "free" advice, and Daley kept the process clean through his autocratic rule. The fear of Daley—his tough etiquette of unspoken rules absolutely regulating behavior and his presence guaranteeing order—was enough to keep the natural anarchy of urban ambition in check.

In 1961, things really began to come together for Berger when he found himself in the same Cincinnati hotel as the mayor, in town delivering a speech to an urban renewal meeting. When Daley was county clerk he used to play gin rummy downtown on Saturdays with Berger's father, in the tax consultant's LaSalle Street office. That weekend in Cincinnati, the mayor promised young Berger his first shot at city contracts. Berger explained,

> I called up his suite after the speech and asked for him. "Tell him it's Miles Berger, Al Berger's son." Sure enough the mayor comes on the phone. Says, "Hi Al." He did that for years, called me Al. He invited me up. I told him about Mid-America [Berger's new appraisal company]. We talked about Dad's business—property tax business, which we still did. I told him we wanted to do appraisal work for the city. He asked if we were qualified, and I told him we were as qualified as any other firm. He said he'd look into it. Three days later I get back home and Jim O'Donahue—I never could get him on the phone—all of a sudden calls me and it's "Miles, this is Jim," and that's how I got started doing—maybe I did some appraisals for him—then I broke into Land Clearance.

Miles Berger continued throughout the 1960s to reward the mayor's trust.

Arthur Rubloff fatally mistook this young Jewish man on the rise as *his* personal insider. Rubloff decided that with the possible exception of Daley's press secretary, Earl Bush, Albert Berger's son Miles was one of the few Jews close to the mayor. He could count on him.[31] The miscalculation was understandable. Rubloff had established his career at a time when ethnic politics were everything. He made much of Berger's position and assumed the younger man would give him another way into City Hall.

Rubloff was not the first real estate professional to recognize how important it was to get close to local politicians, but he managed it with rare élan. He wasn't like the old-time curbstoners—fly-by-night property hustlers who met pols hunched over their drinks in the steamy joints on Block 37. Rubloff's design was always to appear as if he were doing it all for a higher public purpose, out in plain view.

With the help of a full-time publicity agent, his name above all others became linked with the brokering, managing, and trading of land. Like a courtier building his own palace near the king's, Rubloff installed his own offices on the fourteenth floor of the Brunswick Building, where he had a view out his windows of Daley Plaza below, City Hall to the left, and Block 37's Dearborn-Washington side on the right. From the days of his first office—a hallway in a friend's building—he had been in the habit of raising his desk a few inches off the floor so a visitor looked up at him even when he was seated. Down the hall, a gallery of plaques and signed photographs of the developer with important people, was a kitchen with a fine chef worthy of a head of state. A full-time staff served formal meals at lunchtime.

Near Rubloff's office there was a vault that held the gifts dispensed throughout the year to his business associates. He knew exactly what he gave and the price he paid. All details were meticulously recorded in a logbook, such as who had received the oversize monogrammed General Burnside shoehorns he was especially partial to. His secretary kept a special calendar, revised monthly, recording the birthdays of important people and the presents they had been sent in the past. An important alderman like Thomas Keane, even after he had done time for mail fraud, was dutifully sent a small fruit basket on his birthday, every September 29. The columnist Irv Kupcinet—because he often got Rubloff mentioned in the newspaper or spotlighted on television—got a ten-pound chocolate bar; important women received the five-pound version. Every instance of his generosity was noted, no matter how small. Rubloff loved the personal touch, a show of gallantry. Expensive perfumes for the wives of businessmen, Gucci leather for the politicians' girlfriends, a glowing letter for his executives, a cane for his younger brother, regular wining and dining, were all recorded dutifully, preserved in his files. This was a businessman's archive, a waxworks of power where he could browse anytime he needed reminding of his own importance.

In this strictly nonliterary need to write everything down, Rubloff imitated the mayor. Daley religiously kept a diary back home in the modest add-on to his bungalow he called a workroom. Every day for the mayor was the same. Even if he had an evening political event he returned home to have dinner with his family. Every night before he retired, he went downstairs to study briefing books, lift weights, and write. This writing was not

personal—he was not introspective and rarely reflected on important public events of the day. Daley's journal was a boiled-down list of favors. Written in a private shorthand he had perfected as a schoolboy, the mayor
carved his hieroglyph of power: whom he saw that day, the favor requested,
the favor deferred or approved. But never denied; he always left the deliv-
ery of bad news to his aides.

Yet, even for the mayor, dealing with Arthur Rubloff was a challenge.
The developer added a B-movie theatricality to normally somber business
transactions. His irritating Marx Brothers confusion of clown and gentleman—his way of getting position—took some getting used to. Rubloff,
who always created enough agitation to mask, ever so slightly, the pleasure
of moneymaking, jumped at the opportunity to help Daley out with his redevelopment problems.

Since the war, he had struggled to lend his name to some important civic
project. In the early 1950s, he began planning and arranging the financing
for a 150-acre civic extravaganza on urban renewal land north of the
Chicago River, which the developer and his publicity agent first called
Project X—suggesting that he and Enrico Fermi were working on another
atomic bomb—and renamed the Fort Dearborn Plan when it was made
public, cleverly recalling the city's beginnings as a garrison town. Among
other radical changes, Rubloff's plan called for the relocation of all of
Chicago's major public buildings.

At Fort Dearborn, Rubloff emulated his model, William Zeckendorf. In
1946, Zeckendorf convinced John D. Rockefeller Jr. to buy eight acres of
land for $6 million (seventeen dollars per square foot) for the new United
Nations headquarters. He had seen the underlying value where no mortal
had seen it before by "visualizing the area without slaughterhouses . . . all
the land around there blossoming and becoming worth forty or fifty a
foot."[32] Before word got out, Zeckendorf had packed himself off to Europe
and had surrogates buy up seventy-five separate parcels for $3 million
(nine dollars per square foot) around the perimeter of the future UN. The
formula of combining needed public improvements with the accompanying private profits from trading land at the periphery was just what Rubloff
had in mind for Chicago.

Rubloff's enlarged scale of ambition propelled him beyond the gray-
suited businessmen who also made huge deals but kept the details private.
Instead of keeping secrets, Arthur Rubloff proclaimed everything in advance. The developer proudly saved the headline, in Yiddish, from the *Jewish Daily Forward:* "Jew Is Creator of a Plan to Build New Center for Four
Hundred Million in Chicago."[33] But the private redevelopment scheme,
many times larger than New York's Lincoln Center, was abandoned by

Richard Daley during his first term, though the new mayor kept the accompanying legislation, tailoring it to establish the Public Building Commission.[34]

In rejecting the Fort Dearborn project, Daley had humiliated Rubloff
in front of his downtown sponsors, including the heads of Chicago Title,
Marshall Fields, and the architects at Skidmore. But in getting as far as he
did with normally reluctant businessmen, Rubloff had impressed Daley. So
the mayor kept him nearby, skillfully hinting without any promises that the
developer would participate with him in future urban renewal action.

Rubloff knew he had lost and bowed out gracefully. "Dear Dick," he
wrote Daley on October 2, 1958, "Yesterday morning the Redevelopment
Committee of the Building Managers Association met in session for the
purpose of discussing the Daley Plan [Rubloff's Fort Dearborn]—and I
gave them a first rate talking to. I told them this was no time to dilly-
dally—and that out of respect to you and in the interest of developing a
better Chicago, they should not only endorse the plan but do everything to
expedite it."[35] Ending with his generous offer of "any assistance," the "Dear
Dick" letter was Rubloff's new calling card, delivered personally to the
center of power.

With the Fort Dearborn debacle receding into memory, Rubloff spent the
last years of one decade and the majority of another waiting for the city to
make its move on the North Loop—and nothing ever happened. And then,
unexpectedly, Daley finally acted on June 14, 1973. The mayor announced
his North Loop redevelopment plan at a press breakfast held at the Drake
Hotel. Without informing anybody in the Department of Planning, the
mayor, in response to a routine question, proclaimed that he was about to
renew the entire North Loop. Lewis Hill remembers clearly what happened next. As soon as the mayor finished his remarks, Hill's phone started
ringing back at his City Hall office. Reporters were asking him what the
North Loop project was. Nobody had ever heard of it before. Was it true
that the city of Chicago was prepared to bulldoze nearly thirty acres of its
own downtown? It was London blitzed, another earthquake in San Francisco, a terrorist blowing up the New York Stock Exchange. But Chicago
wouldn't wait for a disaster, like the 1871 fire that leveled these same blocks
a hundred years ago, it would demolish by plan. More than fifty functioning buildings, close to seven full blocks, were all ready for execution.
Hill—who hadn't thought about downtown urban renewal in years—recalls thinking, "Oh shit, Rubloff did it again."

. . .

Rubloff understood that the delay in redeveloping the North Loop had created a lucrative spread between the land's bottomed-out current status—head shops and dilapidated office buildings—and its improved future value. Direct government interference in markets invariably distorts values as entrepreneurs exploit the city's mistakes. Social scientists John R. Logan and Harvey G. Mitlitch surmise that "Property prices go down as well as up, but less because of what entrepreneurs do with their own holdings than because of the changing relations among properties."[36] The city unwittingly was about to create an enormous economic bonus in the North Loop that would take special skills to collect.

These were the same odd mix of talents that Rubloff and other unabashed land traders had perfected over decades. City governments are consistently outmatched when it comes to extracting the spread between the current and underlying value of commercial property: the *rent gap* between a property's current and future cash flow.[37] Rent gap is real estate gold or oil, once you find a way to extract it from the land.

Rubloff hit his first big strike during the last years of the Depression when he first settled on a destroy-in-order-to-save-it strategy for distressed downtown properties. He had never been initiated into the civic etiquette of preservation. Newer was better for Rubloff; he lacked any inhibition about leveling monuments. Like every other soul in real estate with too little business after the crash, Rubloff roamed the downtown until he knew every Loop property from basement to attic. He romanced the building engineers, janitors, and elevator operators until he had an insider's view of the physical and financial condition of every building. Simply by showing a little interest and doing small favors, he learned about the broken boilers and who was still paying rent, all invaluable information for a bargain hunter.

People had a habit of confiding in him. He had a gift for putting seemingly unrelated facts together; the stuff his competitors were too busy to notice. In 1938, Rubloff had discovered from reading the morning newspaper that the city of Chicago in digging a State Street subway tunnel had undermined the foundations of the venerable Masonic Temple. Across Randolph Street from Marshall Field's, on the prosperous east side of State Street, the skyscraper with its observation tower was a prime downtown destination from the day it was built in 1892. For a short time the world's tallest building, the skyscraper had retail on the lower floors and was topped by professional offices and lodges for the Masonic order. The huge complex was a wonder of modern organization of the sort Henry Blake Fuller wrote about in *The Cliff-dwellers*. Fourteen passenger and two freight elevators, two five-hundred-horsepower Corliss engines, eight steel boilers, six dynamos, eight large pumps, and miles of electrical wiring were all examples of the same improbable new technology—going full tilt in the heart of the city— on exhibit contemporaneously at the 1893 world's fair.

When Rubloff began his building inspection, the Masonic Temple was in miserable shape. In 1922, the Chicago Order of Masons had sold the building at a loss to a group of local investors who renamed it the Capitol. The new owners quickly accumulated $4.5 million in debt and filed for bankruptcy in 1937.[38] Rubloff learned from the papers that it would cost an additional $100,000 to fix new damage from the subway tunnel borings. The rest was pure improvisation. Dismissing the forlorn building as a "pile of Romanesque Architecture," Rubloff approached the creditors with a proposition. While insisting he loved the "superb architecture," he suggested it was pure sentimentality to try in any way to save this once-elegant structure. With the soft soil rocking under the bankrupt pile of steel and stone, this masterpiece was only a liability on one of the busiest corners in the world.

Rubloff's appeal to the beleaguered owners was to have them, in effect, look under the building, to the ground. After years of neglect, value in the Loop had shifted from the architecture—which had sold at a premium when it was new—back to the land. No matter how grand their architectural pedigree, older buildings were a financial disaster. With imposing charts and figures, he demonstrated his point that more than 220,000 square feet—including almost 50 percent of the tower elegantly reserved for a sixteen-story skylighted interior court—was unrentable. The building as it stood was worthless; it could never get out of debt.[39]

Rubloff proposed what he called a supertaxpayer: a new two-story building designed to fit exactly on the footprint of the old. A "taxpayer" had no architectural pretension. It was built to secure one's title to the land and pay a modest profit until a better deal came along. With the addition of rentable space at the subway level, a total of sixty thousand square feet, he calculated that the New Capitol Building could produce an annual gross return equivalent to that of the original skyscraper, with none of the staggering expenses. Rubloff calculated that one *new square foot* was 7½ times more valuable than one of the old.[40] With the new building loaded with retail businesses geared to the life of Randolph Street, including a six-hundred-seat newsreel theater, value was moved back to eye level and to the mezzanine, where the architects put plenty of glass for commercial displays. In demonstrating that the Masonic Temple was twenty stories too high, Rubloff revived the value of the land and changed the character of the New Capitol property. No longer at the rump end of State Street bring-

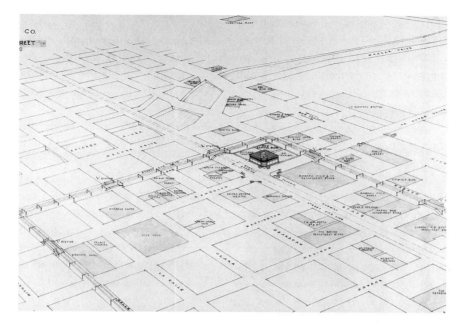

Rubloff's supertaxpayer (1939)

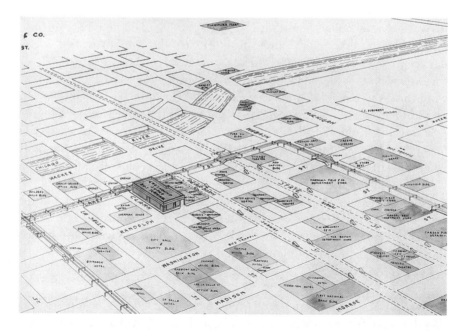

Rubloff's earliest North Loop plan (1939)

ing up the rear of a line of more successful buildings, this supertaxpayer was repositioned to face west toward Randolph and its bustling entertainment district. He successfully demonstrated that to accrue the full advantages of "an improvement which will unquestionably develop this location to its highest and best use under present-day conditions," the ancient skyscraper had to go.[41]

In his ceaseless maneuverings to make money, Rubloff had contributed a powerful conceptual element to a conventional real estate transaction. He radically reimagined the land, thinking of it not as something fixed for eternity but as malleable. The troubled property was staged to exploit the city's original east–west axis—essentially abandoned from the time Chicago's great nineteenth-century land baron Potter Palmer rotated Chicago's commercial district to the north–south by buying up a mile of State Street after the fire.[42] Rubloff's New Capitol was at once shifted out of the prestigious retail orbit of State Street, where it couldn't compete, and aligned with the successful Rialto along Randolph, where it could.[43] In a midwestern city that shut down early, the Rialto—four blocks along Randolph between State and Wells—was going day and night. By cranking the property off State Street and facing it in a more favorable direction, Arthur Rubloff had accomplished the impossible. *He moved land to improve its location.*

A population of insomniacs and stay-outs were the ones he was after with his twenty-four-hour Newsreel Theater. Quoting "confidential information" from an unspecified source, Rubloff gave the combined paid attendance (10,512,027), during 1937 to 1938, of only five of the theaters nearest the New Capitol's State-Randolph corner. Throughout his career, Rubloff would use the magic of numbers, calculated down to the last integer, to provide real estate dealing with the aura of scientific precision.

The value Rubloff had added only continued to accrue. In 1949, the Capital Building Company nearly doubled its money.[44] At the very moment when the suburban exodus was beginning and the economics of the Loop were changing forever, Arthur Rubloff had discovered a radical formula to counter the trend. He made big money in just the spot where the other pros were losing their shirts.[45] Rubloff's love of the bulldozer began at the corner of State and Randolph, where he first gambled and won with the notion that large amounts of money would surely follow bold plans.

Daley's Drake announcement of June 1973 surprised the developer as it had the mayor's closest aides. For years, he hadn't heard anything directly out of the mayor's office. Always the public optimist, Rubloff interpreted

Daley Plaza (1977), with Block 37 in the background

the mayor's remarks as confirmation of his deal with Hill and Berger. Rubloff, earlier in the year, mainly out of frustration, had gone public with his own preliminary ideas for the area. Even though the mayor, at his press breakfast, credited the Department of Planning, his concepts were indistinguishable from the ones Rubloff had presented to a handpicked group of business leaders in March. Rubloff's blueprint was made official on October 3 when the Urban Renewal Board commissioned a $96,000 feasibility study, incorporating the developer's plans of the area. The city had done no independent planning, and the study was paid for by the developer and an organization of downtown businessmen.

Through default, Rubloff had become the planning department's back office. Hill recalls that it was a little after the mayor's Drake announcement that Rubloff got some funding at the First National Bank to help develop *his* master plan for the area; it was also about this time that the developer started showing off a big Loop model with new buildings scattered among the old. With Daley's implied (and undenied) endorsement, Rubloff attempted to seize the initiative, compelling the city to go forward with its plans to acquire all twenty-seven acres. Once that was done, he knew it would sell the blocks to him for next to nothing. According to the city's own definition of blight, the land had to be nearly worthless commercially to justify a taking. Rubloff was merely holding the city to its own rhetoric. In return, he would develop the choice parcels himself and sell the rest to clients such as Hilton at market rates. He'd make a huge profit before a single building was up.[46] In Lewis Hill's opinion Rubloff wasn't interested in developing anything. He "wanted to buy wholesale and sell retail," but it was Arthur Rubloff whom Hill, acting on Daley's orphic mumblings, had put into this extraordinary position.[47]

Remarkably, right from the beginning, the North Loop was already out of Daley's control. All Rubloff had to do was look out his office window to get Block 37 right in his sights. A better view than the mayor's. Who had set up whom? How did it happen? How for five years did Arthur Rubloff become the exclusive planner of the North Loop?

As early as 1970, Rubloff was hearing from his sources—the same Daley loyalists who had been feeding him information for years—that the city had banked close to $44 million, not yet allocated for a specific urban renewal site.[48] Government subsidy like this, no matter how meager, was catnip to developers. Even if it weren't true, Rubloff could use it as an enticement for private investors leery about getting entangled in messy city politics, especially in Chicago. Rubloff presented himself as someone able to handle politicians.

With his political bona fides established, Rubloff began to approach the biggest Canadian developers, such as Cadillac Fairview and Olympia and York, hotel chains such as Hilton and Omni, and venture capital firms such as Charles Allen and Company, trying to tap their direct line to billions in financing. Promising tax money as a way to underwrite the expensive project was Rubloff's in with conservative financiers whom he encouraged to confuse the city's passive support of a complex redevelopment deal with the "full faith and credit" of the United States, which underwrote Treasury bonds and insured them against default. In this way, between 1973 and 1978, Arthur Rubloff improvised a nifty pyramid scheme in the North Loop, with the unwitting city providing all the collateral; he was trying to capitalize the profits and socialize the costs.

In 1971, already secretly preparing to develop the North Loop, Rubloff had spun off an entity called the Arthur Rubloff Development Company. The accounting maneuver removed him officially from the intense day-to-day chores of the real estate business, although he continued using the cash-rich brokerage and management operations to pay his expenses. This divesting of direct control, he told associates, was part of a retirement plan, but for a gentleman used to waking early, seeing dozens of people, and making fifty calls a day, it was hard to slow down. Even his art collecting was frenetic. The bronzes, ivory carvings, and glass paperweights— counted in the thousands—any art work he could hold in his hand. After he cornered the market in paperweights he sent duplicates back to his dealer to offer at auction. He then forgot about them, went to the auction, and bid up the price. With his failing vision and bad eye for art, Rubloff wound up buying back at a premium the dregs of his own collection.

Development for Rubloff was like collecting. He had never really built anything himself during his long career, always hedging with partial ownership of many successful projects. The North Loop, he hoped, would change all that. It was finally the "big one," a monumental collection of buildings right in the middle of the city. He had tried twice before: once with North Michigan Avenue, which proved to be less of a development deal than a brilliant promotion, and then with Project X. He had no political standing—he was not in the government nor was he given any official authority—but he had a wonderful instinct for opportunity.

Rubloff used his earlier "planning" failures as dry runs. As extensive as the North Loop plan was, it was still only a fifth the size of Fort Dearborn and arguably no longer at odds with Daley's own plans for the area. Rubloff persisted in calling the North Loop the Chicago 21 Plan, to echo the Central Area Committee's and city's official designation. Chicago 21 was the city's master plan, or, more properly, its wish list for future development of its central square mile. The renaming suited Rubloff's sense of himself as a city booster, above politics and not in it just for the bucks.

State Street at the time of Rubloff's "great idea"

The intentional confusion helped. In reality, there was no city plan. Arthur Rubloff was, in fact, the first planner of the North Loop. No one in the mayor's office was about to stop him. Recognizing there was to be no resistance, he immediately honed in on three blocks on State Street between Washington and Wacker. On Blocks 36 and 37, he had plans for a retail mall and public library and a hotel for Block 16. He said anything that would make the development appear sufficiently dignified, with a clear public purpose. But it always retained his stamp. A library in a mall was a wacky combination for anybody except Rubloff, whose idea of literature was a Christmas catalog from a Bond Street haberdasher.[49]

Rubloff's recent experience in development was limited to the California shopping centers he was building with Alfred Taubman. Rubloff claimed to have discovered Taubman, a talented entrepreneur, "wasting" his talents building small strip malls around Detroit. He wanted Taubman more for his contacts with large users of space, such as department stores and hotels, than for his technical experience as a developer.[50] Malls multiplied retail square footage the way skyscrapers intensified premium office space—requiring many more users than even the largest single-store facilities—and combined urban density with suburban control, the security of the locked space. Rubloff's ideal urban place was a perfect hybrid with no identity of its own. He reasoned that if shoppers were ready to spill their hard-earned money in old factory spaces, like shopping mall/industrial park Ford City on the Southwest Side, imagine what they would do, if properly encouraged, on State Street, which for almost a hundred years had been one of the world's prime retail locations.[51]

Rubloff took the unformed idea the back-office planners were toying with when they first approached him about doing something about downtown and gave it a specific shape he could hawk to investors. He made one new idea out of two old ones (combining the suburban mall with urban renewal), redirecting public resources away from the ghettos back again to the rich middle. With visions of something like his own Evergreen Plaza mall only a twenty-minute ride from the best neighborhoods on the bus, eight minutes on the subway or el, he proposed, just for openers, a new multimillion-square-foot climate-controlled Main Street. Snugly fit on two blocks of old State Street was a relocated piece of the suburban dream, with a ten-story central library thrown in as a bonus.[52]

What was good in the 1950s for Chicago's Southwest Side, he reasoned, was right in the 1970s for downtown. He quickly renamed Block 37, calling it Block 1, and made it the center of his plan. In his mind, not one of the old buildings in the North Loop was worth saving except for the Reliance Building, already declared a city monument and virtually untouchable any-

"Junk" on Block 37

way. After the public outcry that followed the demolition of the Garrick Theater in 1961 and Chicago Stock Exchange in 1972—two downtown landmarks designed by Louis Sullivan—the city council passed a handful of ordinances that offered special protection to a few best examples of the city's celebrated commercial-style architecture. However, most of the city's fine stock of historic commercial architecture remained completely unprotected or had an empty endorsement from the National Register of Historic Places. The federal government could only make recommendations. The National Registry is only advisory and has no statutory power.[53] A building's inclusion as an architectural snail darter on the National Register paradoxically made it more of a target.

Never bothering to wait for the city to condemn the land, Rubloff began working without any proper authority, declaring all the North Loop "junk," a collection that included several buildings already cited for their historic or architectural merit by the bureaucrats in Washington. Rubloff persisted in describing Chicago as "a lethargic city" and offered that "about 80 per cent of the buildings in the Loop are obsolete and should be demolished, but nobody has the courage to go ahead and start it."[54] With a grant from the Greater State Street Council and a little of his own money, he hired Charles William Brubaker, president of Perkins and Will, to draw up some plans.[55]

On February 6, 1973, months before the city's announcement of any formal urban renewal initiative, Brubaker presented Rubloff with an estimate of ninety-six thousand dollars to prepare some plans and build a large presentation model for three blocks on State Street. Rubloff, who was mainly self-educated and still signed his name in the blocky, distinctively crabbed handwriting of an immigrant, marveled at Brubaker's facility as a draftsman. He admired Brubaker's uncanny ability to draw instantly what his client was thinking, effortlessly producing sheet after sheet of pen-and-ink sketches. Each drawing had a neat three-dimensional look that anyone could understand. Rubloff's intention, from the beginning, was to use Brubaker's work as the basis for all his future claims on the land. In the absence of any comprehensive North Loop plan, Brubaker's vivid drawings gave the developer credibility with the politicians and cynics in the real estate trade. The architect's easy freehand planning lent the inchoate North Loop initiative a reality it lacked in fact.[56]

Rubloff never bothered with the niceties of prior ownership or longtime leases on the subject blocks. A prospector driving a stake into the land, he cried "Eureka," and waited for the rush. Brubaker's sketches were his hurried claim. All Rubloff's efforts were aimed at making himself indispensable to the process. Before the city made its move or any other private developer got wind of what he was doing, Arthur Rubloff, with money in his pocket and a plan for the future, planted himself in the neglected middle of town.

Because malling had replaced planning, there were no committees to consult, no global abstractions about the welfare of man, no detailed plans, only one massive interrelated architectural complex with walkways under and bridges over the once-threatening streets. If others followed Rubloff's lead, the city could be rebuilt all at once in thirty-acre chunks, in what were called superblocks, over at Perkins and Will. Then the good—films, libraries, performing arts, and shopping, especially shopping—would win over the bad, the peripatetic, aimless, and disordered life outside. Independent of the weather, secured, turned in on itself, turbulent urban life would then be tamed, recapitalized, and made to pay handsomely. Reclaiming the center, malling out the shock and funk that had finally brought even the indomitable Richard Daley to his knees, Arthur Rubloff offered to save the city, even if he had to do it all by himself.

Rubloff figured that he was working unopposed in the North Loop. The Central Area Committee issued its long-awaited master plan, *Chicago 21: A Plan for the Central Area Communities,* in 1973 but seemed more interested in the area of the Loop south of Jackson Street. Daley was employing his familiar divide-and-conquer strategy, in effect having the Central Area Committee and Arthur Rubloff both thinking they had his full attention and the authority to move ahead. After the mayor's sudden death on December 20, 1976, it was clear that no single entity in the city was in control of planning. Every special interest, including Rubloff with his jump-start in the North Loop, claimed to be carrying out Daley's will.

Rubloff's familiar repertoire of secret plans, private luncheons, unveilings of scale models, leaked documents, his illusion of complete control, would in the past have been effortlessly parried by a healthy Richard Daley. But the mayor wasn't well throughout the seventies, and Rubloff's machinations further burdened an overwhelmed city government never quite recovered from the troubles of 1968.[57] The mayor's decline in office produced the sad spectacle of key government agencies filled with brilliant second bananas, all unable to make the simplest decision. When their boss died, two very different but ineffectual successors, machine-loyalist Michael Bilandic, followed by a self-professed reformer, Jane Byrne, created a power vacuum that put the whole North Loop up for grabs. Others who got a shot at building in the Loop got it only as a result of the city's inability, without Daley at the helm, to follow through on its trumpeted development initiatives in a timely manner. This governmental inaction combined with Rubloff's ceaseless inveigling produced a free-for-all, destined to yield disappointing civic results. Rubloff's Magoo-like bumping into authority, once thought amusing over at the Hall, inadvertently swamped an already weakened, leaderless, nearly bankrupt city government in the booming private capital markets of the 1980s.

At the very moment the city of Chicago, under court directive, was decentralizing and disbanding its ancient political machine and needed centralized leadership the most, there was no one to lead.[58] A private-development frenzy had already been unleashed with no sober public authority left to restrain it.[59] The melancholy result was too many insolvent sixty-story skyscrapers, costing between $100 and $175 million apiece to build, subsidizing tenants with rent concessions and other enticements to make the buildings appear prosperous and occupied.

. . .

A closer look at Rubloff's North Loop plan is necessary to understand how radically the rules had changed just as another, even more powerful, group of entrepreneurs was awaiting its chance to play the great game. While the city spent the 1970s getting the legal authority to condemn, take, and transfer to new owners private commercial property, Arthur Rubloff was busy scaring up billion-dollar investors for the land he was "certain" the city of Chicago would make his at bargain prices. Essentially left alone to fantasize what he would build over the compacted debris of his competitors' buildings, Rubloff hired more architects, commissioned appraisals, lured investors, and tried to interest Canadian developers in some of the best blocks. He went out of state and then out of the country for his financing. In this way, Rubloff successfully marketed himself as the ambitious outsider's best way into City Hall. Letting them think that his enterprise was too big to fail, he passed around what he unfailingly claimed to be "confidential" government documents and promised to deliver the mayor of Chicago to his potential Canadian partners, Cadillac Fairview and Olympia and York.[60] He put on quite a show.[61]

Arthur Rubloff made commercial real estate glamorous, while involving government in the process to enlarge the scale of his deals. At the helm of the North Loop redevelopment in the beginning of 1973, he must have felt that all the pieces of this crazy puzzle had wonderfully fallen into place. Instead of behaving like a good citizen following carefully considered public policy initiatives, he was leading. The long years of hanging around City Hall had paid off. Daley's precipitous political swoon had finally cracked the machine. Arthur Rubloff simply walked through the breach ahead of everyone else.

In the early years of the North Loop Daley considered Rubloff merely a stalking horse. He had tried playing him off against the more cautious types on the Central Area Committee, which included corporations, utilities, and big retailers—businesses that must be located downtown but are basically hostile to Democratic politics and entrepreneurs.[62] Headed at its inception by the chairman of the Chicago Title and Trust Company, Holman Pettibone, the CAC had been, from the early days of Daley's first term, the city's watchdog. And Pettibone, whose title company had a monopoly on all land transfers within the city and collar counties, was in a particularly good position to oversee Chicago's development activities. Most CAC members lived in the suburbs and only commuted to Chicago, publicly disdaining quid pro quo urban politics as a primitive throwback to the frontier days. The Central Area Committee's true interests were never immediately com-

Arthur Rubloff posing in
front of his model (1973)

patible with those of the mayor. It always took some convincing. Rubloff
came in handy because he had a line to the entrepreneurs, a working relationship with the State Street crowd, and the ability to move fast. In addition to bringing in the executives at Marshall Field's and Commonwealth
Edison, Rubloff was also useful for stimulating the glacial planning bureaucracy on the tenth floor of City Hall. Luckily, the discouraging subtleties of power were mostly wasted on Rubloff. In his own mind, at least,
he had so completely charmed his way into the inner circles of the Daley
administration that City Hall was busily doing his bidding.

Rubloff had no doubt that he had earned a monopoly over the whole
downtown—and, more important, that Daley saw it his way too. When
Perkins and Will completed its scale model of the redeveloped North
Loop, the developer gallantly invited the entire Central Area Committee
for an advance look. Most dutifully came to his offices on the morning of

February 4, 1974, not quite certain that the mayor hadn't gone mad and put Rubloff in control. Preening in front of the model, giving interviews to reporters, alluding to this major retailer and that world-class financier he had all lined up, Rubloff was so high he could have started the demolition with his own fists.

The bluff worked. The Central Area Committee effectively dropped out of the North Loop, concentrating its energies in other key areas of the downtown that did not require government subsidies. For a few silver platters of scrambled eggs, steam-tray sausages, and a model paid for by the State Street Council, Rubloff had bought some time as he waited for the city to take the land and give him title.[63] Once he had that in hand, he could offer the land as his equity portion of a redevelopment deal with an investment bank or insurance company, conveniently providing the rest of the required capital in debt. No money out of his own pocket. Just another pure deal.

If everything kept going smoothly, he would be part of several billion-dollar deals as the entire North Loop, along with some contiguous properties of which he already had a piece, got redeveloped. Rubloff still had a stake in The Brunswick Building, an older low-rise on Wabash, and the Trailways Bus Terminal on Randolph Street; he also managed or brokered several other parcels of real estate in the redevelopment zone. He was using real estate he didn't own to control huge amounts of capital, drawn from every civilized corner of the globe. Rubloff had improved on Zeckendorf's method. Zeckendorf had unfortunately gone bankrupt a decade earlier, after mistakenly using personal guarantees or recourse loans to finance his empire. That wouldn't happen to Rubloff; that was the "beauty part," he said, of having the city as your partner. Arthur Rubloff co-signed nothing; he didn't have to. Down at the Board of Trade, where billions in futures are traded daily, they call it laying off risk, or finding the next-best fool.

So Rubloff continued "developing" in the absence of any real property to develop, and the mayor continued proclaiming all sorts of progress in his crusade to bring back tens of thousands of Chicagoans who had decamped to the suburbs. Daley likened the effect of Chicago 21 to the 1958 Central Area Plan, which he claimed was responsible for a $5 billion building boom, "one of the great acts in the renaissance of the city."[64]

From the Great Depression to the beginning of Daley's first term in 1955 there had not been a major commercial building erected in the city. Under Daley (1957–73), Chicago experienced a true building boom, putting 22 million square feet of new office space on line. The city was careful to position the North Loop as simply a continuation of this natural process of recapitalization. Lewis Hill, then commissioner of both the Department of Urban Renewal and the Department of Development and Planning, referred favorably to Perkins and Will's initial three-block scheme. However, he refused to release any studies and was careful not to mention Rubloff in any official capacity. Following the mayor's explicit direction, Hill would not acknowledge that the North Loop was in reality a joint venture with ancient Arthur Rubloff doing all the venturing.

But in September 1973, City Hall officials, using Rubloff's appraisal figures without attribution or independent audit, pegged the initial land acquisition costs at only $25 million. From only the first three redeveloped downtown blocks, they confidently maintained that the city would benefit from $500 million in new construction and a tenfold increase in commercial property taxes. This remarkable windfall was being guaranteed four years before a single dime was committed to the project, four years in advance of the legal authority to redevelop, five years before the first official plan, and nearly a decade before the first North Loop demolition took place.

Ready or not, the starting gun had fired in 1973, setting events recklessly into motion: lawyers were retained, ward politicians alerted, appraisers set to work; architects and engineers were busily designing as all the early money that could be extracted in fees started to flow. The initial idea of North Loop redevelopment, carelessly spitballed out of the mayor's office, announced impulsively over breakfast at the Drake, and further articulated by Rubloff, had somehow become a most awkward inevitability. With no official government plan, no financing, no real authority, Arthur Rubloff installed himself as czar of the North Loop as if he were old Daniel Burnham himself.

Fronting a giant public project was the highest form of status in the city. Since the World's Columbian Exposition, hosted by Chicago in 1893, the city had been obsessed with comprehensive plans. The architect-businessman Daniel H. Burnham had assembled a group of prominent American architects, mostly from the East Coast, to design what they called the White City for the exposition. Temporary steel-frame sheds, lathered with white plaster to simulate ageless neoclassical detail, were an immensely popular aspect of the fair, which was visited by millions. The fair suffered a devastating fire shortly after it closed in 1894, which melted the minimally fireproofed architecture in a few hours. The architecture's disappearance in fact just intensified it in memory. It's the lost Atlantis to which all subsequent planning longingly refers.

The 1909 Chicago Plan proposed that the entire city be transformed using the White City model. Permanent neoclassical buildings at a uniform cornice line, as in Paris, would replace the hodgepodge of existing architecture. Several elements of the plan were enacted over time: the elaboration of the park system, protection of the lakefront, large avenues such as Congress Street and Wacker Drive, ceremonial entrances, monumental sculptures framing roads that go nowhere. The plan's existence in fragment, recalling the popular fair's catastrophic demise, tended to reinforce rather than diminish it as an idea. In Chicago, the Plan Commission, a group of civic leaders originally responsible for implementing Burnham and Bennett's recommendations, were in later years the mayor's guide to matters having to do with land use. In Chicago, the Plan Commission is commonly confused with an actual planning department, which the city lacked until Daley's first term.

Before Daley, planning in Chicago was effectively left to the businessmen, with the mayor's office offering belated approval. Any kid brought up on the *Wacker Manual* or in the Museum of Science and Industry, the only building restored after the fair, knew two Chicagos. There was the gritty mercantile and industrial reality interposed with the genteel, fanciful, planned fragments, visible everyday on a bike ride near the lake or a walk downtown. At the time the North Loop was locked in the planning department's back offices, the city had not yet completed a plan. A longtime alderman, Leon M. Despres, one of the few authentic independents ever to sit on the city council, observed Chicago's surprisingly sclerotic history of planning: "Chicago's housing, urban renewal and metropolitan problems require the best planning available. The department is permitted to plod along on an announced project to unveil a 'comprehensive plan' at the end of 1962—just in time for the next mayoralty election. Such grandiose blueprints, however beautiful, are always out of date even before they are revealed."[65]

It took considerably longer than Despres imagined, until, in fact, December 1966, before John G. Duba, commissioner of development and planning, finally produced the city's long-awaited Comprehensive Plan. By the time Rubloff really started gearing up for the North Loop, the city had issued a few more versions of Duba's herculean feat, filled with more pretty pictures, flowcharts, and site plans with multicolored arrows. These belated public-planning initiatives were bracketed by the even grander Central Area Plan and its expansion later into the *Chicago 21* document—two exclusively *private* efforts. A later chairman of the Plan Commission, Julian Levi, arrogantly suggested that realism should dominate planning over at City Hall: "The thing I always find discouraging is that people talk in glowing terms of these plans, without specifying how we get from here to there.

The Rialto (looking east; Block 36 on the left, Block 37 on the right) in the early 1970s. In the right foreground is the north side of the Daley Center, with the parking garage that replaced the Garrick Theater across the street.

What is a realistic price tag? Where will the financing come from? These things need a hard look."[66]

A real plan with a realistic budget, work schedule, performance criteria—this was something new, and it really wasn't the sort of planning Rubloff or most politicians had in mind. "Planning" was one of those talismanic words in Chicago, like "clout." On its own, "planning" never had much meaning, but was awfully useful if placed in the right sort of incantation. In this environment, Rubloff, the broker, property manager, developer, philanthropist, art connoisseur, was a planner too. Born before the Chicago Plan was first announced and schooled himself on the *Wacker Manual,* he knew how profitable it could be to cloak a real estate play in official rhetoric.

Chicago's North Loop was better than an ambassadorship to some out-of-the-way country. Give a few million to both parties every four years, and

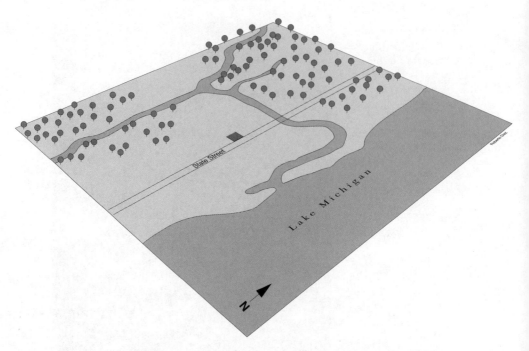

Block 37 superimposed on a computer map of Chicago as it might have appeared before the 1830 platting of the city. The area between Lake Michigan and the future State Street is mostly landfill produced from the rubble of the 1871 fire.

if you're lucky they reward you with a stint in Upper Volta, to be a slow-moving target for terrorists. This was the kind of prize for being old and rich that his cronies down in Florida lorded over him every winter. But that was nothing, Arthur told them, back in Chicago he *was* the government. Sort of. Arthur Rubloff was never more in love with himself. Acting downright governmental, entering into solemn agreements with those stiffs down at the State Street Council, and dressing the part, Arthur Rubloff, nearing eighty, felt reborn.[67]

Rubloff immediately set to work with his (three) renumbered State Street blocks between Washington and Wacker. These were significant proprietary acts, given that Rubloff did not yet own any of the land and never would. Renaming the land effectively dislodged the property from its long history. Blocks 37, 36, and 16 were older than the town itself, named before Chicago was incorporated, appearing in James Thompson's 1830 and James S. Wright's 1834 survey maps as if they had been the white man's forever. Rubloff's new classification echoed the original act of conquest, when the

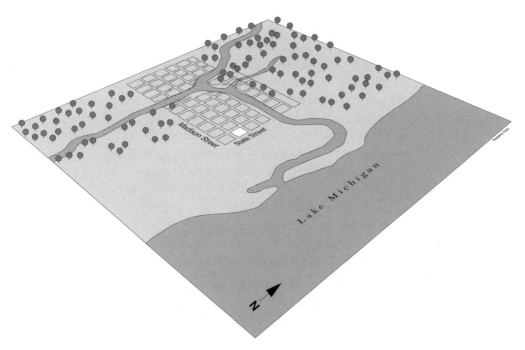

Computer rendering of Block 37 (shaded area) after Thompson's 1830 survey and map of the city

first square miles of Indian lands were purchased at a penny an acre and subdivided for resale.

Rubloff further assumed control by employing the mayor's own consultants. Along with William Brubaker at Perkins and Will, Rubloff retained Skidmore's Roger Seitz, and Miles Berger. Berger was so discreet in the exercise of real political power that he was virtually unknown to the public at large. He ran his own appraisal firm, Mid-America Appraisal and Research Corporation (MARC), and maintained his father's tax-consulting business. Albert Berger, whose first big clients in the 1920s were Chicago Motor Coach Company, W. F. Hall Printing, and the Yellow Cab Company, knew his way around Cook County government, particularly the office of the assessor. In real estate, a bad tax assessment can quickly turn a profitable deal sour. Many a sale for a commercial building falls apart at the last minute because of a failure to get the taxes under control. Rubloff knew of the Bergers' reputation for providing a developer a favorable tax situation. In the old days, he had retained the elder Berger and was eager as he geared up for his last real estate extravaganza to see how well his son Miles played the game.[68]

By deftly exploiting the shifting nature of political influence, Miles Berger had penetrated deeper into politics than his father had ever been able to do. He understood early on that one gets things done in American cities not through graft, which can land one in jail, but by overcoming the bureaucratic process. Influencing government, local lobbying, was now a profession practiced from the safety of the city's finest towers and not at the seamy ward level. Berger understood zoning, appraisal, real estate financing, and taxes. He had the names and private numbers of those in City Hall and the county who could make things happen. Unusually patient, never with his hand out, always publicly generous, Berger made his way. He was by his own definition only a real estate adviser, prudently counseling clients on how to move their projects through a maze of regulations and unseen complications.

Getting things accomplished in a big American city requires a certain sort of expertise not normally available in universities and graduate schools of business. For example, to get a zoning variance for permission to cut a curb for a new driveway or to clear an alley for a skyscraper requires the same two-page application and a nominal fee. Aldermen used to handle both, receiving in return more "consideration" for an office tower built in their territory than for a driveway. Zoning matters in the neighborhoods are still handled by the alderman, often through a committeeman or Democratic precinct captain. A generous contribution to a politician's kitty is considered just compensation for facilitating the process. Often an actual facilitator, like a grimy character out of Dickens, is hired to stand in line at the various governmental offices to make sure everything goes smoothly. For generations of ward bosses and their hangers-on, moving permits through the Hall was generally considered blue-collar work, hardly requiring the legal acumen of a Learned Hand or Louis Brandeis.

Facilitating was one of several lucrative franchises disturbed but never completely eliminated with the introduction of serious governmental reforms. Beginning in the 1960s, political influence simply moved up from the tavern to the corner office, naturally becoming more profitable when it could no longer be practiced so overtly. Gone were the days when elfin Paddy Bauler danced a jig in public, proclaiming, "Chicago ain't ready for reform." Alderman Bauler did business in his bar, receiving petitioners as if he were the pope, never living long enough to see that reform politics with its myriad of new regulations and prohibitions would be better for his business.

Miles Berger was one of the few able to accommodate the change from Baulerism to the new corporate style. He was as comfortable with the powerful zoning attorneys, partners in the city's white-shoe firms, as he was with the old cigar-chomping pols. The difference was only the scale of money involved. It might take just a few thousand dollars in contributions to a powerful alderman's campaign to keep him helpful. At minimum, it would set a developer back tens of thousands in fees for the same zoning consideration when handled by establishment law firms like Sidley and Austin or Mayer, Brown and Platt. Lawyers mystified the approval process, and politicians went along with the change, simply following the lead of a formidable lobby of new professionals cashing in on their old turf.

Miles Berger

Berger followed the trend. He had learned the real estate business at his father's deathbed. At the age of nineteen, dutifully writing down the intricacies of the ad valorem tax law in blue examination books, Miles Berger mastered a potentially lucrative subspecialty. He never gave a second thought to returning to Brown University to complete an undergraduate degree in religion.

Negotiating taxes, an accepted part of doing business in the city, was thought, at best, to be at the border of respectability. Berger aggressively improved upon the company's original businesses with a long list of pro bono activities to raise his own reputation in high civic circles. He was an invaluable resource for the corporate money managers, turning, in the 1970s, to commercial real estate investment as an inflation hedge. Berger knew the financial angles as well as the political.

At the time Arthur Rubloff retained him, Berger was already a member of the Illinois Revenue Study Commission, chairman of the Chicago Real Estate Board Tax Committee, and, most important among his various civic duties, vice-chairman of the Chicago Plan Commission. The developer had correctly surmised that there was no greater power broker in the city, particularly following Daley's death, when there was hardly anyone left from the old regime who knew enough to move forward a large civic project. Only well after the fact would Rubloff figure out that this brilliant public servant had dipped into the old developer's pocket and helped put the North Loop in other hands.

Specifically, he needed Berger's authority with the politicians as an appraiser. There were better technical firms in town, but only Mid-America had a lock on city business. Mid-America's calculation of land values would prove more important to Rubloff than all the expensive engineering and architectural studies. He knew that Berger and his key partner, Leonard Worsek, were the ones the city would consult to set property values in the North Loop. Mid-America was the firm to *quantify commercial blight.*

Not surprisingly, it generated figures that encouraged Rubloff. MARC estimated that the developer would have to pay only a little less than $3 million for nine acres, an average of about $300,000 an acre—considerably less than he would be set back for a lakefront lot out in the northern suburbs. Using industry-approved methods of calculation, Leonard Worsek scientifically set the value of Blocks 1 and 3 (37 and 16) at $10 a square foot and Block 2 (36) at $5. Mid-America's price tag for Block 37 alone was $1.035 million.[69] Rubloff could now cash in on all the paranoia and fear that Daley had centered on the downtown.

Armed with these low-ball estimates, verified by the city's own respected professional appraisers, Rubloff began serious negotiations with investors. Brubaker's sketches showed a forty-story (1.4 million square foot) office building and a 500,000-square-foot mall for Block 37, a five- to seven-story department store and ten-story central library for Block 36, and a thirty-story (one thousand room) hotel/convention center and television studio for Block 16. The three blocks, bought for next to nothing, would multiply in value as the land was built up. Like a city slicker smelling oil and effortlessly separating a hick from his dusty tract of land, Rubloff was confident of the astounding future worth of property he persisted in public to call junk.

Cheap land in the center of town started the feeding frenzy that got the North Loop going in the 1970s. The city never bothered doing its own independent appraisals. Daley simply accepted MARC's numbers and used them as a further demonstration of the area's economic deterioration, somehow neglecting to read the small print. While Rubloff was prepared to offer only ten dollars a square foot for Block 37, he expected the city to pay more than one hundred dollars to purchase the various parcels from their lawful owners before it passed them on to him. Miles Berger, who was a confidential real estate counselor to the mayor at the same time he was advising Rubloff, argued that this deep discounting was still a good deal for the city. The ten-to-one write-down of land, a single expense, would be offset by the annual ten-to-one increase in property and sales taxes. Broken-down Block 37 was paying less than $1 million in taxes in 1973. With all of

Brubaker's architecture in place it would pay nearly $9 million in property tax alone. Add in all the new jobs downtown and other improvements in the area, and Berger was offering the mayor a 2-million-square-foot golden goose, just for openers.

After Daley was gone, when Mayor Bilandic was uneasily in control, Miles Berger was still there, more powerful than ever. His real estate appraisals were now recycled as official city documents, the city paying his firm seventy-five thousand dollars for the same analysis he had done for Rubloff in 1973.[70] This was textbook pure dealing. With Berger so cleverly inserting himself between the businessmen aching for a piece of land and the city eager to get a quick return on its investment, every person wishing to do business in the North Loop had best go through him.

In February 1978, following MARC's projections to the letter, the city of Chicago's price tag for the entire North Loop was still only $40,794,965. But five years had gone by, and people were alerted to the city's plans. Property owners on the redevelopment blocks who had been renting space for as little as sixty cents a foot suddenly saw an opportunity to make some money themselves. They awoke to the fact that their land, now officially designated a commercial slum, was, with the exception of one small building at the corner of Dearborn and Washington, worth far more flattened than it had been when fully leased out.

Rubloff knew intimately the old owners of blocks like 37; he had brokered their property and worked out their leases for more than half a century. Once he went public, he worked hard trying to complete a redevelopment deal before all the retired judges, bankers, and politicians who had been holding land since the 1940s started to fuss, claiming their share of the ride up in values. The city too wanted a timely completion of a deal before speculators started bidding up land prices.

Still encouraged by Miles Berger, who in fact was even then helping the city sell off "his" best blocks, Rubloff rushed to lock up his financing. He nearly closed a joint venture with Olympia and York (50 percent) and Allen and Company (25 percent) on June 6, 1978. The venture was to start with 488,645 square feet—two State Street blocks (37 and 36), one on Dearborn, and another on Wabash that later fell out of the plan—that he would purchase from the city for a bargain $24 million.

Rubloff didn't bother informing his new equity partners that these parcels were just the castoffs from the original North Loop plan and that he had already been stripped of half his empire. Berger and Hill had plucked out the properties that could be most easily developed, exploiting the developer's contacts with the Hilton Hotels Corporation and the new Republican governor of Illinois, James R. Thompson.

As the city began talking directly with Hilton, Rubloff was still presenting himself as an essential middleman. The city wanted Hilton to build a hotel–convention facility on Blocks 16 and 17, from Wacker Drive, along the river, down to Lake Street, between State and Clark. And on a site directly north of City Hall, between Randolph and Lake, bordered by Clark and LaSalle, shoehorned into the original redevelopment district, Governor Thompson commissioned a new state office building. These three blocks were the new core of the North Loop. As 1978 began, Rubloff, completely undercut, was left to fend for himself.

It was impossible to complete a transaction without the city behind him. Having successfully demonstrated that private financing was available in hundred-million-dollar increments, Rubloff had outlived his usefulness. The lame-duck planners in Bilandic's City Hall thought they now knew enough to beat the private sector in the great game.

Bilandic, in addition to the North Loop, had a few other public works headaches. Principally, Chicago had received $2 billion in state and federal grants to build the Crosstown Expressway, a north–south trucking link between the city's two main arterial roadways and Midway Airport. In the last years of the Daley administration, public opposition to the Crosstown had been fierce. Neighborhood groups, the grassroots organization in the outer wards, would not accept another expressway tearing up schools and churches, displacing thousands of residents from their homes. The Crosstown eventually was defeated, but it was an irritant throughout Bilandic's abbreviated term (1976–79).

The North Loop, like the Crosstown, proved more a distraction than a cause for Mayor Bilandic, who though he had been the city council's and organization's select candidate to finish off the Boss's sixth term, knew little of the old Daley agenda or how to make it work. Bilandic left the decisions to Rubloff's old professional contacts and tried acting mayoral. He and his fashionable wife, Heather, got dressed up a lot and were seen at the ballet and opera, thus breaking one of Daley's first rules of power: politicians should never appear self-aggrandizing or stray too far from their political base. During most of their surprising tenure, government was on hold as the Bilandics, black tied and begowned, moved from charity ball to ribbon cutter as if they were the Duke and Duchess of Windsor. The North Loop, particularly, was left somehow to develop on its own.

Rubloff's initiatives were still encouraged, but the city essentially did nothing to make them happen. Nor did it bother considering the disastrous effects of a simultaneous private and public negotiation—both parties claiming equal authority. Rubloff continued to present himself as the North Loop czar, while no single individual within the government claimed as much. Investors such as Olympia and York and Hilton, with expensive properties worldwide, were justifiably confused about who really spoke for the city and not above playing one off against the other.

During Bilandic's term, the Department of Planning spent a desultory year or so coming up with a North Loop redevelopment plan that it hoped would qualify for as much as $25 million in federal aid through a new funding formula—Urban Development Action Grants (UDAGs). The $44 million that the planning department had supposedly already earmarked for the Loop had evaporated at the time of the Bilandic succession. To supplement the meager federal subsidies—unrecoverable North Loop costs were already estimated at more than $200 million—the city prepared a hastily conceived application to the Department of Transportation for $12.8 million to tear up State Street. This resulted in a street narrowing transitway limited to bus traffic that killed off the last vestige of department store retailing in the southern part of the Loop. Within a few years after the mall was completed in 1980, Sears, Ward's, and Goldblatt's abandoned their flagship State Street stores, accelerating the deterioration of the area.[71]

Still, Rubloff didn't give up, although he made some cosmetic changes. He relieved Perkins and Will of its architectural duties and hired architect Helmut Jahn to "redesign and modify" Brubaker's model of the whole North Loop. But it was all too late for the old developer; he was being squeezed out for good. Cadillac Fairview came and went in 1977, as did Olympia and York in 1978. Serious developers were skeptical that Rubloff could deliver on land costs as low as three dollars a square foot. Also, with Berger and others in the city dealing directly with Hilton for Blocks 16 and 17, they questioned his real influence. Looking around the Loop, as the 1970s came to an end, Olympia and York saw its competitors willing to pay up to three hundred dollars for comparable sites.[72]

Instead of meeting the Canadians' realism with a more sober reassessment, Rubloff simply became more fervid and desperate to please in the face of their obvious skepticism. Out of the air, like a circus performer twirling a stack of plates on a stick, Rubloff wrote a letter (May 1, 1978) "off the record" to Gregory Dillon, a key Hilton executive. He was offering a generous tax abatement from the city, knowing all the while that the county and *not* the city was central to the process, carefully assuring all parties involved that he was acting merely to "hasten the negotiations." He appears

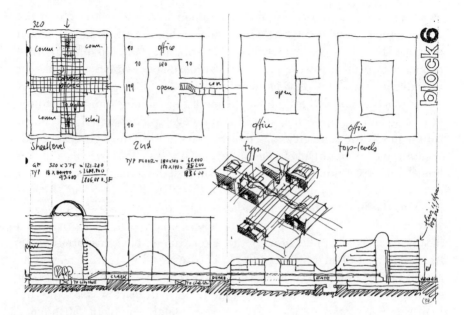

Helmut Jahn's North Loop drawings (1978)

to have been goaded on, if not officially by the planning department, then by Miles Berger personally.[73]

The damage was done. Rubloff had gone ahead and promised tax breaks specifically to Hilton and Olympia and York, knowing all the while that they were a long shot. He already had in his possession two negative legal opinions. In fact, one of his first acts in developing the North Loop had been to hire, in early 1973, attorney Newton Minow to investigate the legal hurdles to commercial tax relief in the district. Minow was not encouraging, so Rubloff just retained another lawyer: in 1978, he asked Jack Guthman, like Minow a partner at Sidley and Austin, to review the facts. Guthman reiterated in even stronger language the difficulty of providing selective tax relief for private projects. But Rubloff kept these findings secret, observing the client-lawyer privilege by never bothering to inform the city or his prospective partners that abatements were *impossible*. So at the very worst time, the city imprudently reasserted responsibility for a project that was already well out of hand.

National retailers like J. C. Penney, hotel chains like Omni and Sheraton, who had already been in extensive negotiations with Rubloff, fled when it was clear that the developer was not going to get control of the North Loop in a timely manner. When the moment was right Lewis Hill advised the mayor to take over the Hilton negotiations for Blocks 16 and 17 and use the state's claim on Block 34—Rubloff's preferred site for a new State of Illinois Center—as proof of progress on the North Loop.

No one in the city felt any need to inform Rubloff he was out. He figured it out in time, but not until the private development interests were already profoundly alienated from the public process and the once-serious urban renewal effort, going back to Daley's second term, was fatally derailed. The joke was finally on the city, with its unprecedented statutory authority to condemn a third of its best commercial land and buy it at market rates for resale. No one in government could reliably distinguish between fact and fiction, policy and promise, much less find a way to make a success of the country's largest urban renewal project. Well after the Canadians and Rubloff were gone, Chicago was unalterably attached to a billion-dollar redevelopment effort that it had no idea how to effect. With no investment capital, either public or private, and its only significant tenants a nontax-paying entity (state of Illinois) and another asking for near forgiveness of taxes for a minimum of thirteen years, Rubloff's North Loop plan and now Bilandic's (or Berger's, as it is referred to in several internal planning documents) were in serious trouble. All the promises, sales tricks, seductions, had stuck to the project as if they were law.

Exceedingly low land prices, unrealistically low condemnation costs, and, for the two prominent blocks on Wacker Drive, a whopping $70 million tax abatement guaranteed the North Loop would be stillborn in its original form. Once the next wave of speculators came on the scene, they started batting around the carcass before the corpse was cold. No plans, no rules, no bigger predators, just a lot of meat out in the street.

Rubloff never did get his joint venture going and was permanently out of the urban renewal business when Mayor Bilandic lost office to an upstart politician in 1979. Promising to destroy the old Daley machine and rid the city of its "cabal of evil men," Jane Byrne became mayor. She tried reforming in her first year, battling with the police and firemen's unions, vowing to put Chicago's finances in order after she discovered her mentor Daley's habit of submerging debt in the mazelike complexities of the capital budget. Mayor Byrne even fired Miles Berger, who had been on the Plan Commission for nearly fifteen years. She would reappoint him less than a year later, at about the time she gave up reforming, and promote him to czar of the North Loop.

.   .   .

When Rubloff first went public in 1973, no one ever imagined that he would persevere so long. He was now out, in part, because he had overestimated Berger and Hill's dependence on him. They had no intention of letting Rubloff and his pals develop the North Loop and then collect a fortune from the subsequent steep rise in values. Berger had set the values so low in the first place just to get things going, and not to put money in a competitor's purse. Miles Berger wasn't playing for short-term advantage; he intended to be around a long time.

Right from the outset, as a highly visible public official, Berger prominently took the high road, rescuing himself from developing any of the North Loop, a business he never had much interest in anyway. With the help of a public relations firm, he presented himself as a simple, concerned citizen with more than a decade of selfless public service already behind him. Berger presented his professional expertise to the city as matter-of-factly as he would order a fine wine with dinner. A manner seasoned by noblesse oblige and self-effacement was his preferred personna. Miles Berger invited others to think of him as the anti-Rubloff, or counter-Rubloff, while he remained diligent and active in his varied private real estate operations. Particularly after he rose to the top of the beleaguered planning hierarchy, Berger, *not* Rubloff, was a politically smart corporation's contact at City Hall. The transformation was complete.

He was invariably in possession of reliable information and knew how to parcel it out. For example, when the North Loop deal was heating up, in early July 1978, Berger learned that Fidinam (USA) Incorporated, a Swiss investment company with offices in Chicago, had offered Hilton $135 million in funding. By December of that year Norman Perlmutter, an old friend and future partner at Heitman Financial Services, replied to Leonard Worsek that he was prepared to offer Hilton's North Loop operations $140 million in financing. Pending acceptance of the conditional UDAG to the city of Chicago, Heitman was eager for the business.

On June 28, 1978, the same day Fidinam made its offer to Hilton's Corporate Financing Division, the hotel's Chicago lawyers, George Cowell and Oscar D'Angelo, wrote to Lewis Hill that they had been meeting with his (Hill's) "representative, Miles Berger." Berger had so perfectly situated himself in the middle of the deal—between the city and entrepreneurial business interests—that, at times, he must have felt that he was negotiating with himself. Professional ethics had so eroded in America that almost everyone was prepared to mine the lucrative seams between business and government.

In most cases government was overmatched. The best and the brightest stayed out of public service, which had been badly stigmatized through most of their adult lives. Those remaining were either career bureaucrats riding the job out to retirement or a few ambitious, highly talented ringers, like Berger, who volunteered to even the sides. In the public-private business environment of the late 1970s and 1980s, all of this double-dealing, pro-bono-ing, was just another way to wealth.

The city would never quite escape Rubloff entirely. Berger and Hill might have picked his pocket, but Rubloff, who really wasn't ever in it just for the money, had his revenge. Rubloff had worked the territory too long not to leave some mark. He left it on the North Loop deal, somehow poisoning all future negotiations. Even though his own lawyers had severely questioned the practicality of downtown tax relief—at the center of one of the world's most lucrative retail districts—Rubloff offered it anyway. Olympia and York and Hilton Hotels were promised expensive tax concessions that no responsible administration could ever meet. This was in addition to the corporation's radically reduced land costs and veto power over competing developments. Hilton had somehow gotten the idea that in agreeing to build in the North Loop it had gained control of central area planning.[74] Rubloff's curse. When the tax abatement was officially denied and Hilton announced on March 4, 1982, that it was formally withdrawing from the North Loop, three more years had passed. The North Loop Redevelopment Project was a decade old, with no progress to report.

Between May 22, 1979, and January 22, 1980, the Byrne administration was active in de-Rubloffization. A series of letters, memos, and meetings between the Department of Planning and large national developers indicate their willingness to realize Rubloff's scheme without him. Before Rubloff was completely out, two new commissioners of planning, Thomas Kapsalis and Martin Murphy, each followed up with Olympia and York and presented himself directly to the Rouse Company and Portman Properties, large national development firms, to see what they could do on their own. As they saw it, the only thing wrong with the Rubloff plan was Rubloff.[75] But without Rubloff at the center of activity the whole contraption of secret side deals and empty promises inevitably fell apart.

As time passed with nothing happening, the whole North Loop, under the imminent threat of demolition, became a free-for-all. Individual owners of even the tiniest parcels of land hired the best condemnation attorneys to fight demolition; neighborhood activists fought commercial tax concessions; and preservationists perversely listed the architectural merits of what Rubloff emphatically dismissed as worthless. They all piously fought redevelopment as they gleefully watched their property values rise.

It was Fort Dearborn all over again. Arthur Rubloff did all the work, and at the last minute someone took the project out of his hands. That was politics. But this time it was somehow different for him. He knew he was at the end of the line. Rubloff couldn't help feeling that he had been responsible, at least in part, for the accelerated decay of the Loop. The postwar success of his revived North Michigan Avenue had further crippled State Street. And now that he had a way to reverse all that blight, he was being denied. Maybe it was just old age that had permanently frustrated his ambitions, but the North Loop had unquestionably gotten away from him.

Toward the end, nobody was telling him anything. Things got so bad that Rubloff had to hire Tom Keane Jr., the son of former alderman and Daley-era power broker Tom Sr., to leak some of the details of the Hilton deal back to him. In a confidential memo to Rubloff dated July 16, 1980, Tom Jr. confirmed that the city had agreed, in May, to sell Hilton land for fifty dollars a square foot and that Baron Hilton was dictating conditions. Rubloff easily decoded another interesting tidbit provided by Keane. The cash the city needed to buy land for resale was being underwritten by a generous line of credit from Continental Bank, although Mayor Bilandic in 1977 had announced that the city would meet its financial obligations with bonds. It had all the marks of a fix. No bond issue meant no public review. This was a fact that Rubloff filed away for possible later use. If by some miracle he were ever to get back in the game, he might be able to embarrass someone—if there was anyone left in the city who was still embarrassable.

Perhaps Rubloff got the last laugh after all, as land prices soared and the city's own estimates for buying the condemned property doubled and then doubled again. Just at the moment the city was most committed to the urban renewal effort, Rubloff told a reporter at *Forbes* that the North Loop project's time had passed. "You couldn't possibly get it off the ground now," Rubloff chided in March 1980. "Four years ago I could have built that mall on State Street for $45 a foot. Today it would cost $85 or $90. I had the funds and the backing and the people to do the job and, unfortunately, Mr. Daley dies."[76]

Nonetheless, it took him another year to admit to his financial partners that the game was over. On March 16, 1981, he reluctantly sent the "North Loop material" from the aborted Olympia and York/Charles Allen/Rubloff

Development joint venture back to Albert Reichmann, who along with his brother Paul headed O & Y, in Toronto. But he still couldn't let go. And in July, he followed up with a personal note to Reichmann, expressing real bewilderment that their development never went ahead. Nearly in his ninth decade, Arthur Rubloff, with no trace of irony, blandly described the madness he himself had set in motion. He reported to Reichmann that the Canadians and Germans were busy buying up everything in sight, paying as much as one thousand dollars a square foot for raw land in Chicago. Land not very different from that the city was once willing to trade him for ten dollars a foot was now being bid up one hundred times. Now that Rubloff was out of the game for good, he wanted to reassure his friend that most of the Loop properties weren't worth pawning anyway. But he couldn't avoid being just a little wistful. At these inflated prices, he confessed to Reichmann, he wouldn't mind selling everything he had. With that little piece of old business completed, he signed the letter "Art" and took the next plane to Palm Beach.

Rubloff gave away close to $100 million upon his death in 1986, at age eighty-three. With this final act of generosity, he had hoped to complete the metamorphosis from broker to city builder. Yet even in his absence, he is still remembered as a deal maker and not the true philanthropist he became. A colleague of Rubloff for almost forty years thinks that in the colorless world of business "Arthur was absolutely in a class by himself." His personality was so large that he could always overcome other people's inhibitions; he would find a way to complete a deal. The Rubloff executive continues, "If Arthur was determined that you were going to become his client and his friend you might as well relax and enjoy it because there was no way in which you could resist it."[77] Buildings he had to demolish, the few he developed, the many he managed, were often just tiresome afterthoughts to the architecture of the deal. The great game; that's what he loved.

III ▌ THE BOYS ON THE BLOCK

In the last days of 1980, a black limousine moved slowly through Chicago holiday traffic. Bruce Graham autocratically directed the limo from the back seat, all the time lecturing a younger man seated to his left. Graham's attentive passenger was Lawrence F. Levy, a client for whom the architect was designing a new skyscraper. Bruce Graham told his new client fabulous stories about how architecture was reshaping America. Levy couldn't get enough of the architect's spiel, although he thought he had heard some of the same stories before.

Graham had the driver take the car into the old downtown, around Block 37, one of the key pieces of the North Loop. Situated strategically, with the Daley Center and City Hall on the first two blocks to the west and Marshall Field's across State Street to the east, this three-acre block was a real prize—if he could ever get his hands on it.

Graham rhapsodized what he planned to do with "visionaries" like Levy right here in Chicago. Chain-smoking cigarettes on a cold day with the windows closed, he disappeared in the smoke, spinning tales about rebuilding the city. His voice floated in the car, disembodied. "Vision, art, courage . . ."—like violin music at a Hungarian restaurant.

The value of downtown land had been disguised by decades of abuse. Black teenagers were milling around the video arcades, killing time before catching a show at the United Artists Theater, which like all the former first-run theaters in the Loop was currently showing action films and exploitation fare such as *Blacula*. On the Dearborn side Levy could see the sign for Mayors Row, an old City Hall hangout, invariably in the newspapers as a site for political payoffs; and farther down the street he caught a glimpse of the dilapidated U.S. Shoe Repair, squatting in the same brown Tobacco Road lean-to where the Mayflower Coffee Shop had operated since the Depression.

Graham had the car stop in front of 30 West Washington, one of three tall buildings on the block. Preservationists praised the terra-cotta of the facade, but in the low winter light it was hard to make out any of the Art Deco details. Covered with years of grime and pigeon droppings, 30 West Washington was a hard sell as an architectural masterpiece. But Levy knew by now that he wasn't on a personal architectural tour. Graham had brought him to this spot for a reason. This sham of an office building was the home of Stop and Shop, where ladies in fur wraps would have their chauffeurs double-park while they made a tour of the caviar and fine wines.

Lawrence Levy

Stop and Shop was the place where Dad, on his way back from work, bought the best wines and cheeses. Special cuts of meat, Maine lobster, exotic fruits, were all presented exquisitely in showcases: all manner of delicacies with the store's own label as a guarantee of quality. Candy eggs in different sizes, from canary yellow to robin's blue; jelly beans separated by color in big vats; mountains of wicker baskets were available at Easter. Walls and ceilings, pink and copper, painted to look like fine marble, set off the dioramas of food in their fancy cases. Levy remembered marveling at the place when he first came to Chicago.

Gaper's, the area's finest catering operation, was run from this building, as was Hillman's, a midprice supermarket that was a few steps down, in the basement. There was a wholesale produce operation, meat cutting, poultry packing, in the four sub-basements, and mostly vacant offices in the higher floors of the seventeen-story building. With this old building and the other high-rise shtetls on Block 37, Bruce Graham was putting Levy in position to play the great game.

The city's Department of Streets and Sanitation had already strung the trees with thousands of twinkling white lights, providing an incongruous Currier and Ives backdrop to the frantic Christmas shopping. North Michigan Avenue had effectively displaced the old State Street corridor with its celebrated department stores and funky entertainment district off to the

United Artists Theater and Bensinger Building on Randolph Street in their last days

Stop and Shop and Hillman's (30 West Washington)

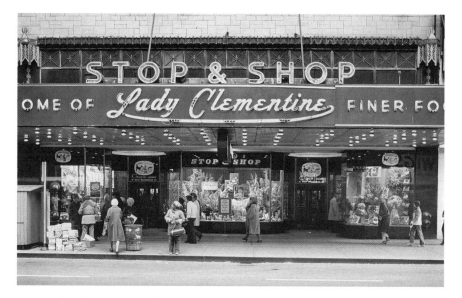

Stop and Shop marquee and display windows

west on Randolph. This northernmost third of the three-mile avenue—extending from the city's historic downtown to fashionable East Lake Shore Drive—was once only little more than a confused collection of a few distinguished Art Deco buildings, artists' spaces, parking lots, and one prominent billboard advertising Seagram's whiskey.[1]

Yet in the thirty years following the Second World War, developers, following Arthur Rubloff's lead, had transformed the street. North Michigan now has Cartier's, Saks, and even a prosperous twin of the city's own Marshall Field's, whose original, one of America's last great emporiums, is only a mile south on State Street. Business jumped the Chicago River, effectively cloning itself in the new malls and fancy high-rises along North Michigan, a seesaw prosperity that successfully remade an undervalued part of town at the price of marooning the historic downtown.

Commercial Chicago in 1980 was effectively cut in half, a result of nearly forty years of social and economic turmoil. Two downtowns competing unequally with each other. In the late 1940s, the city had revived the long process of rebuilding itself north of the river that had begun in 1920 with the completion of the Michigan Avenue Bridge. This was an area that had grain elevators and active industrial lofts well into the current century. Successfully luring back some of the business it had lost to the steady exodus of whites out to the suburbs, the center of old Chicago is now improbably on the wrong side of the river.

The steep decline of a self-confident white-and-black middle-class city that had occurred for the most part silently for suburbanites and "lakefront liberals,"—the prosperous middle class still remaining close to the downtown—and dramatically off in the twenty-four poverty areas, city neighborhoods like Lawndale, Woodlawn, and Englewood, was beginning to be felt in the Loop.[2] Retail businesses had lost their primary clientele and were forced to survive by carrying off-price merchandising targeted at those who couldn't afford to leave the city.[3] Those rich enough to live outside the city or in its best residential areas no longer shopped in the historic downtown but patronized the new shops north of the river, housed in glitzy suburban-style malls.

Before the Great Depression, the downtown had accounted for 78 percent of the nearly $2.7 billion of retail sales generated annually in the entire metropolitan area. By 1965 the downtown share had fallen to just over 50 percent and by 1972 to about 40 percent.[4] Of these declining revenues, Michigan Avenue had captured the biggest share. Battered by the suburbs, the city was put irrationally in competition with itself. State Street's great department stores, unable to meet the competition, one by one began to close.[5] As the 1980s came to a close, only two of the retail giants remained on State Street.[6]

Responding to the regional pressure on its sales, including that exerted by its own successful suburban stores, Marshall Field's duplicated its State Street headquarters, miniaturizing to fit a tighter, more practical space near the top of Michigan Avenue and sharing the prime site with a formerly remote East Coast rival, Lord and Taylor. The new location, completed in 1976, was called Water Tower Place, after the Gothic waterworks that had miraculously survived the Great Fire a hundred years earlier. Field's had the best space in Water Tower, one of the first of the now-familiar vertical urban malls. Clad in marble, fitted with a glass elevator shuttling through a yawning atrium space mirrored in glass and chrome, Water Tower Place legitimated the same urban style that reached an apotheosis of excess in New York's Trump Tower only a few years later. In Water Tower Place a waterfall divides the up and down escalators, hanging vines and potted trees make for a hybrid environment where outdoors is inside, streets are stacked on top of each other, and the imagined security of the suburbs is imported to the center of town.

Mixed-use skyscrapers like Water Tower, with famous department stores on the levels closest to the street, specialty retail on the floors above, movie theaters, restaurants, condominiums, and hotels, is the contemporary formula to stem the inexorable flight of population and tax base away from the central cities: sprawling up rather than out. The special irony for Chicago was that North Michigan Avenue—the city's most successful urban development initiative, privately conceived, executed, and financed—and not the hated suburbs had finished off its downtown. As the last decade began, progress and its shadow were only a bridge apart, that is, before all the money began to flow and skyscrapers, each with nine-to-five populations the size of many a small midwestern town, were planned for every square inch of the Loop.

By 1980, redevelopment was almost completely out of the hands

Bruce Graham

of the professional planners and finally within reach of speculators and their architects. This was why Bruce Graham was so interested in taking a Christmas drive with Larry Levy.

Chief design partner and head of the Chicago office of Skidmore, Owings and Merrill, Bruce Graham was only in his twenties when he joined SOM in 1951. His considerable talents as a designer and promoter accelerated the firm's already legendary expansion and helped it grow further into a multinational corporation employing thousands of architects and engineers. SOM's product was large, reliable commercial buildings, designed, engineered, and marketed from a single source. By the time Graham brought Levy into his confidence he had learned on his own to play the great game quite well.

Working for Gerald D. Hines during the Houston oil boom in the 1970s, Graham observed that architects were critical to the new private-sector redevelopment projects. The new-style developer needed a compliant professional to help him fatten construction budgets and justify expensive space-wasting luxuries. Simply by defending the "art of architecture," Graham found he got bigger fees and more notoriety. Architects were gaining celebrity status in the 1970s as their flamboyant efforts became associated with $100 million deals.

Hines became the architect's model of the enlightened developer. In a series of audacious buildings he quickly transformed the image of the builder from a penny-pinching Babbitt to a cultured patron of the arts. Hines had started with Philip Johnson and went down the list of famous architects whom he hired to design high-rise offices all over the country. Although the same size inside—1 million square feet plus—Hines's buildings always offered some distinguishing feature that set them apart from the competition's. For Hines in Chicago, Graham designed Three First National Plaza (completed in 1981), a glass tower with an angular saw-toothed facade.

Graham was simply following Johnson's example. Philip Johnson had set the trend by cutting in half a classic International Style skyscraper of more than a million square feet as matter-of-factly as if he were slicing a quiche for dinner guests. As with everything he did, Johnson sliced with flair. Done at a forty-five-degree angle, the cut transformed one seventy-story glass box into two, each with a unique chamfered top. Reassembled on the same base and linked by a triangular lobby that Siamesed the skyscrapers at their feet, Pennzoil Place (1976) was a sensation in flat, sprawling Houston.[7] Better yet, the project was a gold mine. Claiming that the architecture's pure geometry—accentuated by the bronze glass endlessly reflecting itself—was more like sculpture than real estate, Hines brokered the space at a three- to four-dollar premium per square foot. This was worth millions to the developer. When asked what was so special about Pennzoil Place, Hines explained. "In a competitive job market," he told an interviewer in 1982, shortly before the Houston real estate market tanked, "people want to work for a company that represents more than a commodity in space."[8]

Name-brand, eye-catching architecture—always with some gimmick, always big—was thought in the 1980s to be money in the bank. And architects proved to be so cooperative; they loved the limelight and the big money. Just the sort of economics Bruce Graham claimed to have invented when he was busy romancing a client anywhere from London to Dubai. But to keep the big projects coming, Graham knew he had to keep an eye on politics. To this end, he and William Hartmann maintained SOM's long-held position as the de facto technical planning arm of the city of Chicago. As the 1980s began, Graham was at the height of his influence.[9]

Graham hadn't been working with Larry Levy for long when they took their tour together of the Loop. The young developer was just at the construction stage of a mixed-use complex at the northern end of Michigan Avenue, on the west side of the street across from the venerable Drake Hotel. Levy had purchased the land for $7 million in 1978 from two families who had inherited the property but had no plans to develop it themselves. Once the locale for some of the city's most fashionable shops, the land had been vacant for a decade. Only a forlorn open-air parking lot remained when Levy first saw the property.

Graham got involved with Levy shortly after he discovered that this new-comer had gotten hold of the corner, a prominent intersection where the avenue dramatically meets the lake. Graham had always wanted to build a tower there and had thought any of the known developers in town would come to him first. Graham proved himself misinformed. Busy traveling to other projects, the city's premier architect found that he had lost the chance to build One Mag Mile on the corner of Oak and Michigan. In his absence, Levy had already hired Richard Barancik, a Chicagoan specializing in the design of luxury apartments. Barancik's reputation for never putting design over the financial considerations of a real estate deal appealed to Levy, who had just gone out on his own, working a high-risk niche of the business he didn't really know.

Levy researched Barancik's nearby work, such as 990 Lake Shore Drive, an architectural eyesore but one that sold out quickly and retained its owners. The young developer admired Barancik more as a businessman than an architect: his buildings didn't make it into the *AIA Guide* to architectural monuments but they could be aggressively marketed and steadily, along with the rest of the market, increased in value. Barancik's bullheaded, analytical approach to high-rises was Levy's own. Levy told his architect how much money he wanted to make, and the architect went off and designed the envelope. Bullish, with a barrel chest and abbreviated neck, Barancik had the sort of physical confidence that got people to do what he wanted. His odd certainty that he was a great architect, in the same league with I. M. Pei and Richard Meier, didn't hurt either when he was trying to move a difficult project ahead. And his plan for Levy worked well, at least in the beginning.

So Levy should probably have put Graham off, explaining politely that he already had an architect. He could have agreed to work with Graham some-time in the future, offering some lame excuse of the sort Levy had perfected in dealing with people he no longer needed. But he couldn't resist being courted by anyone important, particularly a Chicago legend. It seemed only yesterday to Levy that he was working for Joe Beale at Hawthorn Realty, trudging haplessly through wet farmland with a goofy smile and a plat book under his arm, looking to build future suburbs and industrial parks in the Chicago outback. Using his dowser's instinct for a bargain and Joe Beale's capital to close the deal, Levy had worked his way right up to president of Hawthorn. The Hawthorn partnership came to control thousands of acres, creating edge cities complete with wholly self-sufficient business, retail, and residential districts, right at the crossroads of the interstate highways. Prior to moving his operations downtown, Levy had already displayed his considerable abilities and made a name for himself.

Everything was going great before the 1973 Arab oil boycott precipitated

a small real estate crash that continued over the next few years, forcing interest rates to double and stay high. The value of Levy's long-term leases,
the mainstay of his operation, was cut in half. But that was the past. Two
years is ancient history to a broker, and Larry Levy was soon back in business. He had learned the hard way that the old real estate ethic of buy and
hold had no future. In the new age of property swapping, funded offshore
and through Wall Street, the money was made—through fees, refinancing,
and quick sales—before a building was ten years old. He vowed next time
to be sure to grab all the money up front, before some arcane economic
cycle or crazy Arab screwed up his business.

In 1980, nearly a year before the North Loop got his attention, Levy, still
in his thirties and only recently on his own, was suddenly in the position of
developing a $120 million project in the big city without a cent of his own
money. All that steady work in the suburbs had made him, in the view of
the trade, bankable. Little more than a decade separated Levy from the
dark hustling days when he had trouble raising enough credit for a car loan.
Now he had a bona fide track record, a reputation in an unsentimental
business where "credibility was king." Michael Silver, a broker famous for
negotiating cheap leases for his well-heeled professional clientele, explained Levy's magic of turning debt into cash: "If you were credible with
your bankers, enjoyed a good relationship, there was nothing to it. Easy
done." Hawthorn Realty had underwritten Levy's new downtown interests,
and brilliant Joe Beale was still out in the burbs.

That's how fast the development business could change. Levy wasn't
going to get caught unprepared and wasn't about to turn away the head of
SOM, begging for a chance to work for him. Less than a year before their
Christmas limousine ride, Graham had talked about them making history
together, just the sort of empty language Levy, a great salesman, used himself to close a deal. But being wooed is, as he should have known, different
from wooing. He hired SOM to do the commercial and retail parts of the
building, roughly one-half of the million-square-foot pink-granite skyscraper, and got good value from Graham's firm. It was responsible for all
the structural and mechanical work, including the heating, ventilation, and
air-conditioning (HVAC). Richard Barancik was kept on to do the apartment tower, where Levy figured all the fast money would be made.[10]

Graham predictably did not get along with Barancik, whom he profes-
sionally disdained. In design conferences Barancik got into the habit of de-
spoiling Graham's beautiful colored drawings with a black marking pen.
Levy didn't pay much attention to the histrionics and got a lot of work out

of both men. Barancik's plan to provide maximum livable space for each apartment fit nicely into the SOM structural scheme. Long ago, Bruce Graham and his close engineering partner, Fazlur Khan, had devised a system of bundled tubes, which effectively reduced the amount of concrete or structural steel necessary to build skyscrapers of fifty stories or more. This architectural and engineering innovation made building tall economically possible. Using the SOM structural system, developers could reach up high, where they could charge premium prices. The result for speculators like Levy was dramatic. Now anyone willing to take the risk could develop structures reserved in the past for build-to-suit corporations or big financial institutions. The Khan-Graham approach to skyscraper design allowed smaller, lighter buildings to be locked together to create a taller, cheaper whole. The method had been tested successfully at Chicago's Sears Tower (1974), still the world's tallest building.

For Levy's more modest project, the architects bunched three hexagonal tubes, providing the maximum number of lake views and increasing the building's floor-to-area ratio, or FAR. The permissive Chicago zoning code allows a building to occupy a whopping sixteen times its ground area without a special variance, a legal allowance to build more space. Levy's One Mag Mile project earned an FAR of almost double the usual limit.[11]

Barancik delivered a workhorse of a product that Bruce Graham enhanced with his pedigree. Larry's fledgling Levy Organization, founded in 1978 with younger brother Mark, was offering affordable luxury with the snob appeal of brand-name architecture, only a traffic light away from exclusive East Lake Shore Drive. For Larry Levy—who as a business student at Northwestern University in nearby Evanston once sold mattresses out of a derailed boxcar and hustled cheap airplane charters to Europe—having the designer of the world's tallest building on his payroll was all the proof he needed that he was a big-time developer.

On December 1, 1980, with no buildings or model apartments, Levy opened the sales office for One Magnificent Mile. Well before the end of the month, 25 percent of the most expensive condominiums had been sold, more than $20 million worth without even a hole in the ground to show for it. Graham thought he had in Levy a young guy with a talent for raising money who still could be manipulated. With Levy feeling so good about his debut performance, it was the perfect time to set him up for the next project. As head of the Central Area Committee, Graham prided himself on knowing a little earlier than most what was happening in town.[12] Although immediately afforded the pomp and status of a city planning document, the

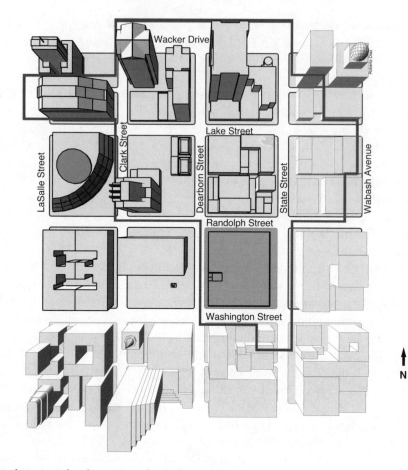

North Loop redevelopment and TIF district

Central Area Committee's 1973 *Chicago 21* had been produced exclusively in the offices of Skidmore, Owings and Merrill. So intertwined had SOM become with the city's Department of Planning that it was in the end impossible to tell the difference between an actual city initiative and one originating at Graham's firm. The latest of these efforts was merely the latest iteration in the redevelopment of the North Loop.

Since the previous summer, Graham, along with Skidmore planner Roger Seitz and associate architect Joseph Gonzalez, had been working for Charles M. Shaw, a developer whom Mayor Jane Byrne, after only reading a magazine profile, had contacted and impulsively hired to oversee the entire redevelopment district. Shaw had built a large, architecturally distinguished apartment building right on the shore of Lake Michigan, at the foot of Navy Pier a decade earlier and had made the national press after developing the air rights above New York's Museum of Modern Art. Museum Tower, designed by Cesar Pelli, provided luxury condominiums and expanded MoMA's office and exhibition space. This public notoriety was somehow enough to assure the mayor that Charles Shaw could manage the largest urban renewal effort ever attempted in this country. She soon signed him up, offering him 2 percent of all the work done by other developers and one of the three-acre blocks to develop personally. At 2 percent, as all the blocks were built out, the job of gatekeeper would earn the developer a minimum of $20 million for doing next to nothing. The mayor wanted Shaw to think that she had turned over to him the absolute power to decide who got to build in the North Loop—a nice bonus for just getting your name in the paper.

Brought on board in the summer of 1980 to pick up the pieces of the Rubloff initiative, Shaw would spend only seven months in the job. He never got a signed contract from the city, nor did he receive much cooperation from the mayor's real estate brain trust, which included two aldermen, Edward Vrdolyak and Edward Burke, plus Charles Swibel, three of the "cabal of evil men" whom the mayor had successfully run against as a reformer only a year before. Impossible for him to see it coming, but Shaw's real use was as a time server.

With Skidmore doing Shaw's master planning, engineering, and site models for most of the North Loop, Bruce Graham was certain to get a big share of the architectural work, a big chunk of $60 million in total fees; that is, if everything went according to plan.

But things never went well. Only a few months into the job, Graham already knew Charles Shaw was on his way out. By late November, the city still had not consummated an agreement with the developer. Graham had heard Shaw's lawyers were about to pull the plug.[13] That's when he first thought of promoting Larry Levy as a little czar of his own.

In his own right, Larry Levy, while getting established as a developer, had been trying his luck in the restaurant business. In 1978, the Levy Organization had taken over D. B. Kaplan's, a delicatessen doing no business in a remote location in Water Tower Place. Levy quickly turned the operation around with clever salesmanship, purveying the illusion of a neighborhood joint where the waiter knows your name and stuffs your sandwich with a few extra slices of meat. Just for you. Soon there were D. B. Kaplan's in Atlanta and Minneapolis, a D. B. Levy in Los Angeles, Dos Hermanos Mexican restaurants, and cafeterias cutely named Eaternity. He had several of his restaurants arrayed together in a food court on the prominent mezzanine level of Water Tower Place. Ethnic theming that provided a sense of place in the dead space of malls was Levy's main contribution to the restaurant business. His formula allowed developers to put marginal, leftover areas to highly productive use. When successful, his restaurants, often deep within an amorphous mall space of hundreds of indistinguishable stores, became a point of destination. People didn't simply find themselves at one of his restaurants after an exhausting day of shopping; they *planned* to go there. Levy saw that restaurants used intelligently in the real estate game could ameliorate the anonymity of modern urban architecture on an even grander scale.

So when Levy thought about the Stop and Shop Building on Block 37 with its large marquee advertising itself, he got the picture immediately. Imagine a quality institution, in business for a hundred years, that he didn't have to invent or hype. Gaper's, operating out of a small kitchen on the third floor, went all the way back to the Chicago Fire, when it was called Tebbitt's and Garland, a real carriage-trade operation serving the Palmers and Swifts. Larry wouldn't have to sell it with stupid puns like the "Ike and Tina Tuna sandwich" or with waiters in sombreros. Stop and Shop had real class with real tradition: its own private label, Tegar; a fruit man selling only premium size-eighty-eight oranges; a butcher who cut prime aged beef; and ladies snacking on dainty sandwiches in the Tiffin Tea Room on the mezzanine. Larry Levy had only been in the food business for two years but knew a downtown institution when he saw it. He didn't need Bruce Graham for that.

Better yet, Stop and Shop was in trouble; it was no secret. Once a bigger operation than the Jewel supermarket chain, it "got killed," according to one of its owners, when it expanded to the suburbs in the 1960s and went head to head with Jewel. Its core business was always on Washington Street and in Hillman satellite stores in black neighborhoods. Stop and Shop, Gaper's, and Hillman's had been owned since the 1920s by two old German-Jewish families, the Sterns and the Loebs, who built the building on Block 37 after moving from a smaller site across Washington Street.

Here was the gist of Graham's pitch to Levy. On November 13, 1980, more than a month before their limo ride into the Loop, Shaw and Skidmore had presented their North Loop concept publicly. Mayor Byrne had pressured Shaw to show something despite his complaints that he and his architects were not ready. At a packed event held at the Conrad Hilton Hotel, Shaw uncomfortably unveiled his ideas. The mayor spoke first: "For millions of persons throughout the country and the world, the Loop identifies Chicago and, indeed it is Chicago. . . . It is precious to our heritage, and it is equally precious to our future." Shaw attempted to keep up the cheer, but with little substantive work completed, his presentation came out fatally vague. He added that he wanted to "give people the opportunity to participate twenty-four hours a day in a city they are part of."[14] But what could he say? He had been undermined and set up to fail.

Scheduling the morning announcement for the Hilton and not City Hall was calculated to remind the new county assessor, Thomas Hynes, how important the hotel chain was to the North Loop. Byrne knew that fellow Democrat Hynes was in a rival political camp and unlikely to grant what was now "her" project a valuable tax abatement. The unveiling proved to be a political and architectural disaster.

The press, local and national, after one look at the developer's proposals for multiple underground passageways and sky bridges over downtown streets, took to calling the scheme Mole Town. On February 10, 1981, only three months after unveiling the Buck Rogersish plan, Shaw was dismissed. Without soliciting other bids, the mayor offered him a prime site in the redevelopment district where the Greyhound Bus Terminal was scheduled for demolition.

This private offer was done directly counter to the existing North Loop plan, only recently reaffirmed by Byrne's own planning department and handpicked Plan Commission, which still demanded a comprehensive multiblock approach to redevelopment. Dealing had replaced planning so completely in the city of Chicago that the mayor was giving away downtown blocks, potentially worth billions, as casually as if she were trading houses for hotels in a friendly game of Monopoly.

Shaw eventually turned down the mayor's offer. He had learned that the city's quid pro quo was to save and restore, at the developer's expense, the Selwyn and the Harris, two rotting former legitimate theaters that had been gerrymandered out of the redevelopment district. This was a sop to preservationists, busy organizing against what they feared was surely to be the wholesale demolition of the area. Built as a pair in 1923, the two crumbling brick boxes had somewhat distinguished terra-cotta facades in English (Selwyn) and French (Harris) ornament, but all of the expensive walnut panels and careful gilding had long ago been stripped by scavengers from the interiors. As far as Shaw was concerned the theaters were ugly and potentially expensive squatters that would occupy a quarter of a block for which he might have other, more profitable plans.

Soon after getting the boot, Shaw held his own press conference, in which he emphasized his distaste for politics, and left public life for a while, but not before negotiating with the city a couple of hundred thousand dollars in expenses and a new job. With its North Loop tax break looking as if it would never work out, Hilton hired Shaw directly.

Shaw's was the last attempt to redevelop the North Loop as a single entity. After he withdrew no one again would propose to develop the entire site in a rational, integrated manner with all the buildings scaled to each other, divided and apportioned intelligently into residential, retail, and office uses. The North Loop would be offered wholesale, block by block, to the highest bidder, in precisely the manner the city said it would never consider. On April 9, 1981, two months after his resignation, Charles Shaw billed the city for $593,564.51 (fees and expenses) for less than a year's work, proving he could play all the angles pretty well himself.[15]

At least since the "unveiling," Graham had known that the Shaw-Skidmore project would never go forward. More important, he recognized that the North Loop as a coherent urban renewal effort was dead. Work wouldn't be handed down from czars but from ambitious neophytes like Levy, who needed experienced veterans at their side. SOM had been the third local firm to have tried its hand at the entire renewal area, and now it had blown it. The firm was right out in the open and made to look foolish with its work for Shaw. Graham took the criticism as a public humiliation, potentially disastrous for business. All the uninformed talk of moles and Buck Rogers made him sick. For the first time in his career, Bruce Graham was having trouble getting his phone calls to the mayor's office returned.

But Graham had a knack for distancing himself from failures and quickly changed strategies. He understood that the city was fatally committed to taking the land through eminent domain, with or without a plan. Having made commitments to the federal government in order to qualify for a $25 million Urban Development Action Grant and having passed all the enabling legislation, the city had to move forward in some manner. Block 37 and all the other designated blocks would eventually be demolished. With Charles Shaw gone, there still would be the pretense of a North Loop plan for all twenty-seven acres, but in fact it would be a free-for-all. All this flattened land, compliments of the government, would inevitably spill onto the private market; first come, first served. Little guys like Levy would then have a chance and SOM another shot. Block 37 wasn't seven megablocks, but sandwiched between City Hall and Marshall Field's, it was prime real estate right at the heart of Chicago, a perfect encore to Graham's Hancock Building (completed 1969) on North Michigan Avenue and Sears Tower in the Loop. Any architect worth his fee could settle for that.

The Selwyn and Harris Theaters as porno houses (late 1970s)

Graham figured that Levy had a few months' head start on all the big local developers such as JMB (the country's most successful real estate syndicator, perfecting the idea of taking prime commercial real estate and selling it off as shares), Metropolitan Structures (an active Chicago company), and the out-of-towners like Gerald Hines, with whom he was currently working. As a syndicator of real estate and an adviser to giant pension funds, JMB was an especially attractive client. It managed billions in prime commercial and retail land held in several successful partnerships, offered to the public through a few select Wall Street brokerages. Graham would have to compete for these developers' business against local architects such as Helmut Jahn, who had taken over C. F. Murphy Associates (renamed Murphy/Jahn in 1981), Skidmore's most serious rival for high-quality work. The potential payoff for an architect who captured this business was well worth the effort of sucking up. JMB alone could afford to employ Graham's firm for decades all over the world.

However, winning any one of these downtown projects would take a little extra imagination. Murphy/Jahn also had a reputation for political influence as great as SOM's, earned for completing successful public works projects during the long Daley administration. Graham reasoned that a head start was all Skidmore required to get back in the North Loop. And this time Graham wouldn't have to deal with the Department of Planning and a government unsure about its next step. Development was where it should be, according to Graham, right on the private side. With Levy, he figured, he had the closest thing to a patsy he could find. To help consummate the romance, the architect even got the young developer nominated to the Central Area Committee.

But Graham badly miscalculated the situation in at least one respect. As soon as he started spilling the dirt about Block 37, he lost his edge with Levy. Once the young developer had time to think about what Graham had revealed about the North Loop, he began devising his own angle. By giving Levy inside information, the approximate timing of Shaw's departure and the change to a block-by-block auctioning of land in the North Loop, Graham had unintentionally made himself expendable. The balance of power had already shifted. Larry Levy was now in control, even if his architect didn't know it yet. He didn't own Block 37; in fact he didn't have a clue who did, but even while Graham was busy blathering on about his plans Levy already had his next move. He quickly authorized the architect to work up a scheme for the whole block.

While he waited for Graham to deliver the preliminary architecture, Levy made it his business to find out as much as he could about Stop and Shop and some of the other concerns on the block. Levy considered himself a visionary of sorts. Industrial parks, shopping centers, malls, took vision, didn't they? You had to trust tomorrow and take the risk. How different was downtown from the boonies, where he controlled thousands of acres? All he needed was a few of these run-down properties on Block 37. Then anyone from the Canadian Reichmanns to Texas developer Trammell Crow would have to deal with Mr. Larry Levy if he wanted to do business in Chicago. Bruce Graham called it a preemptive position on the block. Levy was confident he already knew how to pull it off.[16]

So Larry Levy had an early holiday that year. Block 37 had fallen out of Santa's bag and had unexpectedly turned up under his tree. As 1981 began, the city was still trying to salvage the troubled Hilton deal. Hilton's Chicago agents claimed that it was impossible for their client to build a profitable 2,100-room convention hotel without the Rubloff tax abatement that was now permanently stuck to the project like a bad suit. If nothing else, after two decades of political continuity, the rapid change in administrations would have doomed the deal anyway. It didn't help either that Assessor Hynes was a political ally of future mayor Richard M. Daley. Daley was not encouraging Hynes to salvage any North Loop deal that he hadn't made himself.

In fact, the only aspect of the North Loop going according to plan was the very part the city had the least to do with. On August 2, 1978, newly elected Republican governor James R. Thompson had pushed a $15 million appropriation through the legislature to buy the old Sherman House, an antiquated hotel across from City Hall on Randolph Street.[17] For years, Rubloff had been trying unsuccessfully to convince Thompson's Democratic predecessor, Daniel Walker, and anyone else who would listen, that the site was the best place in the North Loop to put a public building. The Sherman, former Democratic Party headquarters, had become a financial liability for its owners, the Teamsters pension fund. Walker passed on the opportunity, leaving all the glory to the man who foiled his reelection. For months, Rubloff and his confederates had pressed Thompson to resuscitate the plan. Thomas H. Coulter, chief executive officer of the Chicago Association of Commerce and Industry, wrote to the new governor, reminding him that office space was "tight" downtown and that the "north section of the Loop" needed more service-type jobs. Coulter assured the governor that his decision to place a new state office building across the street from City Hall would "inspire" developers, catalyzing a renaissance of the entire area.[18]

Thompson never required all the civic stroking. A bruiser of a Chicago attorney permanently on the outs with the organization that ran the city, he simply got a kick out of razing the epicenter of backroom deal making. Replacing it with an open, round glass structure in the critically approved postmodern style added a nice final touch but was almost beside the point compared with the pleasure of demolition. Once he had finally agreed to Rubloff's blandishments, the governor made it clear to the Democrats in City Hall that the North Loop's firstborn would be his baby.

Thompson's personal selection of Rubloff's architect, Helmut Jahn, from among twenty competing designers ensured him notoriety. Right from the beginning, the state of Illinois structure was never intended to be just another government building with minimal detailing, somber colors, and numbing anonymity. Thompson was convinced that Helmut Jahn would deliver what the governor described as "an award winning edifice" and do it quickly. Only three weeks after signing his design/engineering contract on August 6, 1979, Jahn had produced for the governor's pleasure eight radically different conceptual schemes. Thompson chose option 8, the most architecturally daring and most expensive.

While the state of Illinois was admittedly a good anchor tenant, in effect adding an extra renewal block to the original plan, Jahn's creation also presented some vexing problems for City Hall. The building was not exactly what the North Loop needed: an energy-hogging, tax-exempt government office could never deliver the power-of-ten increase in property and sales taxes specified in the redevelopment plan. Furthermore, Thompson's Taj seemed to undermine completely the only convincing rationale for attacking commercial blight in the first place.

Nor did it help, from the city's point of view, that Thompson moved effortlessly through the approval, financing, and condemnation stages of the project. His sublime competence and imperial manner made the Chicago politicians look even more pathetic as they dithered away for another three years failing to condemn even a single parcel. Assembling the state of Illinois site took the governor less than sixteen months from the project's original announcement (August 2, 1978) to the acquisition of the last of twelve separate parcels (April 15, 1980). Only Daley had ever done it faster, blitzkrieging the Civic Center site in the 1960s. And also like the old mayor, Thompson kept land prices down, relatively immune from the sorts of speculative activity already plaguing every inch of the city's portion of the North Loop.

Not until August 21, 1981, after a request for proposal (RFP) was answered and accepted, did the city's first true North Loop project move ahead, eight years late. Even then, the Transportation Building, a glorified indoor garage and office building, was only a small slice of a redevelopment block and not the two-block Hilton extravaganza so widely promoted. As the city fumbled with botched agreements and hastily improvised RFPs, the Republican governor looked more like Daley's true heir than any Democrat running for election. But not to worry—nothing worked as planned in the North Loop, even Thompson's part.

Rubloff's ghost didn't wait until he died in 1986 to start haunting the downtown. Before additional millions were spent to fix the cooling system, offices under Helmut Jahn's glass domed State of Illinois Center (completed in 1985) got as hot inside as 115 degrees Fahrenheit. The state's own Environmental Control Office had to send workers home early the first summer the building was occupied.[19] Final costs more than doubled from a low of $87 million to well over $180 million, including the expensive modifications to the prototype cooling and heating system.[20]

Beleaguered contractors worked at shrinking the swollen budget. Project manager Frank Conroy proudly saved $364,000 by removing, at the last moment, hundreds of office doors. Governor Thompson took a creative angle, never retreating an inch. He implied that no doors, open-atrium design, glass everywhere, fulfilled architecturally his campaign pledge of openness in government, an allegory for the new order in Chicago. Here he was, the state's chief executive, out in the open with nothing to hide—the only true democrat in a hopelessly corrupt city. How about that?

Thompson was liberating Chicago, crushed under one-party rule for a hundred years; he was giving her more light. All ambitious politicians use architecture symbolically. Daley had been a master of it. Thompson looked at his *grand projet* as merely a continuation of a lifetime's hard work rounding up and prosecuting pols, a sport he had pursued lustily, a few years back, when he was United States attorney for the northern district of Illinois.[21]

Bruce Graham was busily educating Larry Levy to these and related matters. Doing his own snooping, Levy found that in most respects Graham's story checked out. There was no longer any North Loop redevelopment plan, only the authority from the city to get title to the land and sell it immediately at a discount to a private developer. Levy decided he had as good a chance as any of his competitors. Developer Richard Stein was already working with Skidmore on the Transportation Building. Levy continued calling around, including a talk with his friend Barry Neckritz, the attorney for Hillman's and Stop and Shop.

After New Year's 1981, Levy began focusing all his attention on the Stop and Shop property, having satisfied himself that the business there was in real trouble. Thirty West Washington, where the Stern-Loeb grocery and catering operations had been located since the 1920s, offered him the best chance of getting a toehold on Block 37. Arthur Rubloff's more exotic efforts at capturing the whole North Loop had quickly receded into folklore. And, Levy figured, even if Rubloff hadn't completely succeeded in involving government directly with high-stakes private development, there was no reason why he might not make the gambit work for him.

Most of the hard work was over, particularly the fervent constitutional battles initiated long ago in Daley's law department. The takings clause of the Fifth Amendment to the United States Constitution, later broadened by the Fourteenth Amendment to apply to the states, maintains, "Nor shall private property be taken for public use, without just compensation." The amendments' intentions were to inhibit wholesale confiscations of property, such as were planned for the North Loop, and to bar government from compelling one class of people alone to bear public burdens that, in all fairness and justice, should be borne by the populace as a whole.[22]

A city council ordinance of March 28, 1979, establishing a formal North Loop Blighted Commercial District relaxed these fundamental protections. With this last in a string of time-consuming and expensive legal steps, the city superseded all previous land claims and moved immediately to re-claim private property in the redevelopment district, including Block 37. In all, twenty-seven acres, 52 buildings, 1,060,200 square feet of office area, 196,800 feet of retail, 9 theaters, 10,200 office jobs, 2,595 retail jobs, and close to 1,100 part-time jobs were slated for "improvement." On Block 37 alone, fifteen of the sixteen buildings, housing 384,300 square feet of office space (3,840 employees) and 73,800 square feet retail (1,300 employees), were demolished in the winter of 1989–90.[23]

Having languished over most of Daley's last three terms, governmental land-use authority was ironically expanded at the very time land values, on their own, were rising to unprecedented levels, particularly in the central business district. The city of Chicago was actively in the real estate busi-ness, providing expensive subsidies and broad condemnation authority at precisely the moment they weren't needed. Property that hadn't changed hands in generations spilled out, all at once, onto the market. Such a radi-cal reshaping of landownership, originally meant to benefit the city as a whole through a carefully staged redevelopment strategy, was manna to an entrepreneur like Larry Levy, who suddenly had an unobstructed path to one of the best square blocks in America.

Only vaguely aware of what the city was doing and caring less, Levy just kept making deals. Through the beginning of 1981, One Mag Mile was leasing up, he was opening at least one new restaurant every quarter, and he had commercial property in the suburbs. It was uncanny: only two years in the development business and everything was going his way. He re-members walking down the street, hearing people whisper, trying to recall his name as he passed. He recalls them saying, "That's the guy who bought the property at Michigan and Oak." He adds, "They would try to meet me. And the mayor asked to meet me. And all that kind of stuff."[24]

And then things just got better. Leo Melamed, autocratic head of the Chicago Mercantile Exchange located at 300 West Washington until the early 1970s, hired Levy to handle the exchange's real estate interests, in-cluding, most important, the choice of site for a new 250,000-square-foot trading floor and two 1-million-square-foot office towers. Melamed, who had made and lost several fortunes trading futures, was a lawyer by train-ing and a published writer of science fiction. He was also a realist. In 1972, with economist Milton Friedman providing academic ballast, Melamed es-sentially invented the financial futures business. For nearly every following year, the Merc grew 40 percent. Melamed, who had been actual chairman of the Merc for only two years (1969–71), had continued as special counsel to the exchange's board of governors and chairman of the executive committee, which gave him more power with less formal accountability. In the exchange's real estate dealings, he was king.

Levy approached the Merc after he learned that Melamed had solicited proposals from veteran developers. Melamed hired Levy, a relative outsider, to evaluate them, including one from Tishman Speyer, on whose property the Merc's trading floor was currently located. From Melamed's point of view, Levy earned every dime he made. For one thing, it was Levy's idea to take Joseph Fujikawa's conservative, typically bare-bones Miesian scheme and make it look more up-to-date. He conceded that Fujikawa was a fine architect. After all, he had solved the difficult technical design problem of a clear-span trading floor. But to market a building in the 1980s and command premium rents, a broker needed more than brilliant engineering. The Merc, growing at a much faster rate than the rival Board of Trade, wanted its new building to be more dignified: Fujikawa-like function plus something classical. Levy determined that the frame should be clad in granite. Sure, he knew that the Mercantile Exchange would never stand at the foot of LaSalle Street, but a couple of million square feet on Wacker wasn't bad for the former Butter and Egg Board. Cast in stone, brand-new, the Merc made the Board of Trade look like a relic.

The Merc was just the sort of commission Levy craved. No committee to negotiate with, one guy making all the decisions; Levy knew it was what he called a slam dunk. With Leo Melamed watching over him, guaranteeing nearly 60 percent preleasing of the first tower, the Merc's in-house developer risked nothing. As effortlessly as a currency trader figured complicated swaps between the yen and dinar, Levy calculated in his head all the years of fat fees and the promise, not so far down the line, of a gigantic bonus when the second tower was completed and all 2 million square feet were built out. Better yet, all this came at the very time he was completing his first solo development project in town and was wondering what he was ever going to do with Block 37.

Levy made sure that he was the Merc's only link to the booming real estate markets. While Melamed watched billions an hour flowing through his vast trading networks, he hardly had time to reach down to pick up the spare millions that were still locked in the ground. Levy didn't mind bending down. Working the land was his way to a fortune. For openers, he had an exclusive: choosing a developer for the Mercantile Exchange. His relationship with Melamed gave him instant credibility with the downtown real estate crowd. Like Rubloff before him with Marshall Field and his friends, Levy suddenly found himself in the big time.

Better yet, for most of 1980 to 1981 Larry Levy was on both sides of the development game. Specifically, he used his unique position to gain access to JMB and to Metropolitan Structures and its rich new fifty-fifty financial partner, Metropolitan Life. He understood as well as anyone that the commercial real estate business had changed radically. Wild inflation made it unprofitable to hold land indefinitely. Financing alone could quickly bankrupt a project.

Yet, before Levy could exploit the profitable subtleties of modern mortgage financing, he had to figure out a way to get the building out of the ground. This was where the risk was, along with huge up-front costs he might never recover. One-million, or more, square-foot office towers have staggering initial expenses. Once up and operating, however, a single $100 million investment (figuring, on average, construction costs of one hundred dollars a square foot in 1980), with each of its square feet fully occupied, produced a steady flow of cash. With demand picking up, tenants were signing leases indexed to inflation. Since no economist predicted a near end to inflation, a thirty-dollar-a-foot rent in a new building in 1980 was marketed as a bargain by people like Levy who pointed out that commercial rents were likely to be as high as seventy dollars in 1990.

Big insurance companies such as the Prudential and MetLife wanted an equity position in real estate. The first line of modern developers in the 1970s had successfully demonstrated that large office buildings produced fast capital gains. Institutions were slow to figure this out, providing builders a flood of debt with no equity position. When a high-stakes modern developer sold or refinanced, sometimes in fewer than five years after the building was topped off, the lender could bank his safe 3 percent profit (the spread between what the money cost and the rate charged), but could only watch in awe as the $100 million tower was refinanced for $200 million or sold to the Germans or Japanese for $250 million, while the developer paid off the loan, settled a few expenses, and pocketed the rest.

Lenders, who for decades were at the fat end of real estate, buying money for 3 percent and lending it out at 6 percent nearly risk free, were encouraged by their boards to be more aggressive. Why should developers, who had none of their own cash at risk, reap huge rewards while the lenders were left with the scraps? This changed quickly in the 1980s. The commercial banks, whose losses were indirectly insured through federal government agencies such as FDIC, were formerly in real estate deals for fewer than two years, profiting handsomely from high-interest development and construction loans. Insurance companies traditionally took out the construction loans, taking 80 to 100 percent of a project's entire debt in the form of mortgages. However, as the new decade began both were suddenly eager to be codevelopers, in effect becoming partners with the same sorts of businessmen their executives consistently blackballed back at the country club.

This new sort of codevelopment deal was just the thing to initiate Larry Levy into the high life. He took to calling himself the Mercantile Exchange's personal developer. And Leo Melamed encouraged him with the news that the Merc would have direct ownership of its trading floor in any new building. This amounted to nearly a $40 million equity stake in a $350 million project. Melamed's financial commitment gave Levy an unbeatable advantage in negotiations with at-risk developers who would actually raise the bulk of the money and get the new Mercantile Exchange built. Ten percent equity financing and a 60 percent prelease commitment were significant lures. With Leo Melamed's considerable resources behind him, Levy was a match for any developer in the business. At the time he was wondering what to do with Block 37 in early 1981, he was right in the middle of negotiating for the Merc.

Every developer, banker, and broker suddenly wanted to be his friend. Between the exchange and its member firms, Levy could ante up a 600,000-square-foot user; the Merc's own commitment to the project virtually assured short- and long-term financing. With the deal all but settled, Levy was suddenly in a position to bail out a much bigger fish. Holding land bought on spec, paying taxes and expenses, the country's richest developers were betting on high inflation in the real estate market and praying for a rich user. Larry Levy knew what aggressive developers needed, and not knowing how long it would last he made the best of his unique position as middleman. He had no idea then that his good fortune in having gained Leo Melamed's confidence at the Merc would directly affect the future of Block 37.

Flush with Mag Mile's flurry of December condominium sales, Levy gave Bruce Graham the go-ahead to do a single-tower scheme, right in the middle of Block 37, imagining à la Rubloff that the whole site would be flattened. This bought him some critical time during the late winter and early spring of 1981. Soon after he had seen the downtown property he called some people he had been cultivating at the Prudential.[25] Like other insurance companies, Prudential had been long dependent on the steady income generated from expensive whole-life policies. Increasing financial deregulation in the 1970s depleted what had seemed to be a bottomless money machine. Consumers now purchased cheap term policies and wised up to more lucrative investments in the new money market environment. And the normally conservative insurance companies, which had for a century enjoyed wide interest spreads, were abruptly entering, with fat wads of money, the shadowy urban real estate markets.

With years' more experience than its new competitors, the Prudential thought Block 37 was worth taking a crack at.[26] Through an equal partnership with a developer like Levy, the Prudential hoped to own a first-class asset that would in a short time pay for itself, gambling that at some date not too far in the future the building(s) would be refinanced or sold, the old mortgage paid off, and the profit split between Levy and itself.

While the Prudential busied itself with running the numbers, holding meetings, and drawing up drafts of the joint-venture agreement, and Skidmore made drawings and models, Larry Levy had almost effortlessly ratcheted up his business another notch. Every move he made seemed to be right, like a great shooter in the zone. Later, when he bought a tiny piece of the Chicago Bulls, he would watch Michael Jordan from his courtside seats, wondering how much more he might have accomplished had he been given some athletic ability and Jordan's instinct for the basket.

Levy's deal at the Merc foreshadowed his maneuvering on Block 37, but in ways that would surprise him many years later when the whole business started to go bad. Principally, his representation of the Mercantile Exchange brought him back into contact with Neil Bluhm, who along with Judd Malkin was a major partner of JMB.

In late 1969, Bluhm had gone into business with his old University of Illinois fraternity brother.[27] Malkin, an imaginative financial analyst who had been educated as a CPA, was the perfect foil for Bluhm. He was then president of a public company that held the seventeen-state (Midwest) distributorship for Jaguar, Toyota, and Triumph automobiles, while Bluhm, also a CPA, was practicing law at Mayer, Brown and Platt, one of Chicago's premier firms. Malkin's natural reserve coupled with Bluhm's selling skills put them right in position to exploit the changing corporate view of real estate as an investment vehicle. Their first big break came when John Coleman, who ran the venture-capital arm of Continental Bank, bought a 10 percent equity position in their fledgling company. This was right before JMB, in 1971, launched its initial public offering.

Malkin and Bluhm's edge lay in offering to the public what had been closed-door, private syndications of the sort perfected by William Zeckendorf Sr. and some prominent California property developers after the war. These early JMB partnerships were different from the first real estate investment trusts that had been wildly popular in the late 1960s but failed miserably in the 1970s. Effectively, the REITs were large pools of capital looking for real estate. What JMB offered its select investors—mostly wealthy doctors and lawyers with a minimum of five thousand dollars to put at risk—was Judd Malkin's and Neil Bluhm's strict underwriting criteria and nose for first-class property. Unlike the REITs, which exploited long lines of credit provided by clueless desk jockeys remote from their property back at the bank, JMB went out to the field. These were experienced guys who lived the real estate business and its fast track to the good life.

The REITs usurped the role that mortgage bankers had played in the past. Traditionally, the mortgage bankers borrowed money from the banks and re-lent it with a spread to the real estate developers. Before real estate suddenly became glamorous, it was incumbent upon the banks to underwrite

Neil Bluhm

the credit of the mortgage banker—his experience and reputation—and it was his professional obligation to underwrite the credit worthiness of the developer and the project itself. JMB's original niche was in the place of the old middlemen, those knowledgeable real estate professionals unceremoniously removed by bankers to increase their own profits. So with JMB acting the supervisory role of the circumspect mortgage banker, some real quality control in investment, as well as a deep understanding of the underlying asset, was salvaged.

Then by the mid-1970s, Wall Street started its "go, go, go thing," securitizing property, raising lots of money, and taking a big cut.[28] Banks played their part by lending money to the real estate investment trusts and fattening their piece with new fees of their own. The banks got themselves in trouble when they started generating vast profits on a simple earnings-per-share basis, thereby neglecting the sort of sound lending and investment strategy that had drawn them to real estate in the first place. JMB was a very modern company with an old ethic. Hard-earned expertise was the only thing that mattered. Just as the banks were abandoning prudent underwriting, JMB renewed conservative investors' faith in real estate as a slow but reliable asset. Like a wise old family retainer Judd Malkin provided an air of stately caution, while Neil Bluhm and Stuart Nathan, JMB's head of development, navigated the world of high finance.

In those early years when JMB was creating its blue-chip reputation and the whole company consisted of only six or seven people, including secretaries, JMB made most of its money on commissions from real estate transactions. For example, the company might buy a property, paying the owner a commission (a finder's fee), and then resell it, all the time retaining a fee for putting the deal together and another for syndicating. Finder's fees, acquisition fees, fees too new to have names, were all prime cuts from the same cow. The partners' thinking was: they'd make a deal today, finish it, raise money, and there'd be so much money to cut up. In the early years it wasn't so much a business as it was a transactional arrangement. And it wasn't all that profitable in the beginning. Their real estate trading operation required a dramatic change of scale. JMB's goal was to transform itself into a proper business. Bluhm and Malkin took a giant step in this regard when they acquired Equities International, solely for its client list. An established company, Equities International was doing public syndications on a more regular basis. Its roster of pigeons was just what JMB required to grow.

By bringing its partnership units down to five thousand dollars, JMB appealed to a large unexploited consumer market. Its pool of potential investors was enormous. For people frustrated with the low interest paid at banks, JMB provided an inspired alternative. Courtesy of Malkin and Bluhm, those who regularly bought common stocks and bonds could now knowledgeably enter the commercial real estate market, formerly the preserve of coupon clippers and wealthy professionals. The first offering of JMB Properties, a division of the parent company, was a portfolio of carefully chosen real estate with proven cash flows or high rates of capitalization, paying between 8 and 9 percent annually.

That first public offering, Carlyle I—a $7 million portfolio of California apartments—came out in 1971. The name, a complete invention, had high-class associations of grand hotels and summers in Newport. Carlyle was sold through the large wire houses (brokers) who needed some new real estate products to offset the loss of the REITs. Carlyle II, in 1972, raised $16 million. Large retail brokerages like Shearson and Merrill Lynch did not want to underwrite their own programs. They increasingly depended upon Malkin and Bluhm's knowledge of both the financial and "real" side of real estate. And JMB proved Wall Street right by assembling a portfolio of prime West Coast properties just in time to sell on the booming California property market, where values were soaring with the first hit of OPEC inflation.

JMB assured investors that they had in Carlyle a coupon, marketed on the expectation that the investment would pay off in ten to fifteen years, that would outperform corporate bonds, perform as a partial tax shelter, and have an excellent chance of capital appreciation. But Carlyle wasn't the only innovative real estate–based financial instrument. An additional spin-off, JMB Income Properties, changed the mix a little between capital appreciation and shelter. From the beginning, these products were fine-tuned to attract the same money stream that traditionally found its way into the bond market. Continuing to stress the fundamental economics, JMB downplayed the syndications as tax shelters, continuing to prosper as competing national firms, such as VMS in Chicago, went bankrupt soon after the tax laws changed in 1986.

JMB's programs—Carlyle I through XVI, Income Properties (twelve issues), Mortgage Partners, Carlyle Income Securities, shopping center syndications, and some private offerings—were a conservative investor's dream: real estate that behaved like a bond with an equity "kicker." JMB made it all seem as natural as letting your Uncle Manny do your taxes. It was easy to think of Judd Malkin and Neil Bluhm as the same guys to whom you entrusted the bake sale money back in high school: audiovisual nerds who wheeled around the overhead projector, were in the mathletes, and would have gone to MIT if they had had the bucks. Good folk doing fine deals was the reputation that JMB assiduously cultivated and to a large extent earned over two tumultuous decades, during which most of the real estate profession was involved in unabashed, old-fashioned wheeling and dealing.

Just about the time Larry Levy started in the development business, Malkin and Bluhm had a billion-dollar operation going at full tilt. JMB was involved in the ownership, management, and leasing of real property, a conservative cover for a fundamentally radical securitization of land. But even before a single caisson was in, the money was already flowing from the various financial transactions in which the company had a hand. And it didn't stop there. When the building was up and running, JMB collected management fees and leasing fees. Front end, back end, the money was reinvested as soon as a commercial bank cut the first check for the construction loan. Borrowing capital, debt in $100 million chunks, is how a New Age real estate pro only *starts* making money.

Depending on the size of a deal, an acquisition fee can be as low as 8 percent for a large project and as high as 20 percent for a small one. In addition, JMB cleverly improvised on the old formulas, providing services like the JMB Insurance Agency to insure its own properties. The insurance operation turned out to be so profitable that it was later offered, in Stuart Nathan's words, to the "outside world," providing insurance for other developers.

All told, this real estate attracted billions in capital, inciting normally cautious financial types to relax their underwriting standards. Wealthy individuals, institutions such as hospitals, universities, and giant pension funds, all wanted in, ignoring one glaring imperfection in their new sure thing. Unlike the first generation of postwar towers, built to suit Fortune 500 corporations as "homes" for their workers, flashy new skyscrapers were completely speculative ventures, erected with no specific use in mind.[29] They were giant vertical airports with no planes set to land. Beginning in the late 1970s, sixty-story towers couldn't go up fast enough. And, paradoxically, just as the demand for commercial real estate predictably had once outpaced supply, now the population of users of expensive Class A space remained flat. New office towers were built simply because there was money available to build them. Think of your town's proudest office building as a three-dimensional junk bond with money leaking from the front end and back. Who could resist such a flood of money flowing through the same hose? Each fee was a pinprick, a little hole spurting money into a common well. At the end of the 1980s, *Forbes* listed Bluhm and Malkin with more than a billion dollars apiece in their private accounts.

Through it all, JMB maintained its reputation for being above the battle—better behaved than the more predatory real estate firms that made it big and then quickly disappeared. As of summer 1992, JMB had real estate in its own account worth $5.7 billion out of a total $21 billion under management—73 million square feet of office and industrial space, 93 million square feet of shopping malls, nineteen thousand apartment units, and eight thousand hotel rooms—and employed thousands.[30]

In the 1980s, nobody played the real estate game better. Coming out of the previous decade cash rich and confident of its position atop the increasingly competitive world of real estate financing, JMB wanted to broaden its influence, no longer content simply to passively profit off the speculative bubble that drove Loop values from a high of $301.50 a square foot (JMB's 1979 purchase of the city garage on Wacker Drive) to more than $1,500 a square foot in 1989 (Manufacturers Life Insurance Company's $1,658 purchase of the southeast corner of Monroe and Wacker and a Saudi businessman's binding agreement to buy 303 West Monroe for $1,482 a square foot). JMB plunged into development and the bold outright purchases of some of the world's finest properties.

In their first decade, they grew from successful investors and pension advisers to land barons, rivaling and then surpassing the Reichmanns after the Canadians floundered on London's Docklands, a sprawling mixed-use development that was meant to supplant the city as England's financial center. JMB focused on established businesses, purchasing Cadillac Fairview in 1987 from the Bronfmans and Reichmanns, Urban Investment (Chicago) in 1983 from Aetna, and Amfac properties (Hawaii) from Alcoa in 1988, in the process acquiring for its portfolio prestige properties like Chicago's Water Tower Place, Los Angeles's Century City, and Houston's Houston Center. JMB owned department stores, shopping malls, and office towers all over the world. None of this was lost on Larry Levy when he was choosing a site for the Merc. He was in the enviable position of being able to do Neil Bluhm a favor.

For its debut in development, JMB started big, purchasing at auction, with no guarantee of a future user, the land on Wacker Drive which the Chicago Mercantile Exchange now stands. In 1979, three hundred dollars a foot for land was considered a fortune, particularly if you could not be certain of averaging out your cost down to ten dollars a square foot. For an 83,835-square-foot site, 2,225,000 square feet of building would be required to make the deal work. Where Malkin and Bluhm were nearly flawless in their understanding of the financialization of real estate, they were neophytes at the development end of the business. Taking a raw piece of land, raising money, overseeing construction, and then managing, in all its variations, the completed building were a reach for even an established firm. And to complicate things further, JMB's opportunity to enter the development business came at an unusually turbulent time, when real estate was fast replacing the energy markets as the quickest way to vast wealth.

JMB had for a decade involved itself exclusively in the glamour end of its business, as the commodification of real estate reached the ultimate stage, joining other more portable objects of wealth in the world's trading houses. The actual object of desire—be it gold, oil, diamonds, or downtown land—in the end is simply the basis or starting point for speculation. In each case, the commodity's *perceived* future value, rather than its actual scarcity, is where the real treasure lies.[31] An architect who designs a glittering tower with a cathedral-sized lobby and rich appointments is simply setting the jewel. Gold is traded in ounces, oil in barrels, diamonds in carats, land in square feet. The trick to trading land, rather than simply farming or renting it, is to celebrate the aura of location—its spatial uniqueness and special sort of scarcity—while, paradoxically, finding a way to securitize and render it as a truly liquid commodity. Land can obviously never be as portable as gold or diamonds, flow as freely as oil, but as a magnet for cash it certainly works just as well. Referring to commercial property as an aggregate of square feet retains the lure of uniqueness while conferring the practical tag of unit value, critical to modern exchange.

Speculative bubbles rely on the availability of capital in huge multiples of the underlying asset.[32] They always thrive where there is no traditional market balance, no equilibrium between supply and demand, a relaxation of the classical rule that, at least in theory, sellers should equal buyers. The real estate bubbles of the 1980s were driven by a situation in which there were many more buyers than first-class properties and locations. Cash was abundant. JMB thought of Chicago real estate as the third crest of a fifteen-year tidal wave of money.

First, in the mid-to-late seventies cash went overseas to service Latin American debt. This recycling of Arab petrodollar deposits produced huge paper profits through wide interest rate spreads. At an unprecedented scale, the simple principle of buying money cheap and selling it again at a fat premium undermined the banking system. The concentration of bank debt proved fatal when the large American banks were unable to sell Latin American bonds on the market. This was the period the New York banks were savaged at their own hands, after having competed ruthlessly to lend billions to Mexico and Brazil.[33]

The second wave, in the early 1980s, was fueled by post-Arab-boycott oil and energy cash, savings and loan money freed through deregulation, and pension funds that sought high total returns from real property. Even small-town banks, formerly restricted to lending on local residential mortgages, were given wide latitude. They poured out billions to large Wall Street brokerages that packaged—bundled together—their loans and resold them on the public market.[34] No lending institution was immune. During this period Chicago's biggest bank, Continental Illinois Bank and Trust, had to be bailed out by the federal government. Continental had lent promiscuously to deep-gas wildcatters through a correspondent institution, Penn Square Bank, operating out of a shopping center in Oklahoma City. Forced to compete with the returns of natural-gas leases and other quick-rich schemes, real estate bottom lines were dressed up to look more appealing to Wall Street. Calculations were no longer made on a simple cash-on-cash basis that added up a building's rental income and subtracted the operating expenses and taxes, but on a total-return basis, which pretended to know the property's value decades into the future. Instead of old-fashioned estimates based on arithmetic and sober experience, the future asset value and income stream of the new generation of skyscrapers were figured on early spreadsheet computer programs.

These projections satisfied the appetite for junk-bond-level interest rates while underplaying the risk to unsophisticated investors, new to commercial real estate but already addicted to double-digit returns. After all, a developer could always point to the building itself as the ultimate collateral, implying that the financing was as solid as the steel frame. As long as inflation kept prices rising, no one was ever going to question the accepted accounting model for calculating commercial property and see that it was based upon a simplistic straight-line linear model of the future and contained several highly questionable assumptions.

No critical thinking was required or encouraged. It wasn't quite dreaming that you might win a fortune at three-card monte, but contemporary real estate accounting required its own sort of magic thinking. Played on a computer and not on an old corrugated carton, internal rate of return (IRR), the decade's most popular form of analysis, was a key feature built into the new software. The IRR was calculated by putting several variables into play, most notably the widely accepted prediction that inflation would continue growing at better than a 10 percent clip. With a press of a key on a computer keyboard, a broker with only *Sesame Street*–level math could generate a total return in seconds. He could just as easily work backward, determining a particular annual return of, say, 15 percent, and know to a tenth of a percentage point the rate of inflation fifteen years out. The total return, sometimes figured as far into the future as the year 2020, took the combination of forty years of rent rolls, refinancings, accelerated depreciation, taxes, rollover, and lease renewals indexed to inflation, and an anticipated capital gains bonanza when the building was sold. Average investors who couldn't pass geometry were instant Einsteins with days of complex calculations completed in seconds.

Nearly half a century of inflation had helped lull investors into thinking that real estate prices would continue doubling and redoubling for another generation or two. As the eighties began there was not a single active real estate professional who had lived through the Great Depression, no one who had experienced the terrifying experience of property values crashing to zero overnight. Rather than dwell on the past, a new breed of CPA and MBA, born and bred in the booming postwar years, prepared pro formas, handicapping the performance of million-square-foot buildings years before the first tenant appeared on the site. Pro formas based on the new math of IRRs were crystal-ball predictions of how a building would perform once it was totally leased out and operating.

The pro forma, doubling as a prospectus, usually included a fancy architectural rendering and some short biographical essays on the project's general partners. A little calculus, some purple prose, the pro forma was a literary hybrid. Privately printed in numbered copies, the pro forma sold an expensive piece of architecture in advance of the fact.

Pie-in-the-sky profits, a beautiful new tower in the middle of town, fine people running the show, all added up to make a normally hard-boiled businessman giddy with anticipation. Many a pension fund manager looked around in the 1980s, watching from the sidelines as all the new wealth was being made in real estate, wondering how he might dump off a few hundred million in treasuries, with their razor-thin profit margins and boring predictability, and buy a little property. Can you blame a guy for dreaming that an office building he knew rationally to be a net liability when he bought it was "actually," in the oracular language of the IRR, paying 20 percent a year and bound to make him a fortune?

Generated at the touch of a finger, discounted annual returns induced the first group of Lotus 1-2-3 eaters to invest fortunes in Sun Belt real estate, most notably in Houston, Dallas, and Los Angeles, and then finally back in the old cities like New York and Chicago. Not a few made fortunes as advertised, thereby encouraging even more to play at this new science of numerology.

The final speculative wave was effectively driven by the reverse of the first when Americans, who never really critically assessed the value of the underlying asset in Latin American lending or in their own property, were replaced by the Japanese, who made the same mistake with American commercial real estate. When the United States was still the world's largest creditor nation in the seventies, the New York banks sustained crippling losses by playing the spread on Third World loans, which were seemingly safe because they were backed by the full faith and credit of sovereign nations. The opposite occurred in the mideighties, when the United States abruptly became a net importer of capital. This time the Japanese were playing the spreads: the value of their currency (yen increasingly strong against the dollar) and the wide gap in interest rates. High American interest rates doubled and sometimes tripled stable Japanese rates of 4 and 5 percent. With forecasts of total returns gassed up to approach 20 percent, plus a snob-appeal first-class asset (skyscraper) by a world-class architect, Chicago real estate sucked Japanese and other offshore capital to the city. Japanese investment in American real estate through 1990 was $70.72 billion. In the peak year, 1989, the Japanese had $1.9 billion invested in the Chicago area alone.[35] Investors were not often reminded that in place of their cash, developers were only promising paper returns. Real estate might be made to look like a bond or security, but real property has no par value. There is never any assurance that at some specified future date an investor will get his principal back. Downtown land was always an ideal candidate for a big bust. If real estate ever acted contrary to the pro formas, one would be lucky to get back half of his original investment.

· · ·

Larry Levy's choice of JMB to develop the new Chicago Mercantile Exchange cemented a relationship with Neil Bluhm that carried over later in the summer of 1981, when Levy needed help with Block 37. Levy, always pretty much a fringe player in big-stakes real estate transactions, managed to captivate Bluhm through a mix of subtle sycophancy and shrewd dealing. Bluhm was a natural businessman who had never bothered to acquire any polish. He had a perpetually unpressed look that belied his new wealth. Now that he could eat at the best restaurants, have boxes at the opera, symphony, and Cubs games, he tried to look a little more elegant, at ease with the trappings of success. Levy, with his trendy restaurants, cocky regimental mustache, bantam confidence, and calm recklessness in pursuing self-advancement, hypnotized Bluhm. He liked the way Levy dressed, his ease with strangers, the whole package. And now Levy had produced a big user for JMB's expensive land. The Merc deal put Malkin and Bluhm into position for the single biggest payday in their company's history.[36] What wasn't there to like about Larry Levy when he first started talking to them about Block 37?

As the Merc's leasing efforts intensified, Levy had frequent contact with Bluhm and matter-of-factly started talking about "doing something in the North Loop." Bluhm was naturally intrigued, still seeing dollar signs every time he looked at Levy. The timing of Neil Bluhm's ardor proved to be excellent for Levy, who as the months passed was starting to have serious problems with his financing on Block 37. The Prudential, which had seemed eager in the beginning of the year, began slowly retreating; Levy couldn't close the negotiations.

The big insurance company, naturally conservative about risk, became increasingly nervous about the economy, now deep in the recession brought on by the Federal Reserve Board's tightening of credit. There were other problems too. Levy, who did not yet own a single parcel on Block 37, was beginning to test the insurance company's patience, blowing in its ear about the city's imminent plan to condemn. Still the Prudential kept him on the hook, recognizing that the city would most likely pick an established developer or one who already had a position on the land. For his own part, Levy knew he wasn't big time and was only attractive to a financial partner and the city if he brought with him to a deal a few key properties, preferably distributed in all four quadrants of the three-acre block. Even if he finally signed on to a joint venture with the Prudential, it might still be good for future business to tantalize Neil Bluhm and Bernard Weissbourd, head of Metropolitan Structures and JMB's development partner at the Merc.

Levy understood his position. He had worked hard the first half of 1981,

Bernard Weissbourd

trying, like a proper developer, to come up with some credible architectural scheme to show his money partners at the Prudential. All the time he was desperately trying to buy up whatever he could. He learned more about Stop and Shop and started romancing Gardner Stern Jr., son of one of the founders. Junior was watching the store while John Loeb, scion of the other founding family, was off in Europe. In Loeb's absence, Levy put on his show with Stern, unwrapping a great plan for bringing the Sterns' family business—a Chicago institution—into the modern age of retailing.

Stern was still swooning when he told John Loeb what had happened during his absence. A meeting was set up at the offices of Skidmore, Owings and Merrill so the young developer could personally show Loeb, a much harder sell, some of what Stern called "Levy's great ideas."

Late in May 1981, Loeb went down to the Inland Steel Building, a gem of an office building designed in 1955 by Bruce Graham and Walter Netsch, where the firm still had its offices. Walking the few blocks from Washington to Monroe, Loeb moved architecturally forward in time from the nineteenth to the late twentieth century. Across the street from Inland Steel was Perkins and Will's sixty-story First National Bank and Helmut Jahn's newly completed Xerox Centre, with its elegant round corner and spiraled cornice. For Loeb, who confessed that he rarely walked downtown, the short jaunt was strangely disorienting: his family's proud real estate at 30 West Washington suddenly looked a thousand years old.

Bruce Graham, Larry Levy, and Levy's brother Mark were ready for him in one of the presentation rooms. The lights went down. John Loeb was shown a block he had gone to work to everyday for more than twenty years, and it was completely transformed. Nothing remained of the old buildings. In the month he had been away, Larry Levy had shanghaied his life. Here a business, more than a century old, in a building that went back nearly sixty years, was made to vanish right in front of him. Loeb studied the colorful renderings and models—listening all the time to Bruce Graham's patter—and couldn't help feeling like the schlemiel who leaves his car with the keys in the ignition and finds it gone when he returns. Here was the confident head of Skidmore with two guys he had never heard of—Larry Levy all suited up and full of charm and his brother Mark dressed like a slob, nodding compliantly—talking about their plans for his business on a block on which they owned not one square inch. Loeb admits he arrived there in a "crummy mood" but got to feeling a lot worse looking at Graham's design, a monolithic tower set right in the middle of the block. These weren't doodles, sketches done after hours, but a real architectural scheme, nearly fifty thousand dollars' worth, representing months of work.

Worse yet, other respectable businessmen were taking the Levys seriously. Even before Loeb, the first property owner on the block, got a look at the project, the Prudential Insurance Company had deliberated on a commitment of more than $100 million in financing, based on the same crazy scheme. He couldn't help fantasizing on his way back to the office that he might discover the whole block demolished in his absence.

Undeterred by the "crummy mood" in the room, Levy began to pitch his plans for Stop and Shop and Hillman's as if he were the head of city planning and any final disposition of the North Loop remained simply a bothersome technicality. After "about thirty minutes of propaganda," the lights went up, and Loeb asked some questions. In this building that appeared to him to be a slightly more tasteful, but just as expensive, Water Tower Place, Levy guaranteed him eight thousand square feet on the Washington Street side mezzanine and fifteen thousand square feet in the basement for Hillman's. As Loeb tells it, Levy had it all figured out to the last cent. Rents would be forty-two dollars for the mezzanine, twenty-five dollars for the basement. Loeb concluded that Levy had seen the Water Tower rent schedule. Loeb had only recently seen it himself and had reluctantly turned down a deal there because he "couldn't make the numbers work."

This was madness. Loeb was currently paying only between eight dollars and ten dollars a square foot for his entire operation. He told Levy that to make Stop and Shop work, he required at least twenty thousand square feet, and twenty-five thousand to thirty thousand square feet, also on a main floor, for Hillman's. Already getting up to leave, he told the brokers that the rent for Hillman's should be no more than 1 percent of sales, and that Stop and Shop could be 2 or 3 percent of sales. The business also required its own receiving dock and alley. Shutting his briefcase, he loosed his parting shot: "I'm sick and tired of people telling me what's going to happen with something that I own. You guys don't even have the decency to ask."[37]

None of this bothered Levy, who had calculated in advance that he knew more about the food business after a couple of years than John Loeb had learned in a lifetime. In fact, he confessed to feeling a little sorry for the Sterns and the Loebs. It was natural that fellows who had inherited their daddies' business would be a little "behind the curve." Sure John Loeb was angry. Levy understood. He was proposing to knock down the family empire, quarter his space, and quadruple his rent. But he was confident he could make Loeb see that everyone would make out better in the end if the two families would just let him use the cream of their operation, Gaper's and Stop and Shop, to billboard his new project. The only thing left in the financial ruin of their business was the invaluable pedigree of their name. He didn't bother telling them that.

Larry Levy made a play for Loeb's business only to get at his land. Graham's architectural show was only the first tack. If Stop and Shop had been agreeable to coming into the development as a tenant, he could have used it as leverage to get other retailers without having to front any financing. Fronting a partnership with the Loebs and Sterns was simply the easiest way to position himself between the owner of the land, Woodman of the World Insurance Company, and Hillman's, Inc., which had only months earlier signed a new thirty-year lease.

Bingo—Larry Levy, without a dime of his own money, discovered a way to gain a solid position on Block 37, although he still would have to find some way to make a deal before 1981 was over. Business had been starting to turn down. He could feel it slide at his only other development project. Since the December 1980 rush on condominiums at One Mag Mile, he hadn't sold another—and wouldn't for more than two years.[38] Without a parcel of land on Block 37, all Levy had in May of 1981 was plenty of expensive architecture and no financing.

John Loeb had no interest in working with Levy and made it clear that if the developer was hungry enough for his family's property he should buy the business, and even before leaving SOM's dog-and-pony show he told Levy as much. Loeb's resistance suggested to Levy that Block 37 wasn't going to get developed as easily as Bruce Graham had made it seem. It was only another instance of the rubric that in the real estate business it was best to ignore bad news and just continue moving forward. Once he captured the Stern/Loeb business, he'd keep the marquee names, Stop and Shop and Gaper's, and off-load the rest; on-site chicken plucking, meat cutting, and wholesale produce were not what he had in mind for the new downtown. He instructed his attorney, Paul Rudnick, and his accountant, Howard Bernstein, to open negotiations while he concentrated on circling the block, looking for his next piece of land.

He immediately followed up on one of Graham's first observations about the block. The architect had mentioned that Samuel Zell had purchased the leasehold for the Unity Building (127 North Dearborn) within a month after city council approval of the amended North Loop Guidelines. Beset by his new problems at One Mag Mile, the frustrating details of closing the negotiations with the Prudential for Block 37, and the leasing over at the Merc, Levy forgot about Zell until he read about him in the papers. On February 26, 1981, Zell had written Mayor Byrne, professing his readiness to preserve and rehabilitate the building for use as his own corporate offices. Here Levy had himself believing that he was the only wildcatter on Block 37 and discovered that Zell had beaten him to a claim.

Samuel Zell and the late Jerrold Wexler, another legendary Chicago speculator, were the direct descendants of Arthur Rubloff. They were pure land traders, developing nothing unless backed into a corner. Zell had acquired the nickname Gravedancer, because he specialized in buying up distressed properties, sometimes at as little as twenty cents on a dollar. Looking closely at the Sidwell map, which detailed real estate transactions on Block 37 over time, Levy was delighted to discover that the property lines of 30 West Washington and 127 North Dearborn touched at the rear of both buildings. Any person who controlled the two properties effectively cut a diagonal right through the block. Two buildings, like a well-placed knight and bishop, could dominate half the board.

Levy called Zell, recounting what he had read. Zell confirmed his interest in the Unity Building. Zell, trained as a lawyer, liked the idea that he would house his various businesses in a tower that had briefly been the address of Clarence Darrow, around the time of the Leopold and Loeb case. Of course, it hadn't escaped his notice that 25 percent tax credits were available for those interested in rehabilitating historic structures. He quickly retained a young architect, Kenneth Schroeder, and gave trompe l'oeil artist Richard Haas a deposit to see what they might do with the old building. The building at 127 North Dearborn had begun life listing five degrees to the south, sinking into the muddy subsoil immediately after construction in 1892. It was never clear how Richard Haas, famous for rendering false classical fronts on anonymous buildings, was going to paint over this problem.

In turn, Zell also learned that Levy was trying to assemble some land, maybe only the south side of the block. Levy needed to talk to him. Zell, with a condemnation order hanging over the entire North Loop, responded, "Let's talk; you never know," already setting Levy up before the younger man had a chance to run his own con on him. Anticipating his meeting with Zell and making the best of it in advance, Levy let the Pru know, at about the second-draft stage of their joint venture, that he was

Unity Building and Commonwealth Edison substation

making progress toward getting the west side of Block 37. After Levy's call, Zell was never as keen to renovate the Unity, a building he only weeks earlier had called a "jewel."

In fact, as a speculator Zell was in fine shape. He had made a deal back in November 1980 with the Lanski family (who had owned the property since 1945) for a thirty-year master lease until the year 2010 on a building that was almost 90 percent occupied when he assumed ownership. In return for the leasehold, he agreed to pay the Lanskis total rent of nearly $6.5 million and supplied them with an unrestricted $300,000 security deposit, on which—at a time when interest rates were up to 20 percent—he required only 6 percent interest. This was a hefty security deposit to pay if Zell really was interested in occupying the building for thirty years; the arrangement only made real sense if he intended to be in and out of the transaction fast. The Lanskis and Zell had essentially agreed to a clever profit-sharing arrangement: the family got to pull out $300,000 in nontaxable cash from the old building, and Zell put himself between the fee (the deed to the land still held by the Lanskis) and the city's North Loop Guidelines that directed a taking of the entire block by the city through eminent domain.

This seemingly innocuous transaction with the Lanskis, Zell, and longtime partner Robert Lurie set a new, considerably higher value for the property. Discounted back, the leasehold on this leaning tower now had a price tag of more than $2 million. For $300,000 down, Zell, now with Larry Levy on the hook, was in position to make a quick profit of close to 700 percent. Zell's Unity Building play would immediately begin the actual spiral of North Loop land, inflating its cost to the city by five to ten times what it cost before the first successful speculator arrived. Sam Zell's arrival on Block 37 marked the formal beginning of the eighties downtown land grab. What was still officially blighted land now had a Tiffany price tag.

Levy moved swiftly into real negotiations with Robert Lurie, agreeing to pay Zell $2.1 million for the lease and an additional $2 million for his option to purchase the fee at some future date directly from the Lanskis. Significantly, at the same time, in a separate deal memo, Levy agreed to give Zell/Lurie 2 percent of his share of any future joint-venture agreement to develop the entire block. He also pledged to send Zell/Lurie copies of any future partners' financial statements and other pertinent information relating to an ongoing joint venture. When the deal was signed on November 30, 1981, the Gravedancer had made more than $1.7 million in less than a year.[39] By concealing Zell's continuing 2 percent position in a potential $1 billion deal, Levy had provided the speculator with an invaluable window on the closely held financial positions of his competitors. Just for insurance, Levy also bought 111 North Dearborn, little more than a wooden shack, two structures down from the Unity, for $600,000.

After a bad start to 1981, Levy was suddenly having new success. But all this good news was getting expensive. In addition to locking up the two properties on Dearborn, he had come to terms, after almost daily negotiating sessions with John Loeb and the Sterns, for 16–30 West Washington. And this one wasn't cheap. Levy agreed to pay $1.65 million to have their 1980 lease assigned to him and concurrently to purchase all outstanding shares of Hillman's, Inc., capital stock and assume $3 million in long-term interest-bearing debt. At two dollars a share for 477,763 shares of Hillman's, a million here, a million there, Levy was quickly getting in over his head.[40]

Still no commitment from the Prudential. Before he had signed any agreements, around the time he was still courting John Loeb and Sam Zell, he decided to take his first look around the State Street side of the block. Pathway Financial (100 North State), an old Burnham office building, was right on the corner of Washington and State. Next to it was a small taxpayer with a Limited clothing store on the ground floor, in place of the already demolished Roosevelt Theater. A storefront farther north, Levy discovered a remarkable series of small buildings that turned right around the next block on Randolph. These were very old structures built right after the 1871 fire, linked by a common alley. The buildings stopped abruptly at an empty lot, where a fire had burned out a building more than a decade earlier. He remembers thinking it eerie that he was walking in the heart of America's second city and looking to pick up in one shot more than half an acre of land as if he were still beating the cornfields.

All 25,000 square feet from the middle of State to the middle of Randolph, the entire northeast corner of Block 37, was for sale. He calmly offered the owners $5 million more that he didn't have and sat back waiting for the deal to flesh out brilliantly, like all the others. But it wasn't to be. Levy had miscalculated. He had unexpectedly run into a cadre of old political insiders. They had been patiently buying up land in anticipation of something happening since 1946, when one of them, Colonel Jacob Arvey, had first obtained a sneak look at the city's first Comprehensive Plan. Chicago aldermen treated the never-adopted preliminary plan as a treasure map of every foot of future development over the entire metropolitan area. The document proposed 135 miles of new expressways, 360 major thoroughfares, and 300 miles of secondary roadways. Funding of these traffic ways alone was a Marshall Plan for the downtown.

Arvey, who had no professional interest in real estate, was the lawyer for an inventive local banker, George D. Sax, who wanted to open a real consumer bank, the first on State Street. Sax, who invented drive-up-window banking, was a colorful downstate figure who made his first fortune manufacturing punchboards. These were originally an innocent merchandising technique for marketing chewing gum, but became infamous in the 1930s as a colorful vehicle for the neighborhood numbers rackets. Sax made good use of his selling skills when he moved permanently to Chicago.

In the late 1940s, George Sax came to know Arvey in relation to a certain real estate problem concerning his bank. The Exchange National Bank had a national charter but a precarious hold at its prominent LaSalle Street location. George Sax was Jewish on a completely Gentile banking street. He prospered in businesses proper bankers disdained, like providing the daily cash deliveries for the city's currency exchanges. More prominent now than ever in Chicago, as traditional institutions have fled the inner city, currency exchanges are poor men's banks. Trading money in surprisingly high vol-

Block 37, Randolph Street side

ume at exorbitantly high fees, they are a high-margin operation for those willing to trade at the limits of respectable business. For Sax, the purchase of State Street land was a hedge against the time he would inevitably be forced out of his LaSalle Street lease.

Arvey did all of Sax's legal work, putting him in a good position with the Democratic organization. For his conscientious work Arvey was rewarded with a minority position in each of the land parcels purchased by the Sax-controlled Jewell Development Company, a form of tribute to the Colonel. He split this extra commission with his firm, Arvey, Hodes and Mantynband (later Arvey, Hodes, Costello and Burman).

Following the Second World War, Colonel Arvey, Barnet Hodes (a one-time corporation counsel), and several prominent Cook County judges, for almost forty years, all got in on the northeast corner of Block 37. A lark, an investment for the kids, when they first started collecting these odd pieces of land, the properties soon got to be an embarrassment. Mostly vacant above the first floor, stinking of urine and filled with retail sharpies that the owners hadn't seen since their West Side days, this corner of the downtown until Levy arrived was hardly their Klondike load.

The first person Levy approached was Howard Arvey, adoring son of the colonel, who was still a law partner of Scott Hodes, son of Barnet, in the old family firm. Both Arvey and Hodes had inherited from their fathers a minority interest in the block. No longer politically influential, the law office still had contacts with all the various real estate interests on Block 37. In the summer of 1981, Levy hadn't been lucky enough this time to run into a fellow speculator like Zell, or a good businessman like John Loeb ready to get out of a family operation gone sour: this time it was the heir to a waned political dynasty who was clever enough to realize what the young developer was up to. By shooting his mouth off, Levy instantly raised the value of the property in Arvey's mind five times what he had thought the firetraps were worth and started him thinking about making more.

When the city chose Levy and his joint-venture partners to develop Block 37, Sidcor (a suburban real estate company that had purchased the Sax and Arvey interests) sued the city, filing a traverse against the taking of its land. On December 12, 1986, a judge settled the case, directing the city of Chicago to pay Sidcor $14,907,667. Land appraised in 1978 at less than ten dollars a square foot (written-down price to a developer) and at one hundred dollars a foot (actual cost to the city) was driven up to more than five hundred dollars a square foot when the city actually had to buy it in 1986. (Four entire blocks in the original North Loop plan, including 37, had been budgeted at only $23 million.)

Levy understandably never had another conversation with Howard Arvey or any of his partners. He unfortunately learned, as he later admitted, that the Arvey group was very sophisticated. This was useful knowledge, but it came a little too late, just as the world started falling in on him. The Prudential abruptly withdrew from the Block 37 deal in the summer of 1981. Citing fast-rising interest rates and expensive prior commitments, the giant insurance company canceled every new unsigned development project. Almost overnight, Levy was looking at next to $10 million in new land purchases, fifty thousand dollars in useless architectural work, and a reputation that wouldn't be worth a damn if he couldn't figure a way out. Thinking back on the period, Levy remembers, "I was ready to throw up. I was very frightened."[41]

But he had also learned after years in the unpredictable real estate game to keep his hand concealed and an optimistic smile on his face. He installed his mother as official greeter at Kaplan's, for that touch of authenticity, and left the day-to-day operations of the restaurant business to his brother, freeing himself to concentrate on the Merc and his other development interests. There things weren't going so well. Both Mag Mile and Block 37 were big headaches and getting very expensive. The mixed-use tower on North Michigan was getting built very slowly, and the apartments were not selling at all. As August 1981 rolled around, he was about to sign off on nearly $6 million of derelict Block 37 properties, with no cash in the bank. No wonder he felt sick to his stomach.

After the Prudential cut him loose, Levy poured all his energies into the Merc. He went as often as possible to the JMB offices in the Hancock Center, getting as close as he could to Neil Bluhm, never letting on that the Prudential deal was starting to go sour. He used his borrowed stature with JMB to regale Bluhm with the Levy Organization's great plans for the North Loop.

Levy had known for a while that JMB and Met Structures were interested themselves in developing a block. They would bid equally against other developers once the city, now without "coordinator" Shaw or a legal redevelopment plan, got around to issuing an RFP. Levy was mounting an expensive campaign to win a preemptive position on Block 37, where he was a front-runner. His rich partners at the Merc didn't own anything on Block 35, north of Randolph between Dearborn and Clark, where the Greyhound Bus Terminal had been operating for almost fifty years.

While Levy was busy working all the angles, his Block 37 partners were distracted elsewhere. Bernard Weissbourd, who ran Metropolitan Structures, went ahead and retained Helmut Jahn, then working on the State of Illinois Building, to prepare a design for the Greyhound block. Weissbourd showed Jahn's plan to Neil Bluhm; Bluhm and Malkin then agreed to be partners with Met Structures in the North Loop. They hadn't even begun to consider Block 37.

Barney Weissbourd had already helped elevate Jahn to the highest ranks of American architects. Another Chicago developer, Harvey Walken, had hired Jahn to design a tower (1 South Wacker) in 1979. Walken's financing came from Metropolitan Life, which insisted that Metropolitan Structures be brought in as the development partner.[42] Joining Walken as codeveloper, Weissbourd got a chance to see the young architect in action. Jahn had all of Mies van der Rohe's facility and Germanic certainty, coupled with a taste for designer clothes and fast cars. A Mies for the eighties. This in Weissbourd's mind put him a cut above Joseph Fujikawa, who had been assigned the majority of Met Structures design work since 1969. Furthermore, it didn't hurt either that Jahn reportedly had Mayor Byrne cooing in his presence.

Weissbourd's choice of Jahn was especially significant in the elite world of skyscraper architects. Metropolitan Structures, in 1959, was the successor firm to a prominent business begun by Herbert S. Greenwald, an unusually cerebral man in the action-oriented development racket. Employing only one architect, Ludwig Mies van der Rohe, he became famous worldwide as a sensitive architectural patron. He brought status to a marginal profession. With his pipe, relaxing in a book-lined office, he was the picture of a man of high sensibility, adding luster to the marketplace's daily combat.

Talmudic scholar, philosophy student at the University of Chicago, art lover, a salesman, Herb Greenwald displayed a wild mixture of American attitudes. He brought an unmistakable virtuosity to the square business environment of the fifties. With Mies perfecting the formula of steel-frame and glass-curtain wall, Greenwald had a product to meet the first wave of postwar prosperity. He gave people great architecture they could afford. High-rise Levittown with style. First the daring apartments in Detroit, Hyde Park, and on Lake Shore Drive, then the government buildings and corporate headquarters—Miesian architecture in America was Bauhaus workers' housing, upscaled. Greenwald's developments had just enough sumptuous detail—green marble and glove-leather furniture—to satisfy the new hordes of university-educated consumers. And because it was a relatively simple formula, Miesian architecture was profitable.

When Greenwald died in an airplane crash in February 1959, his lawyer took over the eccentric company and transformed it into a consistent, profitable, mainstream business. Barney Weissbourd didn't have the typical developer's MO either. He held a Ph.D. in chemistry and before becoming a lawyer had worked on the Manhattan Project. Metropolitan Structures kept on hiring Mies, and even after the master's death in 1969, they employed the Office of Mies van der Rohe to design a veritable farm of flat-topped steel-and-glass towers on the air rights above the Illinois Central tracks along the lake. The complex was named Illinois Center.

Larry Levy had taken to walking the few miles from his apartment in Lincoln Park to work at the Hancock. It took his mind off the failure of the Prudential to come up with the money he needed to continue on Block 37. He'd look over at the lake, at the sailboats and the girls sunning themselves on Oak Street Beach, and as he was strolling he'd make himself concentrate on how unbelievably lucky he was. Out of hometown St. Louis, brokering the biggest real estate deal in town, opening a new restaurant every few months, and watching his own skyscraper grow out of the ground. Block 37 was going to be his monument, the Levy Tower, right in the city's bull's-eye. He had done his part, hiring that prima donna Bruce Graham, listening to the Sterns and Loebs moan about a great business they had turned to shit. Then the Prudential, without any warning, left him holding the bag. It was hard to get that out of his mind.

He was almost at the end of the walk, about to put on his daily smile for Neil Bluhm, when he figured it out. This was always how the best ideas came to Larry Levy. No planning, no strategizing, just natural, like singing in the shower. He thought, "Why not simply let Neil know that I might be interested in doing a joint venture with him if things ever went south with the Pru? I'd keep him informed. Give him the courtesy of first refusal." Before he reached the Hancock elevators he had worked it all out in his mind. It went something like this: "Neil, if anything ever happened to the Block 37 deal I'd want you to be the first one to know, blah, blah, blah." He figured (correctly) that once he had Neil Bluhm on the hook, Barney Weissbourd would follow. After their first successful joint venture at Illinois Center, JMB and Metropolitan Structures had an understanding that they would offer each other a piece of every new deal.

And that's how FJV, the Block F (latest designation for 37) joint venture, got started. Metropolitan Structures and JMB immediately reimbursed Marla (Mark and Larry Levy's corporate entity) for all its real estate costs in assembling the three strategic parcels on Block 37, plus $1.9 million in cash to operate Hillman's, Inc. Just like that, Levy was out of harm's way with millions in running-around money. In exchange, the two real estate giants got Larry Levy as an equal partner in a gigantic joint venture in which they were going to have to pay all the bills. How's that for luck?

Around the time the bruisers from Streets and Sanitation were again stringing the trees with Christmas lights, Larry Levy was officially in business with two new partners who had the ability, all on their own, to make the Block 37 redevelopment a reality. He'd be working directly with Stuart Nathan at JMB. Nathan was initially cool to the project, but was persuaded by Neil Bluhm and Barney Weissbourd to give it a go. But Nathan was suspicious of Levy and wondered openly what in addition to the three land parcels—the buildings Levy already controlled—he brought to the joint venture. In little less than a year, Levy had parlayed $6 million in personal liabilities into a one-third interest in what was, even then, shaping up to be a $600 million project. But after the Mercantile Exchange had worked out so well, Bluhm and Weissbourd, who each thought the other more keen on making the Block 37 deal, would have followed Levy anywhere. All through the spring of 1982 FJV worked out the details of its agreement and waited for the city to move on the rest of the block.

On March 4, 1982, the city's deal with Hilton officially fell apart. The hotel company announced plans to rehabilitate the Conrad Hilton on South Michigan Avenue with its new developer, Charles Shaw. Assessor Hynes had tried negotiating a compromise to the original $70 million abatement, including a plan that would index future tax breaks to the hotel's occupancy rate. But even for a company lured to the site with assurances of veto power over other North Loop redevelopment blocks, a healthy discount on the cost of land, and other considerations, Hynes's careful deliberations proved to be too much of a waiting game. In the three years since Mayor Byrne proudly announced Hilton's participation in the North Loop, nothing good had happened from the corporation's point of view. Land values in the blighted district had spiked up; tax protestors and architectural preservationists had had time to organize. The McCarthy Building, built within months of the Chicago Fire and still standing on the corner of Dearborn and Washington, became the center of a legal battle that would delay the redevelopment of Block 37 until the last year of the decade. In this contentious environment, where no one on either the private or public side even pretended to be in control, Hilton simply withdrew from the North Loop.

Facing an imminent reelection campaign, this setback left the Byrne administration with $50 million already spent in acquiring the North Loop land and only two flattened blocks to show for it. The mayor and her allies were eager to get the North Loop going any way they could. They would listen to anything reasonable and put a series of "tombstones," boilerplate announcements, in national papers like the *Wall Street Journal,* requesting proposals for mixed-use projects on one or more blocks.[43] Full blocks of downtown land were passing from a public entity—which held it only to resell—to private hands, just as Bruce Graham had said they would. Larry Levy, who had done his homework and already acquired three parcels, was there when opportunity presented itself.

Levy and his two partners at FJV even had a plan to dangle in front of the city. They could get their hands on all the capital needed and had an architect then very much in favor with the politicians. Ironically, Bruce Graham was out as soon as Levy's Prudential deal broke down. Barney Weissbourd had been feuding with Graham in his autocratic role with the Central Area Committee. Graham had insisted that Illinois Center—isolated by a severe level change—be opened up to Michigan Avenue. The feud was rancorous enough to poison the two to each other permanently. So Graham's whole brilliant rationale in giving Levy the first word on the North Loop troubles had backfired because of a minor feud with a big moneyman that the architect had conveniently forgotten. Graham was out, and Helmut Jahn was in. Levy's dutiful protestations to his partners had little effect.

Jahn's flashy modern style had become synonymous with the speculative building craze remaking Chicago piece by piece. Mayor Byrne liked his verve. He wasn't the sort of architect to be hired by the boys in the Eleventh Ward, who were running the city when Mrs. Byrne first came up in politics. They were conservative when it came to presenting themselves publicly; they liked fat classical columns and heroic paintings. It took self-legendizing Big Jim Thompson to stick it to the local cretins.

The State of Illinois Center was a critical commission for Jahn. Having already secured a reputation among architects, he had struggled to sell his unorthodox buildings to developers. The State of Illinois had both secured his reputation in Chicago as architect of the city's most audacious building projects and brought him, as the eighties began, into the full light of international celebrity. But it was with this building that he first outran the pack of globe-trotting architects, divas all competing for the same roles. It showed how much influence an architect could have on even the most conservative, tightfisted client.

Jahn's State of Illinois Center attacks the street with a sumo wrestler's belly. The flying saucer form, hollowed-out glass atrium, American high school colors, and fun-house elevators provide the building with an aggressive counterimage to the austere neoclassicism of traditional civic architecture. Governor Thompson, who got it built at about two times the cost of a comparable private office building, loved the notoriety. Anonymity through the propriety of the classical orders might have seemed appropriate for a less self-assured time. That was back when the day-to-day workings of a young government or trading on LaSalle Street needed borrowed grandeur: the elephantine sureness of fluted columns and Latin mottoes cut in stone. Then thick-walled classical architecture provided government and moneymaking with a symbolic parity.

Banks with propylaea and cathedral-sized banking floors, government buildings with cracked linoleum and proper Corinthian pilasters hung as decoration, were presented with the same architectural solemnity. Through the formal architecture of the neoclassical City Hall and County Building and the LaSalle Street banks, the normal deal making and hedging that really run a healthy American city were artfully slipped from one realm to another, private to public and back and forth, the way a nimble close-in magician palms a deck of cards.

At the beginning of the 1980s, when Block 37's final act began to unfold, the drama of dealing, public and private, came out for once in front of the formal proscenium, not intending to reveal any secrets but simply to revel in itself. Postmodern architecture with its pasteboard classicism was the style in wide favor as curtain-thin scrims, stretched tight like wallpaper over the structure, replaced all the sturdier illusions of imperial order. The thinness was right for a time when the new nine-to-five urbanites were no longer working class but graduates of the best universities and professional schools, elite locales where they had perfected their appreciation of irony. The "po-mo" mix of imagery, from Palladian cutouts to Piranesian vaults, from banks to beauty shops, robbed classicism of its last shreds of meaning. Postmodern architecture was perfectly tuned to a new audience of art consumers. Architectural detail was simply fashion, transforming a once closely regulated academic language into babel. Whether in slavish mimicry or fanciful recombinations with the same lack of materiality, the fancy elevations of commercial buildings and their cavernous lobbies were empty oracles to a remote power. Clean cash, capital flow, financial gods, were all evoked in the echoing voids. No one did the conjuring better than Helmut Jahn, who in draping the material still managed to retain some of the most beloved modern iconography, particularly the technological grandeur of the Crystal Palace and the great European railroad halls.

The stone was no longer load bearing, the skin sometimes as thin as glass. The classical allusions were mostly arbitrary on office buildings built on spec. All told, the architecture was perfect for an audience raised in the suburbs and nurtured in adulthood on David Letterman and *Saturday Night Live*. In the middle of a wild economic boom, the post-Vietnam generation had returned to the downtown to work for a while, just for the bucks. These young adults had no real politics, only visions of early retirement, babies nurtured in the calm of a well-provided middle age, nannies to do the hard work, lots of exotic travel—the sorts of things worth working for. No protest. As a sign of quality, young men and women chose serious architecture with plenty of historic details in the newly gentrified near-in Chicago neighborhoods where they lived. But these wonderfully successful professionals didn't need the sincerity of the old architecture at work. Back at work on Monday they liked a good architectural gag.

Their offices were all in buildings that played some sort of urbane in-joke, of the variety Letterman likes to pull on a polite Bangladeshi or elderly lady who doesn't quite get it. Amiable, obvious, ultimately harmless humor with an edge. Above a typical empty three-story lobby outfitted like Hadrian's villa, all these expensive skyscrapers are simply huge standardized boxes, encased in a hard shell. One box on top of another. The joke is that these fifty-story stacks of minimal boxes, all as essentially the same inside as Ramada Inns, are dedicated to making money out of air. No product is ever manufactured; nothing tangible is ever produced. A contemporary skyscraper is basically only a series of anchorages, slips for fiber-optic lines, networking computers, Quotrons, faxes, and phones. The architecture provides something solid to make more material the essentially amorphous quality of modern life. Altogether billions of billable hours are logged over the phone. With such opportunities to make a fortune downtown as a lawyer, an accountant, or an investment banker, a young person after her eleventh hour at work thought it nice to have a touch of irony in the architecture, a successful allusion now and then to a vanished permanence.

Helmut Jahn's State of Illinois Center was a critical addition to the architectural representation of the new age of money. In his own way, the young architect was helping government to shed its pretensions, its advertised distance from private money grubbing, and to present itself as just another consumer service, best suited to a mall with lots of glass, food courts, and visual distractions. In Jahn, public officials and private developers had a perfect ally who didn't register the difference between public and private life. Government buildings that looked like malls and private offices treacled with classical detail eroded the boundaries further. Consuming licenses and permits, ice cream or boats, were all the same to Jahn, who had grown up in postwar Germany, where all the fustian Roman architecture had been blown to smithereens. A neutral, eye-catching, high-tech modernism was Jahn's way to level class distinctions. He was, in the State of Illinois Center, an architectural Barnum, democratizing art by offering it up to the widest range of public taste.

This was architecture for Everyman in the sedating familiarity of the reconstituted suburban mall relocated to the middle of town. To make sure his real audience—the clients who paid for his tours de force—wouldn't miss the polemic and think he was just pandering, Jahn added a row of flattened classical columns to mark the entrance, made of the same alloy paneling used to clad the unglassed portions of the rest of the building. The trick for Jahn was to combine the high-mindedness and rigor of the great modernists, Mies van der Rohe and Eric Mendelsohn, with the aesthetic populism of John Portman, who first transported the mall from the suburbs to the heart of the city. Portman had created the hybrid in Atlanta by capturing the excitement of the circus tent or state fair and sealing it in the aspic of glass-box postwar American urban architecture. Jahn took Portman a step farther. Large outdoor plazas had distinguished Chicago's best public buildings since Mies designed the three federal buildings at the south end of Dearborn Street. Jahn incorporated this within the State of Illinois Center, now the James R. Thompson Center; only in his version of the public building, the plaza is inside, ringed by a semicircle of offices centrifuged out to the edge.

Helmut Jahn delivered an unusual product, always animated by at least one distinguishing idea that gave the work a custom-tailored quality. Unlike other architects who followed Mies, his big buildings never looked off-the-rack. He was the perfect Reagan-era architect, when vast sums were available for million-square-foot office buildings that no one really needed. At a time when the space behind the facade was identical, no matter who the architect was, the packaging of urban skyscrapers was critical. Like Philip Johnson at his prime, Jahn offered his clients a hook—a stylistic one-liner to distinguish their box of air from a competitor's. When the commission was extraordinary, his incomparable facility in manipulating form produced a really fine piece of design. The United Terminal at O'Hare Airport, the sleek Mendelsohnian curves of the low-budget Xerox Centre on Monroe Street, and the detailing at McCormick Place showed what he could accomplish if everything was right.

Jahn's work was everywhere in town, but Block 37 was the most important site he'd ever had a crack at. He could see all the buildings on the block whenever he went up to the cupola at the top of the old-fashioned skyscraper where Murphy/Jahn has its offices. The cupola, a speakeasy during the Capone era, was the firm's presentation room. Off to one side was a scale model of the city in which Jahn-designed buildings prominently figured throughout the downtown. Important clients, politicians, and journalists took the trip up to the dome in a private elevator, a rickety low-technology relic of gangster Chicago. The brief vertical trip provided just the right touch of nostalgia for Jahn's rich international clientele. Lunching on poached salmon, arugula, and a crisp Montrachet, they could talk about how the architect planned to save the city. After a meal and a tour of the model, Jahn would take his guests to one of the oversize windows, for a look down at Chicago. Architects call this looking out and down the eye-of-God perspective.[44] It suited Helmut Jahn just fine. Transforming seedy Block 37 into something completely new was the sort of center-stage civic commission that made practicing architecture worth it all.

FJV promised the city to tap hidden profits and revive Block 37 from its long economic swoon. In return for its acceptance of risk and the expectation of its huge capital investment, the city council formally approved FJV's bid in 1983 and granted it exclusive redevelopment rights to the block.[45] In return, the developers agreed to pay up to $4 million to preserve some old buildings conveniently out of the range of their bulldozers and dazzled the

The headquarters of Murphy/Jahn behind the Trailways bus terminal on East Randolph (1970s)

city with their projections of more jobs, bigger assessments, and fattened tax rolls: all an accepted form of tribute for the right to build on land that they had no hopes of acquiring on their own. These three real estate developers thought they had found a way for the city of Chicago to help make them richer.[46]

Only a few years into the eighties, FJV was ready for a new downtown real estate boom. The first surge of new office construction had already begun in 1979. Between 1979 and 1981 alone, developers had produced 4.5 million square feet of new office space. During those boom years, when FJV initially considered a radical makeover for Block 37, there was a rock-bottom vacancy rate of only 4 percent in Chicago. Banks, insurance companies, pension funds, individuals in REITs, were throwing money in their way to build downtown buildings so large, combining as many disparate functions as a small city or suburb, that many had to be approved separately as planned unit developments (PUDs). Daytime populations in the tens of thousands on one block, all huddled together making inflated professional salaries, paying rent, and looking for places to shop, were a downtown conquistador's dream; the maps to this El Dorado were already spread out in every developer's boardroom.

This was the eighties and no normal recovery from a normal downturn in the business cycle. The signs were all over the place that something was different. There was money everywhere and fewer bureaucrats and Cassandras to slow you down, bum you out. Abruptly deregulated financial markets excited normally sensible people who for years had been content to squirrel away their hard-earned cash in passbook accounts paying miserly interest. These sober souls were now seeking double-digit Las Vegas returns on their savings, eroded by years of steady inflation and their own prudence. But this assumption of dangerous risk never really registered, because the investors never saw the change. It was as if Granny and Professor Chips had taken out all their cash from the friendly neighborhood bank, dumped it into a sack, and walked across the street to the bar and put it on the backroom table where the boys were playing poker. And with the fancy prospectuses, listing billions in successful real projects already up and running, it looked like every hand was a full house. The risks were invisible. No one was being openly conned. Monthly financial statements figuring in the market value let you keep close tabs on your investment. Only old ladies used banks in the eighties.

The problem was that the language of discounted values, internal rates of return, capitalization rates, were hieroglyphics to anyone but a statistician. The gobbledygook of a brokerage account was like the mass when it was still in Latin. You relied on someone else to know what was going on and were reassured that big returns were there. With paper profits growing each month and celebrated sales or refinancings of projects reaping hundreds of millions in profits, no one had much incentive to question the basic assumptions behind the math.

Yet, these weren't the biggest factors inflating the real estate bubble. By 1982, when FJV first made a play for Block 37, a dramatic cultural change had occurred. Over the years, people had come to see property differently. With Americans taking on unprecedented levels of consumer debt, earning two incomes per family rather than one, their savings down, they came to view their primary real estate, their homes or condos, as investments more than shelter. Home prices beat inflation each year after the oil boycott of 1973 sent consumer prices out of control. House buying, previously considered a long-term commitment to place with typical thirty-year fixed-rate mortgages, now was viewed as the demotic way to wealth. Flipping and refinancing a home, taking the spread between the market value and purchase price (predictably higher because of constant double-digit inflation), and taking it out in cash or buying a newer, bigger home and mortgaging it to the hilt was an unacknowledged form of speculation. Paying off big debt with cheaper money in the future put at risk what was typically a family's largest single investment. More dangerous still, risk was submerged. First a younger generation, free of the experience of the catastrophic drop in values during the Great Depression, and then its once-prudent parents took the bulk of their equity, the collateral for their upward mobility, and eventually let it all ride on "sure thing" investments that proved as reliable as the daily trifecta.

Real estate, traditionally a slow-moving insider's market, was suddenly viewed paradoxically as a hedge on inflation and a safe haven for hard-earned money. As a result of these perceptual changes, property just a few blocks away from Block 37, only recently thought too expensive to build on at a third the cost, was suddenly appraised at more than one thousand dollars a square foot.

In the midst of all this swashbuckling the city bumbled along, offering some of the best land in Chicago at fire-sale prices. On Block 37, FJV agreed to pay $151.50 a square foot for all the land it didn't already control on the entire three-acre site. The city accepted its $12,583,430 bid on May 3, 1983, and froze the price at just the moment values were escalating most radically.[47] It took another four and a half years, until September 23, 1987, for the city to sign a redevelopment agreement that officially land-banked the property to the developers' advantage. FJV had to pay taxes and carrying costs on only the quarter of the block it had already purchased on its own. Until it took title two years later, in December 1989, the city was, in effect, FJV's partner, subsidizing its deal even further than what turned out to be more than a three-to-one write-down for the land. The city paid close to $40 million for property that it had committed itself to sell, years earlier, for $12.5 million—cheap land in the center of town, where not another inch was available for development at this grand scale. All this suggested to the three partners that there remained plenty of room to build more when they hired Jahn to design their 2.2 million square feet.[48]

Nonetheless, nothing much happened on Block 37. Committed to developing the land since 1983 and having invested nearly $3 million in preliminary architectural work, FJV waited seven more years to get started. The optimistic tone of Mayor Daley—the eldest son of the man who had first conceived the North Loop two decades earlier—on the day when the old buildings finally came down in 1989 had to be balanced against FJV's frustration at the city's inability to act in a timely manner. After a decade of negotiation, lengthy condemnations, lawsuits, and protests from preservationists, what had seemed like a bargain in 1982 was looking less attractive every day.

The developers looked on apprehensively as the mayor finally got the long-awaited demolition under way. Downtown Chicago, the mayor promised, would be a place where "people will live, work and play, a place that is alive long after dark." Remade Block 37 would add 10,500 jobs and $9 million in sales taxes. A "milestone," Daley concluded.[49] For what came to be nearly a billion-dollar project before the bottom fell out, the city's less than 10 percent contribution in the form of discounted land made Daley feel pretty good. The downtown goose was still laying golden eggs. Larry Levy struggled, at the start of the demolition, to put it all into words: "We all thought that this particular project had a lot of civic pride and responsibility to it that we all wanted to share in."[50]

Larry Levy was not used to making speeches. He was better one-on-one, getting close and making the sale. Corn-beef sandwiches, or distressed property at bargain prices, Levy always made it seem more appetizing than it later turned out to be. He set you up and then, like all great salesman, he walked away and let you sell yourself. JMB, the billion-dollar real estate syndicators and pension fund advisers, along with Metropolitan Structures, responsible for millions of square feet of impeccable glass-and-steel Miesian boxes, were there to provide financing, building, and engineering. When asked what he put into the deal, he said self-deprecatingly that he was the partner in charge of coffee. Larry Levy had sold these big-time developers on this marooned strip of downtown as effortlessly as he hawked a fat slice of cheesecake at Kaplan's.

IV THE WAY THINGS WORK

Stuart Nathan was enjoying the real estate bubble of the early Reagan years. With Block 37, he had a clear shot at rebuilding a large chunk of the downtown he had first visited as a kid from the Northwest Side. Failure was unimaginable. Even the old bureaucracies entrenched in City Hall were singing the praises of privatization and deregulation. The scuttling of the earlier North Loop master plans played into the hands of the professional real estate interests, especially those powerhouses like JMB and Metropolitan Structures, who in a pinch could provide their own financing. The city was out of money and required a rich development partner to fill all the holes it had so intemperately dug.

In the first months of 1983 Stuart Nathan reluctantly surveyed the property his senior partners had inherited from Larry Levy. Nathan was preoccupied with finishing the Merc and didn't initially share Bluhm and Weissbourd's enthusiasm for the deal. However, as he got more involved he began to see the site's potential, its essential character under the ruin of a hundred years' worth of accumulated masonry. He concluded that Block 37 was no ordinary piece of real estate. Situated between Marshall Field's on State Street and Daley Plaza, the block was the natural bridge between the city's commercial and public zones. By opening an attractive route from the west side of the Loop to State Street, a redeveloped Block 37 might reasonably attract a whole new population. A look at the old city maps shows a designated street, Court House Place, running right through the middle of the block, terminating at City Hall, site of Chicago's original courthouse. An impeccably designed, well-situated retail mall linking State Street to FJV's two new office towers at the back of the site could possibly restore Court House Place, currently a back alley, into a commercial thoroughfare.

Nathan also reckoned that the time was right to give the job of remaking the crumbling downtown over to a professional businessman like himself. The city had led the redevelopment effort unsuccessfully for more than a decade, trying to retain control while paradoxically inventing a mechanism that made unproductive land directly available to private interests. By the time the North Loop condemnations were completed, six Chicago mayors, including its first female and first black chief executive, had settled on a unique category, "economic blight," that permitted them to remove commercial property from its rightful owners and trade it at will. A neat sleight of hand that deftly hid a tough fiscal program behind a social screen, this permissive form of urban renewal was only a matter of money.[1]

At the time JMB got involved, the higher social rationales for the wholesale expropriation of private property had been so eroded by tax protests and preservation battles that the city had little left of its reputation to lose. The outgunned professional staff at the Department of Planning concluded that the developers had won enough concessions to go ahead and tap the land's hidden value based on their own calculations of profit. Why not drop all pretense of city planning or any of the other rhetorical flourishes that obscured modern land trading? In that way, at least, the city could never be accused of collusion if things ever went horribly wrong.

Nationally there had already been a significant shift in the way public officials viewed their central business districts. Since the election of Richard Nixon in 1968, the federal government had become increasingly reluctant to fund the cities. Big-city mayors were in a fix. They were hesitant to raise property taxes that would further alienate their nearly absent middle class. Cities required new sources of capital, and the people they were most likely to get it from were not about to put up with the old rules.

This was the political environment throughout the seventies and eighties, during which time office towers relentlessly replaced public works as a means of massive urban reinvestment. To any eager public officials, skyscrapers were Grand Coulees set on their end: great vertical dams, diverting capital right into the middle of town. New office buildings were sold as giant accumulators of capital. In 1983, when Stuart Nathan first got control of three acres of dirt-cheap downtown land, this was the kind of city building he had in mind for Chicago. A redeveloped Block 37, put back on the tax rolls and generating a bonanza in rents, was private enterprise at its best. If he could only get started.

The new focus of Nathan's ambitions was a place long singled out by moralists and social reformers as a public menace and finally declared an abomination in Mayor Byrne's much-delayed execution order of 1982. Echoing her esteemed mentor, Richard J. Daley, she called it an area of "commercial blight," coming as close as any politician had to naming that awful thing imperiling the American city. For FJV's three development companies, who owned some of the fanciest real estate in the city, this piece of moldering property was, to say the least, an unusual prize.

FJV had signed its deal with Chicago in 1983 to tear down Block 37 and rebuild it, but it had had nothing much to show for it. For the next six years the city struggled to condemn out the old owners, delayed with nuisance suits and bugged by speculators trying to jack up the price of these derelict properties.

Stuart Nathan

Until Illinois passed its first quick-take statute during the condemnation proceedings on Block 37, a demolition permit could not be issued until every owner on the block had received "fair market" compensation in exchange for the city's right to raze his buildings. Employing this new law, a judge could assign a tentative award pending a later trial and permit the building to come down. In all cases on Block 37, landlords received higher final awards. (One case involving the McCarthy Building was finally settled by a jury on July 29, 1995, six years after the five-story structure was destroyed.) Even with quick take, it took years of delay before demolition began on Block 37, and then only after the developers agreed to lay out the money.

Publicly committed to invest vast amounts of money in a risky urban renewal site, FJV is still out in the cold. What happened to these clever entrepreneurs who had cut what looked like a slick bargain at the height of the 1980s real estate boom? After the boom suddenly went bust, they found they owned little more than a junkyard, a black hole for more than $100 million in public and private investment.

Stuart Nathan waited for the city to do its part of condemning and getting title to the land, watching helplessly as his competitors beat him out for the lawyers and high-class service businesses whom he hoped would occupy his transformed Block 37. Other developers, such as John Buck, Miglin-Beitler, and Stein & Co., built quickly during the eighties on land they had acquired through exclusively private transactions.[2] Their developments in the old downtown, west of Clark Street, were direct competition—more of a threat than the new office towers on North Michigan Avenue—to the North Loop redevelopment. FJV still awaited the arrival of the bulldozers as other luxurious buildings opened for business, picking off tenants, one after the other, from the same exclusive list. Nathan could only stare at his funky, down-at-the-heels block as the delays mounted. All this hassle for a piece of decaying real estate that no one, until FJV put its money down, ever seemed to give a damn about.[3] For a businessman like Nathan, used to barking out orders and getting his way, negotiating the rights to this block was like spending a decade in line at the Department of Motor Vehicles.

Nathan, a nail biter in the best of deals, was especially agitated. After his initial skepticism about contracting with the government on a project of this size, he had committed himself completely to it. And everything went brilliantly at first. All the decay, the slummy character of the block, had been in the developer's favor when he negotiated the purchase of the land in 1983, locking in a bargain price of $151.50 per square foot. With the pieces they already owned, FJV would control a whole block. The city had inadvertently helped him land-bank three acres, freezing the value at an early 1980s level and demanding payment only in 1989, when he could pay it off with inflated dollars. And he knew personally how much of a bargain it was. Just a few years before, he had paid more than $300 a foot for a lousy parking garage on Wacker.

Nathan would have years to reflect on the way he, an unsentimental businessman and lawyer, had become hopelessly ensnared in city politics. JMB normally flew above the flak. The company's fortune had been made treating real estate mathematically, like any other commodity, taking the best cut, assigning it a value, and dividing it into smaller units to be syndicated all over the country. Nathan's firm looked at a skyscraper or a regional mall as it would a stock or a bond, sold and traded like any other financial instrument. He and his partners prided themselves on marketing the romance of property ownership to a sophisticated, wealthy clientele; and now somehow they were in business with rank amateurs, civil servants who couldn't begin to appreciate the elegance of these deals.

If JMB had only kept clear of development. Everything else continued to go smoothly: purchasing, repackaging, and retailing existing properties, extracting money at every step like a troll under a bridge. Nathan should have known that developing Block 37 was a whole different game and extremely risky. Right out of law school in the early 1960s, he had seen how the big money was made in Chicago, and it wasn't by sticking your neck out like this in public. Working for Colonel Arvey himself, he had observed firsthand the way street-smart politicians put businessmen like himself straight through the ringer.

All the reasons and complicated business plans aside, the truth was that Nathan, who had a well-earned reputation as a tough negotiator, had fallen in love with development. The idea of having a hand in revitalizing the city's historic downtown captured his imagination. Developing an urban renewal site into the Taj Mahal, having your name connected with that forever, that would be really something. And the joke was that JMB and its partners would make just as much money as if they were putting up another stupid mall in Orange County.

So a city that had already spent billions, over only two decades, in state and federal aid, and was desperate to save itself, found businessmen happy to rescue it for a price. Having already lost their sustaining manufacturing industries and abandoned by their middle class, Chicago politicians were not in their best bargaining position. Admittedly, FJV and the city of Chicago were a crazy marriage of ambitions. The city had failed at least two times to create a workable master plan for the North Loop. Now, along with its new corporate partners, the mayor's office was going to give it one last try, hoping that this once-brilliant crossing of streets in the heart of town might revive. After all the false starts, Block 37 was given a reprieve.

Abandoned by good people afraid for their safety and avoided like a bad melon even by the smart shoppers and thrill seekers who had stubbornly, against all odds, kept the place alive, the block that planners called "key" in their first studies was finally, in 1983, on track again for improvement.[4] But this was not to be. The plans first concocted during the time Kennedy was president were still incomplete as the 1980s came to an end.

At the start, FJV was mostly unaware of the political details. The project appealed to its vanity. Restoring one of the city's great historic sites had a particular pull on the developers as Chicagoans. Replacing a clutter of old buildings, still crowding the block, with two towers and a mall was also good business. They were exploiting an economy of scale that effectively transformed 115,000 square feet of ground into 2.2 million square feet of leased space. A completely redeveloped block was a new economic entity nearly twenty times the size of the existing collection of odd-sized lots.

Taking land to its highest and best use, or creating value, is what developers call the way they make money, gobs of it. And for a time developers

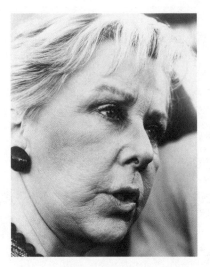

Mayor Jane Byrne

actually do create value, just as a grain trader at the Board of Trade gets cash in January for a June wheat contract. Buying land at a low price, fattening it up, and trading it high are the essence of the business. But unlike an old-fashioned landlord, farming his monthly rents, a modern developer extracts, through financing, years of future value before a building's first day of operation. A property's refinancing or sale retires the original loans and leaves the trader with cash that he can immediately divert to other purposes. In the 1980s, developers created a commodity better than oil or gold, because in theory at least it was endlessly multipliable. Its means of production was controlled by a relatively small group of men with a stunning access to capital. A tall commercial building creates a commodity, new rentable air, and sets the price. Anyway, this was the way things were supposed to work: a barely plausible pas de deux that seduced normally unexcitable businessmen to sign a risky futures contract with the city of Chicago.

To aggravate matters, FJV hadn't gone into a pure deal with a powerful all-controlling civic force like Richard Daley, but had entered into a strange contract with one of his unlikely successors, Jane Byrne. As with every booster and effective actor before her, Jane Byrne decided to make her reputation by building. She began with a dusty document, *Redevelopment Plan for Blighted Commercial Area, Project North Loop,* that she found in her fifth-floor office, only days after moving into City Hall.[5] Mayor Byrne would use this vague Bilandic- and late-Daley-era document, the North Loop Blighted Commercial District, approved by the city council on March 28, 1979, as the legal precedent to initiate a wild process of land trading and swapping, a high-finance version of the same overheated mercantile environment that the blighted commercial area plan aimed at eradicating.[6] By the end of her term in 1983, Byrne had completely stopped governing and was simply improvising. She had unwittingly become a broker serving exclusively private interests, merely replacing one old breed of capitalist in the city with a newer, richer variety.

. . .

Richard Daley had given the young widow her political start. Mrs. Byrne had come to him with her story of finding a calling to public service after attending a John F. Kennedy campaign rally. She showed him a treasured relic of that day: a newspaper photograph of her fatherless daughter, Kathy, sitting in the president's lap. Little fatherless Kathy, the daughter of a gallant marine aviator killed serving his country, the murdered Catholic president, and this brave young woman asking for his help; it was all too sad. Awkward with most women, Daley was intrigued with this independent middle-class Irishwoman.

In the summer of 1964, he found her a job in a local antipoverty agency. In her autobiography, Mrs. Byrne describes how the Chicago Committee for Urban Opportunity worked. "Instead of federal funding going directly to social service organizations, the money went to City Hall, which funneled it to the Chicago Committee for Urban Opportunity. This agency was treated as another branch of city government." So when the mayor cautiously gave her this first job, he made sure she got a political lesson along with a paycheck. Jane Byrne was a good student. She recalls, "He wanted control of the federal funds for two specific reasons. There'd be a political benefit because the agency dispensed thousands of jobs, and there'd be personal aggrandizement, because Daley's name would appear on each and every check."[7] Later, when she herself aggressively went after HUD money, pitching a brightly colored tent for a lavish press party on a block of the North Loop, it was meant as homage to the man she called Buddha.

But in the act of tailoring her own larger-than-life ambitions to his frame, the bantamweight, humorless Mrs. Byrne neglected her model's reserve and his rare, six thousand rpm squeal of godly delight when he was surprised or especially amused. She was too easily vindictive and neglectful of the necessary stroking required for unprincipled loyalty. Qualities he would never have accepted in a man, Daley overlooked in this driven young woman.

Because Daley never completely trusted any man, Jane Byrne was able to get close to him. She patiently moved in until she was able to usurp the vast authority left unassigned upon his death in 1976. With Daley gone, Byrne had the imagination to fictionalize a united Chicago out of the same North Loop plans she would ridicule Daley's successor, Michael Bilandic, over during the primary in 1979. This made her seem like a natural leader, a unifier, in sharp contrast to the bickering men involved in the Balkanized ward wars initiated within moments after the boss expired.

Michael Bilandic dutifully served out Daley's sixth term, but expectations for how the city viewed business all changed when with no warning Byrne defeated him. Under Daley, the city decided to ante up a premium cut of its downtown and offer it at a bargain price to all comers; it happened, no matter how mad the deal might appear. Without Daley, the city was suddenly more like New York or any other older American city, pretty much ungovernable and up for grabs. For months during the primary campaign, Byrne pilloried Bilandic as the machine's stooge, an incompetent—no small matter in a town that has "The City That Works" plastered on everything from el trains to garbage trucks. She assured the crowds that real men make sure the trash is picked up, streets are lighted, and snow removed.

Her point was made conclusively when a giant snowstorm hit the city weeks before the primary. The Department of Streets and Sanitation failed Bilandic. Daley had packed the huge municipal department with a permanent cadre of ward committeemen and wise guys from the First Ward. For decades they had answered to the same boss; it was hard for them to accept he was gone. Snowdrifts, petrified in ice, blocked major intersections. Panicked into doing something that would ease the delays, the Chicago Transit Authority instructed trainmen not to stop at key stations in the city's vast black neighborhoods. Byrne made efficient use of these facts.

Even in his own mind never much more than a caretaker, quiet Mike Bilandic had trouble defending himself against a woman. Fighting back felt to him like slapping his sister. He was too courtly, too immersed in the old system. She said anything that came into her head or startled him with carefully crafted insults prepared by her second husband, Jay McMullen, a former real estate reporter for the now defunct *Chicago Daily News.* To Byrne, a laughable underdog at the beginning of the race, the party faithful were irrelevant. The Organization had had its time. She viewed the unlucky incumbent as a screwup with a particularly galling weakness: he was unable to control the great Chicago machine, that customized instrument of power Richard Daley had perfected in the course of twenty-one years on the job. The machine was broken.

Ironically, Bilandic's failure was for Jane Byrne more instructive than all of Daley's cool successes. She recognized the necessity of quickly demonstrating her own untested competency. This desperation to be taken seriously, particularly by men, made her overanxious for a big score.

The florid-faced, crackling little woman made the North Loop her cause, trying to succeed at something that had frustrated Daley and baffled Bilandic. With lots of the planning already done, the North Loop, she hoped, might improve her odds of achieving a visible success early in her first term. This was the complete extent of her analysis. Planning was just politics.

She was, in fact, like any other classic Chicago politician, trying to make a name. She too would chase the glory of planned development, the ultimate measure of one's civic leadership.[8] Substance in these planning matters was less important than intent. Taking on the big challenge was enough. When, starting in the late forties, Mayor Martin Kennelly built a string of city garages in the Loop, the City Hall press office treated them as if "honest Marty" had built the pyramids. Downtown parking was his complete answer to the disaster of suburban flight. Sure, he didn't get re-elected, but he retained a measure of self-respect and got to campaign as a builder.

By honing in on the North Loop, Byrne thought she could control the unpredictable building game.[9] In a series of early press conferences she announced that Hilton was going to build a twenty-one-hundred-room convention hotel at the top of the North Loop to replace, among other gems, one of Kennelly's city garages and the infamous Shangri-La Theater with its nightly fare of porno films. She reassured taxpayers that she would get the state and federal governments to pay for a good part of her renewal effort.

After wasting her first year in office fighting a losing battle with the city's powerful municipal unions and trying to pay down a $102-million deficit left by the departing machine, Mayor Byrne made peace with the City Council's evil cabal. To be sure of getting their attention, she installed them in her inner office on the fifth floor of City Hall. As 1980 began she belatedly started getting things done, building cleverly on initiatives already in place. She made a point of using private developers, sidestepping the city's planning bureaucracy wherever she could. Her principal motive was to avoid the career people still loyal to the organization, now headed by Richard M. Daley, Buddha's son. Go with them—bureaucrats who had been on the tenth floor since the department's creation—and they would find a way to make her fail. Worse than that, she was convinced that the young Daley would find some way to grab the credit even if she succeeded. She was encouraged by the way Governor Thompson, coming as he did from even farther outside the normal Chicago political channels than she, had managed to get the State of Illinois Center up and rolling in only a matter of months. She recognized that the building had been Arthur Rubloff's and the governor's accomplishment, but she didn't mind taking some public credit for the giant potbellied civic mall, built during her early days as mayor. Since it was built on a city redevelopment block, she thought herself justified in calling it part of the city redevelopment effort. Until cost overruns, nearly two times the cost of a comparable commercial building, made the State of Illinois Center a liability, she let on that it was *her* first success in the North Loop.

In the rest of the North Loop she was no luckier than her two predecessors. After a fast start, Byrne too got bogged down. But her signature style of mock planning was in place. The tone of her four-year tenure is captured by a series of farcical turnarounds, capped by the ascendancy of Miles Berger as North Loop czar on February 13, 1981: the same man she had unceremoniously replaced as plan commissioner and castigated as a do-nothing Bilandic holdover during her first days on the job.

With the Bilandic-initiated HUD grant for $25 million still pending, like money left under a mattress by a poor uncle, Byrne felt that the momentum was there, if she could only learn to stay out of her own way. To keep things going, she announced on July 20, 1979, that Chicago's initial contribution to the North Loop project would be $50 million in loans. This is a highly irregular, expensive form of financing that has the important advantage of less formal public scrutiny.

But costs inflated quickly. In April 1980 the city council approved loans of $55 million to acquire land in the North Loop area. These loans plus interest were paid off in September 1982 when the council approved a $65.5 million *bond* issue. The bonding occurred after the project gained momentum and was widely perceived as an integral piece of planning for the entire city. The mayor delayed going to the city council for long-term bonding until the project, through her constant promotion, became an inevitability. From Daley, she had learned that the success of any large civic project was in inverse relation to its perceived costs. Letting the public believe in the beginning that it was being treated to a free lunch, in the form of Bilandic's pending UDAG application, gave her time to line up the real financing when she finally received a proper development plan from her Department of Planning.

Fifty million dollars in loans was money Byrne could get her hands on immediately. Her real estate advisers reminded her that Bilandic had made the mistake of waiting for a proper plan. Look what had happened to him. Why wait? When Byrne first presented "her" North Loop concept to the Plan Commission, she waved a thick document in front of the commissioners. The men, who all owed their appointments to her, enthusiastically supported their diligent new leader. At least one of the new commissioners was impressed with this woman, only a few months in office. After the whirlwind meeting was over, he took a look at the heavy document she had dramatically placed facedown on the long conference table when she left the room. Between the two carefully printed covers he discovered a sheaf of empty pages.

Mayor Byrne, more than her two predecessors, thus bound her future to the uncertain fate of the central area, a decision that would make her particularly vulnerable to bad advice from a gang of downtown interests that Daley for years had kept at bay. The old Chicago rules had been reaffirmed in the 1950s by political insiders like Harry Chaddick, author of the permissive zoning code, and Charles Swibel, after twenty years still head of the catastrophically mismanaged Chicago Housing Authority. Swibel and Chaddick were again proffering advice and were joined in her administration by Jay McMullen and ambitious young aldermen, such as Ed Vrdolyak, who already dominated her city council. Her election was a signal to these interests that the old Chicago rules were back in operation.

The mayor's deepening dependency on Charles Swibel was especially damaging. Swibel continued to run the CHA as a branch of his private real estate interests. Samuel Pierce Jr., the head of HUD during the second half of Byrne's term, found in a 1982 audit that the CHA was in "a state of profound confusion and disarray." Swibel, a dapper trader of confidences and inside information, would have been right at home in the nineteenth century when Chicago was run out of the back room of a saloon. Byrne's new Plan Commission chairman, Miles Berger, said Charles Swibel "was like horse shit all over the road," convincingly trading influence even when he didn't have it.

Although his influence with Jane Byrne was real. His "no problem" approach to government fit the mayor's desire to get things done fast. Knock down more than fifty buildings and get billions to finance the rebuilding, "No problem, mayor." This bluffing and bullying approach to governance, a bit out of date at the time, was somehow reassuring to the mayor. She never seemed to notice, as some of her plan commissioners warned, that he was "very talkative" about the North Loop. For instance, he felt no conflict of interest in advising Hilton's lawyers where to "break the price" when negotiating with the city for the first two North Loop blocks. Originally willing to pay close to a bargain one hundred dollars a foot, Hilton contracted to pay fifty dollars a foot and looked forward to an expected $70 million forgiveness of taxes. Each dollar per square foot that Swibel graciously saved the hotel chain cost the city millions.

Ever teetering over the edge of respectability, Swibel, during the Byrne years, had many a gent writing him "Dear Chuck," soliciting his opinion on important matters of state. Important operators at all levels of business who prided themselves on not wasting time with underlings knew that

Swibel was the mayor's gatekeeper on all matters concerning development. One of these influential civic leaders was Lewis Manilow, who for years had been publicly decrying the city's woefully lean menu of downtown culture. He didn't really bemoan the loss of most of the jazz clubs, movie houses, or cabarets: he hungered for more ballet and big-production theaters, a new culture zone for upscale entertainment. On Randolph Street, where down-scale popular art once happily thrived, he envisioned modern dance, ballet, and straight plays struggling on subsidies. After all, Chicago already had a fine opera house, a world-renowned orchestra, and a wonderful museum within a five-minute walk of Randolph and State. Once the Loop was properly cleared—neutron-bombed of its disorderly population of black and Hispanic teenagers—the wonderful buildings would remain.

Manilow, a lawyer, art collector, and Democratic fund-raiser who had inherited a fortune from his developer father, knew where to go for a job requiring political influence. He wrote to only four people: Mayor Byrne, Miles Berger, Charles Shaw, and Charles Swibel.[10] He wasn't discouraged after getting nowhere with the mayor. Charles Shaw was sent a copy of the request simply for good form. Only Berger and Swibel could do him any good. Manilow wrote to them on the same day. Now that all the North Loop movie theaters were demolished or scheduled to be taken down, he argued, there was room for a theater row extending west from the Chicago Theater on State Street to the Selwyn and Harris Theaters on Dearborn. As with many a movie palace before them, the Harris's and Selwyn's last incarnations were as porno houses. These two nice little boxes with Renaissance facades were perfect, Manilow suggested, for dance and legitimate theater. The Woods Theater (now demolished), a dilapidated movie house that appeared on no one's preservation list, was thrown in to heighten the dense Shubert Alley effect. A separate citizen's group proposed to preserve the four-thousand-seat Chicago Theater on State Street.

Preservation, in the mayor's opinion, was just another special interest, one her advisers could easily dispatch. She knew that Berger and Swibel finally didn't give a damn about any development that wouldn't make it on its own in the marketplace. Manilow might just as well have saved his stamps.[11] But in these two odd men, who never overtly acknowledged each other publicly, Manilow had at least found the right guys. His failed foray to them reveals how completely trading influence had replaced governance in matters of planning. As of 1996, Chicago still had no theater row. However, the promise of a new upzoned entertainment district remains an unrealized inducement for comprehensive urban renewal. Nothing gets built, but the money flows with no recognizable civic benefit. In fact, the melancholy result of nearly two decades' worth of cultural enhancement is that the city continues to commit millions to subsidize private ventures with no commercial future (currently a new Goodman Theatre on the same urban renewal block where the Selwyn and Harris stand in ruins with newly sandblasted facades). In belated recognition of the city's historic weakness for blandishments of desultory philanthropists and perennial fixers, the Daley administration in 1994 successfully sued the "nonprofit" corporation running the Chicago Theater to get back some of its more than $16 million in defaulted loans.

Swibel was the past master of such schemes. In his prime he would settle for nothing less than representing both sides; he had so beautifully perfected the art of negotiating with himself. Whether or not Jane Byrne ever focused on Swibel's life in the shadows, no one will know for certain. Swibel died of cancer on January 19, 1990. However, she consistently left unchallenged his con man's air of certainty and became increasingly dependent on him and his pals to make policy.

While Swibel encouraged the mayor to move forward on the North Loop, in private he parlayed his insider knowledge of this one gigantic undertaking to prove his general importance. His influence was at its height in 1980, when he flew to Washington with Lewis Hill, the recently deposed head of Chicago's Department of Planning, and a young deputy commissioner. In the nation's capital, Charles Swibel, without portfolio, was representing the city's downtown development interests at HUD. This was the same agency then actively investigating him for twenty years of mismanagement as head of the Chicago Housing Authority. Breezing into the HUD offices, greeting everyone by his or her first name, he walked right into the secretary's office. Mayor Byrne had provided him with a list of eleven city projects requiring federal funding, including the North Loop. No detailed plans, no careful budgets, just a list. A week later, Swibel sent the deputy planning commissioner back to Washington to fetch the signed federal commitments to fund the projects.

The best example of Swibel's brand of complicated hustle, weaving politics and cash, concerned one of the city's most prominent architectural monuments. Swibel persuaded William McFetridge's powerful Janitor's Union to invest its pension money in Marina City, architect Bertrand Goldberg's utopian mixed-use project on the north bank of the Chicago River. When they went up in the early sixties, Goldberg's corncob skyscrapers became immediately identified with the new Chicago, audaciously rebuilding itself. Swibel was effectively the developer and later manager for Marina City, where he originally did a lot of good, providing subsidized middle-class housing for those priced out of the downtown housing market. In addition to bringing people back to live downtown, the investment proved successful for the union.

But, typically, Swibel couldn't resist playing every angle. Allowing nothing to exceed his reach was the principal source of his professional pride. After the original investors were paid off he deliberately drove Marina City into economic ruin, disturbing the scheme that had been carefully balanced between the profit-making businesses (garage, office tower, and retail) and rental housing.[12] When the subsidized rental apartments went on the market in 1977 as condominiums, he and his political buddies bought up scores of units at the insider price and resold them at a handsome profit. Alderman Ed Vrdolyak, Byrne adviser and a future mayoral candidate, was one of the intimates who benefited from the condominium conversion. He was part of a group, concealed in a land trust, that owned forty-seven apartments, worth more than $2 million. By the end of 1978, Swibel had earned a profit of $6.25 million through the sales and a five-year contract paying his management company $107,000 annually. All this was accomplished with only $1,000 down.[13] After the financial gutting was concluded, Swibel allowed the building to deteriorate so badly that Marina Towers wound up in the hands of a local receiver and eventually on the books of the Resolution Trust Corporation.[14]

In the 1960s, Continental hired Swibel to manage a troubled piece of downtown real estate. In appreciation, the CHA chairman shifted the authority's lucrative development fund to Continental in a non-interest-bearing account.[15] On April 12, 1982, after a HUD investigation irrefutably linked him to two decades of mismanagement, the mayor reluctantly accepted his letter of resignation from the CHA. But he was not quite ready to retire from public life. Immune to public shame, choosing to view his dismissal as a lucky break, Chuck Swibel was now blessedly free of all the thankless public service he had done for Chicago's poor.

Already camping out in Byrne's back office and finally relieved of his civic duties at the CHA, Swibel suddenly had more time to concentrate his energies on all the monster deals downtown. The city's professional Department of Planning, the Chicago Plan Commission, and four other agencies responsible for downtown redevelopment looked on dumbstruck as Jane Byrne, listening to the reckless advice of Charles Swibel and other real estate "experts," pushed forward in the North Loop. A real estate extravaganza, backed with the full prestige and legal resources of municipal government, produced just the sort of gambling action mixed with public confusion that had made Charles Swibel a very rich man.

Always trying too hard to be taken seriously, the tiny mayor, overdressed and breathless, pitched some tents on the first of the forlorn renewal sites and threw a party with good wine and fancy hors d'oeuvres. There she initiated the public selling of the North Loop plan to anyone who would listen. Whatever her original intentions, Mrs. Byrne, a sorcerer's apprentice with the powerful tool of eminent domain as her mop, began cleaning out the center of town and put Chicago's most valuable land up for grabs.

She had good reason to think she might succeed where others had so miserably failed. At the time Byrne was elected in 1979, the office market was strong in the Loop proper and up nearby North Michigan Avenue, but the old core retail and commercial zone had radically contracted, losing half of its major department stores and two-thirds of its theaters.[16] Byrne decided to edit out only one part of the existing Chicago 21 Plan for the central area and add a few key details of her own. The problem was that she was negotiating from a position she hadn't yet secured. The Cook County assessor, not the mayor of Chicago, is the only public official with authority to reduce taxes, and Thomas Hynes had already decided against her. He was determined not to provide a generous tax abatement—a special rate based on 16 percent of assessed valuation rather than the normal 40 percent for all other downtown commercial property.

In announcing that he had turned Byrne's request down, Hynes, on December 8, 1981, offered a compromise, promising to peg Hilton's future taxes to the profitability of the new hotel. Mrs. Byrne stuck stubbornly to her demand for tax forgiveness as well as her support for Hilton's unreasonable demand to control development of the other North Loop blocks. On December 9 Hilton terminated its contract, and the following day, HUD informed the city that the long-delayed UDAG, now pared down to $7.9 million, was permanently on hold. The city would request additional tax deals, but all the blocks subsequently developed were financed privately without them.

Hynes's refusal to go along with the North Loop abatements saw to that. Since the time of Daley's last full term the city had been allowing private operatives to make exotic promises to attract outside capital. But whereas Daley had the power and influence to set things right at the last minute, Bilandic and Byrne did not.

Hynes's reluctance to play along revealed a serious shift of power, one that contributed, ironically, to some of the worst financial excesses of the 1980s. His well-reasoned attempt to keep the politicians from overextending themselves queered the Hilton deal and signaled, correctly or not, that the city could not be trusted in setting up big-money public-private partnerships. It became clear in an instant to everyone that the mayor, already out of money, had been bluffing. Having spent $50 million for the condemnation of the two hotel blocks (16 and 17), Chicago did not have a cent to go further in the North Loop. After Hilton dropped out, the Byrne administration, only a year away from reelection, had lots of debt and nothing but the planned Transportation Building under contract with Stein and Company to show for its urban renewal efforts. This sort of bungling highlighted by a skillful opponent might prove as fatal as a blizzard around Election Day. Byrne shifted gears quickly. She had her planners rewrite the RFP for Blocks 16 and 17, no longer requiring that both blocks be developed together. A local pair of developers, Urban Investment and Development Company and Libra (Eugene Golub), came up with a more modest hotel scheme. This idea never came to fruition, and the project was further scaled down, until, in desperation, the succeeding administration accepted a bid from Stouffer to build a midpriced facility at the corner of State and Wacker. By then, however, the North Loop plan was completely in tatters. Anyone with the slightest interest in building on potentially the most valuable property in the country was given a silver shovel and a permit to break ground.

However, at the time Mayor Byrne digested the full effect of the Hynes mutiny, she was still trying to salvage some of the more grandiose aspects of the original twenty-seven-acre initiative. In 1982, the only site retaining any of the glamour of the old Comprehensive Plan was Block 37. If she could pull off on Block 37 any of what had been intended for the two-block Hilton site, its central location and prominence might be enough to run for reelection on. A block with two stunning towers on Dearborn and a multistory retail mall across from Marshall Field's was the whole North Loop plan in a nutshell. Byrne looked at the brilliance of the State of Illinois Center, then under construction, and took note that property values were already climbing in the area of the new building, especially the ground under the Greyhound Bus Terminal.[17]

If she weren't able to act soon in the North Loop, even with her powerful condemnation authority, she might not be able to afford the land she needed. Jane Byrne loved the fact that Helmut Jahn was FJV's architect and that the developers were proposing a new government building to be housed in one of their towers. Little Jane Byrne in a bigger building than Big Jim Thompson, down the street on Randolph. Just as things were looking real bad she had discovered Block 37. But it was a little too late.

All the delays had created a special problem on this key piece of real estate in the North Loop. Mayor Byrne's desperate reversion to a block-by-block redevelopment strategy favored the existing landlords on Block 37 more than any others. Concealed for years under layers of arcane trust arrangements and protected like the gold at Fort Knox by the Illinois blind-trust statutes, the old landholders were forced into the open. Most of them had encamped on the site between the last Depression years and the conclusion of the Second World War. They had purchased depressed downtown property for themselves as an irreducible piece of America. The land, as good as the country itself, they reasoned, would in later decades yield its true worth and underwrite a university education or a new business for a lucky heir.

These owners of Block 37 had been awaiting condemnation since they bought their first thin parcels more than forty years back. But it never came, and the Loop, once the location for some of the highest property values in the nation, never went up in value. They kept up their payments—taxes and minimum maintenance—renting to small retailers and peddlers who paid on their lease but gave the area the look of a souk. Above the ground level one was lucky to rent for more than a dollar a foot. The respectable doctors and dentists had long ago evacuated the block, moving east one block to Wabash, and ragtag semiprofessionals did business on the upper floors behind lettered window signs. Frequent fires in the old, poorly ventilated buildings made the place unattractive to all but marginal businesses. As a Bedouin seeks water, many an improbable commercial enterprise, dowsed for low rent, relocated and thrived on Block 37.

Then in early 1981, Larry Levy, looking for more bargains, moved around the corner from Washington to State and hit a trip wire. Offering Howard Arvey and his partners $5 million for their tumbledown corner extending from mid–State Street to the middle of Randolph, he effectively set the value at a level their dads had been awaiting for years. On the morning of the day Levy came a-calling, Howard Arvey figured the whole mess was worth about a million dollars. At that he'd have been happy to vacate just to get away from the legal wrangling that had developed between the various ownership interests for nearly half a century. But this new figure changed everything. Five million dollars was worth negotiating over. Levy must have carelessly spitballed the number on his way to see Arvey, but now it was law—the absolute minimum anyone would have to pay for the northeast corner of Block 37. By the time it was all over, the city would wind up paying nearly $15 million just to knock it down.

Howard Arvey followed his father in representing the sons and daughters of politicians, judges, and professionals who had bought downtown land after the war.[18] In addition to the Stern, Loeb, Crown, and Sax families, land or leaseholders on Block 37 included the Bensingers, Lanskis, and Cuneos, who had all learned the real estate business as part of their liberal education. Land the old men had once passed around as effortlessly as the sports page at the Covenant Club was now, thanks to the city, put into the hands of Harvard MBAs and guys with lines of credit for offshore billions.[19] It was suddenly somehow worth a fortune. Levy's overeagerness helped them see that.

The failure of the landholders to create a large consolidated piece of the block couldn't be blamed on outsiders or politicians. Fathers, mothers, brothers, sisters, sons, and daughters, now all beneficiaries in land trusts most of them had known nothing about until the patriarchs died, were in no position to make the sort of complicated financial deals required in the 1980s. At the end of a decade of free-base capitalism, before the crash cut real estate values in half almost overnight, office property nationally was worth more than $1 trillion, accounting for 11 percent of the total stock of nonresidential and residential property. Alan Greenspan, chairman of the Federal Reserve, was worried that financial transactions were conducted at such high speed that nobody could understand them anymore. He belatedly warned, "We must all guard against a situation in which the designers of financial strategies lack the experience to evaluate the attendant risks, and their experienced senior management are too embarrassed to admit they do not understand the new strategies."[20] American real estate worth $8.777 trillion was close to 1.5 times the gross national product and three times the national debt. Mom-and-pop operations, at a manageable scale, were driven out of the market by fiber-opticked, wire-transferred, Eurodollar megadeals that treated big buildings like pinochle cards.[21]

The closest any of the old-timers had ever come to assembling a significant part of the block occurred in early December 1963, when Colonel Henry Crown and George Sax met together in a downtown joint to discuss their common interests on Randolph Street. Crown owned the United Artists Theater on the corner of Dearborn Street, separated by only one thin building from the Sax interests, and had a piece of the Roosevelt Theater just south of the Sax property on State. The Crowns preceded the Saxes on Block 37 when they bought the theater as distressed real estate right after the Depression.

Crown's main link to the establishment had been Walter Heymann, for years the number-two man at the First National Bank of Chicago. Long regarded as one of the city's finest bankers, Heymann never became president of a LaSalle Street bank. In real estate before the war, Jews were excluded from top positions in establishment downtown firms. But Heymann, more than any of his contemporaries, was able to respond to the coming crisis. Most property owners in Chicago began to suffer the steep deflation of their real estate as early as 1927. Unable to keep current on interest and taxes, the rest were brought down in the October 1929 crash. En masse, they returned their mortgaged properties to their bankers. Prominent banks, like First National, soon had huge inventories of worthless land and properties with no obvious buyers. In the case of commercial properties held in trust in Illinois, most went back to the title company, where a trustee legally held the defaulted deed. This would not have happened in most American cities, where the title company only guarantees ownership (title) and does not stand in for the legal owner or beneficiary. Because of the blind trusts the owners of record—not the actual landowners—were often only expediters in these big institutions.

Heymann had learned his trade as chief executive of the West Side Trust, a small bank that financed the predominantly Jewish wholesale businesses clustered around Wells Street at the edge of the Loop. Until the Glass-Steagall Act (1933) outlawed interlocking bank directorships, he kept his affiliation with the West Side Trust while he worked full-time for the downtown bank. This provided him unique access both to immigrant cash businesses and the capital resources of the First National, the world's largest savings institution. Heymann recognized that if he offered a deep enough discount on quality properties, there would be buyers. This way the property would not have to be written down as a total loss. When things inevitably improved the bank would participate on the upside. Getting new buyers would, in effect, put the property on ice but safely within the bank's reach.

Heymann knew exactly how the plan should work. All he needed was a precise triage, selecting the good real estate from the bad, so he could act as a reliable middleman. In addition to Henry Crown there were plenty of successful entrepreneurs who had rarely ventured past their own neighborhood. All hungered for downtown land. Colonel Crown was a typical candidate on Heymann's list. His line of work was Depression-proof: New Deal public works projects for which he provided all the concrete. Crown's company, Material Service, had always received large construction loans from Heymann, and the two had developed a close personal relationship. When the bank foreclosed on Chicago's oldest hotel, Heymann naturally first went to Crown to see if he could take the Palmer House off his hands, which he did. But it was almost as an afterthought that Walter Heymann really created the bridge between the Jews and the entrenched real estate elites. When he led Henry Crown and a few others of his most trusted clients to the inventory of distressed properties overseen by Newton C.

Farr, a director of Chicago Title and Trust, Heymann brokered his most unlikely alliance.[22]

In later years, most vocally in the forties, when he was president of the National Association of Real Estate Boards, Farr was reviled by civil rights activists as "one of Chicago's most intransigent defenders of restrictive covenants." He steadfastly advised the real estate fraternity to "hold the line" against blacks seeking better housing in white areas of the city.[23] As a director of CT&T, a position he had virtually inherited along with his father's real estate business, Farr had a real power base. There he got a good look at the "bushels of bonds" representing failed real estate deals that came flooding back for review at the title company beginning in 1927. Farr got to know the critical details of the confidential blind trusts, stacked like empty pizza boxes to the ceiling of his office.[24]

Downtown land, particularly when it was available at five or ten cents on the dollar, would make fortunes like Crown's, earned in a more combative style, appear more respectable. At places such as the Covenant Club, the transformation of money from entrepreneurial businesses to mainline investments was called koshering. The only thing the old-timers needed to complete the ritual was a conservative businessman: Heymann. A skilled negotiator, whose brother, Edgar, headed the Saxes' Exchange National, Heymann was especially comfortable doing business with Chicago's big banks, the title company, and them. The word went out among Crown's cronies that Walter could help get them "a piece of downtown."[25]

Discreet and self-deprecating in manner, Heymann personified the "think Yiddish, speak British" camouflage of those men who first broke into the city's highest business and professional circles. He was impeccably honest: the perfect insider to deal the old families out and the new ones in. By offering on a first-come basis prime slices of the Loop at a big discount, Heymann had discovered an ingenious way to raise cash on nonperforming real estate and solidify his reputation with his directors at the bank at the same time.

By treating these returned properties—conveniently graded and classified as "nonbook" assets—separately accounted for—Heymann kept at least the First National from liquidating prime downtown land that he knew, if he were sufficiently patient, would recoup and eventually exceed its precrash value. Men like Heymann and Farr shuffled the deck for all those who followed. Falling land values after the Depression made it possible for people who once could only dream of owning a single building downtown to choreograph the control of an entire block. Heymann and Farr had done their part, leading them to the best bets. In the process, the nature of the real estate business changed again from a small conservative trade where everybody knew each other to a high-risk occupation more like swapping pork bellies. Real estate was elevated to a glittering great game of trading and brilliant deals, no longer a patient affair. The arriviste money-moving gang that settled on Block 37 in the 1980s was its natural heirs.

There were no more successful real estate operatives than FJV in the city when simply as a legal convenience it invested in Block 37. If everything had gone ahead right on time, FJV could have justified the politicians' gamble and profited handsomely in the process. Everyone would have won. Helmut Jahn's architecture would by now have recentered Chicago's office and retail trade on the west–east axis, from the prairie to the lake, right through the center of the block. Once reclaimed and outfitted in the newest style, this run-down part of the city could finally be put back on line as a workhorse producer of tax revenue, proving right the optimistic projections of a whopping power-of-ten increase in all taxes and employment. More space for the developers to rent, more jobs, more space for politicians to tax, a perfect arrangement all around. At the beginning of the 1980s, such utopias seemed realistic. With the poor safely out of the downtown, there would be only shimmering towers and great glass emporiums, gushing money for education, police, fire, and welfare on land presently taxed no more than vacant land. A single-class urban paradise that multiplied capital for the businessmen who took the risk and incumbency for the politicians who found another detour around raising property taxes out in the wards where the voters lived.

Helmut Jahn was hired to provide the narrative for the metamorphosis. Over a decade, Jahn prepared six different architectural schemes for Block 37. Rich imagery in the form of sketches, drawings, renderings, and precise scale models were first used by his clients to convince the bankers and other financiers to start raising close to $300 million to get the entire project built. After this fund-raising was under way, but well before ground was to be broken, these same architectural images—refined to accentuate the sumptuous interiors—were recycled to convince lawyers, accountants, and bankers to pay nearly thirty dollars a square foot in rent on a slice of downtown that formerly claimed little more than a dollar a foot for office space. Ground taken to its highest and best use, buildings reaching up to the sky where the offices rented for as much as fifty dollars a square foot, were the fool's gold of the 1980s.

On dense urban blocks like 37, cultivated from a mix of labor and salesmanship, arid land was made lush from the same drive to enclose and control that had settled the American frontier. Manifest Destiny, confined to

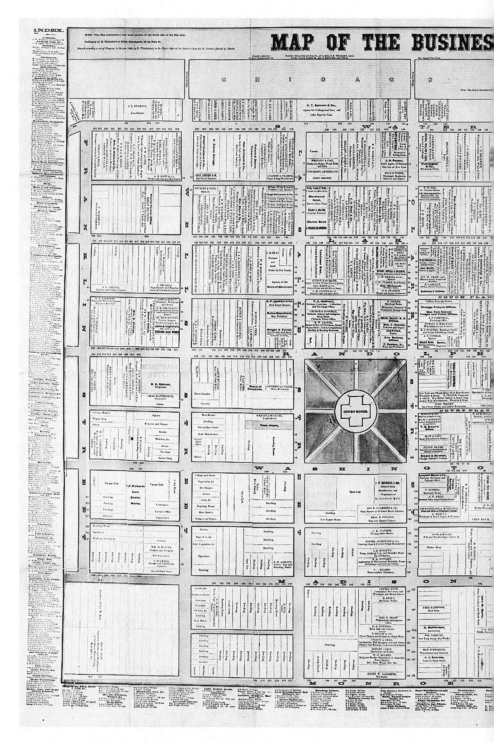

Dense business district (1862)

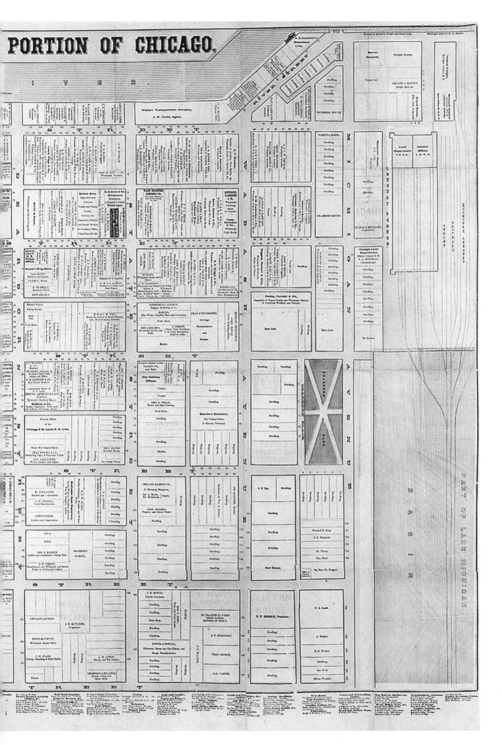

the tightest spaces, spawned a rambunctious manner of civilization. All this frantic activity was tied to the frenzied accumulation of money and striving to make a name. In 1990, when the last of the abominations on Block 37 finally tumbled down, the city was enacting the countermyth to its high rhetoric of conquest. The uncensored urge that settled the country also left an exotic collection of very human things on the land. Block 37 was no longer thought to be a proper monument to progress but a disorderly, built-up, real place that needed a complete overhaul.

Broken off from the rest of the moraine, farmed with buildings rising above the flat prairie, Chicago's downtown began as second nature. Here the steady push out from the East Coast was stopped, its ambitious population collecting rather than dispersing farther west. Backed up against Lake Michigan on the east and looped by a river that forked sharply to the north and south, Chicago owed its density to the fact that the most developed part of downtown was so contained—fewer than forty city blocks in all. A farmer needed acres of rich loam in southern Illinois; a Chicagoan needed only twenty feet on the street to make his fortune. Selling shirts, peddling health cures, giving advice, no more tilling the earth but finding fresh schemes to farm the air above one's matchbox of precious urban ground developed the core square mile of downtown.

The right to vote and to own land outright or fee simple, meaning that the ground, buildings, and air rights were the fee holder's exclusive property, had originally brought a crowd of independent businessmen to Block 37. For more than a century, until the bulldozers were finally lined up to level it again, even flatter than a real prairie, these pioneers and their descendants had continued subdividing the original eight lots, sometimes trading as little as five feet at a time. The pure order of the grid envisioned by the United States land ordinances of the late eighteenth century was fractured in practice by speculators. City blocks were jigsawed into odd permutations. A prominent commercial property like the old Kranz Viennese specialty shop had one entrance on State and another on Randolph, wrapping itself like a boa around the larger and older Springer Block, one of the few remaining fire-era buildings, on the northeast corner.

Peeling away the layers of ownership, leasing, and subleasing on the block, one can still imagine the shadow of the Cartesian grid that sliced up America during the first years of the Republic: equal sections mathematically divided in exact square-mile portions all over the country and then locally broken down further into blocks of about 100,000 square feet until they were parsed further still into eight long city lots. The earliest national grid, enclosing the country's abundance into rectangles of affordable, endlessly exchangeable parcels, had its desired Platonic clarity. When it was originally platted, the founders imagined all the surveyors' carefully drawn and measured right angles as God's mind imposed autocratically on the land.

The country got older and this divine clarity, represented in evenly drawn and apportioned property lines, abraded with the actions of brokers and traders. And at the end, right before the lots on Block 37 were reassembled and transferred to a single trust, before the heavy machinery had leveled the architecture and scraped the ground flat, the old place had come to look more like a cracked eggshell than the mind of God.

Trussed up and ready to be devoured in one big bite—that was how architect Helmut Jahn pictured the block as he waited in 1982 for the land to be leveled and prepared for him. One hundred and fifty years of history erased in an instant. To this architect, full of the conceit of saving the city— an act of hubris satirized as far back as Aristophanes—the old block was not being demolished so much as being placed, after so many years of neglect, safely in his hands.

Yet, before any of the architect's ideas could ever become deeds, the city still had a good deal of work to do. As of August 14, 1982, the Department of Planning had not yet begun evaluating sixteen different proposals from twelve developers. In response to the Commercial District Development Commission's original newspaper advertisement, local real estate firms had cobbled together the vaguest sort of narrative for the North Loop redevelopment blocks. Details could come later; most developers were simply concerned with not being left out of one of the biggest downtown land auctions ever. They were merely keeping their place in line, including FJV, who submitted its first plan at the same time as Sidcor, its only competitor for Block 37. Already inundated with a pile of dense reading material, the CDDC started readying a second RFP (issued on November 1, 1982). This one attempted to clarify the North Loop Guidelines, particularly for the two Wacker Drive blocks (16 and 17) once Hilton was permanently out of the district. All the tedious public notifications and careful documentation were part of the Byrne administration's program to maintain a veneer of legality now that most of the initial North Loop rationales had evaporated.

In fact, after Miles Berger replaced Charles Shaw, the city planning effort was actually revived for a while. From February 1981 through the RFPs in August 1982, the city formally abandoned their *grand projet* approach. Berger was helping the Byrne administration divest costly city land in an orderly manner—one small piece at a time. In addition to the successful bid for the Transportation Building (Block 18), on April 20, 1982, the CDDC signed an agreement to rehab the Delaware Building, a landmark built right after the fire on the northeast corner of Dearborn and Randolph (Block 36); ABC began remodeling the State-Lake Theater Building June 3, 1982. None of these initiatives were sufficient by themselves, but taken together they appeared to justify the city council's agreeing to issue $55 million in bond anticipation notes with plans to retire them later with the formal $65 million North Loop bond issue.[26]

With credible proposals in hand, Chairman Berger could take considerable credit for having professionalized the city's redevelopment effort, long in disarray. Outwardly, he was refreshingly democratic in his approach. He encouraged public interest groups to have their say on taxes and architectural preservation, the two most controversial aspects of urban renewal. Hours of hearings were held, mountains of transcripts distributed, until everybody was talked out.[27] He was careful to let the mayor take the lead. Mayor Byrne pledged an "open, fair and orderly process" in the selection of developers, with all construction to be under way by 1986.[28] The mayor was advised to preempt the preservation battle by volunteering to save eight buildings, none of which, of course, were in the way of the really big projects.[29] As a sop to Manilow's group, the Selwyn, Harris, and Chicago Theaters were spared, along with some small office buildings. The Reliance Building, one of the few designated city landmarks, was also saved, but was never actually on a North Loop redevelopment block to begin with.

By appearing to be a preservationist herself and by putting everything out in the open, the mayor could still choose whomever she wanted to deal with in private. She knew that Berger was very effectively taking care of all of that. Important civic types like Manilow would have their say and would get a shot at a theater row. The city even devised a formula that stipulated that the developer of the rest of the Greyhound block—a site large enough for two towers—would help pay for the theater restorations. But Berger knew the Selwyn and the Harris were disasters. Every engineer who had ever taken a close look at them complained that they could never be properly insulated against the noise and vibration from the Dearborn Street subway. For starters, it would take more than a million dollars apiece simply to shore up the floors.

Piety was Berger's game face. It was only in private that he really got the chance to show his mastery. Sure, he had his own opinions, but he knew that his value to the mayor was his insouciant air of objectivity. More than any of the men that offered their counsel, Berger had real ties to the old system. When only a kid, he had hung around with Mayor Daley and James Downs as they reconfigured the downtown. He was also there with Rubloff in the dinosaur days. He knew by name all the snapping turtles who were down at the bottom of those secret land trusts. The mayor had once impulsively pledged to reveal all the underlying North Loop ownership, parcel by parcel, and it took all of Berger's considerable skill to help get her out of that one.[30] She was also helped by planning commissioner Martin Murphy, who concocted some legal-sounding rationale for not naming the owners immediately, though he promised it would all be done in due time. But except for Berger and a few aged pros, the planning department and certainly the mayor had no idea who owned the land they so avidly sought.

Berger's invaluable role in the North Loop process was to try somehow to clean it up. His first significant contribution was to de-Swibelize the project's financing. To keep the North Loop within his sphere of influence, Swibel had arranged a $50 million line of credit from the Continental Bank. At the time (July 20, 1979), Mayor Byrne had declared proudly that "this offer by Continental Bank is another example of the confidence of the financial and business community in this administration." A brief thirteen-page guideline was enough for Swibel's bankers, who, in a further show of appreciation, offered the unrestricted use of their depositors' money at 40 percent below prime. Desperate to fund the two Hilton blocks in the face of the county assessor's mounting objections, Byrne had abandoned Bilandic's planned bond issue. With Cook County looking over her shoulder, she didn't want to involve any additional government agencies. But as she took office, HUD was questioning the city's application for a UDAG of any amount. Cheryl Wright, HUD's local administrator, was most critical of the city's lack of private financial commitments, the absence of a true redevelopment plan, and particularly its intention to demolish landmark buildings. She reminded the city that Federal Urban Development Action Grants were specifically *not* to be used for taking down architectural landmarks. The preservationists set their sights on Block 37, where most of the monuments were located. Because of the city's refusal to stick with a coherent preservation scheme, all federal funding to the North Loop was suspended. In the end, Chicago never received a cent of UDAG money—the original collateral used to get the project started.

Berger had nothing personal against preservation; after all, he lived in a landmark on Astor Street himself. But he understood clearly what was happening. The Landmarks Preservation Council of Illinois (LPCI) that had formed in the early 1970s, during the losing battle to save Louis Sullivan's Chicago Stock Exchange, had reorganized in response to Rubloff's "it's all junk" North Loop declaration. It had allied itself with concerned architects such as Walker C. Johnson at Holabird and Root and Ira Bach at the city's advisory Commission on Chicago Historical and Architectural Landmarks. Since there were theaters sprinkled on most North Loop blocks, LPCI made a practical alliance with Lewis Manilow's performing arts coalition. In January 1981, less than two months after Shaw's Mole Town presentation, LPCI published an impressive document entitled *The Feasibility of Incorporating Landmark Buildings in the Redevelopment of Chicago's North Loop.* Funded by Chicago Community Trust, Continental Bank Foundation, and Joyce Foundation, and under contract with the National Trust for Historic Preservation, this richly illustrated pamphlet, pulled together in only a few weeks, was more a comprehensive planning document than anything the city had produced in fifteen years of study. With almost everything on three sides of Block 37 proposed for preservation, Berger knew he might as well forget about any federal assistance. He treated the booklet as if it were the *Communist Manifesto,* so contrary he felt it was to the city's plans for the North Loop.

Berger proved right in taking the document seriously.[31] At the time it was published, he knew that preservation was not what the city had in mind when it first officially sought condemnation power back in the early seventies. At best, rehabilitation of these deteriorating shells would increase their use, but in no way could they ever come near producing the ten-times increase in property and sales tax the city required. The bonanza was only gained from tearing down 300,000 square feet of ruin and replacing it with 2.2 million square feet of new architecture. Those opposing preservation argued that every building spared was potentially blocking a similar multiplication of value. It was a purely economic argument.

The LPCI proposed to save as many as five old buildings on the block and wrap them with an awkward band of retail stores along State Street— a new cummerbund on a rented tux. The preservationists were concerned with both the architecture and the varied economic and social life represented in the odd collection of buildings. Once they were gone, the hundreds of businesses and organizations that had found their way to blocks like 37 would be lost to the city forever. There would be no place for them in a homogeneous downtown of great towers and thirty-dollar-a-foot-plus rents.

The LPCI scheme tried to integrate the existing tenants with the gang lured by the redevelopment. An awkward mall hollowed out through the middle of the block, linking Daley Plaza to the main State Street entrance of Marshall Field's, brought the new and old uneasily together. This was all well intentioned, but as far as Berger's Plan Commission was concerned, preservation only meant trouble. He particularly didn't like the fact that the LPCI had gotten establishment backing from the Chicago Community Trust and the Joyce Foundation.

These were the people who had real influence in the city. Unlike the tax protesters and community groups, they could truly gum up the works before anyone had time to clue them in that they might be acting against their own interests. The equalized assessed valuation in the district was $53,158,199 before the proposed redevelopment and would be $622 million if it happened.[32] No new big buildings downtown meant an inevitable rise in corporate taxes in the existing central business district and higher levies out in the neighborhoods. Chicago just couldn't afford preservation. Berger wondered privately whether or not he should give some of these do-gooders a peek at what their new tax bill would be if they actually managed to preserve all those miserable buildings.

So Miles Berger began his reign by trying to limit Swibel's inordinate influence on the mayor in matters concerning downtown real estate. It was one thing being head of the Plan Commission—there wasn't one Chicagoan in a thousand who knew the difference between the commission and the city planning bureaucracy—and quite another to play out in public. Within days of his new appointment the new downtown czar substituted a regular bond issue for Swibel's funding plan, the standing five-year, $50 million line of credit from Continental. Berger knew that every reporter in town would eventually follow the line of credit back to Swibel, whose cash always came from Continental, where the CHA did its banking.[33] Berger had also heard on good authority that Swibel was about to sell his Madison-Canal property to two heavy contributors to the Byrne campaign, developer Daniel Levin and construction executive James McHugh. Congressman Dan Rostenkowski and former Park District commissioner Dan Shannon (manager of Rostenkowski's "blind trust") were also involved. If Swibel was already profiteering on Madison Street, in the West Loop, his "help" would be poison. Swibel and his group had already induced Congressman Rostenkowski to write an unprecedented exclusion into 1980 federal tax legislation that allowed them to build more than two thousand units of luxury housing with low-moderate-income HUD rent subsidies on the old West Side urban renewal land, formerly called Madison-Canal. No need for Jane Byrne to suffer a political embarrassment that Berger knew was avoidable. In keeping Swibel clear of the North Loop, Berger figured that he had already earned his keep.

Into early 1982, the czar deftly shepherded the city's most complex development projects, some that had languished for years. With little fanfare, he had accomplished what Rubloff and Shaw had failed to do. Conspicuously refusing to develop any part of the North Loop himself, he maintained a consistent stance of nonpartisanship. Sure, he was the one who had first told Howard Arvey about Sidcor, the development firm that came to represent the former Sax-Arvey interests on Block 37 in their competing bid to the city and eventual suit against FJV. But that was bound to happen; Berger knew everyone in real estate, and everyone came to him for advice.

It was he who had helped put the mayor in position to run a successful Daley-style reelection campaign. After a rocky start, she could now point to some real accomplishments. Rebuilding the North Loop was something everyone could see. The downtown was experiencing a building boom, and there were construction cranes all over the Loop. Who'd blame her for taking credit for it all?

But one thing Berger couldn't completely control was Jane Byrne's continued loyalty to Charlie Swibel. He knew nothing good could come of her continuing dependence on Swibel for real estate advice. Just when he successfully lobbied Swibel out of one area of planning, he was back in another. Keeping him in her administration had already cost Byrne plenty, especially with moderate blacks who had very publicly abandoned her opponents and won her election. She did herself permanent damage waiting until the last moment to force Swibel's resignation as CHA chairman and then perversely replacing him with a series of appointments that seemed directly aimed at irritating minorities. The mayor handed her opponents an issue and plenty of time to organize against her.

Relegated for decades to ineffectual complaining, the protesters had an economic cause that would have consequences for the day-to-day life of the Loop. Linking a neighborhood issue to the arcane workings of downtown power made them a political threat rather than just a quadrennial social annoyance. Specifically, objecting to a white-majority board that administered the almost 100 percent black population in Chicago public housing, the anti-Byrne forces boycotted the mayor's favorite downtown extravaganza: ChicagoFest, later renamed Taste of Chicago, an annual summer promotion of the city's food businesses and tourist industry.

The successful boycott made Byrne suffer her own version of the Bilandic blizzard. She was shown publicly to be vulnerable, and the inchoate black protest movement surprisingly effective. Around that time, Harold Washington, a black congressman and former promachine Democrat, was persuaded that he might win if he ran against Byrne. He had run for mayor in the late 1970s but was defeated in the Democratic primary. His chances looked better this time. Leading up to the Democratic primary, anti-Byrne forces registered fifty thousand new voters in a city where black and white voters were evenly divided.

Then Berger's own luck really began to take a turn for the worse. His youngest brother, Robert, and three other men were indicted on racketeering charges and two counts of mail fraud for bribing officials of the Cook County Board of (Tax) Appeals to reduce assessments. The government charged that Robert Berger was part of a scheme to obtain $135 million in fraudulent tax reductions. In addition, Robert, president of the Berger family tax-consulting company, testified to having paid a four-thousand-dollar bribe to the deputy commissioner of the Cook County Appeals Board.[34]

On February 22, 1983, Harold Washington won the Democratic mayoral primary. And then in little more than a month, with only 51 percent of the vote, Harold Washington would go on to defeat the Republican challenger, Bernard Epton. Washington was Chicago's first black mayor, with what he generously interpreted to be a mandate to change business as usual. He thought his supporters expected him to begin reversing the flow of capital to the downtown and find a means to start it flooding into the residential neighborhoods—to stop a trend in place since the Second World War. The inner city was increasingly poor, segregated completely from the rich enclaves clustered near the lake and cut off from the tantalizing prosperity out in the suburbs. Chicago—African Americans and poor whites—saw Harold Washington as a way to protest the old order.

Although the bulk of Mayor Washington's support was black, he narrowly outpolled Epton among white ethnic voters who historically voted along strictly racial lines. This oddity was particularly significant given that Washington captured only 12 percent of white votes citywide. (Chicago at the time was evenly divided between whites and blacks at nearly 40 percent apiece with Hispanics at 14 percent.) Whites who voted for Washington could register their own sense of disenfranchisement in a city that favored flashy downtown skyscrapers over

Mayor Harold Washington (1980s)

schools, police stations, and firehouses in their neighborhoods. In the past, in appreciation for its loyalty to Democratic politics, the white working class was rewarded with secure patronage jobs in huge municipal departments such as Streets and Sanitation or the Park District. At the same time, back in the wards where they lived, these same loyalists were displaced by interstate highways and blockbusting real estate scares. So the white liberals remaining in the city, the generic poor, and any other Chicagoans who thought themselves excluded from the main financial benefits of a prosperous, single-class central business district figured they had nothing to lose giving Harold Washington a chance. Hardly a real mandate, but their trust was enough to motivate the congressman, son of a Democratic precinct captain, to give the job a try. Remembering all the time to keep a lid on the sort of deal making that had made him an able South Side machine Democrat under black ward bosses William Dawson and Ralph Metcalfe, Washington took office in the spring of 1983.

Independent, erratic, willful, a voracious reader, Harold Washington was not the usual cut of politician. A big man who preferred the chaos of his book-strewn living room to the ceremonial dinner, he also favored junk food, hounding around, and, on his own schedule, giving a rousing speech. He often forgot to pay his utility bills and once spent thirty-six days in jail for neglecting to file four years of income tax returns. Washington didn't give a damn about money or personal gain, yet got into trouble for the matter of a few hundred bucks. He had a self-admitted tendency to be easily bored and was sometimes negligent in his law practice. The local bar removed his license for five years after it was charged that he had collected on legal services never provided.

None of these indiscretions ever added up to a premeditated pattern of deceit or corruption. Instead, ironically, his candor and nonchalance about his own failings helped him with the voters sick of the piety and staged sincerity of most professional politicians. With a nature so charmingly anarchic, Harold Washington never considered making adjustments to the way he conducted himself publicly. A large man with a deep, loud voice, he employed a Teddy Roosevelt–style oratory and had the ability to register the shock and aspirations of his constituency: the gift of improvising politics to give inchoate feelings form.

Nonetheless, soon after he took the oath of office, the very contradictions that made him so compelling as a candidate threatened to undo him. Yet, Washington was not about to be trapped into the permanent role of a populist permanently running against the downtown. The new mayor understood as well as any tested white politician before him that one-third of the city's tax base was contained in less than one of the city's 224.2 square miles.

He knew that he had no choice but to keep money invested downtown. But it wasn't so easy. Washington understood as well that he had to do the compromising without alienating his core followers back in the neighborhoods, all aching for a bigger share of the city's tax dollar. For a cunning ward politician who had attracted all of the black vote, "except for the accidents," as Epton put it after losing the mayoralty, Washington recognized that he had a potential gold mine in the office buildings perpetually under construction in the Loop. Furthermore, he was willing to do business with what the old machine regulars still called Republican interests, without appearing to be their man. To this end, he persevered in recruiting a new type of politician into his administration. Unfortunately, Washington was running against patronage and the old system at the very moment his partisans were first tasting citywide power and required the freedom of wide executive appointment power. His corporation counsel, James Montgomery, frequently argued for greater latitude in hiring, another name for the kind of patronage that progressives had fought against during their long years out of power. In this environment, Washington's choices for cabinet-level positions were especially sensitive. The new mayor was being watched by both sides to see if he would break faith with those who had put him into office. All the time he was eager to show results.

His choice to head the Department of Planning was Elizabeth Hollander, a respected community activist who had made her political reputation in public interest advocacy groups such as the Metropolitan Planning Council. Like the mayor, she lived in Hyde Park. It might as well have been St. Petersburg. The home of the University of Chicago, Hyde Park has its own brand of politics, an odd mix of cultural leftism and economic conservatism. It is integrated racially, along class lines, but not socially. With its back to the lake, the neighborhood is surrounded by some of the poorest census tracts in the city. In the late 1950s when the area looked as if it were going to be overrun and university officials were threatening to relocate the campus, Julian Levi focused the city's urban renewal and conservation efforts directly on that area, where he also happened to live. Levi took down thousands of housing units, relocated poor residents, and built new apartment houses and undistinguished commercial strips. At the time Elizabeth Hollander took control of the planning department, Hyde Park had stabilized, particularly in the area directly under university control called the Golden Rectangle. With campus security and city police combined, the rectangle has the third-largest police force in Illinois.

Hollander had a very able deputy, David Mosena, who later headed the department under Richard M. Daley. Mosena was a professional planner who had helped revive the department's sagging morale under Jane Byrne.

But planning in the Washington administration, in the beginning, was not so different than it had been under Byrne. Well into 1985 Miles Berger was still chairman of the Plan Commission, after graciously agreeing a year earlier to step down. Two years into Washington's term, seventy-three major appointments were stalled, including that of Walter Clark, vice-president of Citicorp Savings, who was supposed to take Berger's place. Washington was having trouble getting his way with a partisan city council, divided consistently twenty-nine to twenty-one against him.

But having Berger around turned out to be a lucky break. In his final act of de-Swibelizing city financing he helped point Mayor Washington in the direction of a new state bonding program called tax increment financing (TIF). Tax increment financing would prove to be an unexpected short-term blessing for the ill-starred North Loop.

Washington was generally successful in acting on some of the last Byrne-era initiatives, including a city council ordinance (January 18, 1983) authorizing acquisition of property in the "blighted North Loop" and a second RFP for a "mixed-use development on Block 37." His Department of Planning submitted a staff report (August 23, 1983) to the CDDC recommending that approval be given to negotiate a redevelopment agreement with FJV, based on its May 3, 1983, offer of $12,583,430 for Block 37. Harold Washington's planning department, like the two hapless administrations before it, had inherited the North Loop Redevelopment Project without quite knowing what to do with it. Specifically, the problem was how to finance its implementation.

Harold Washington had a lot of other things on his mind and, not exactly by choice, left downtown planning to the professionals—his well-meaning commissioner and a few quality staffers—where it had never been before. The planning bureaucracy had traditionally been kept too far from the political action to follow the intricate moves of Hill, Downs, Chaddick, and Berger as they remade the downtown. In effect, the official Department of Planning had always been a spectator in the great game. With little preparation it was now suddenly cast onto the Machiavellian field.

Yet, if power had been gracefully relinquished in a constitutional manner, Mayor Washington might have had a real chance to reform the entire urban renewal process. But from the start, his administration was under siege. Those same men to whom Jane Byrne had once contemptuously referred as a "cabal of evil men" now had firm control of the city council. Whereas Byrne, after a year's rebellion, brought the aldermen Edward Burke and Eddie Vrdolyak into her confidence, Washington, on principle, refused to compromise with the politicians who firmly controlled the council and weren't about to take on another partner. Waiting for power since, as young men, they engineered Michael Bilandic's ascendancy over the more direct claim of a black alderman, the "Eds" now wanted to run the city themselves. The mayor was in the unenviable position of having his enemies "outside the tent pissing in," rather than, as Lyndon Johnson sagely advised, "inside, pissing out."

In addition to obstructing key appointments, the city council voting bloc refused to pass the mayor's budgets. For more than three years—most of Washington's first term—very little got done. Chicago was suffering from the big-city equivalent of a constitutional crisis. A *Wall Street Journal* reporter described the city as Beirut on the Lake, and the epithet stuck. Frustrated as needed initiatives were stymied, locals took to calling the three-and-a-half-year stalemate the Council Wars. Chicago's hosting a 1993 world's fair, its major urban renewal projects, virtually anything requiring a city council ordinance, were stalled.

The effect of this cruel game of political chicken was especially harmful to the North Loop. Redevelopment deals negotiated during the waning days of the Byrne administration and signed after Washington assumed power were left to the bureaucrats. Although Commissioner Hollander attempted to get the city the best deal possible, her inexperience as a planner and lack of familiarity with the way business was conducted inside City Hall made her an easy mark for developers and other special interests.

But she too might have had a chance if city government had not been so divided. Every redevelopment initiative she tried was met by determined opposition, with one notable exception: the city did manage to go forward with the creation of a tax increment financing district for the North Loop. Keeping strictly to the lines of Rubloff's original twenty-seven-acre redevelopment area, the oldest part of the downtown finally had a reliable form of public investment. Tax increment financing was a clever scheme the Illinois state legislature had created in 1977 to help municipalities fund their own redevelopment plans.[35] TIF was a thinly disguised form of profit sharing for cities in the process of being redeveloped with private capital. Developers took their money up front, while mayors got it for up to thirty years on the back end in the form of taxes. In theory, at least, everyone made out.

With federal aid to the cities diminishing, state governments were being asked to fill the gap. TIF was a way for the legislature, controlled by downstate rural and suburban politicians, to avoid raising state taxes to fund large urban projects. Tax increment financing districts had the added benefit of appearing to broaden home rule powers that the cities had only grudgingly been awarded since Daley Sr. won the state's first meager concessions to local control in 1970.

TIF works like a futures contract or legal Ponzi scheme and is capable of generating millions annually in funding. Once a district is drawn up, thirty-year bonds are issued. In the case of the North Loop, the city raised a total of $222 million, including the original $65 million in general obligation bonds, to leverage an anticipated $1 billion in private investment.[36] This money was earmarked for all the outstanding land parcels, including nearly $33 million for the part of Block 37 not already controlled by FJV.

But there is a diabolical catch. Unlike general obligation securities that were figured in the annual municipal budget, TIF bonds are retired from taxes collected directly from the new buildings already up and running in the district. For example, in 1994, real estate taxes from Leo Burnett, R. R. Donnelley, and Chicago Title—million-square-foot-plus skyscrapers— and all the other new buildings or renovations, including the Transportation Building, Stouffer's hotel, and the ABC headquarters in the refurbished State-Lake Theater Building, were paid directly into the North Loop. The taxing scheme produced so much income that the bonds were all retired in less than seven years. In 1994, with twenty years still remaining in the life of the TIF district, North Loop buildings were throwing off $11 million a year, free and clear. At the end of the year, the city of Chicago had $50 million in cash that could only be spent within the seven-block district itself. So while the neighborhoods continued to be chronically underfunded, state law prohibited any TIF district funds from being diverted out of the downtown. The blighted downtown ironically became a magnet for cash, just as the long-dead Mayor Daley had fantasized.

Yet, with a city council on a permanent job action (1983–86), none of this did the incumbent mayor any good. To further intensify his problems, the Eds presented Mayor Washington with a piece of legislation guaranteed to drive the development community mad. On November 6, 1983, the mayor's council opponents began to formalize an ordinance that would require every downtown landlord to collect a 6 percent tax on leases. The lease tax was a diabolical strategy to alienate the mayor from the last of his white liberal support, most notably Barney Weissbourd, an outspoken Washington booster. Advertised to raise $76 million, the new tax was accompanied by a two-dollar-a-head rollback of the city's employment tax and a 1 percent reduction in the hated sales tax.

The mayor calmly took the bluff and used the anticipated $76 million to balance his budget. Using his opponent's weight against him, Washington did not offer any obvious resistance—a nice bit of political judo that was not

wasted on his renegade city council. Quickly the mayor's move was countered with the creation of an organized opposition headed by four prominent development firms and fronted by lawyer Jack Guthman, head of the
city's own Zoning Board of Appeals. With the mayor's budgets in perpetual
trouble, there was considerable movement toward compromise. For example, on August 26, 1985, the council proposed a linked-development tax that
would enable the city to collect a two-dollar-a-square foot exaction fee from
every new downtown building. This tax was to be paid before a building permit was issued and annually for the initial four years of a skyscraper's operation. Not as lucrative as the original lease tax, the linked-development
proposal would conservatively spin off millions.[37] The money could then be
diverted back to neighborhood development projects. All the time, the $11-
million yearly flow of TIF money was left undisturbed, flooding into the
Loop and reserved for the mayor's discretion.

None of these compromises proved acceptable to either side, and the
developers began to increase their pressure. On December 29, 1985,
Richard Stein threatened to back out of the North Loop if the lease tax was
retained.[38] To make his point stronger, Stein added that AT&T was considering canceling its lease at his privately developed tower farther west in the
Loop. Washington did not relent. Acting together, the development community tried again, this time with litigation. On December 30, 1985, Jack
Guthman filed suit against the lease tax, claiming that it was an illegal property tax under Illinois law. The law never was applied, and a compromise
involving a mixed bag of taxes equaling the $76 million was finally negoti-
ated more than three years into Harold Washington's first term.

Harold Washington was more effective during his aborted second term. In
1987, powerful aldermen like Ed Burke abruptly started doing business with
the mayor. Burke reluctantly concluded that with blacks making up 40 percent of the population, an African-American mayor might have the job forever. No one knew it at the time, but Washington had less than a year to
govern. In the short months left to him, the mayor continued to use the populist rhetoric of restoring power and bringing needed capital to the neighborhoods that had elected him. But, like every skilled big-city politician
before him, he relied primarily on the downtown to keep him in office.

Washington was not going to get in the way of a real estate boom that between 1979 and 1986 alone had pumped $11 billion into the central area,
particularly Wacker Drive. Richard Stein told the *Los Angeles Times*, "Developers build because we have money from lenders. We don't base it on
supply and demand."[39] In fact, the entire western section of the Loop,
starting with LaSalle Street, was choked with new construction. In the first
seven years of the 1980s, with plenty of out-of-town capital, developers

using only the statutory provisions of the city's zoning laws rebuilt the downtown.

Some projects begun during Washington's tenure were so large they reached beyond even Chicago's permissive code. Developers further multiplied rentable space with expensively negotiated planned-unit-development variances. Only a few years into the boom, insurance companies and pension funds had already financed more than 30 million new square feet of Class A office space, a third of all the space built in 115 years. The frame around the old core, consisting mostly of private projects that, like the new AT&T and Morton International headquarters, required not a cent in subsidies, prospered.

Ironically for Mayor Washington—the savior of the excluded neighborhoods—the fattened goose of downtown development was laying golden eggs. Even the North Loop with its costly three-to-one write-downs on the cost of land was beginning to pay off. Stein's Transportation Building and Elzie Higginbottom's apartment complex were under construction. Successful agreements were being worked out with John Buck and the Prime Group for two skyscrapers on the second of the two original Hilton blocks. There was even a deal finally with Stouffer. Critically for Washington, who couldn't afford to be associated with any land giveaways, these redevelopment deals were now negotiated without any tax abatements.

Regardless of the change in administrations, the real subsidies were still cleverly submerged in the discounted price of the land. In a parody of conventional financial wisdom, the city *bought high and sold low.* Given the actual price of the land, these redevelopment compromises would take years to really pay off. This blighted property, proclaimed worth next to nothing at the start of the two-decade redevelopment effort, cost the city, in actuality, an average of nearly three hundred dollars a square foot, with some parcels valued at close to six hundred dollars. They were contracted to sell it at between fifty dollars and two hundred dollars a square foot.

But it wasn't all yet a complete disaster. As each new building in the twenty-seven-acre North Loop TIF district went up and onto the tax rolls, its entire property tax payment was fed back *exclusively* into the district. The city had some cash—lots of it, in fact.

Even with the city finances coming under some control and FJV prepared to start developing Block 37 as early as 1983, the Washington administration spent four more years accomplishing next to nothing. From the days in the early eighties when HUD had first been critical of the city's failure to have a coherent preservation policy, the Department of Planning seemed paralyzed. Too many buildings of historic or architectural signifi-

George Landfield's rental marvel (1980)

cance were threatened by the North Loop project. And after almost ten years of vacillation, the city would conclude that it could not go forward if it had to meet stringent preservation requirements. This was particularly true of Block 37, where most of the designated North Loop "monuments" were situated. But this new realism came too late, only after the city council had somehow decided to preserve a piece of one tiny building at the corner of Washington and Dearborn. This unexpected humane act, later reversed, as it turns out, was enough to delay the project permanently.

The McCarthy Building had been owned since the forties by George Landfield, who had turned the hundred-year-old structure into a rental marvel. While other buildings on the block were struggling to keep half occupied, the Landfields had a full house in their five-story wreck. Doctors, lawyers, hairdressers, small businessmen, ground-floor retail, were shoehorned into every available square foot. More than sixty people in all worked in the McCarthy's twelve thousand square feet. It produced more than a quarter of a million in gross rent, $125,000 net profit for Mr. Landfield, who in later years ran the building from happy retirement in Sedona, Arizona. Some of Landfield's tenants shared the same secretary; others time-shared the office space itself. Even the roof was rented annually for a large billboard. This was dense-pack capitalism, albeit a little comical, like the Marx Brothers' stateroom in *Night at the Opera.* Anyway you describe it, the building had been wildly profitable for nearly half a century.

On June 6, 1984, paying not a bit of attention to any of these real estate realities, the city formally designated the facade of the McCarthy, completed in 1872, less than a year after the Great Fire, a protected architectural monument. The city council was effectively following the already superannuated 1982 version of the North Loop Guidelines, pledging to conserve the McCarthy along with at least three other threatened structures on the site. Preservationists had been seriously misled. The building had historical value only because the scores of office blocks exactly like it— there used to be four on the Dearborn-Washington corner alone—had already been demolished. The McCarthy was merely the Landmarks Preservation Council of Illinois's last stand. Instead of resting its case on the building's dubious architectural merit, the council would have had a better chance preserving it as a monument to free enterprise. Particularly as the real estate business approached its apocalyptic collapse at decade's end, the McCarthy, without a single lien, no debt, was one of the few solvent buildings in any big-city American downtown. For that alone it should have been saved. But it wasn't.

FJV was not unsympathetic but remained frustrated by the perpetual political foreplay. At its own expense, it analyzed moving the building on a giant skateboard diagonally across the site to the Randolph–State Street corner. They were pretty much losing their minds. No insurance company would underwrite the five-hundred-foot trip. Then studies to preserve the limestone facade revealed that it would turn to powder if removed. Only a death notice settled the matter. On September 22, 1987, the city council officially *de-designated* the building as a landmark—an unprecedented reversal—and set the stage for its eventual demolition. The Landmarks Preservation Council immediately sued the city, delaying demolition of the block for an additional two years. When it lost the suit, the delays had taken the project into 1989. Anticipating some of these difficulties, the city had prudently filed for quick-take powers.[40] The McCarthy Building, demolished in 1990, was still in litigation in the summer of 1995. Quick take allowed the city to move more quickly, but made it more difficult to estimate final costs. Then again, as the decade came to a close, everything was out of control. Out of the hands of politicians, deaf to the blandishments of developers, and into the clutches of pure speculators out to build nothing.

In a highly inflationary period like the 1980s, every day of delay meant

What FJV and architect Helmut Jahn had in mind for State Street in the early 1980s

that clever condemnation attorneys working for the owners could present steeper comparable values. Two of the best, the late Thomas Burke and his associate William Ryan, represented most of the privately owned parcels on Block 37. Thomas Foran, former Chicago Seven prosecutor now in private practice, had the rest. With land in the most expensive districts of the Loop selling for as high as $1,500 per square foot, Burke, Ryan, and Foran dramatically raised the final price of Block 37 land.

Elizabeth Hollander oversaw the negotiations for most of the North Loop blocks and watched helplessly as land values tripled. Block 37 received most of her attention. She was basically resigned that the other North Loop sites would be developed privately, just as if the city had never become involved with its quarter-billion-dollar commitment to underwrite rebuilding.[41] Made to look like suckers for subsidizing millionaires, at least she made sure the city was paid a high price for its complicity.

Before the McCarthy Building was officially de-designated and effectively traded, Hollander exacted a commitment from the developers to contribute up to $4 million for other North Loop preservation projects that they had nothing to do with, including the Reliance Building and the Chicago, Selwyn, and Harris Theaters. All this legal extortion of the private sector put the city in the odd position of holding its own monuments hostage. For enough money, any building could be taken down.

This preservation roulette on Block 37 actually accelerated after the city backed down on its own written commitment. The first official versions of the North Loop Guidelines promised to provide a *service tunnel* that ran from lower Wacker Drive, near the river, for two blocks, south to Block 37.

Without direct underground service to the block, any one of Helmut Jahn's six schemes, amounting to more than $9 million worth of paper architecture before he was finished and effectively off the job, required that the McCarthy Building give way to a street-level service ramp. The developers used the glitch to get their own valuable concessions. Bernard Weissbourd testified that the city, in agreeing to vacate two feet of Dearborn Street in order for the architect to hide the Commonwealth Edison substation—the only "monument" successfully spared demolition—had already saved FJV $27 million.[42] If the city was going to hold them up for $4 million in public improvements, Weissbourd figured, the least the politicians could do was save them some money somewhere else on the block. No one, on either side of the deal, wanted any close scrutiny of the service tunnel–preservation trade.

This was why Hollander never publicly blamed the developers for the McCarthy fiasco and joined with them to defend against the LPCI suit. But all this dealing by Commissioner Hollander had come after a public pledge never to trade monuments. It further weakened the city's stature and undermined its word. As Harold Washington's handpicked liaison with the development community, Hollander was especially sensitive to charges of old-fashioned wheeling and dealing. But what was she to do? Out of money and out of time, the city had no choice but to come to closure.

Like almost everything else, planning under Washington had this unfortunate quality of last-minute invention. No one could put pressure on the developers to fulfill their side of the bargain until the city had delivered on its. Before the service tunnel was cavalierly offered as a planning concession, no one had ever bothered pricing out the real cost of the improvement, a complicated piece of engineering that was meant to run under the densest section of the downtown. When the Department of Planning belatedly figured the costs, it discovered a proper freight tunnel would cost at least $10 million, and there was no guarantee that the costs wouldn't severely escalate nor that a tunnel could actually be excavated through the aggregated mass of foundations on neighboring Block 36.[43]

Lawyers, architects, parking consultants, engineers, and assorted professionals all continued to make money on this perpetual nonstarter. And all the old guys were gleefully cashing in—the Crowns, Saxes, Arveys, Epsteins, Mantynbands, and Klutznicks, families prominent in business and politics—whom Arthur Rubloff had first led downtown in what now seem like almost prehistoric times. Only the new, fancy breed of developers, like Bluhm, Malkin, and Weissbourd, was stalled. The Washington administration tried everything in its power to make the last piece of the North Loop fall into place. After all, FJV had enough civic spirit to retain a semblance of the comprehensive planning that had once been the main component of the urban renewal effort and intrinsic to its legal rationale.

But all of Hollander's machinations and the developers' countermoves merely added to the costly delays that had plagued the project from the start. The final blow came when Harold Washington, Daley-like, died of a heart attack the day before Thanksgiving 1987, only seven months into his second term. This act of God consigned Block 37 to an additional two years of inaction while an interim mayor, Eugene Sawyer, filled out Washington's term. The election in 1989 of Richard M. Daley was not in itself enough to get FJV's $600 million project out of the ground. Yet, only a few months into Daley's first foray into the family business, the sixteen buildings on Block 37 at last had an execution date.

V THE PRICE OF PROGRESS

On a cold Sunday in late fall, two men work together downtown, breaking up old plaster with hammers and crowbars. One reaches in with his pliers and pulls copper wiring out of the wall, arching his back, pulling hard as if he's hooked to a marlin. The tug-of-war ends when his partner, standing at his side with fence cutters, snips the wire jacketed in white plastic, twists the thin copper into a coil, and carefully places it alongside the pipes, electrical fixtures, and other valuables fished from deep inside the broken walls. Gone junking over the weekend, the two industrious scavengers will get a few hundred dollars for the scrap.

Only a few days earlier, on October 17, 1989, Richard M. Daley was also working outside. The newly elected mayor of Chicago smiled as a Caterpillar 973 tractor rode through the display window of a shoe store on the west side of State Street directly across from Marshall Field's. The old facade split in one shot; thick walls peeled away just enough to expose carefully painted squares of color in the interior. Floors and ceilings tipped together in the shell of the old masonry, Mondrianed pieces of a cracked coconut. It was a ceremonial first pitch for the benefit of the dignitaries who would all be gone when the heavy work began later that day with a whole fleet of cranes and wreckers.

Daley politely declined a turn at the stick controls of the red-and-yellow bulldozer. Images of failed presidential candidate Michael Dukakis in an M1 tank or of Jane Byrne swinging an iron ball through the lobby of the Shangri-La Theater must have made him pause. Short people in big machines, the inevitable newspaper picture was inevitably a little unsettling.

The mayor, his blue suit powdered with plaster dust, spoke for the city: "We take a giant step forward today to rebuild our central business district."[1] One of his police officers from the Loop Tactical Unit was more direct. Police Sergeant Greg Couchrene called it "crime prevention with a wrecking ball." He added, "That whole strip is neutral ground for gang bangers. It's where they strut their stuff. They go in that arcade, blow their last quarter, then rob somebody for 'L' fare home. It's no loss as far as I'm concerned."[2]

In little more than two years, the mayor promised, great towers would rise, along with a cathedral-sized shopping mall on State Street, replacing the junk that had

Mayor Richard M. Daley (1989)

accumulated on the block. The city was waging a holy war for a place where progress had unaccountably stopped—Third World Chicago, not out in the ghettos, but right in the center of a ring of streets housing international corporations, financial markets, and three-hundred-dollar-an-hour lawyers.

Daley, who had inherited Harold Washington's order to knock down Block 37, was in the odd position of defending his old rival's program from attacks by preservationists, tax protesters, and businessmen forced to relocate. But Daley knew an urban renewal effort was needed. Otherwise, the land would continue to run down, because no private individual had the authority to break the hundreds of long-term leases, subleases, and complicated mortgages on the blocks. The space in the successful old buildings was rented by the floor or office, and in some cases by the room. A lawyer, for example, who needed an office only when he wasn't in court in the morning could share with a dentist who needed it only in the afternoon. It added up to thousands of people with some financial connection to the block. An "intricate pattern of property rights" had rendered the land useless to rich investors of just the type the city was courting.[3] Landlords and lessees were like wrestlers hopelessly entangled in each other's arms and legs; they required a referee to pull them apart.

Property owners released from old restrictive leases were reluctant to rent out their property again on an extended basis, particularly with the threat of imminent condemnation. To keep the retail profitable, landlords sought out big-volume businesses—electronics stores, head shops, record stores, theaters, and discount clothing outlets—that were willing to pay high rent, on a short-term basis, for the opportunity to operate in one of the world's busiest commercial corridors, across from Chicago's finest department store. It was still a bargain to these tenants, playing instinctively what game theorists with their sophisticated mathematical models call the prisoner's dilemma.[4] One step above a squatter, a businessman in a run-down store has no motivation to spend a cent more than his rent. On Block 37, the immediate winners of this invidious comparison between the improved and derelict were the job-lotters, who with no calculus or academic theory found new ways to make money. No need for fancy shops or soaring towers: they prospered in a style offensive to the old families and new high-finance entrepreneurs alike.

Loaded with cash from pension funds and insurance companies looking for fat returns, the new money caste aimed to push out the squatters all in one shove. Big-time developers didn't understand how the old-timers had survived so long on 37 and were never really curious enough to find out. The answer might have surprised them. Developers in the rest of the Loop, busy building sanitary new skyscrapers, perceived Block 37 as the most blighted, but it was, in fact, more profitable than it had ever been—a prisoner's riddle all its own.

The three businesses joined together in the development company called FJV ignored this crucial paradox at their own peril. Compliments of Chicago's generous interpretation of its powers of eminent domain, FJV now controlled a full city block and was out to make "serious" money on an exponential scale.[5] FJV took title to the land late in 1989, after the demolition was completed, still publicly confident that it could cure this chronically sick strip of downtown. Its approach was to favor the highest office floors and ignore the ground, except in the State Street portion reserved for six stories of retail, a vertical mall of Disney-like stacked city streets. The Water Tower Place formula imported to the Loop. This was a risky strategy, since the only reliable economic engine of the block from the days of its first settlement had been the thin strip of linear footage nearest the street, where long-term renters conducted their retail businesses. "One up, one down"—space on the ground floor and mezzanine—was the age-old formula. The consequence of these development decisions was a fatter, taller architecture in the planned towers on the Dearborn side (including nearly half of Washington and Randolph) that permitted the developers to transfer value up. This was the hidden jackpot on Block 37. Having the whole three-acre block at its whim was the key to FJV's making full use of the air rights.

Since Mies van der Rohe in the 1950s perfected glass-and-steel buildings on stilts, modern architects had learned to use the first thirty feet of a high-rise simply as a formal entrance piece, obliterating the city's indigenous commercial-building type. Mies's rigorous rationale provided no room for the foul stores and rough trade that went on in the streets of Chicago. A high-style type, intended originally only for inner-city residential use, was adapted indiscriminately for strictly commercial purposes.

The transformation worked very well. The bases of Mies's tall buildings were reserved for a hollow lobby, security desk, and elevator core. Nothing went on at the bottom of a Miesian skyscraper. The lobbies were stripped bare, clad in green marble, and fit with a spare selection of the architect's rich leather-and-chrome furniture, in which no one ever sat. Sanitized neutral spaces, these were simply attenuated entrances that led to the elevators and the floors, where the building really started. No distracting clutter or disorder was experienced on the ground. Mies accomplished the setbacks, typical of Art Deco buildings in which the tower was progressively thinner than the base, in one slender form and still avoided the stigma that had been attached to even earlier skyscrapers. Some of the earliest tall towers, providing the large floor plates attractive to big corporations anxious to have as many workers as possible on the same floor, were as wide as they were tall. These were dense, bulky piles of steel and masonry that achieved their huge surplus of cubic footage by blocking a neighborhood's precious available light and crowding the street. New York's Second Equitable Life Assurance Building (1915), the modern model of the FAR hog—twenty-five times its ground plan without setbacks—fomented the outcry that led only a year later to the country's first zoning code.[6]

Mies came to America right after the great Art Deco skyscrapers were in place. Buildings with ever-larger FARs, such as the Empire State and Chrysler Buildings, were planned under New York's 1916 zoning ordinance. In the city's densest corridors, skyscrapers were still permitted to rise 250 sheer feet above the street and cover up to 90 percent of the site. This equaled the bulk of more than one-half the Equitable Building, which at 1.44 million square feet was only forty stories tall. As a bonus for limiting the base to about twenty-five stories to avoid the "canyon effect," an architect was allowed to build up, creating the characteristic ziggurat profile of skyscrapers designed in the 1920s.[7]

Mies then went one bold step further by getting rid of the sheer wall of the base, the vestigial architectural relic of robber-baron capitalism. Abandoning ziggurats and maintaining a constant building width, Mies created a new aesthetic. He aired out the tower of the Equitable years and made high bulk acceptable again. His great skyscrapers were dense but light. Adding abundant glass framed within carefully detailed steel, he made these mastodons appear transparent and lithe. In the interiors, Mies's lobbies mediated between two elements, providing a transition from the foul street to the elegant upper reaches. The new space, treated with conditioned air for its own atmosphere, was marketed at a premium to accountants, lawyers, and the expanding financial markets, all rising in place of the bawdy American industrial city. Skyscrapers made space out of air.

And in place of the street, as they hid behind the self-serving pretense of creating new public space, postwar architects designed uninhabitable plazas to the last square inch. In return, developers received bonus FAR to go higher. Cities—flat broke and desperate for open land—granted these ill-considered zoning variances. But without a thriving perimeter, whether it is packed with upscale retail consistent with the desired new order of the city or more like the disordered market it seeks to replace, high-rise architecture abandons an economic mainstay. This oversight has been especially fatal to buildings of an earlier time. Having been superseded decades earlier by more modern office space, only those supported by retail could be kept alive. Once the base of urban architecture was superfluous, the old buildings themselves were doomed, having lost their last compelling rationale for preservation.

In the 1980s, as Block 37's optimistic new owners prepared to borrow hundreds of millions, they never quite acknowledged, even to themselves, how extreme this change was. The piece of the city FJV was drawn to had endured, amazingly unaffected, as other developers with big plans came and went. Coming close to demolition several times, the block was always saved at the last minute. Neither the politicians nor the developers ever fully appreciated the reasons for its stubborn endurance. A disquieting set of facts relevant to its economic survival holds the clues.

Even a quick review of the block's economic history reveals that it had been profitable only in that narrow band of space closest to the street where merchandise was advertised, bartered, and sold in one swift transaction. On-the-fly businesses that were suited to the marginal, Casbah spaces belting the block's entire perimeter did well. New architectural formulas attuned to the ground, not the skyline—more street, not more space in the air—was what the old city needed. Architects needed to stand Mies on his head.

Nothing less than an act of heresy for modern architects was required—to put the ground rent back. Welcoming pushy crowds and random activity on dense city streets was the only way to reverse the decay that had given the block its death sentence in the first place. No more buildings were required that vacuumed people off the street, rushed them up to private offices, and contained them nine to five until it was time to evacuate the town for another day. The answer lay at ground level and not in the air, as the architects and their financial backers had long maintained.

But no one thought of reclaiming the street in time. FJV still thought the big money was to be made high above the ground, with program-driven financing schemes that not a soul could clearly explain, and in retail malls that shut out the street. The Block F joint venture let the bulldozers bury any further reminder or misgiving it might have had, even fronting the money for the cash-poor city to finally get things on track.

Not only buildings were leveled in the 1980s. Development also violently displaced an earlier generation of businessmen. With no small degree of skill and guile, the former downtown owners knew how to make big bucks on small margin. Without spending the millions it took to put up new buildings, they rode in Cadillacs and had time to go to the club for a game of cards and a steam. Two cultures collided on that day when National Wrecking went through the wall. The individuals to be evicted had no debt because they could get no credit; the group evicting them, with the city's help, was more than 70 percent in debt and used no cash of their own.

Block 37 had survived in its terminal state for so long only because money wasn't made on complicated leases, legal fees, or projected capital returns, but on the hoof. These no-frills businesses found ways to exploit a new hip clientele with plenty of cash to spend on bongs, disco, and horror films, as the landlords were subsidized for keeping their land "asleep"—as an experienced speculator like Colonel Crown called it. It was always "expensive to buy money."[8] Wait and the payoff would come when the property, with the old buildings cleared off, was put to a higher use. In the meantime, you were paid to sleep.[9]

The barkers outside the Designers Mart on Washington Street yelled out the day's bargains; the buxom woman who ticked like a metronome back and forth on a swing over the sidewalk lured customers into the greasy spoons on Randolph Street. Block 37, always a poor cousin to the carriage-trade businesses to its east and the fine offices to its west, was at its economic peak only after the Second World War. Ironically, its reprieve arrived at the very moment American cities, including Chicago, first became conscious of their permanent decline. By exploiting the most primitive stage of capitalism, the quick-buck businesses—occupying the ground floors of the buildings in such rapid succession that some were gone before they had a chance to put up a permanent sign—provided Block 37 with a brief second chance.

On a more analytical level, this oscillation of ground values downtown signaled a change at work in the urban ecology. The steep downward trend, experienced as a carnival of bargains on Block 37, was like a forest fire clearing away old growth. Low prices allowed new players to enter the market, to break the old monopolies. Monopoly requires a stable environment in which the buying and selling of merchandise is ritualized and controlled. In the place of competition, in which price is negotiated and fought over hand to hand, value, in a monopoly environment, happily embraces Adam Smith's metaphor of an invisible hand. For the monopolists during prosperous times, a self-stabilizing market that favors them with most of the business is their heavenly reward for lending their money. Their god is the Enlightenment figure of the watchmaker who, after completing creation's clockwork, exits, leaving only the shadow of his genius to be perceived in the endless intricacies of his craft.

Economist Robert Heilbroner sees this self-serving interpretation of Smith's *Wealth of Nations* at "the base of the sanguine expectations for capitalism in our day." He adds, "They are not 'scientific' predictions, in the sense of relying on laws of behavior as immutable as the law of gravity. Perhaps some propensity other than the desire for an augmentation of fortune will arise one day to give a regularity to the way we interact, or, some substitute for private property will instill in us the kinds of price-sensitive behavior on which a capitalist system depends."[10] Meanwhile, during periods when capital is held tightly and credit is difficult to come by, the active, democratic, blood-sport side of making money is relegated to the margins.

On LaSalle Street, the city's central financial corridor, palatial main banking floors, half a football field in length, transformed the profane act of commerce into the sacred. At the Continental Bank there were murals depicting heroic episodes from the city's past, inspirational quotations set up high near the coffered ceilings, and a Bernini-like array of columns that ennobled the procession from the front door to the teller's cage. On a mezzanine speckled with handsome desks the more involved acts of banking could be done at a volume only a little higher than a discreet whisper. Aisles and nave were encircled by the executive offices, intimate chapels off to the side. The architecture was meant to elevate the lending, depositing, and withdrawing of money. A theatrical space encouraged suspension of disbelief, aristocratic flimflam to disguise the arbitrarily high premium extracted from a clientele with no real alternative to doing business there. For an activity Karl Marx disparagingly dismissed as "fictitious capital," lender and borrower alike had a place that gave their lives some measure of solidity.

Another prominent downtown monopoly, Chicago Title and Trust Company, used stately architecture, too. It was called the Supreme Court of Washington Street by the big-time lawyers who had to have their deals approved by the company, which was born when all the original land records in the city were destroyed during the Chicago Fire of 1871. Clear title to real estate was preserved only in the records of the abstract men, who copied documents for attorneys. These scriveners, the human Xeroxes of the day, joined together, pooling their abstracts, to form the Title and Trust Company, which continued until the late 1960s to hold a monopoly on title insurance for property throughout the city and Cook County. Chicago's official land records are a composite of abstracts and later originals that provided the title company with more authority than the government itself concerning the crucial issues of ownership.

A cadre of title officers, night-school lawyers, accountants, the lowest professional rung, had the last word on real estate deals. On their own authority, these meticulous form readers could delay a transaction for the tiniest of oversights. At Christmas their desks were covered with gift-wrapped liquor boxes and other tributes attesting to their unequaled power to delay—"the enemy of all deals."

Through the late 1960s, all real estate transactions anywhere in the metropolitan region had to pass through Chicago Title, which exacted separate fees for title searches, insurance, and, like a funeral home, the use of its wood-paneled rooms for closings. Signing the deal, exchanging ownership of property, were done with the same solemnity for a $2 million penthouse as for a $20,000 bungalow out in Cicero. A commitment to amortize up to thirty years of mortgage debt was observed at the title company with all the whispered civility of a church service. In a distinctly modern iteration of the honored Jeffersonian notion of landownership, decades of indebtedness were celebrated with a title officer as minister. A deed for real estate, a tiny piece of America that for a fee the title company insured to be uniquely yours, made it official. Ceremony made the inevitable exchange of cash, really the only point of the exercise in the first place, simply a bothersome afterthought. Demeaning details were lost in the pageantry.

"Part of God's estate in the Globe," Henry Ward Beecher called real estate more than a hundred years ago. When you are contracting with God in a profitable way, he added, "a parcel of ground is deeded to you and you walk over it, and call it your own, it seems as if you had come into partnership with the original proprietor of the earth." Any design claiming to be serious architecture was required to complete the effect.

. . .

In the retail district on State Street, Marshall Field's did business in a palace with gilded columns, painted ceilings, marble floors, and baronial wood everywhere. Field had cornered so much of the world's mahogany for his store that he sold the surplus at a handsome profit in the 1920s, to Continental Bank for its new headquarters. The architecture added value to each tiny unit of merchandise, reaching markups of 300 percent when it came to furniture, cosmetics, or designer clothing. All this value added was banked by the department store.

Marshall Field's, Chicago Title, and Continental Bank had set up housekeeping in some of the large trees before the ecological balance in the Loop was seriously altered after the Second World War. A war then developed between the monopoly interests happily in place and the catbirds invading their nests. For owners on the down-and-out side of State Street, on Block 37, the first stage of the downtown invasion was profitable. Landlords welcomed hard-working retailers willing to pay high rent to be down at street level on State, where they could undercut the retail behemoths. Relying on established businesses like Marshall Field's, Peacock's, and even a more modest retailer such as Carson Pirie Scott to keep prices high, the catbirds perched right across the way and got the bargain hunters. As the Superfly clothing store Arrowsmith and Company and Cheap Willy's restaurant moved in, the large-overhead, full-service stores that maintained an aura of exclusivity were especially hard hit. They found it increasingly difficult to maintain a premium price for merchandise when the environment in which they did business seemed to change overnight from Fifth Avenue to Penny Lane.

This, Gilbert H. Scribner Jr. considered a frightening trend that required his immediate attention. He detailed the Loop's precipitous down zoning and identified it to his clients as the first serious general challenge to the city's business and real estate monopolies. His conclusions appear in a series of meticulous appraisals for the First National Bank, beginning in May 1952. Scribner was a principal in Winston and Company, one of the city's blue-chip real estate firms since 1891. A few such firms effectively set real estate values up through the Second World War. Their conservative appraisals provided a benchmark in place of a true market. Building owners, until the war mostly prominent local and East Coast families, could trade land through their brokers without haggling over price. Land traded within a narrow margin. There were no radical spikes in values of the sort sure to attract speculators. These reports were simple narratives of the urban condition. In the closed world of commercial real estate trading, they were the insider's equivalent to a private posting of stock prices.

But something had gone wrong. Along with the deterioration of downtown property there was an accompanying trend that concerned Scribner. A new group of owners on and around Block 37 had crashed the party. Their activities, protected by the secrecy of blind land trusts, had eluded the conventional radar, but Scribner knew hustlers were around, and he sounded the alarm. He wrote to Martin O. McKevitt, a bank vice-president: "Omitted are the sales of the leasehold interests at 150–154 North State Street, 156 North State Street, and 9 West Randolph Street. These have been omitted because the consideration is not a matter of public knowledge; however, there has been a very rapid turnover of controlling interest in the immediate neighborhood of these properties in recent years, with control passing from old well-established Chicago citizens to groups of *acknowledged speculators who are not generally conceded to have the best interest of their neighbors or the street in mind*" (emphasis mine).[11]

Specifically, Scribner was warning that this "passing" of control from "well-established Chicago citizens" had consequences that you didn't need a real estate genius to point out. The "acknowledged speculators"—code for "Jews" and other outlanders—had placed guys with pinkie rings, cigars, wads of bills tied with rubber bands, behind the counters of once-fine State Street stores. Somehow, when the proper retail establishment wasn't looking, Roosevelt Road—a main off-price retail corridor just south of the Loop—had transposed itself into the Loop—merchants like Mr. Dopp, who sold leather goods and invented a prized product called a Dopp kit, in which men all over America transported toiletries. Dopp was a railroad jobber, buying boxcar-sized inventories of damaged or leftover goods and reselling them. He was the natural heir to the pushcart peddlers, no-overhead retailers who along with the sodbusters settled the West. To understand Scribner's alarm, imagine, in New York, bustling Orchard Street businesses moving one morning, unannounced, into Trump Tower. Half a mile from the Federal Reserve and the Board of Trade, Block 37 was, during its last days in the 1980s, a place to witness unencumbered, undisguised money changing. Chicago's affluent white middle-class population commuted from the suburbs only to work. Commuters didn't linger after hours.

Little was done to reverse this trend. Solutions to the failing downtown were principally economic. The architectural solutions merely exacerbated the problems of dangerous streets and empty properties. It took a while to find a formula that would allow the new scale of buildings, like the multi-million-square-foot Prudential Building that when completed in 1956 was the first new office building in the city since the Depression. Until the expanded use of eminent domain, old blocks, like 37, had become odd amalgams of small lots that couldn't be added together to form a superlot capable of supporting a modern skyscraper. Value had diminished, reverting back from the total area of the land to only a small, intensely used strip of linear street frontage. Without a tall building, an old block's value was still effectively locked away. No single owner could yet control enough of the block to build at the scale needed to tap the surplus value. This new square footage in the air was like oil waiting to be extracted from deep in the land. A skyscraper was just a massive oil derrick turned upside down, drilling the sky.

Even Thomas Jefferson and Alexander Hamilton, adversaries in most other matters, agreed that fee-simple title was as important as the right to vote.[12] Both considered it desirable to make land in America an easily disposable asset that government regulated only minimally. This was a direct reaction to monopolistic English land grants such as the Grosvenor family's five-hundred-acre parcel in central London. Since the seventeenth century, the Grosvenors have enjoyed a fat annuity from the leaseholds of all the property in what is now Mayfair, Belgravia, and Pimlico. The fees are never sold.

The founders reacted violently to any such permanent restrictions on the outright trading of land. As a consequence, the first government sales of frontier land in the 1780s gave owners full possession of a rectangle, scribed on the surface but theoretically extending endlessly into the sky or as far down as the landlord could bore. The bigger the property's original outline, the greater its potential volume. Divided properties were less valuable than consolidated ones. Fractured ownership on Block 37 made for small lots, additionally difficult to join together in Chicago because of the regulations governing blind land trusts. This worked wonderfully when downtown land was all owned by the same few families and institutions. Land deals could then flow effortlessly from one trust to another with the price left unreported except to the intimate circle of owners and their handpicked real estate advisers.

Trading was thus restricted to a small cartel that, in effect, had inside information on the land's current value. There was no true real estate market because there was no reliable public information concerning price. An interested buyer couldn't just contact an owner and make him an offer; there was no easy way to find out who the owner was. Blind trusts mystified landownership, restricting knowledge to a specialized white-collar caste who knew how to find out, for a fee, the same information offered for free and considered public information in most American towns. For just this reason alone, intelligence concerning land was raised to a fetish and high-priced professional specialty in Chicago.[13]

The promise of future riches encouraged landlords to hoard property, treating well-located urban lots a bit like prime agricultural land, let out for as long as a hundred years at a time and farmed in the form of leases. Monthly rent payments, returning close to 10 percent with modest escalating clauses to keep the rent current with inflation, made for a secure investment. All this began to change in the Depression when the old families sold off their land or the banks foreclosed on properties from which the cash equity had been removed earlier to play the booming stock market.

Capitalism before the Great Depression had been played exclusively as a Monopoly game through interlocking of corporate boards and the day-to-day collusion of men belonging to the same social set. But their monopolies began to leak as the real estate that they had gathered almost as an afterthought became distressed. This was the most visible part of their failing empires. Entrepreneurs for whom land trading was the only avenue to wealth knew exactly what to do next.[14]

Block 37—the low number designating it as one of the original fifty-eight three-acre rectangles of land downtown, platted before the town was incorporated in 1833—was always a precious piece of land. Different from other nearby parcels, like Block 39, reserved for a county courthouse, or the old blocks around Monroe Street retained as school sections set aside for future educational uses but leased out to individuals, all lots on Block 37 were owned fee simple.[15] Local and state authorities were required through the original federal land grants to reserve certain central city blocks for schools or other public buildings. Reuse of the reserved land was thus limited to long-term leaseholds. This made neighboring land held fee simple, free of restrictions governing its sale and trading, ever more valuable. With the old owners doomed and every bit of history that had ever attached itself to Block 37 over its long life about to be erased, FJV arrived on the scene.

One hundred and fifty years earlier, civil engineers in the employ of the young federal government, measured and drew lines in the middle of nowhere so that politicians might find an efficient way to turn land, America's richest asset, into cash. Land sold and traded today still bears the mark of the original eight lots of 1830 that first partitioned all of Chicago's downtown blocks. Land was subdivided expressly for resale to pay for the Illinois and Michigan Canal, planned to begin in the city at Bridgeport on the South Branch of the Chicago River. Linking the Great Lakes to the Mississippi River, the canal made Chicago the West's central city. The land auction produced a speculative fury—a classic twenty-year boom-and-bust cycle— that lasted well into the next transportation craze, even before the canal was completed. As railroads made canals obsolete, Chicago effortlessly accommodated the new technology, fitting iron tracks along the old canal right-of-ways. Speculators traded and retraded the rest. The city's first official designation was Section 9, Township 39, Range 14, one small square of the giant American checkerboard.

"Wild land," uniformly cut from the same grid, produced the boom of 1883 to 1836.[16] When the land rush started, Chicago had fewer than four hundred residents and just two hundred houses. In only two years the population multiplied ten times. Using frontier land as collateral, the state banks of Illinois and Michigan issued millions of dollars in unsecured notes. A contemporary observer noted that an "evening purchaser" paid "ten times as much as the price paid by the morning buyer for the same spot."[17] Until the inevitable bust a year later forced banks to liquidate their holdings, these fly-by-night institutions were richer on paper than many an East Coast rival. Bankers might lose their jobs, banks might fold, but to a hardened real estate investor, using credit and little money of his own, this sudden reversal of fortune was no problem. The federal land survey had irreversibly put Chicago real estate into play. With all that wild land laid out in front of him so neatly, a trader worthy of the name would find a way to make money. He started simply by dividing what he already owned into smaller pieces.

Generally, as property left government hands and entered private estates, the big lots were sliced into ever thinner portions, many times deeper than wide.[18] Retail businesses worked only the thin edge nearest the street, leaving their back rooms for storage. Eventually big landowners and small multiplied the space further by building up, stacking narrow slices one on top of the other, advertising new upper-floor businesses with painted signs on the window glass. Commercial real estate, until the advent of the pure business block after the 1871 fire, was always oriented toward the street, densifying up in the narrow zone above the sidewalk. Landlords partitioned vertically as freely as the government, eager to settle the prairie, had portioned the land horizontally. As professionals, inventors, and service businesses, which did not require the eye-level presence of traditional retail business, moved up in a building, the space in the air became more valuable. Engineers and architects allowed landlords to build higher until old families and new—McCormicks, Fields, Loebs, Sterns, Leiters, Levys, Nashes, Crowns, Cuneos, and Colons—all had taken a piece, from owning a quarter block, two original lots, to leasing only a closet-sized office on an upper floor. The same drive motivated them all: to control a piece of downtown property where the action and profits were greatest.

From the inception of the United States, the federal government had

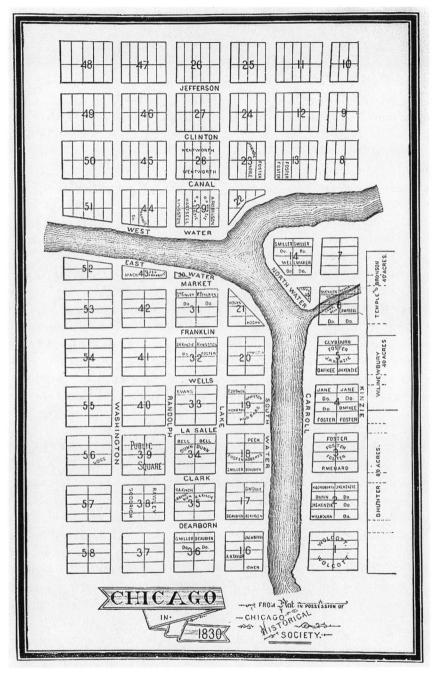

Thompson's plat (1830)

acted as a broker. All land not previously claimed was considered the property of the Republic, treated as an exclusively economic rather than a social resource. Large tracts controlled by Native Americans were bought as undeveloped land and resold as quickly as possible to white settlers to pay off the huge debt incurred fighting the Revolutionary War. In 1833, the Potawatomis sold 20 million acres near Chicago to the United States for an average price of six cents an acre. When resold, a good part of what later became the Loop cost the city's first speculators, John Kinzie and William B. Ogden, $800.[19] Ogden's brother-in-law, Charles Butler, paid $100,000 for 1,000 city lots (150 acres) on the Chicago River's north side, within months of the Potawotomi treaty. No piece of government land was priced higher than any other, a policy favoring those who staked claims earliest in an area near a major lake or river or in a section where improvement was planned. Government ownership of unsettled land was America's purest monopoly and a seemingly endless source of capital.

From the beginning, real estate was favored for its exchange as well as its use value. This made the trading of land for its immediate value at least as important as for any future use. Buying millions of acres for as little as a cent and selling it for a minimum of $1.25 an acre, the federal government treated land as a primary commodity, like grain or lumber, from which it derived a fast cash profit. While landownership soon became encrusted with sentimental associations and nostalgia—"Be it ever so humble, there's no place like home"—American real estate was always at base a reckless and decidedly unsentimental business.

But like all monopolies this one was eventually eroded by overselling and by the same market forces it unrealistically sought to restrain. Holding an exclusive franchise on the Northwest Territory, the United States government set the price, but only through the first sale. The same speculators to whom the government had gladly sold land at more than a dollar-an-acre profit, later, using the federal promise of imminent development, made thousands. The real money is made as the "game shifts from investment to gambling."[20] Chicago developed a whole class of sophisticated buyers who bought up land for the sole purpose of quick resale. As historian William Cronon observed, "Lots that had sold for $33 in 1829 were going for $100,000 by 1836. Such prices bore no relation to any current economic reality. Only wild hopes for the future could lead people to pay so much for vacant lots in a town where the most promising economic activity consisted of nothing more substantial than buying and selling real estate. Speculators dreamed of what the land might someday be, and gambled immense sums on their faith in a rising market."[21]

In Chicago, control of the land quickly passed from public to private hands, radically inverting the source of wealth. To the government that once owned it all, the cash value of an exclusive franchise in land now just trickled back in the form of property taxes. Since municipal governments of the nineteenth century were essentially run on the side by prominent businessmen, lost was any distinction between private and public gain. Urban historian Sam Bass Warner explains, "Those who had private capital, or were bankers or agents for Eastern money, had an enormous advantage. Such men could purchase a whole valley, a promising townsite, whatever they wished. . . . Through large-scale purchases the speculator became a central figure in the allocation of physical resources, and this role was reinforced by his further activity as money lender."[22]

In June 1834, after the announcement of the plan to build the Illinois and Michigan Canal, an 80-by-180-foot corner lot on South Water and Clark Street, near Block 37, sold for $3,500; two years later the price was $15,000. A corner lot at Dearborn and South Water went for $9,000 in March and $25,000 in December of 1835. Banks got into the act by issuing loans against the overstated, not the underlying, value of the land, as they would again in the 1980s. This further inflated the market, until the secretary of the Treasury, in 1836, required banks to pay for government lands in gold coin rather than paper, in effect abruptly turning off credit. A year later, real estate on Block 37 had crashed to ten cents on the dollar, prompting an economist to observe recently, "The history of American banking was strewn with failures, runs and panics that could be traced to an excessive enthusiasm for real estate collateral."[23]

The banks' entanglement with Block 37 began early, as soon as investors saw the larger lots there as capital dams for available credit. Over time, this changed the way credit was viewed, making it appear more like an asset than a liability. No longer purely a matter of debt, a real estate transaction offered a way to get cash out of an investment immediately, like leaving a gold watch at a pawnshop. Banks were attracted to these deals because speculators were willing to pay as high as 6 percent annual interest, two or three times the going rate. Early on, the size of what was built was thought more important than the quality; more building equaled more borrowed money. In an inflationary period, typically a twenty-year cycle of rising property values, the assumption of sale at a higher price was built into the loan. One paid back with cheaper dollars than he borrowed.[24] Architecture, in direct relation to its scale, added cash value to the speculator's investment. More building equaled more money with which to play.

Block 37 received attention because of its central location. Traded and built out completely during its first development phase, between 1840 and 1871, the block became home to a mix of houses, offices, ground-floor busi-

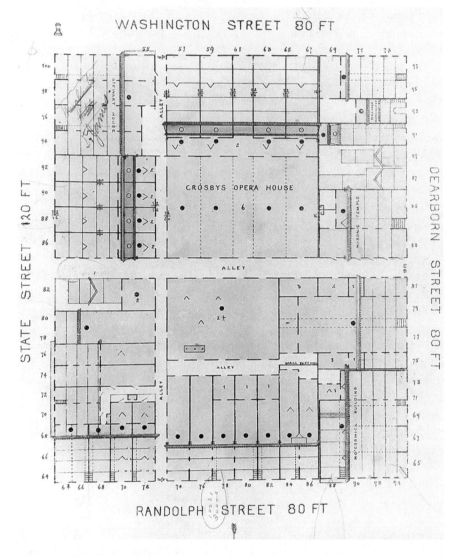

Lot map of Block 37 (1860s)

nesses, and theaters. The Crosby's Opera House on Washington Street, its most prominent prefire building, was a cross between a western music hall and a proper stage. Crosby's first established the site as a key part of the city's entertainment district. All of Block 37 burned to the ground in the Great Fire of 1871, which in less than two days obliterated the entire downtown, destroying 17,450 of the city's 60,000 buildings and doing $200 million worth of damage.

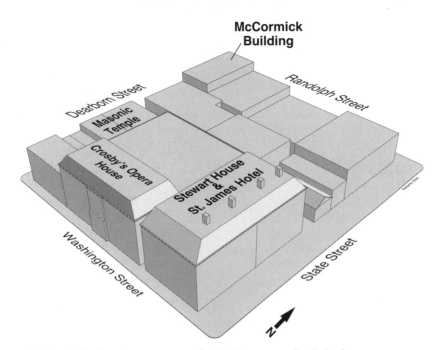

In the decade before the Great Fire, the block was completely built out to an average of five stories. Buildings occupied the site from the lot line back as much as 200 feet.

The disaster also conveniently cleared the block of its hodgepodge of small owners and renters, allowing landlords to take the land to a higher use. This permanently diminished the residential occupancy of the downtown area, where 27,800 people had lived before.[25] Unlike Manhattan, Chicago would never regain its downtown residential character. In particular, Block 37 was suddenly too valuable to rebuild with one-family homes or a sprawling variety theater like Crosby's. Thin residential lots, at least four times deeper than wide, could be put together side by side to increase the total frontage and allow the architects to design taller buildings on a fatter footprint. The result was initially as much as a tenfold increase in rentable area on the best lots. For example, on the Dearborn Street side, land leased, on average, at $300 per front foot the decade before the fire and $1,000 two years after. By 1928, ground values had reached their pre-Depression peak of $23,000, a level not to be reached again until the 1980s.[26]

In the period immediately following the fire, Chicago tripled the value of its land. This was not simply a consequence of the substantial recapitalization of the city from disaster relief and insurance claims. Value was added over the next twenty years in the technologically advanced tall buildings that

Block 37 burned to the ground (1871)

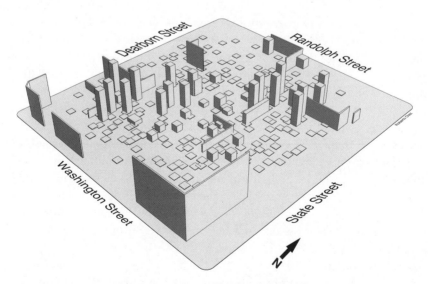

Computer reconstruction of Block 37 after the Great Fire. With lot lines obliterated, businessmen could reimagine the use of downtown space.

Rebuilt Loop after the Great Fire

dramatically multiplied the scale of Chicago's downtown architecture. By adapting themselves to the local business culture, architects, virtually anonymous in most American cities, made a special place for themselves in Chicago. Some, like Daniel Burnham, entered on the financial side into complex real estate deals for buildings they were designing. Perfecting an easily replicable, universally understood container for the city's booming white-collar industries quickly established them as essential players in the land game.

Montgomery Schuyler, America's first great architectural critic, recognized that there was something different about Chicago's unabashed relation to its strikingly commercial architecture. When he came to review the city's new buildings at the end of the nineteenth century, he observed, "[Chicago architects] frankly accepted the conditions imposed by the speculator, because they really are imposed, and there is no getting away from them if one would win and keep the reputation of a 'practical' architect."[27]

Chicago skyscrapers, especially in the supercompressed Loop, were, to a later observer, simply "means to achievement." This old aristocratic prejudice against middle-class business blinded the critic Colin Rowe to the higher possibilities of a clearly utilitarian architecture. In his influential essay, "Chicago Frame," Rowe simply took Schuyler's indictment a step further to convict Chicagoans of what he called "business without inhibition." He missed the irony that commercial architecture in Chicago was the city's highest original art form as a direct result of its speculative impulse, not in spite of it. Rowe's observations, added to Schuyler's, are nevertheless bluntly accurate, although unfortunately moralized: "They [Chicago's original steel-frame buildings] invoked no completely receivable public standards; they stipulated only private gain; and for the taste of the time, which had not yet sufficiently expanded—or contracted—to be able to envisage the *machine* with a poetic bias, they were not so much architecture as they were equipment."[28] Colin Rowe needed only to look a little longer to realize that speculation made visible through architecture *is* the city's "poetic bias." Architecture is, in a city of traders, simply another precious commodity, requiring an efficient market to cash it out. Piers and spandrels cut the meat vertically and horizontally so space could be sold more efficiently from the ground up.

Just as the commodity traders at the Board of Trade use staples like wheat, cattle, and lumber as the vehicle to exchange huge volumes of capital, real estate traders use land aggressively as collateral to raise large amounts of cash. In 1873, at a cost of $150,000, the McCormicks built an office building on Block 37, with a 102-foot frontage on Dearborn and 80 feet on Randolph, a site the manufacturer of agricultural implements had owned since the city's incorporation.[29]

The McCormick Block—the large lot on the northwest corner of Block 37—is an early example of how architects add value to land. Until the Great Fire leveled all the buildings on his eight-thousand-square-foot site, Cyrus McCormick had honored the leases—typically ninety-nine years with an option to renew for another fifty—of small businesses that included a bootery and a small bank. Rather than tie up the land again, the manufacturer hired John Van Osdel to design the biggest building he could. The resulting five-story masonry structure allowed him to move all his office operations away from his new manufacturing plant on the South Branch of the Chicago River. One of the first buildings in the Loop used exclusively for clerical and executive offices, the McCormick Block, fitted out in fine materials, segregated the white-collar administration of business from the gritty making of things in industrial Chicago. The family patriarch, who had begun his life on the prairie scratching out a living with his hands, was

Dearborn Street, Block 37, with the old McCormick property

amused that, bent and weakened by old age, he could effortlessly make a second fortune farming Chicago's downtown land.[30]

After Cyrus McCormick's death in 1884, his heirs asked architect C. J. Warren to design an eleven-story tower to replace their offices. The proposed $600,000 building, steam-heated, electrified, and richly ornamented, represented at least a fourfold rise in value on the land since the McCormicks first rebuilt barely a generation earlier. Even before they began construction, their property dramatically increased in value simply by the family's announcement of Warren's plans. In the end, the Dearborn-Randolph corner proved so valuable that in 1891 Leander McCormick decided not to build anything himself. He kept intact his twenty-year-old office building and agreed to sell, at a stunning profit, the lot directly to the south to Illinois governor John Peter Altgeld. The McCormicks realized that they could get richer by not building and completely avoid risk. A modern skyscraper next to their own more modest offices made their land more valuable with no additional investment.

Altgeld built an imposing structure that he named the Unity, designed by the McCormicks' architect of choice, C. J. Warren. Warren's Unity Building was more than three times the size of the tallest buildings of a generation earlier and five floors higher than a similar tower he had tried to sell the McCormicks. The building cost nearly $1 million, and Altgeld soon went bankrupt when the market changed.[31] These prominent land sales by the city's blue bloods were eagerly handicapped in the press. Horse or land—there was no big difference. According to urban geographer Emrys Jones, "Even in 1880 land inside the Loop was half a million dollars an acre: ten years later it was three and a half million dollars an acre, demanding an ever-increasing intensity of use."[32] A touted rising tide of land values inevitably stimulated other less attractive deals until the market crashed completely in the national economic panic of 1893.[33]

Speculators quickly bought up the other corners to build ever more office space. Back in 1872, the five-story McCarthy Building was put up on the southwest corner, and the five-story Springer Block, the first building demolished in October of 1989, a hypotenuse away on the northeast. Both had basements rented to merchants at a discount. The McCarthy, designed by John Van Osdel, and the Springer by Peter B. Wight, both local architects, were formula solutions to the problem of getting people back to business fast after the fire. By the time they came down, the Springer, renovated by Adler and Sullivan in 1888, and the McCarthy were two of the oldest buildings in Chicago.

Repeated attempts failed to unify the block at the new skyscraper scale. Although the Dearborn Street side offered the best chance, Block 37 never quite made it as a proper business address. The block resisted the singleness of purpose that had established other contemporary skyscrapers. Sandwiched between the entertainment district and City Hall, the block always had two faces, making it a place of transition between the straight and the eccentric—a dizzy sort of indeterminate space that defines great cities as surely as their centers of high culture.

When as late as the forties there were still Jim Crow laws that segregated lunch counters and kept the big hotels white, those unwelcome in the rest of the Loop entertained themselves on Block 37. After urban renewal in the 1950s destroyed traditional shopping districts in black neighborhoods, Hillman's, the only full-service supermarket in the Loop, was where poor people shopped. The store at the time it closed was one of the largest em-

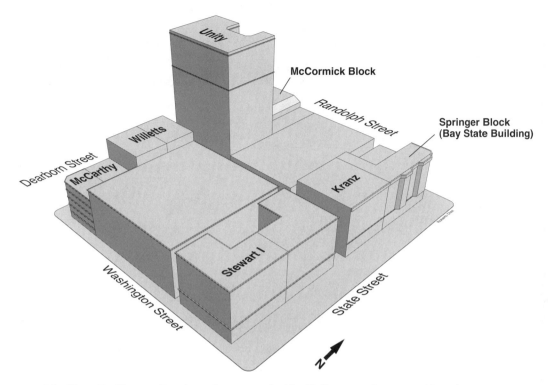

The Unity Building on Dearborn Street was the block's first true skyscraper. Note the McCarthy Building and Springer Block; both figured prominently in the redevelopment efforts of the 1980s.

ployers of blacks in the downtown. But the block was never just a place of work. The east side, where V-E and V-J days were joyously acclaimed, and New Year's Eve was celebrated on the State Street side, between Randolph and Washington. Randolph Street, in the four blocks between State and Wells, was reserved for theaters, lunch counters, all-night newsstands, a pool hall, and novelty stores. The section between State and Dearborn, stripped bare, was until the 1990s a lodestone attracting black teenagers to Block 37. On Easter Sunday, dressed in the pastel-colored gowns and tuxedos they wore to their proms: mating birds in full plumage returning to the spot where their grandparents once paraded.

On Washington Street the food emporium Stop and Shop, a floor up from Hillman's in the basement, was a provincial copy of the food halls at London's Harrods. Stop and Shop was a place you planned for a week to visit. It helped, along with the theaters, Viennese pastry shops, and an old-world coffeehouse on State Street, to give the Loop the feel of a neighbor-

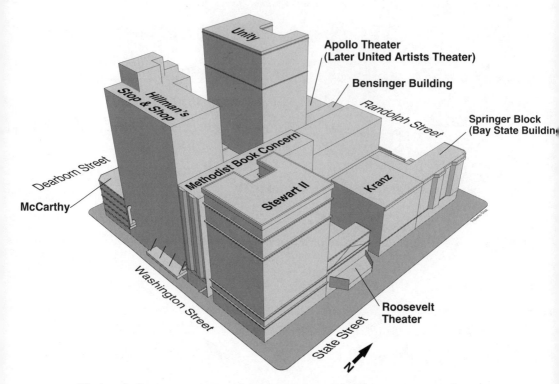

Block 37 built-up to its greatest density, with five tall buildings, in 1930. And so it essentially remained until it was demolished in the winter of 1989–90.

hood. With the exception of Stop and Shop, which limped on almost to the end, these one-of-a-kind businesses with a loyal clientele failed long before the demolition.

Block 37 kept its ragtag character right to the end, remaining an unhomogenized space, never dominated by office warrens, chain stores, or a single class of shopper. There were fewer daily visitors but the place retained its hold. The mad mix of high and low that had always set the block apart from the numbing monotony of the Loop's white-collar respectability persisted despite all efforts at reform. Even the big Unity Building, the block's most distinguished piece of architecture, absorbed the theatrical quality of the neighboring businesses. It became the home to bargain hot lunches in a place called Thrifty 'Thirties, fifty years after the Great Depression. False wood-grained Formica covered all the surfaces, and Depression-era photographs evoked memories of bad times in a clubby atmosphere one step removed from a brown-bag. But this was the first rung on the nine-to-five social ladder, where the lowliest lawyer in the firm or the apprentice salesman could afford, for about three bucks, the status of going out for lunch. After work, Laura Love cut men's hair in an office originally meant for an accountant, on one of the upper floors of the Unity Building. Leaning in just enough as she made her cut, giving a reassuring pat, a brushing of the body, Ms. Love had them lined up all day waiting for a few minutes in her chair. The leaning tower had the odd mix of Rotary International's headquarters and the old speakeasy Mayors Row, where politicians cut deals in the privacy of the tall dark booths. With thick ropes slung over pulleys, gripmen pulled the four elegant elevators to the upper floors. A uniformed operator, with a blue velvet stripe down his gray cadet pants, greeted the lawyers by name and stood "firm and ready" as who he called the "professionals" entered his cab for the bumpy ride up.[34] The Darrow legend brought young radical lawyers to the office space, while downstairs the constant scheming in Mayors Row kept them in business. Federal and state agencies threw a few bucks to patriotic employees when they reported on seditious conversations, overheard in the cabs or common hallways.

During election campaigns the large sign outside Mayors Row exhorted the people to reelect Mayor Daley, instead of displaying its usual list of the day's specials. Fred Winchy, the ancient agent for the building who kept a hundred years of real estate values in his head, used its mixed clientele and theatrical extremes as a special selling point. Every year on St. Patrick's Day bagpipers left the parade route to march through the bar, piping a mournful Irish tune.

In the minds of Chicagoans, Block 37 was always different from that shown on the tourist map of the city. The block didn't make itself felt all at once. Buildings of different sizes, like often-read books replaced randomly on a shelf, recalled collections of experience from the time you were a kid. Layers of memory started from the time your mother took you to the novelty shops or penny-candy stores as your reward for accompanying her on a thunderously boring day of shopping at one of the big State Street department stores. Then there were the Saturday afternoons at the Brunswick bowling alley or waiting as your father had his suit fit at Duru's Custom Tailor; a birthday outing with your friends to a Disney film at the Roosevelt. When you got a little older and could get down there yourself, you watched the men shoot pool with custom ivory-inlaid Rambow and Balabushka sticks on the second floor of a five-story building on Randolph Street. Bensinger's, the Birdland of billiards, where tiny unathletic men as graceful around the green slate-topped tables as Michael Jordan running a three-on-one break with a cigar in his mouth demonstrated Brunswick Corporation's finest

Duru's Custom Tailor in the Unity Building (1980)

equipment. Chicago, the world's largest small city, had a knowable down-town where play was art and good for business:

Later on in life you might have needed the services of one of the few re-maining doctors on the block, somewhere in a back office, away from the street, near the air shaft. Perhaps you required the professional assistance of a cheap lawyer: a divorce, a suspended driver's license, a problem get-ting a building permit. Or your grandmother on a Saturday took the bus downtown, after deciding that she wouldn't throw out her old shoes and needed them redyed. In the Springer Block (sometimes called the Baystate Building), on State Street, they were still manufacturing corsets with real whalebone stays. Your aunt, with thirty of her friends from church, dressed up for an all-expense-paid trip to Randolph Street, where they tested prod-ucts at the Home Arts Guild, a forerunner of today's market research firms. A free lunch, a new lens cap for a camera, buttons for a coat, a new stem for a pipe, that's how the members of a family, each in his or her own way, became acquainted with 37.

There were older memories too, deeper in the past. A great-grandparent who remembered her grandmother going to the Crosby's Opera House or

Springer and Kranz Buildings on State Street (1900)

your great-aunt telling you how after shopping at Field's she took a silver cup and dipped it herself into the polished copper vats at Kranz's, a European-style ice-cream shop with fine Tiffany glass, a family business dating back to the fire. Lots of history crammed into a small space. A rectangular piece of the square mile of the old downtown: manageable, rememberable.

The problem was that when it came time to save the place, it was hard to calculate exactly what it all added up to: all the memories were so different, some so unpleasant. When abortion was still illegal, it was to a block like this that young men led their terrified girlfriends. In a nine-to-five building, tall enough to be celebrated as a skyscraper when it was built, you found a doctor whose address was whispered in the halls back at school.

And there were the movie theaters where the rest of America was imported to the block in first-run movies that you had to see at the United Artists Theater; the last of vaudeville was there too. Across Randolph Street, Stevie Wonder and big Motown revues performed at the Oriental Theater, where Al Jolson once came in the late forties to plug his life story and didn't leave the stage for two hours.[35] But those were the days before the insistent reports of violence, before the universal scorn that made places of entertainment like this off-limits all over America. Now the Oriental has a discount electronics store in the lobby, and the theater is dark, a colony of rats still feasting on popcorn and soft drinks spilled more than a decade earlier. The Roosevelt Theater, on the State Street side of Block 37, was considered so far gone that it escaped the indignity of the scavengers.

The Roosevelt, a once-grand first-run movie house with a dignified Greek Revival facade befitting a bank, was consigned in the end to showing karate films and ghetto fantasies. *Good Guys Wear Black* was the classic playing that day in the summer of 1978 when the city began closing off State Street to cars. The State Street Mall widened the sidewalks and limited access to pedestrians and buses. With this multimillion-dollar plan, Mayor Bilandic hoped to destigmatize what remained of the blighted retail and entertainment districts of the city, but the effort proved wrongheaded. Instead of walling off the "pathological" elements, the mall sealed them in. People felt less safe. One madman in a crowd of a hundred is an entertainer; one in ten is a threat to people going about their business.

Middle-class blacks as well as apprehensive white people stayed away from the Loop. The Roosevelt Theater was the first significant building in the redevelopment area to be voluntarily demolished in the late 1970s and replaced by a taxpayer. It was as if all at once the whole virulent mix of racial fears and urban paranoia of the 1960s had coalesced around this one tight space, overwhelming its last defenses.

Block 37 and blocks like it—sometimes a small city would have only one—was the place where secret and common memories piled up. A Grand Canyon of complex associations, always being added to as space was leased and subleased. From plastic vomit to feature films, jazz and rock and roll, the block over the years offered an archaeology of commerce from elegant to spartan, caviar to three-card monte games. Without any of the buildings, it's hard for people to recall what was there. Few records remain of the block's exuberant life, few images.

Lacking any single example of great architecture, the block was rarely photographed. Generic downtown Chicago, it was easily confused with other places in the Loop. So Block 37 wasn't really missed until people returned, sometimes after long absences, to get a leaky pen fixed or a knife sharpened and found the place gone. Surprised and disoriented, they walked around for a while not knowing quite where they were, because no other block had resisted change so successfully. Except for the taxpayers along State Street, nothing new had gone up on the block since 1930. Odd

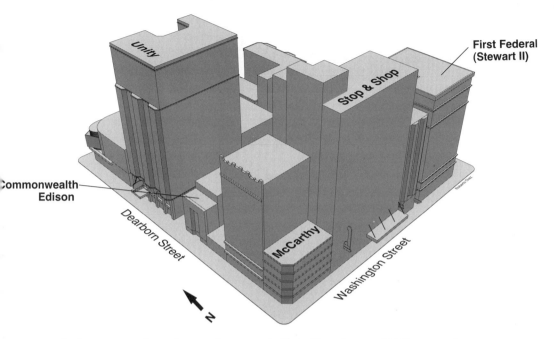

Block 37 nearing the end. Note the New World Building (home of BPI) next to the McCarthy and the United Artists Theater, at the corner of Dearborn and Randolph.

cosmopolitan service businesses—violin makers and dealers in prosthetics—were sprinkled in among the psychic readers and the tailors, barely surviving with the unintended subsidy of low rent.[36] In this way, the block, from head to toe, somehow mediated spatially between the childish lures of whoopee cushions, handshake buzzers, comic books, fart bladders for a teacher's chair, and its various adult offerings, accessible in degrees, from an eight-ball hustle to a "quickie" at lunchtime.

Block 37's persistent defense, up until its last days, was its ugliness. Mosley's Bras and Girdles still had a complete assortment of garter belts in a pantyhose age, its boxes of underwear tumbling into the aisle. At one time or another, Lucy's Restaurant and Finer Amusements, Flo's, the Hollywood Restaurant, De Metz's Candy, Chicago Latin Quarter Vaudvil [sic] Lounge, Rice's Tap and Grill, Morrow's Nut Shop, Pepper's Sandwich, Ace's Coins and Stamps, all had concessions on the block. The block was a carnival, a permanent tent show. Molasses from the caramel-corn joints stuck in the air, sweetening the methane and diesel exhaust.

The cheap rents and tumbling land values also provided a haven for the very people the city held morally responsible for the downtown's decline. Particularly irksome to Daley was a group called BPI (Business and Pro-

fessional People for the Public Interest), which holed up in the New World
at 109 North Dearborn. The building had gotten its name from a Catholic
newspaper that had leased space there for years.

An eccentric businessman and political idealist, Gordon Sherman had,
in 1968, formed BPI as a direct result of what he had seen of the police rioting in the streets during the Democratic National Convention. In 1969,
the organization led a successful "Don't Do It in the Lake" campaign
against Daley's proposed third airport in Lake Michigan, later exposed a
classic CHA contract scam, and fought Commonwealth Edison, its neighbor on Block 37, all from its crowded offices on the thirteenth floor of the
New World. The current mayor's father could not have more vehemently
hated the thin building had it contained Lenin's Tomb.[37]

Directly to the New World's north, the Mayflower Coffee Shop on Dearborn Street was a classic one-arm joint where a busy nine-to-fiver could
grab a sweet roll and a hot cup of coffee and read a newspaper at a chair
fixed with a handy shelf, like a kid's writing desk. Hot fat from the con-
veyor-belted doughnut machine misted the Mayflower's windows, and
brown globs of tallow stuck to the sills.

Later the Mayflower was replaced by U.S. Shoe, with its school of taxi-
dermed game fish mounted on the walls. Inspirational sayings—jock odes
on fishing—were on plaques for customers to ponder as they sat in one of
the chrome chairs bolted to the platform, one high step off the sticky
linoleum floor. You wondered if you'd "rather be fishing . . ." as a courtly
man crouched at your wing tips, sprung tightly in a little ball, shuffling two
brushes and snapping a finishing cloth. This was only one old-fashioned
male ritual, like a Saturday shave at a neighborhood barber shop, that had
stubbornly resisted change. U.S. Shoe was a strange mixture of jive talking
and Victorian reticence, where the shiners offered tips on the races as you
sat, waiting for your shoes to be repaired, in a wooden booth with modesty
panels hiding your stocking feet. Criminal lawyers arguing a case would go
to the valet shop in the back to have their pants pressed during the court
lunch break.

The preservationists forced people to pay some attention to all that
would be lost if the buildings came down. But no appeal to nostalgia was
going to save the block. Sooted walls and entrances stinking of urine and
swamp gas overwhelmed all memory. And in the end, the preservationists
missed the point too. Used to saving one-of-a-kind masterpieces, they
made a desperate stand to preserve one example of nineteenth-century architecture on the site, the last of a once-common breed, the McCarthy
Building. Crowned with a highway-sized billboard, rusting ductwork
crawling across its facade like ivy, the building, a de-designated monument,

was a hard sell in any case: to rewrite architectural history to include a building that no one had ever paid much attention to when there was one like it on almost every corner of the Loop.

The block was only worth saving at death's door, not for its uniqueness, but for its former typicality: a critical piece of the once-dime-a-dozen American downtown. A tough sell. Only after the entire four-block perimeter was trussed with scaffolding and awaiting execution in its last hours could it be fully imagined. A dodo whose mates were already extinct, the block was finally, unarguably unique.

The brief public agitation to preserve the McCarthy Building was one sentimental interlude in a modern history that exclusively contained plans to destroy the block. A contract to demolish and resell was the commitment Richard M. Daley inherited, thirty years after his father first had it targeted. The block's demolition was one of the few goals that had eluded his old man. Thirteen years after his death, it would be the son's success— a wicked gift from the grave.

There were signs that the young Daley might not have such an easy go of it. The job-lotters and off-price schlockateers were now the established businesses. The Chamber of Commerce and Greater State Street Council didn't sanction them. Yet, in a decade that had seen Sears, Montgomery Ward, and Goldblatt's, among other State Street retailing giants, fail, the catbirds were doing all right. Premature, ill formed, colicky, nonetheless the economic opportunists were there as increasingly the more respectable operations evacuated the downtown. Carson's and Peacock's were bankrupt, Field's was sold to out-of-towners, and the Montgomery Ward site had already been flattened for a 1-million-square-foot-plus tower. In this environment of catastrophic business failures and big plans deferred, the seat-of-the-pants retailers looked like Potter Palmers. But even their days were numbered, as storefront rents downtown escalated from the ten-to-twenty-dollars-per-square-foot range to twenty-five to seventy dollars per square foot during one five-year period when the North Loop Redevelopment Project was first openly discussed. At a time when inflation rose 53 percent, rents rose more than 100 percent.[38]

One of the most persistent catbirds, Leonard Begun, had already camped out on the ground floor of 16–30 West Washington Street, where elegant Stop and Shop had run its business behind the large theater marquee. Two years after Larry Levy bought Hillman's, Inc., from the Loeb and Stern families, the food company was facing bankruptcy. He returned the business to the Sterns, who wanted to have one last go at running it. By

1988, formally bankrupt, they moved out, and their building was left derelict. Now in place of beluga caviar and plover eggs were Begun's five-dollar dresses on plastic hangers, bins of pantyhose, designer imitations, silk ties, underwear, and patent-leather shoes. This in a building where Max Adler, vice-president and director of Sears, Roebuck and Company, once had a wood-paneled office on the tenth floor, where he practiced on a Stradivarius violin and had fresh food and delicacies delivered on a silver tray by the building engineer from the catering operations downstairs.

Socks pinned to the wall obscured the trompe l'oeil detailing in the old food hall. Plastering "Moving Out" signs on the windows, Begun had re-named Stop and Shop the Designers Mart and strung an advertising ban-ner from the marquee. It quickly became everything the old store wasn't, crowded with bustling customers for the first time in a decade. But Leonard Begun knew that the party would be over on October 31, 1989, the day the demolition of Block 37 was to begin. Knowing the end was near, he didn't bother paying a dime of rent to his new landlord, FJV.

This was no ordinary challenge. He appealed his eviction to the First Ward alderman, the city council, anyone who would listen. The peripatetic retailer—he had already negotiated a lease two blocks over at 170 West Washington—was at the height of his powers when most embattled. Begun improvised this public appeal only after FJV had bullied him. A master of corporate aliases and CEO of fictitious companies, he proposed that the developers allow Designers Mart, aka Sam's Apparel Mart and Mark Malone Fashions, to stay rent free until the demolition commenced. This agreement was only a technicality, since he hadn't paid rent in almost a year. Still, Begun gallantly promised that if the developers accepted his proposition and gave him $100,000 in cash for all the inconvenience, he'd be off the block in two weeks.

It's easy to see why he wanted to stay. Leonard Begun did two hundred dollars a square foot of no-frills retailing at the same time Marshall Field's was throwing away $120 million in an elegant renovation of its flagship store, trying in vain to come close to his profit margin. Go figure it. Begun's fa-vorite shoppers were the ones who bought most of an outfit retail at Field's and finished it off brand in his shop on the crappy side of State Street. As far as he was concerned all the pomp of upscale retail was a waste of money. Location was everything. Begun boasted, "Everyone gets treated the same whether she's the Queen of Sheba or a hard-working girl."[39]

When the developers rejected Begun's "reasonable" deal, he simply reinvented himself, impersonated a radical man of the people, contacted Operation PUSH to tell them he was protecting minority jobs, and holed up at 16 West Washington like a political prisoner on a hunger strike.[40] Pro-tected by rented guard dogs, he barricaded himself in the store and refused

Designers Mart, relocated farther west on Washington
Street after 1989 eviction

to leave under any circumstances. After police carried him away, he'd just
break into the store again the next day. "We sell cheap and tell the truth.
It's a free country, and I can run this store any way I want," Begun declared.
It was just like war. "We're in a price war with Marshall Field's and Carson's. We were winning. They got jealous. So we have to move. What else
can I tell you? This business needs excitement. That's what happened to
Sears . . . no excitement. Now they're gonna build an office building here?
That's excitement?" The Greater State Street Council took the developers'
side, referred to Begun's store as a "parasite on the business community,"
and welcomed the wreckers.

Overall, the strain proved too much even for Leonard Begun, who died
early the next year at age sixty. His son Marc took over the business, resist-
ing the inevitable lawsuits from FJV, proclaiming that his family was pen-

niless, and continuing to fight for the little guy. "There's ways to stall them," says Marc Begun, "There's always ways."[41]

After the formal demolition ceremonies were completed in November 1989, it took another six months before the last trace of habitation was removed. For nearly half a year, National Wrecking's one-hundred-ton derrick, *Big Mama,* loomed over the site. A three-ton ball crashed through the roof of the biggest buildings, and section after section of once-whole structures were cracked into identical twenty-by-forty-foot chunks. Working methodically, *Big Mama* took about a half hour to extract each messy piece. On the ground, men in dirty-beige overalls, moving slowly under the weight of their steel welding hoods, followed a large claw-scooped tractor as it moved the fallen rubble to the side. The workers cut and cleaned the scrap with acetylene torches, organizing their harvest into piles. Steel beams and sheet iron, fit for recycling, were hauled off first; brick and other masonry were used later as backfill in the old basements to help raise the site back to grade. But before a new skin of dirt and powdered rubble was again drawn taut over the ground, there was a last chance to see down deep. With the walls removed, the floors heaved, the basement of the Springer Block on the northeast corner of the block was like a cracked safe: a vault from the past, exposing briefly to the light those wood foundations from the first settlements and the stacked rubble foundation of a later building, still scorched black from the day the unprotected upper floors vaporized in the convection heat on October 8, 1871.

Behind the barricades in the scaffolded towers a small colony of the homeless lived out the Unity Building's last days. Evacuated of its lawyers, politicians, and Rotarians, the Unity became a home for junkies and drifters who parked their shopping carts, overflowing with plastic-bagged loot, in the silver-plated elevator cabs. Others ventured alone to the upper floors, where politicians once rented cheap space for campaign headquarters; one of the bigger suites was still piled with Harold Washington literature. Water and gas service to the building had long been shut off.

At night the homeless huddled together on the Unity's ground floor, where the vestibule walls were ornamented in four kinds of imported marble. Behind an ornate glass-and-bronze door there was a small rotunda where the kids smoked crack; the old-timers sat in the dark at the long bar of the deserted Mayors Row restaurant, sipping Ripple from cracked crystal cognac snifters and watching the rats build a nest in the old piano.

United Artists Theater awaits demolition (1989)

Demolition of Block 37 (1989–90)

Where lawyers, aldermen, and judges once traded secrets and passed money, most of the joint's current regulars just sacked out, sleeping papoosed in the high booths, stealing a little warmth and privacy.

The Unity was eventually rid of its accidental tenants after a mysterious fire on January 18, 1990, accelerated the demolition. National Wrecking billed the city nearly $500,000 for the demolition and retained the right to sell the valuable scrap. The block, more than once, had been officially declared worthless when it was whole. But Humpty-Dumptied, sorted and shipped, the ephemera of Block 37 still fetched a good price. Select examples of Art Deco ornament, detachable chunks from the terra-cotta facades, were dusted, cleaned, and sold one by one at auction. These suddenly valuable "artifacts" or "architectural fragments" are now scattered all over the country. A conversation piece placed strategically in a converted loft or left at poolside, a handy thing on which to drape a wet towel.

Wood was burned in oil drums during that first winter after the block was leveled. The windblown flames gave the blasted place a garish red glow. It was vacant once again, more than one hundred years after the Great Fire had, in less than an hour, reduced the teeming block to ash. First accidentally, by an act of nature, this time willfully, land where the Potawatomis once camped was made uninhabitable. Barren and dusty, the block this time was purposely, violently removed from the built-up grid, culled out in preparation for "immediate" improvement.

So after nearly two decades of delay, the demolition that was meant to end the stalemate between "legitimate" businesses and the poachers blamed for State Street's ruinous drift proved a disaster. National Wrecking had certainly changed the look of the place from an anarchic zone of commerce to a fenced-in wasteland. From unwanted activity to none, the block is dead.

Instead of instantly reviving the center of the old city—fattening the tax base and enriching real estate investors—the wholesale bulldozing of Block 37 has left a permanent wound at the heart of the city. Consistently pursuing, through several administrations, the fantasy of a single-class affluent downtown, Chicago had little to show for its efforts: only an art gallery for city schoolchildren during the summer, a skating rink in winter, are now all there is to show for volumes of government plans and stacks of elegant architectural renderings. Private developers and the city are already out a combined $100 million with little hope of ever recouping a fraction of their losses.

Something had obviously gone terribly wrong. What had looked like a

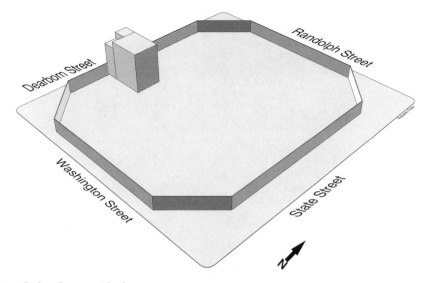

Purified and empty Block 37

billion-dollar sure thing in 1981, when Larry Levy grabbed the first building on the block, had eluded the developers, as it had every other private
and public improver before them. In the ten years since they had fixed
their ambitions to reconstruct the whole block, Chicago had become seriously overbuilt. As six consecutive mayors struggled to get the redevelopment project under way, nearly 25 million square feet of new downtown
office space came on line (more than one-third more Class A space than ex-
isted in 1980). Without the help of any city subsidies other than the usual
fat zoning bonuses, FJV's competitors bought land and built quickly. Their
towers on Wacker Drive and LaSalle Street were already open for business
before the barricades were even up on Block 37. This increased competition for a shrinking corporate population made preleasing of more than 2.2
million square feet nearly impossible.[42]

Men as wealthy as the general partners of FJV didn't get rich watching
others build.[43] Standing still, like a cab stalled in traffic, was costing them
plenty. On the twentieth floor of the Chicago Title Building, the developers opened a leasing office that featured a bird's-eye view of the condemned block and a walk-around scale model of the future development.
The office was opened in the last optimistic days of the boom when this
vivid contrast between before and after—the past framed in a window, the
future in plastic—was thought to be all a "space manager" needed to see
before signing his firm up for expensive new digs. Finally ready to get going
after the preservation suits were settled, the developers went ahead and
borrowed $64 million from First Chicago for expenses, exclusive of the

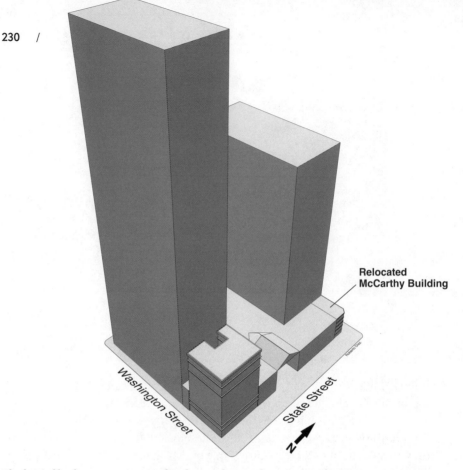

Block 37 if built-out, using one of Helmut Jahn's early massing schemes

hundreds of millions they would require later for construction. This was just for starters—no more than 10 percent of what eventually would be required for the colossal project when all three stages were under way. FJV's own confidential pro formas, or most optimistic financial projections circulated internally and to favored investors, had budgeted $80 to $100 million for retail, $307 million for Tower I, and $160 million for the smaller Tower II. Even using other people's money was a costly business when holding land on which you could not build. Interest rates were near 10 percent when the redevelopment agreement was signed September 23, 1987, and property taxes were $1 million a year; it was costing FJV as much as $7 million annually just to do nothing.

But the developers were in too deep. When the long-anticipated demolition finally arrived in the fall of 1989, they had already run out of time. But

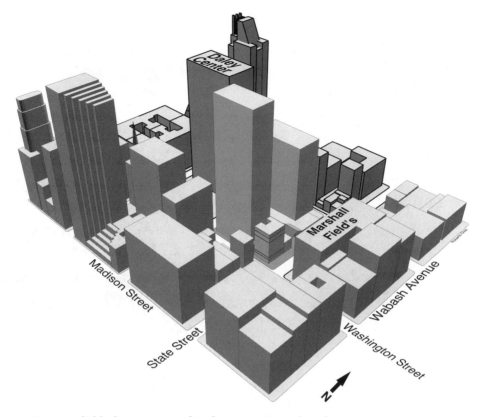

An "improved" block superimposed in the current Loop (1995)

even as the deal began to sour, they continued gamely, trying not to indicate publicly their own despair. There is a press photograph of the three representatives of FJV posed in front of the barricaded block. Bundled against the cold and gamely smiling for the camera, they did not fail to see the absurdity of their situation. Here were three brilliant businessmen who along with the city were the big losers in a two-decade feeding frenzy. With all the costly condemnations, delays, and assorted predevelopment costs, the block had been bid up to a level where no one could profitably build. Asked later what they were really thinking, one replied, "Lined up, with our backs to the buildings, it felt just like an execution."

Looking back at the never-to-be-built architecture on Block 37 evokes the same sort of melancholy occasioned by all the other failed city plans. Together, they are the accumulated records of a serious misuse of public

Stuart Nathan, Michael Tobin, Lawrence Levy, in front of Block 37 (1989)

power and the hubris of downtown land lords. An empty three acres—a lifeless prairie at the heart of the city—is the result of this monumental vanity.

Between 1983 and 1989, Helmut Jahn's inventive schemes changed from bright-colored and rounded towers to more conservative rectilinear architecture. His plans consistently included a great atrium space modeled on the glassed-in crossing of streets in Milan, linking the Duomo to La Scala. The architect studied German cathedrals and how they shaped civic space to find a grand enough scale for his six-story mall. At ground level, the mall was conceived to be no less than a grand indoor avenue, a regulated, climate-controlled, active city street. Passing from east to west wasn't quite the sublime path from the world of God to the high altar of art that it was in Milan, but Jahn's planning was intended to connect Chicago's historic commercial corridor on State Street to the fine open space in front of the Civic Center. In this way, he hoped to revive the city's original east–west axis—from the lake to the frontier—in eclipse since the late nineteenth century.

The architect's Block 37 scheme envisioned a continuous natural movement from the Clark Street entrance of City Hall to the main entrance of Marshall Field's. The scale was monumental and urban. Jahn's scheme for

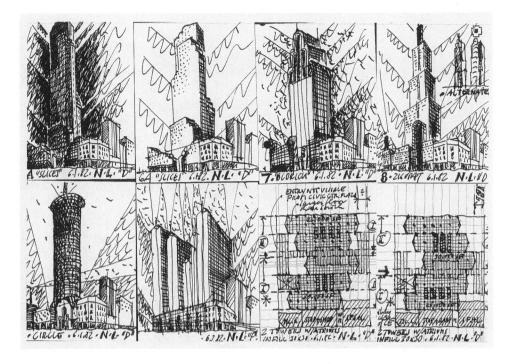

Helmut Jahn's freehand
schemes for an improved
Block 37

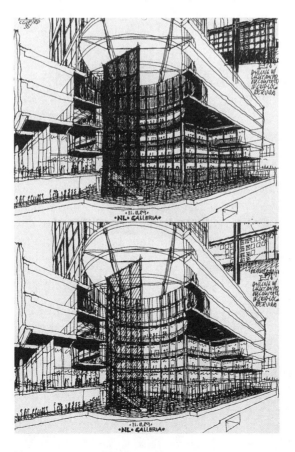

Block 37 had some architectural elements that, at least, tried to address the failing social structure of the Loop.

By opening Dearborn to State on the path of Court House Place, the old alley splitting the block, and dedicating the project's north tower for use as a municipal building, the developers had taken the final step in usurping the public responsibility for city planning. A generation-long trend from Daley (the first), who had supreme power over the Loop, to his son, who barely had enough authority to effect the demolition of a single block, had resulted in the end of planning as a key civic function.

By late 1989, after six years of FJV's failure to prelease one square foot of the block, Jahn had already tried everything to make the project sell. He had gotten rid of the blue skin and curving forms that were a consistent feature of the office towers since the RFP. No one had said it to his face, but blue reminded the conservative business community of the State of Illinois Center down the street, still being excoriated in the press for its cost overruns. "Not sufficiently dignified," the brokers were told; the blue panels reminded these expensive lawyers, FJV's largest pool of prospective tenants, of the rambling high schools they had once attended out in the burbs. A key member of the project team tried to explain the problem: "It had curves; it had the appearance of a lot of glass even though there was a fair amount of stone on the building; but it was a bluish building, and people just weren't responding to it." The market had determined that the architecture was "funny looking."

By the developers' own admission, Jahn's building was not one people could easily understand. This was a big problem at a time when office space was abundant and tenants were scarce. With taxes averaging around ten dollars a square foot, and maintenance another ten, FJV needed to charge a minimum of twenty-six dollars a foot in rent to make the project barely work economically. Everything depended on a popular design. So even with their cheap three acres of land, they had little room to negotiate on price in an overbuilt market. If lawyers and accountants hated blue, Jahn would have to make the skin another color. He tried red, ironed out the curves, made the building straighter.

Principally, Jahn refined the large south tower, limiting the circular elements to the end facing Dearborn, and only then on the higher floors. There was more granite and less metal, red rather than blue—rectilinear forms that would not have been out of place in the expanding office zone along the South Branch of the river, where most of the professionals were migrating.

The design process deteriorated to the point where this world-acclaimed architect was making wild alterations as hurriedly as an agreeable tailor. Jahn made the towers a little smaller, bringing them both down to street level with two separate entrances. Each was articulated differently to distinguish clearly between office and government buildings. Still dreaming that the government would find some way to help bail out the project in the end, he made sure the north tower could accommodate the large space needs of the Cook County courts and toned down the State Street entrance to the mall.

Two big law firms said they liked the improvements in version five and appeared ready to sign on. But they alone were not enough to meet the 50 percent prelease requirement insisted on by Bluhm and Weissbourd. FJV still required a large anchor tenant. At about the same time, the LaSalle Bank said it might be interested in taking a few hundred thousand feet along with a large banking floor at ground level. But these deals fell through during the delays over the McCarthy Building and the city's inability to finish the condemnation process. No sensible businessman would agree to commit his company to pay hundreds of millions over the life of a lease when neither the developer nor the city could assure him that anything would ever be built. Soon the banks and law firms signed expensive leases in other private developments or on the North Loop redevelopment blocks no longer affected by the vagaries of the Department of Planning.

Chicago Title delivered the final blow. The company was shopping for 300,000 square feet and didn't want to move far from its old headquarters across the street from City Hall. Larry Levy had been a company director since the early eighties; his pal Michael Silver was the title company's primary real estate consultant. So the developers had good reason to believe that CT&T might look kindly to taking over a third of their large south tower. Signing up the title company could have saved the whole project at the last minute. But it wasn't to be.

After Chicago Title had signed a deal with another North Loop developer, a senior vice-president confided that he was distrustful of "high flyers" and "quick dealers." These guys "live in a world we don't live in." He added, "JMB people make us nervous. Real estate deals work when you feel comfortable." He neglected to say that Silver, one of the city's most aggressive tenant representatives, wanted a leasing commitment on Block 37 that was so unprofitable for FJV that Nathan had decided to queer the deal. As he calculated, it was better not to build anything than to subsidize a losing proposition deep into the millennium. Chicago Title headquarters is now on Block 35, the site of the old Greyhound Bus Terminal. Its 1-million-square-foot tower has been insolvent from the day it opened.

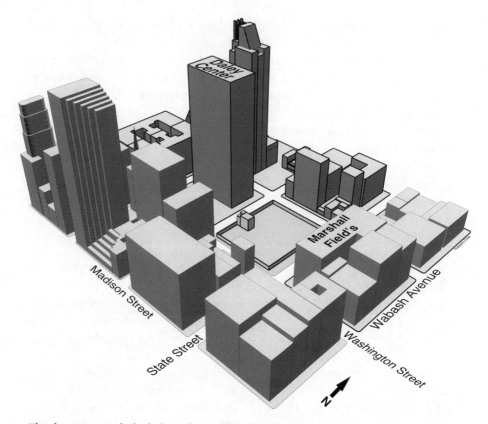

The downtown with the hole in the middle

And then it was *all* over. On December 29, 1989, when FJV belatedly wrote the city a check for $12,583,430 to close the deal, their trophy project now looked to them as inhospitable as the moon. The conveyance of title was originally to take place on February 1, 1988; the twenty-two-month lag cost the venture $7.8 million in interest payments alone.[44] This was in addition to the $10 million they were already out for the pieces they had purchased themselves, and to the $9 million in wasted architectural, engineering, and legal fees. The losses would add up to close to $50 million on a block that they once thought might be worth a billion.

The city had intemperately lured private developers to Block 37 and then marooned them. The city's delays had made them completely miss the market. Then on February 12, 1990, the United States comptroller of the currency issued a warning to the nation's bank presidents that they could be holding large nonperforming real estate loans. He claimed that the government had uncovered "fundamental deficiencies and negative trends" that might have led some banks to compromise accepted lending practices simply "to increase volume and achieve higher levels of interest and fee income."[45] The negative reaction was immediate and dramatic. Within a few months, trillions invested in real estate nationally had deflated by 20 percent to 50 percent.

From the day immediately following the comptroller's decision—when financial institutions abruptly stopped lending money for any commercial real estate—to the present moment, the last chapter of Manifest Destiny was written. Chicago banks alone have written off billions in nonperforming loans. The intricacies of the biggest real estate bust in history can all be understood in microcosm on Block 37—a $100 million hole in the ground, to this day a sad orphan of progress, a memorial to great expectations gone awry.

Demolition complete (1990)

VI FAULTY TOWERS

The ultimate failure of Block 37 was part of a wider international credit crunch in the 1990s that has made the modern office tower extinct. At the start of the decade, office buildings represented 38 percent of all nonresidential real estate and 11 percent of the nation's total stock of property. With a combined worth of $1 trillion, office buildings at the height of the boom equaled nearly 13 percent of the gross national product and a third of the national debt. In less than a decade, however, more office space was constructed in America than in the previous two hundred years combined. A real estate consultant described the change in attitudes that fed the boom: "Before the 1980s, real estate was a residual user of capital; it got what was left over. By the 1980s, real estate had been legitimized as an investment and brought capital from other investments."[1] An analyst for Salomon Brothers added incredulously, "People continued building because there was still a demand to lend on the assets. It was a frenzy—the link between vacancy rates and capital markets disappeared."[2]

Chicago had its own problems with overbuilding. In 1990, 21.65 percent of 122 million square feet of office space was vacant, and the average net rent—exclusive of taxes—in the Loop was $12.50 per square foot, inadequate to service the debt and pay expenses. If 22 million square feet of owner-occupied space was subtracted, the situation was even worse. By 1993, 26 percent of the city's two-hundred-plus office buildings were vacant.[3]

After doing nothing for more than a decade, the panicked regulators belatedly recognized what was obvious all along to every player of the great game. But rather than allow the market to settle—trade down or "clear"—

they abruptly forced the banks to raise cash to cover the shortfall between realistic market value and the developers' rosy projections. Unfortunately, the intoxicated bankers, pension managers, and insurance companies had lent money (sometimes at as much as 115 percent of the project) on these baseless pro formas and without any independent calculations of their own. This instant deflation caught huge money-center banks such as Chemical and Chase Manhattan at a time they had 35 percent of their domestic loans in real estate. Citicorp had 47 percent. One already shaky institution, the Bank of New England, grown fat on paper with speculative loans to developers, shrank in less than a week from a $30 billion to a $20 billion bank before it went out of business.

Scarcity of credit, office vacancies consistently above the threshold 20 percent level, and 2.8 billion new square feet coming on line nationally since 1983 prolonged the crash. And in Chicago, even as late as 1992, new space continued flooding the market. Because of a two- to three-year construction lag, developers and lenders watched in horror as skyscrapers planned in the last years of the boom—$3.4 billion was committed to projects in 1989 alone—were built in the darkest days of the crash. Chicago has a current glut of at least 25 million square feet of Class A office space with an absorption rate of less than 3 million feet a year.[4] Added to the mess was Sears, Roebuck and Company's decision to move its merchandise group to the suburbs—vacating 1.8 million square feet in the Sears Tower, the equivalent of two new skyscrapers.

The Sears action is only the largest example of rental roulette, or monkey-move-up, as brokers call it, that has halved the average "effective rent" in the city from a published rate of twenty-eight dollars to fourteen dollars a foot. Empty new buildings have only filled up at the expense of older towers in a viciously competitive rental market. Given annual property taxes at nearly ten dollars a foot and other expensive concessions from owners meant simply to fill their buildings, there is not a single truly solvent skyscraper—with a healthy cash flow from rent—in an American downtown. It is not unusual for a brand-new building, foreclosed upon and returned to the lender, to be running 30 percent in the red. A $100 million skyscraper in Chicago, completed in 1993 and less than 10 percent occupied, was recently sold for a reported $30 million. Only at a three-to-one discount can the new owner afford to pay taxes, lure tenants, and make a modest profit. The bank that provided the primary financing for the development is now rid of the property, after booking tens of millions in losses.

But the crash was worse for developers, concerned for their reputations or still wishing to remain in business. As their balloon payments—the principal of short-term low-interest loans—negotiated in the late eighties come due in the next few years, developers will continue to turn over the keys to their mortgage and equity partners. Even after other industries have recovered, the 1990 crash will continue for commercial real estate.

Yet, the real victim of a decade's excess has attracted little notice. Soon this disinvestment will have a catastrophic effect on cities still blithely taxing against inflated appraised values, last calculated in the boom. Inevitably, private landlords will ask for tax relief on their prime downtown property as it continues to leak money through the shortfall between declining rent and escalating expenses such as taxes and debt service—the combination of interest payments and transactional fees. In addition to the staggering social problems of education, welfare, and crime, the American city is facing a general economic collapse when the heart of its tax base—the office buildings in its central business district—fails.

Currently in the awkward position of having to operate buildings the size of small cities, lenders might one day simply decide to walk away rather than continue to run them at a loss. This cyclical problem with downtown real estate comes at an unfortunate time, when corporations, because of communication advancements and downsizing, have less need to centralize their operations in dense city environments.

The very real spectacle of boarded-up 1-million-square-foot buildings could well be in our future. Forced to tax their most valuable property as raw land—an average of 10 percent of current rates—cities will go bankrupt. Then everyone will feel the nightmarish consequences—represented architecturally in massive plywooded towers—of a wild real estate boom gone bust. The first wave that evacuated the residential middle class will be followed by a second wave of business, en masse, leaving the central city.

Viewed within its larger context, vacant Block 37 suggests one version of the future. Understanding the forces that created a single, unintended empty place in the middle of one of the world's densest downtowns might forestall the horror of an essentially abandoned center, an urban museum visited only tentatively for its cultural institutions and inimitable historical flavor. As the old city fills up with a dispossessed underclass, the achieving side of the bell curve urbanizes the formerly pastoral near-in collar suburbs and the newly created infrastructure nodes (highways, regional malls, and airports) out on the edge.[5] The city as it has been celebrated for most of human history is in danger of extinction.

A once-confident government that had consciously expanded its powers to reach into the formerly exclusive domain of private property—to fatten its

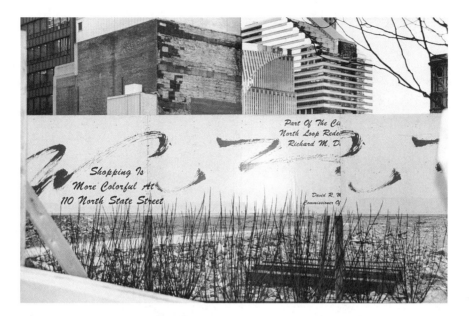

Construction fence after demolition (1990)

tax base and create a misguided utopia of a single-class, prosperous downtown—lost its gamble. The thirty-year war of diverting private capital for
public purpose was lost, with both sides routed in the end. Unthinkingly in
league with the most antisocial tendencies of private capital, municipal
power was employed at an unprecedented scale. The immediate result was
to fracture the fragile economy in place and permanently disrupt an evolu-
tionary process of economic change that has kept the city alive for most of
its history: the downtown was irrationally destroyed.

Ironically, in retrospect, the process of "blighting" that alarmed Daley
(the first) was, in fact, the key to the city's economic salvation. Down zoning is now *planned,* albeit in a more pristine form, for the rest of State
Street. Absent of any hope of attracting rich office tenants to the area, the
city currently welcomes national discount stores even to the formerly exclusive side of State Street. Right alongside where Peacock's, now out of
business, sold Rolexes and pearls, T. J. Maxx and Filene's Basement do big
business.

The sad lesson of Block 37 is that neither the private nor the public sector could find a way to lead the process of redevelopment. Urban renewal
was always in reality a messy business of competing interests that never actually had much to do with all the impassioned rhetoric and beautiful plans.
From the start, Block 37 was simply a zone of opportunity for any party en-

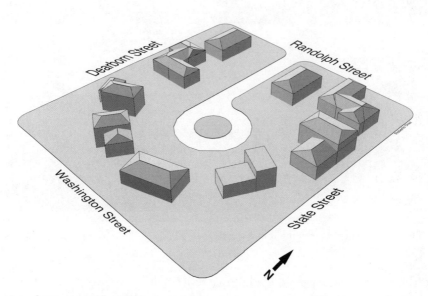

A modest proposal for Block 37. Consider the consequences of the continued suburbanization of the downtown.

amored of the rare chance to control the center of town. Those who still naively think of politics in conspiratorial terms need only review this extraordinary record of high improvisation and managed ambiguity. Almost anyone with sufficient ambition, inside or out of public life, could play at this oddly democratic form of collusion. Access to information and capital, real or faked, is really all it took.

Here on only three acres, private fortunes were made and lost, public reputations risked and squandered. Winners got in early and closed out their positions fast. A public purpose was never served. The speculators and land pirates were rewarded, and the bona fide developers continue to be punished. Larry Levy, who cashed out millions when FJV bought out his interests in the block, has gone on to other things, while his partner in the joint venture remains bogged down in a project from which it will never recoup its investment. The block would have to be worth $1 billion again before the combined public and private money in the project could be successfully amortized in rent.

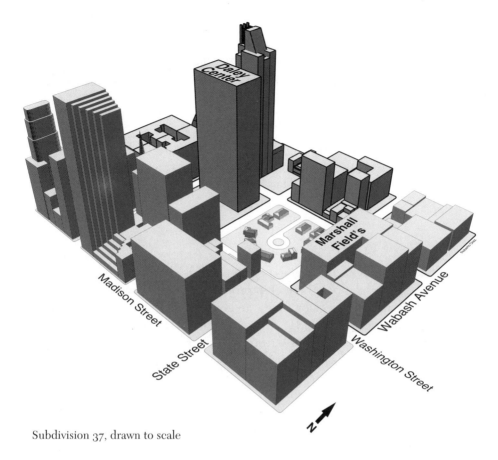

Subdivision 37, drawn to scale

Most of the key players on the public side of the North Loop debacle no longer have positions in government. Miles Berger made out the best, confining himself exclusively at Heitman (an international financial services firm) to the money side of real estate, although he continues to be in demand as a consultant and lecturer on planning issues and recently published an optimistic book on the history of development in Chicago. Jack Guthman, long-term head of the Zoning Board of Appeals, is now in private practice, specializing in regulatory matters. Now that speculative skyscraper development is over for the moment, he has employed his skills in helping casino interests find a way to bring gambling to the city. He understands better than most that a $2 billion downtown gambling complex is just a series of skyscrapers laid on their side.

Elizabeth Hollander is president of the Urban Assistance Program at DePaul University, and most of her former department's professional staff has migrated to private industry. David Mosena, commissioner of planning under Daley (the second) and later chief of staff, is currently head of the Department of Aviation. Former commissioners Lewis Hill and the late Martin Murphy became consultants to the development industry.

Not a single individual with the expertise, political clout, or institutional memory to move urban renewal projects forward is still working for the city. All drifted away, retired out of town, or are dead. The North Loop that began as the crowning glory of civic power under Richard J. Daley is now a beggar, limping along to piecemeal completion in a way that would make the old Boss sick. In an age in which Jane Byrne stars in automobile commercials and Mario Cuomo advertises snack chips, the very idea of public service has been held up to ridicule.

No one involved in the city's last planning fiasco has been immune to failure. The component companies of FJV have all had serious trouble. From its extensive inventory of blue-chip properties—once totaling around $30 billion in real estate, pension funds, and trusts—JMB has steadily been returning buildings to its lenders. By the summer of 1992, its creditors had already realized upon their interest, or foreclosed, on twenty-five properties, forcing the company to liquidate $2.6 billion in assets and write off, as a complete loss, $424 million invested in the Randsworth Trust—a cooperative venture in the formerly lucrative London property market. The following year would be much worse when the new owners foreclosed upon the Mercantile Exchange. And the downward trend continues.

In an international crash that bankrupted the giant Canadian developer Olympia and York and destroyed Trammell Crow Company, VMS Realty, and Portman Properties among other ranking American firms, JMB remained relatively sound, but at a big price to investors and its own reputation. Its brief adventure in the development business proved expensive too.

JMB had to buy back its Block 37 note from the First National Bank at a time when the bank was divesting itself of $2.1 billion in problem real estate loans.[6] Combined with earlier prepayments and accumulated interest over the years, the discounted note cost the joint venture around $50 million. So now JMB and Metropolitan Structures own, free and clear, the world's most prominent hole in the ground. To add to the humiliation, they are obliged to landscape, secure, and pay taxes annually on land no one seems to know what to do with. Still the city persists in condemning additional Loop properties with no immediate plans to replace them. Flush with TIF cash, the Department of Planning has earmarked several old buildings across from empty Block 37 on Randolph Street. In late 1994, Judd Malkin and Neil Bluhm decided to part company. JMB sold its lucrative pension management operation—the core of the company—to Miles Berger's Heitman Financial.

For Metropolitan Structures, the 1990s real estate crash has been even more unkind. Bernard Weissbourd is now retired, but has had to watch Illinois Center—the centerpiece of his personal fortune—fail, building by building. The original Miesian money machine—five impeccably designed million-square-foot towers aligned perfectly to each other like wells in an oil field—have run dry. Nearly 2 million square feet are vacant. Twenty years old and more, these towers are considered antiquated Class B space. In an environment where landlords are paying tenants to move out of older towers, "building out"—extensively renovating—their new suites for free, and subsidizing them with years of free rent, Illinois Center is doomed. Once, mighty Metropolitan Structures descended to building a golf course on some of its remaining vacant land and tried to lure riverboat gambling to dock at its pier. But the final insult for Met Structures arrived at the beginning of 1994, when a speculator from Florida bought the back taxes on the oldest building in the complex for $7 million. It will have to pay Capital Asset Research Corporation of West Palm Beach nearly a quarter of a million in interest to ransom the hostaged building. Cook County treasurer Edward Rosewell called it the "biggest tax sale in the history of Cook County." Typically, tax sales involve two-flats (double-decker apartments) or single-family homes whose owners have fallen on hard times. Rosewell added, "I've been here 20 years and I can't get over it."[7]

Lawrence Levy, the fellow who led all the others onto Block 37, told *Crain's Chicago* in 1991, "Our real estate activities are very quiet."[8] In fact, he has been effectively out of the downtown development business for some time. He was unable to come up with any of the financial guarantees required by FJV's lender, and Levy's one-third stake in the project progressively declined to only a few percentage points, even before the joint venture had to buy back the predevelopment loan. Technically, however, he still bears one-third of the liabilities. He offered the observation, a little late in the game, "There are a lot of times you should not build buildings."

With no development business and few restaurants left in Chicago, Larry Levy now describes himself as an investor. He still has a blowup in his office of Daniel Burnham's exhortation to "make no small plans" and keeps a Quotron near his desk. The beeping little gadget alerts him moment by moment to the smallest activity in the stocks in which he has any interest. As of 1994, he got a restaurant venture, called Dive, going with Jeffrey Katzenberg, formerly president of Disney Studios, and director Steven Spielberg. Submarine sandwiches and fries are served aboard a simulated undersea vessel in Century City, California, as far as you can get

Gallery 37 in place of 2.2 million square feet

from the old American downtown without actually diving to the bottom of the sea.

Sixteen buildings destroyed, hundreds of small businesses lost, thousands of people permanently dislocated: this is the current legacy of Block 37. The city's two-decade crusade to remake itself was not especially successful on its own terms and certainly disastrous for those who made the block their last place of employment downtown. The destruction of Block 37 continues to be a costly failure for the developers and the public.[9]

In addition to the art show in summer and the winter skating rink, Block 37 has been the site of a rock video. Each one of these unforeseen public uses puts pressure on the developers to find a way to leave the block open permanently—to make a $50 million contribution to the city. But this is not going to happen. The city requires some sort of development that will substantially exceed the $1,398,882 in real estate taxes levied in 1982—the last years of the blighted block—one of the prime criteria, justifying the taking in the first place. With FJV paying reduced taxes on what is essentially raw land, frozen at the 1982 level, rather than the $13,453,593 projected for 1995, the city is losing a tax increment of $12,054,712 annually on

Block 37.[10] It is out already at least $50 million itself, the bill for buying out the old owners of the block and preparing it for redevelopment.

The tax increment district currently produces $11 million a year total. All the real estate taxes, including those paid by Chicago Title, R. R. Donnelley, Leo Burnett, and the Transportation Building—the completed elements of the North Loop project—do not yet equal the anticipated windfall on the FJV block alone. Recognizing that something had to be done, the city, in the beginning of 1994, initiated the final act of this municipal comedy by reopening negotiations with the developers.

In the two years since the original schemes were mothballed, Helmut Jahn had been working at radically scaling down the project. He abandoned the 2.2-million-square-foot office/retail development, concentrating only on the State Street side of the block. There he had drawn a modified mall, no more than three stories, that can exploit the commercial opportunities across the street from the renovated Marshall Field's flagship store.

Gone were any plans to build the large first tower, which had doomed the McCarthy Building, and the second tower is now a small park, whose dimensions are the exact footprint of a future skyscraper—to be built if the market ever changes. By conceding that the site can currently support little more than 200,000 square feet, FJV and the city have gone through all this expense and agony to return the block economically to less than it was producing at the time it was legally considered underproductive.

Yet, the block's development even at this scale would allow the developer to cut its annual losses and the city to save some face. Recognizing this sober reality in the spring of 1994, representatives of the city's corporation counsel and Department of Planning and Development began to move toward settling the standoff.

The deputy corporation counsel, Edward J. Wong Jr., made a comprehensive study of the terms and provisions of the original redevelopment agreement and found it "very complex and, in many instances, hard to follow." He was directed by Mayor Daley and then Planning Commissioner Valerie Jarrett to find some way to take control of a planning initiative the city had never regained since the death of the mayor's father in 1976.

Wong's initial findings were not encouraging. He quickly discovered that even though the developers were in technical default—having already paid a total of $4.1 million in liquidated damages and downtown improvements—FJV still owned the block. This gap in the redevelopment deal meant that despite failures and defaults the city had no easy way of recapturing the title that it had blithely quitclaimed—traded unconditionally—to FJV back in December 1989.

The gap left the city in the unattractive position of having to declare FJV formally in default and then within six months buy back the property. For only $12,583,430, the city could buy back those three quarters of the block it had purchased directly or condemned—getting back only a third of what it had cost them. That still left the politicians to acquire the quarter block (the old Levy properties) that FJV had contributed to the project. Though FJV had paid $9,572,372 for the four parcels, the fair cash value had more than doubled, even in a down market, since the redevelopment deal was signed. So even if the city could pull the deal off and manage to buy the block back outright, it would have to spend a minimum of an additional $30 million. At a time when the Board of Education was posting half-billion-dollar deficits, it was hard to imagine that the city of Chicago could divert another small fortune to an empty piece of land that the best developers in the world couldn't do a thing with and the public, kept ignorant of the staggering costs, wanted to remain empty as a permanent public park.

Eager to end this embarrassing stalemate, the city, in 1994, hired U.S. Equities, a private development company, to find some way to complete the redevelopment of the North Loop. USE was to be paid no more than $3 million in fees, over three years. According to the contract, U.S. Equities is to "assist the city in negotiating the most favorable transaction for the city." In effect, the city had officially stepped out of the process, hoping in some way that the private market would save it from itself one last time. This was the same sort of white-knight solution that Daley (the first) had imagined decades back when there were billions in investment capital primed to go downtown.

Ironically, the city was now the only one with cash. Having paid off all the TIF bonds, the North Loop tax increment district was awash with nearly $60 million. By statute, the money could only be used for the North Loop redevelopment district. Since the city was prohibited from using the funds for general operations, Camille P. Julmy, vice-chairman of U.S. Equities, thought TIF money might come in very handy to subsidize a subordinated ground lease or a subordinated second mortgage on Block 37. What the developers had in mind was to have the city use its entire cash reserves to pay for an exclusively private improvement. The windfall—ominously reminiscent of the aborted $70 million Hilton tax abatement—would permit JMB to build a larger mall and attract a first-class anchor tenant rather than the off-price retailers with whom they were increasingly forced to negotiate.

In the next few months, the city, represented exclusively by U.S. Equities, and FJV went ahead informally to hook a major tenant. Although he wasn't yet informed, Helmut Jahn was out as project architect. He was now too expensive and artistically demanding for the sort of supertaxpayer considered for the site. The oddity of two private parties representing the public interest reveals the final depths into which city planning had fallen. Not only was there no pretext of an independent governmental role, but even the appearance of municipal oversight was removed.

In essence, the city was making the same mistake again. By pushing for a deal with Nordstrom, the country's most successful upscale retailer, already prominently placed in many of JMB's best malls, a new group of politicians was trying to distort the market at their own expense. The new Daley administration wanted a major department store, with the prestige of Marshall Field's, to reclaim in the last moment some of the glamour of the original North Loop plan. It could then claim the invaluable political advantage of having finally remade the most celebrated example of the blighted inner city.

In effect, the mayor's office was encouraging JMB to offer the Seattle-based company a sweetheart deal, even though its own attorneys informed it that it lacked the authority to use any TIF money for a "new building improvement that is to be privately owned." This questionable reallocation of TIF funds came, in 1994, at exactly the same time the city was using millions to condemn and demolish several buildings on Block 36 for no apparent reason, pay $1.85 million to "stabilize" the Selwyn and Harris Theaters (in addition to the $10 million used to acquire the Woods and Garrick sites on the same block as part of a new Goodman Theatre complex), and restructure the debt on the Chicago Theater (part of the original North Loop scheme), after the nonprofit development group that bought the property had gone bankrupt and the public was out more than $16 million in guaranteed city loans.

So even though the Daley administration was over its head with other obligations, it continued to prod the developers of Block 37 into a decision they didn't want to make. After all that had gone down, JMB was being used as a middleman to persuade Nordstrom executives that they could come into the Loop risk free. The plan was for the joint venture to finance and build an appropriate facility, then subsidize the rent at single digits as the city found some hidden way to write down the land even further.

The city was desperate, willing to provide a free facility simply to get something going, just to fill the hole. And it thought FJV was eager enough simply to get rid of its property. Somehow it had overlooked the fact that Stuart Nathan—negotiating for the joint venture—had Kmart, with its independent units such as Sports Authority and Borders bookstores, already lined up for the scaled-down development on Block 37. The truth was that after waiting on it for years, Nathan no longer wanted the city as a partner. He did not have to wait to make his point.

In the fall of 1994, Nordstrom withdrew on its own. Publicly it talked

Block 37 on Easter Sunday, 1993

about the older downtowns not being part of its plans. But privately it mentioned how alarmed it was at the particular condition of the North Loop—how it seemed desolate after hours and even during the day, frequented by people who were not "Nordstrom's kind of customer."

In its incomplete resettlement, one block of America is revealed again in a near-primal state. The site's attractive rawness exposes the city ecologically, as second nature—predatory and wild—not simply as an abstraction of advancement. We are in a way lucky to have found Block 37 frozen in a state of progress interrupted. Caught in time between destitution and "improvement," this passionately contested place provides considerable insight into America's hidden order.

Once again, Block 37 is a desolate, flattened piece of prairie, almost exactly a century after Frederick Jackson Turner, in Chicago for the annual meeting of the American Historical Association, confidently announced the end of the frontier. The block's current plight reminds us of the true price paid for the compulsion of reordering and homogenizing that still fuels American desire. Not at the edge but right in the congested middle of the city, Block 37 had civic leaders fantasizing that they had rediscovered the "outer edge of the wave—the meeting point between savagery and civilization."[11] And they went to work.

Yet, what they extinguished on those three acres is already unrecoverable. Through its relentless "improvements," the city has "regressed back to the clarity and predictability of univalence—to the known." The possibility of supporting "an infinite number of superimposed and unpredictable activities" on one block was traded in the end for nothing.[12]

The history of one small place told in all its daunting detail tests the reality against the rhetoric and brilliant invention of American striving.

APPENDIX: NORTH LOOP CHRONOLOGY

1973

February 6   Arthur Rubloff retains architects Perkins and Will for ninety-six thousand dollars to prepare a North Loop plan.

July 1   City releases *Chicago 21* with the North Loop area as the centerpiece.

July 24   Mid-America Appraisal and Research Corporation provides Rubloff with a valuation analysis that officially sets low land values in the North Loop.

October   The Urban Renewal Board authorizes a feasibility study of the seven-block North Loop area. Total land acquisition is estimated at a bargain $25 million.

November 15   The Urban Renewal Board first proposes the Commercial District Development Commission to supervise (provide legal authority for) anticipated condemnations.

1974

February 4   Rubloff presents "his" first North Loop (Perkins and Will) model to the Central Area Committee.

1975

May 8   The city council enacts an ordinance establishing the CDDC. The commission is vested with the authority to designate a blighted commercial area—not less than two acres where 75 percent of the land area is devoted to commercial use. Blight criteria include dilapidation, overcrowding, deleterious land use or layout, failure to produce a proper share of tax revenues.

1976

March   Frustrated by the lack of progress, Rubloff secretly contacts another prominent architect, Harry Weese, to come up with his own North Loop scheme.

August 7   Rubloff again attempts to regain initiative and presents his plan for the North Loop directly to the public. Paul Gapp, architectural critic at the *Tribune,* declares it a "stunning architectural model."

December 20 Mayor Richard J. Daley dies in office.

1977

January   With the city doing nothing, Rubloff accelerates his activities. Specifically, he tries to nail down private financing, still privately negotiating with Canadian developer Cadillac Fairview and a large anchor tenant (Sears and J. C. Penney). He calls his project the Chicago 21 Plan to further confuse it with a real public initiative.

December 7   Rubloff approaches Hilton Hotels claiming that he has in hand commitments with Cadillac Fairview to develop a 1.3-million-square-foot office building; J. C. Penney will occupy a 350,000-square-foot department store as part of a 750,000-foot State Street mall; two developers are said to be interested in building apartments. This is the successful *bluff* that hooks Hilton and gets the city in deeper. All the other elements of the deal evaporate.

1978

January 13   As a hedge against possible failure of a larger North Loop project, Rubloff brokers the $325,000 sale of a Block 37 property. The New World Building at 109 North Dearborn later wins a condemnation award (September 20, 1991) for $2.585 million, an eight-to-one return for the new owners.

March 21   The Department of Planning applies to the United States Department of Housing and Urban Development for a $25 million Urban Development Action Grant for the North Loop, based on a general land-use proposal.

May 1   Arthur Rubloff, claiming that he only wants to hasten negotiations, writes Hilton executives "off the record" that the authorities will provide tax relief if Hilton decides to build in the North Loop.

May 24   Commissioner Miles Berger has the Chicago Plan Commission consider an eight-point laundry list of Hilton demands. The hotel chain, not the city, is dictating public policy. Knowingly or not, Berger has given official sanction to Rubloff's promise of a tax abatement.

June 28   Rubloff writes to planning head Lewis Hill, reminding him that the late mayor (Daley) had put him (Rubloff) in charge of the North Loop. He wants Hill and Mayor Bilandic to honor the Rubloff interpretation of their "special relationship."

July 21   Even as the city tries to conclude negotiations with Hilton, Rubloff executives continue to offer the Hilton blocks (16 and 17) to the Sheraton, Pick, Fairmont, and Loews hotels, stressing in identical letters that the "beauty of this development is that it wipes out all the cancer in downtown Chicago."

August 2   Illinois governor James R. Thompson approves $15 million in funding for a new state office building in the North Loop. The city agrees "in principle" for Hilton to build in the project area.

September 19   After criticism from HUD concerning preservation issues, the city amends its application for UDAG funds to $7.9 for the Hilton Hotel site only, where there are no landmark buildings.

November   The CDDC designates the North Loop project area as "Blighted Commercial Area State-Wacker."

November 9   Rubloff prepares a joint venture agreement to develop the North Loop with Canadian developer Olympia and York (50 percent) and New York investment banker Charles Allen and Company (25 percent). Rubloff retains a 25 percent interest. The deal is never consummated.

December   Rubloff retains Helmut Jahn as the North Loop project architect. Jahn is also Governor Thompson's architect for the State of Illinois Center.

1979

January   HUD tentatively approves reduced UDAG after Hilton guarantees it will not close its Michigan Avenue (Conrad Hilton) hotel.

January 22   Draft redevelopment agreement between the city and Hilton. Rubloff is now out, but the city is essentially agreeing to his terms.

February 21   At a North Loop planning meeting (Plan Commission and Department of Planning), total acquisition costs are estimated at $80 million. Only the year before they were $54 million. The city's chief condemnation attorney, Earl Neal, says he can't begin negotiations with Hilton because there is still no North Loop plan and the city has no money.

March 21   The CDDC submits the *Redevelopment Plan for Blighted Commercial Area, Project North Loop,* to the Chicago Plan Commission.

March 28   The City council approves the redevelopment plan.

April 4   Jane Byrne is elected mayor of Chicago with 82 percent of the vote.

April 11   Chicago Plan Commission approves the North Loop Redevelopment plan and formally accepts the CDDC designation of 26.74 acres in the North Loop as blighted. This is an essential step that will permit condemnation and demolition of the area.

July 20   Mayor Byrne announces that the city will finance the project with a $50 million *loan,* not a bond issue as Mayor Bilandic had planned.

1980

March   The CDDC approves the planning department's *North Loop Guidelines for Conservation and Redevelopment.*

April The city council approves $55 million in bond anticipation notes to acquire land in the North Loop. More than $50 million is required to condemn the first two blocks alone.

May 21 The Department of Planning signs a contract with Hilton agreeing to provide Blocks 16 and 17 at fifty dollars a square foot (at minimum a three-to-one write-down) and requests a tax abatement from Cook County for the entire North Loop.

July 9 Jane Byrne appoints Charles H. Shaw to organize the North Loop project. He retains Skidmore, Owings and Merrill to do his architecture and planning.

August Developer Richard Stein makes a bid for the Transportation Building. It takes a year for the bid to be accepted (August 21, 1981). Eight years into the North Loop project, Stein's building is the first to get a go-ahead.

August 20 County Assessor Thomas Hynes denies city's request to grant Hilton a $70 million (thirteen-year) tax abatement as part of blanket tax relief for the entire redevelopment district.

October 28 Assessor Hynes agrees to reconsider a tax break for only the two Hilton blocks.

November 13 Charles Shaw presents his disastrous North Loop redevelopment "concept." This is the Mole Town scheme.

1981

February 10 Shaw is dismissed after only seven months as North Loop coordinator.

February 11 Mayor Byrne announces that the city will move ahead on the North Loop, but it is the end of any coordinated effort. The project will be bid block by block.

February 12 Miles Berger, head of the Chicago Plan Commission, takes Shaw's place as North Loop czar.

March 3 Miles Berger chairs a meeting between the North Loop task force and Department of Planning. He has prepared thirteen pages of the North Loop guidelines that will be the city's only plan.

March 6 The CDDC approves the Berger plan, which effectively turns over the development initiative completely to the private side. He advises ABC, which is interested in the rehabilitation of a theater building on Block 36, that it must seek Hilton's approval.

March 13 Mayor Byrne announces the city's new North Loop and Redevelopment Guidelines.

April 27 The Chicago Plan Commission approves and amends the guidelines, including the first sensitivity to the preservation issue.

October 22 The city council approves another set of amended North Loop Guidelines.

December 8 The county assessor denies the Hilton tax abatement, suggesting a profit-recapture formula in its place.

December 9 Hilton terminates its contract with the city.

December 10 HUD places a permanent hold on the $7.9 million UDAG.

1982

March 4 Hilton withdraws completely from the North Loop and announces its intention to rehabilitate the Conrad Hilton with Charles Shaw as developer.

April 20 The CDDC signs an agreement for the rehab of the historic Delaware Building on Block 36.

June 3 ABC begins to rehab the State-Lake Theater Building on Block 36. The original Rubloff-Shaw superblock schemes officially end.

June 20–22 The city places newspaper advertisements requesting proposals for mixed-use developments on one or more blocks.

August 14 The Department of Planning announces that it has received sixteen proposals in response to its national advertisements. All respondents are local firms.

August 16 Lawrence Levy writes CDDC chairman Martin Murphy that, on behalf of FJV, he offers to purchase "portions of Block F (37)." He notes that the venture already owns 30 West Washington and 11 and 127 North Dearborn. FJV has only one competitor for Block 37. Representing ownership interests on the block's northeast corner, Sidcor also answered the RFP.

September 16 The city council approves a $65.5 million bond issue for all of the North Loop. This is the total budget for seven blocks. The bond issue *replaces* all previous funding initiatives.

October 12 The CDDC amends the new *North Loop Guidelines*. Each iteration is simply a response to the changing market conditions and availability of public funding. This is *Potemkin planning*—the impression of municipal leadership.

October 13 Chicago Plan Commission approves *North Loop Guidelines*.

October 27 Chicago City Council endorses *North Loop Guidelines*.

November 1 The CDDC "rebids" Block 16, one of the two Hilton blocks, with no mention of any tax abatements.

1983

January 18 The city council passes an ordinance authorizing acquisition of more blighted property in the North Loop and officially terminates the Hilton deal.

February 22 Harold Washington upsets Mayor Byrne in the Democratic primary and sets the stage for his close April victory against Republican Bernard Epton.

February 28 The city issues a second RFP for a mixed-use development on Block 37.

May 3 FJV offers a winning bid of $12,583,430. Sidcor offers $15 million. The CDDC staff report (August 23) judges FJV's to be the only bona fide bid and the developer the one most likely to bring the project to a successful completion.

1984

January   The Washington administration now estimates the cost of acquisition is a minimum of $171 million. Funding will come from designating the North Loop as a tax increment financing district and issuing bonds. The entire increment between the old (depressed) tax base and the new must first be used to pay off the bonds and then later only is to be spent within the seven-block TIF district. (Since the first North Loop buildings came on line, the district has paid off the bonds and accumulated nearly $60 million in cash as of 1995.)

February 29   The Department of Planning, after consulting with civil engineers, determines that it cannot provide a service tunnel under Block 37. This effectively voids the original redevelopment agreement and dooms a city landmark, the McCarthy Building, which must give way to a service ramp now that trucks cannot enter the block underground.

April 10   The CDDC amends the North Loop TIF district.

June 6   A city council ordinance designates the facade of the 1872 McCarthy Building a city landmark.

June 20   The city council authorizes the taking of Block 37 property.

1985

January   The North Loop Guidelines are revised again. Commissioner of planning, Elizabeth Hollander, negotiates an arrangement with FJV, whereby it can "trade monuments." In allowing it to demolish the McCarthy Building, the city wanted a $2 million contribution to the Chicago Theater (saved by a preservation group and later bankrupted with a total of $16 million in city subsidies) and $1 million toward the rehabilitation of the Reliance Building, a landmark office building of great architectural merit, plus up to $400,000 for improvements on the Selwyn and Harris Theaters.

1986

December   The city sells $58 million in tax increment bonds. The budget for Block 37 is $32 million.

1987

March 26   After four years of negotiations, litigation, and delays (until December 1986 the city had no money to follow through on its plans), the CDDC is ready to proceed with a redevelopment agreement and contract for sale of North Loop Block 37.

September   The CDDC issues its revised and amended North Loop Guidelines. Land prices frozen at 1984 levels, when the city first started negotiating for Block 37, have more than tripled in three years. Land frozen at $151.50 a square foot (the price the city contracted to sell for) is now valued by its own appraisers at more than $500.

September 23   A city council joint committee (Finance and Landmark Preservation) votes to *de-designate* the McCarthy Building facade, thus clearing the way for its quick-take condemnation and demolition. (Since 1986, the city council has designated eighty-one architectural landmarks. This is the first de-designation.)

October 22   Mayor Washington signs the Block 37 redevelopment agreement.

October 28   Commissioner of planning Hollander writes to the city comptroller requesting more TIF funds (in addition to the $58 million received in December 1986).

November 25   Mayor Harold Washington dies in office.

December 2   The city council appoints as acting mayor Alderman Eugene Sawyer, who serves until April 4, 1989.

1988

January 1   FJV fails to complete the acquisition. The venture so far has paid only a $1.2 million deposit for the exclusive right to control land worth potentially upward of a billion.

February 1   The deadline passes for the city to convey Block 37 cleared of all structures to the redeveloper.

August 1   Sidcor files a traverse. FJV's only competitor for the block argues among other things that Block 37 was not blighted and that the city never had a comprehensive plan for area. The suit delays FJV an additional year. Sidcor loses the suit, but the delay proved very profitable for the development company, which collected $15 million in cash for its dilapidated properties (more than $500 a square foot).

1989

April 4   Richard M. Daley is elected mayor in a special election. It is for only two years to serve out the remainder of Harold Washington's second term. Daley is reelected for a full four-year term on April 2, 1991, and then again on April 4, 1995.

October   Demolition barricades are erected around Block 37.

December 29   Five years late, in exchange for $12,583,430, the city conveys title for Block 37 to FJV.

1990–

Stalemate: Completely demolished except for the Commonwealth Edison substation that marks the three-acre site like a giant tombstone, Block 37 remains unoccupied. The city and FJV have racked up nearly $50 million apiece in losses. Add to that a shortfall of nearly $10 million in annual property taxes (the difference between the current $1 million annually and the projected revenues that justified the expensive condemnation and demolition). The cost of maintaining an empty space at the center of the city mounts daily. Sears, Montgomery Ward, Wal-Mart, and Sony have all been eyeing the site, but no deal has been struck.

NOTES

I: LORD OF THE LOOP

1. "Jefferson Lecture I.," Washington D.C., Mar. 30, 1977, in Saul Bellow, *It All Adds Up: From the Dim Past to the Uncertain Future* (New York: Viking Press, 1994), p. 131.
2. Chicago delayed rebuilding its downtown. Daley moved cautiously, unlike Robert Moses in New York and heads of other big-city urban-renewal efforts. See Jeanne R. Lowe, *Cities in a Race with Time: Progress and Poverty in America's Renewing Cities* (New York: Random House, 1967), p. 45–109.
3. Brian J. L. Berry et al., *Chicago: Transformations of an Urban System* (Cambridge, Mass.: Ballinger Publishing Co.: 1976), provides a comprehensive statistical profile of Chicago during the Daley years.
4. Nelson Algren first published his observations in *Holiday* and Liebling in the *New Yorker*. Both pieces were soon expanded into books: Nelson Algren, *Chicago: City on the Make* (Garden City, N.Y.: Doubleday and Co., 1952), and A. J. Liebling, *Chicago: The Second City* (New York: Alfred A. Knopf, 1952).
5. Public Building Commission, *The Central Area and the Civic Center Site of the City of Chicago*, 1958, p. 5.
6. The standard Daley-era labor contract was called a handshake agreement. It committed the city to expensive prevailing-rate contracts, providing municipal unions parity with private contractors. In turn, the mayor reaped the widespread political benefits gained from having happy firefighters, police officers, transit and sanitation workers. Chicago was strike free. The real cost of labor peace was lost in a Byzantine system of interlocking local, regional, and federal funding that only the mayor and a few insiders had mastered.
7. Daley managed to maintain the outward impression of cooperation. He farmed out the biggest budget items to agencies with independent-sounding names and sold Lake Michigan water to the near-in suburbs. Agencies such as the Regional Transportation Authority (RTA) received funding from the entire six-county metropolitan area but returned most of it to the Chicago Transit Authority (CTA), the city's own network of buses and trains. In Chicago, public education—the city's greatest single expense—was segregated off to a rich "independent" self-regulating domain, like the Chicago Transit Authority, and the Sanitary and Park Districts.
8. Pastora San Juan Cafferty and William C. McCready, "The Chicago Public-Private Partnership Experience: A Heritage of Involvement," in *Public-Private Partnership in American Cities: Seven Case Studies*, by R. Scott Fosler and Renee A. Berger (Lexington, Mass.: D. C. Heath and Co., 1982) p. 135.
9. See Jean-Louis Cohen and Andre Lortie, *Des Fortifs au Perif: Paris les Seuils de la Ville* (Paris: Picard Editeur, 1991). The authors consider how road building and military fortifications led to social control in Paris during the nineteenth and twentieth cen-

turies. Walling out in the modern European manner was more a "walling in" in the United States. This was not a phenomenon exclusive to Chicago. Only the scale was different. One of the first comprehensive studies of a population behind the walls was Lee Rainwater's investigation of the Pruitt-Igoe projects in St. Louis, *Behind Ghetto Walls: Black Family Life in a Federal Slum* (Hawthorne, N.Y.: Aldine Publishing Co., 1970).

10. Arnold R. Hirsch, *Making the Second Ghetto: Race and Housing in Chicago, 1940–60* (New York: Cambridge University Press, 1983), p. 264. Emphasis mine.

11. Under pressure principally from Southern conservatives, the federal government had provided the cities with inadequate construction budgets. Predictably, public housing projects started falling apart from day one. In one year alone, the CHA paid $7.3 million to repair its elevators, averaging out to $18,000 a unit. See Oscar Newman, *Review and Analysis of the Chicago Housing Authority and Implementation of Recommended Changes* (Washington, D.C.: U.S. Department of Housing and Urban Development, Mar. 31, 1982), p. 12. The audit is for the year 1980, when the CHA paid $7.3 million to maintain its elevators, or $18,000 per elevator per year: "By contrast, NYCHA spends $4,000/elevator/year, or 4½ times less. The private sector managing subsidized housing in Chicago spends between $3,500 and $4,000/year/elevator in maintaining similar elevators (1980)."

12. Hirsch, *Second Ghetto*, p. 109.

13. H. Blumenfeld, "The Economic Base of the Metropolis," *Journal of the American Institute of Planners*, no. 21 (Fall 1955), pp. 114–32; and Daniel Bell, *The Coming of Post-Industrial Society: A Venture in Social Forecasting* (New York: Basic Books, 1973). See also Peter F. Drucker, "The Age of Social Transformation," *Atlantic Monthly* 274, no. 3 (Nov. 1994).

14. See Thomas J. Schlereth, "Moody's Go-Getting Wacker Manual," *Inland Architect* 24, no. 3 (Apr. 1980), pp. 9–10.

15. Daniel H. Burnham and Edward H. Bennett, *Plan of Chicago*, ed. Charles Moore, originally published in two-thousand-copy limited edition by Commercial Club of Chicago, 1908 (Princeton, N.J.: Princeton Architectural Press, 1993), p. 119. Emphasis mine.

16. Walter D. Moody, *Wacker's Manual of the Plan of Chicago* (Chicago: Chicago Plan Commission, 1911), introduction, n.p.

17. Until the Great Chicago Fire of 1871, the city's mayors were all businessmen. Partly as a result of the influx of new sources of capital necessitated by the extensive rebuilding, there was a need for professional politicians. For further background see Robin L. Einhorn, *Property Rules: Political Economy in Chicago, 1833–1872* (Chicago: University of Chicago Press, 1991); Richard C. Ward, "The Enduring Chicago Machine," *Chicago History* 15, no. 1 (Spring 1986); Edward C. Banfield and James Q. Wilson, *City Politics* (Cambridge: Harvard University Press, 1965); and Lloyd Wendt and Herman Kogan, *Lords of the Levee* (New York: Bobbs-Merrill, 1943).

18. Banfield and Wilson, *City Politics*, p. 124.

19. Previous Chicago politicians had used this form of directed development to fund large public works projects, such as the creation of the Metropolitan Sanitary District to fund and administer the construction of the Chicago Sanitary and Ship Canal. The canal successfully reversed the flow of the Chicago River. But no one had ever tried to lead such extensive development downtown, traditionally the realm of the Republicans and well beyond the range of the normal Democratic machine. One of the mayor's confidants from that period recalls, "He'd talk about having total control of the Republican

community. There was no question that they thought him absolutely essential" (interview with Thomas Foran, Apr. 28, 1992).

20. After Congress passed the Economic Opportunities Act in 1964, the mayor, in his role as chairman of the Chicago Committee on Urban Opportunity (CCUO), administered every dollar. See Alan B. Anderson and George W. Pickering, *Confronting the Color Line: The Broken Promise of the Civil Rights Movement in Chicago* (Athens: University of Georgia Press, 1968), p. 136; and Philip M. Hauser, *Integration of the Public Schools: Chicago 1964* (Chicago: Advisory Panel on Integration of the Public Schools, Mar. 31, 1964), pp. 15–23. The most comprehensive study of Daley's administration of federal antipoverty legislation is Nicholas Lemann's *The Promised Land: The Great Black Migration and How It Changed America* (New York: Alfred A. Knopf, 1991).

21. Other cities had barely pretended to have a plan. Pittsburgh's extensive Gateway project was the product of a simple lawyer's agreement between the city's urban redevelopment authority and a life insurance company. A redevelopment contract between the Urban Redevelopment Authority of Pittsburgh and the Equitable Life Assurance Society of the United States, February 14, 1950, was sufficient to start the capital flowing.

22. Ester R. Fuchs, *Mayors and Money: Fiscal Policy in New York and Chicago* (Chicago: University of Chicago Press, 1992), p. 164.

23. Daley succeeded where others failed because he rejected Burnham's idea of moving Chicago's heart west of the river and reaffirmed, rather than abandoned, the historic downtown. Daley built the Civic Center in the same tight corridor between La Salle and State, Washington and Randolph, where the city had first prospered, along the old axis from City Hall, site of the original courthouse to the lake.

24. John R. Logan and Harvey M. Molotch, *Urban Fortunes: The Political Economy of Place* (Berkeley: University of California Press, 1987), explains in detail the phenomenon of captive downtown businesses.

25. This doubling of power was unique to Daley. He told his supporters that he would let someone else take over the party leadership as soon as he took office. But in twenty-one years in the job he never managed to do so. When in 1956 he became chairman of the Public Building Commission, he held all three of the most powerful jobs in the city.

26. Six hundred and forty-eight feet tall, with only thirty-one stories, the building occupies only 35 percent of its site. The architecture provides a minimalist wrapping for more than 120 courtrooms and office space for Cook County, the state of Illinois, and the city of Chicago. See Carl Condit, *Chicago, 1930–1970: Building, Planning, and Urban Technology* (Chicago: University of Chicago Press: 1974), pp. 135–38; and Pauline Saliga and John Zukowsky, *The Sky's the Limit* (New York, Rizzoli: 1991), p. 193.

27. Daley's mastery of the public authority as a way to expedite complex, capital-intensive projects came from his fascination with the culture of politics in the Depression, during the Roosevelt administration. The Tennessee Valley Authority (TVA) was Daley's model of a federal public authority, New York's Triborough authority a regional metropolitan one. In both cases the chief executive had no direct control. Daley's refinement of the public authority would further concentrate power in his own hands. On the history of public authorities as shadow governments, see Annmarie Hauck Walsh, *The Public's Business: The Politics and Practices of Government Corporations* (Cambridge: MIT Press, 1978), and on Robert Moses's use of one: Robert Caro, *The Power Broker: Robert Moses and the Fall of New York* (New York: Alfred A. Knopf, 1974).

28. The original charter passed by the city council provided the PBC the authority to

issue forty-year tax-exempt bonds. On September 20, 1956, the state's attorney of Cook County brought suit in the Illinois Supreme Court, questioning this authority. This was the last effective challenge to Daley's fiscal autonomy. On March 20, 1957, the Supreme Court of Illinois upheld the constitutionality of the PBC but limited to twenty years the maturities of the municipal bonds. The ruling saved face for competing politicians in Cook County but did little more than raise slightly the low coupon on PBC bonds. Chicago Public Building Commission revenue bonds with a 4 percent coupon rate raised $67 million to cover the Civic Center's total development costs.

29. When, for example, in 1968 the PBC involved itself in school construction, it was able to get the Park District to maintain and run recreation facilities for new schools. Daley realized early the benefits of metropolitan government when the city, in 1950, annexed 41.1 square miles of Cook County Forest Preserve land to keep O'Hare International Airport within city limits. The PBC has been responsible for health centers, police and fire stations, the city's junior-college system, and other necessary public projects. High-visibility PBC projects downtown, completed during Daley's twenty-one-year tenure, include a remodeling of City Hall and County Building (a single structure containing both governments) and the old Chicago library (now the Chicago Cultural Center).

30. In a typical year, 1972, Chicago's per capita debt, $304, was lower than all but one city of more than 500,000 population. See also Joe Mathewson, *Up Against Daley* (La Salle, Ill.: Open Court, 1974), p. 81. Mathewson quotes a city official in 1972 bragging that Chicago was in "an enviable position to incur additional debt." See also "Twenty Years of Progress," *Chicago Department of Urban Renewal 1966 Annual Report,* pp. 46–50, and *Four Years of Progress: 1970 Report,* (Chicago: Chicago Department of Urban Renewal), pp. 38–43.

31. The mayor's relationship with the downtown Chicago banks was so good that he had uninterrupted access to a $100 million line of credit. In turn, Daley kept the businessmen happy by maintaining an excellent credit rating that helped leverage more and more private capital. Chicago at the height of Daley's power, 1955 to 1968, was a great capital risk. Among the original members of the PBC were Henry Crown, head of the Material Services Division of General Dynamics; Willis Gale, head of Commonwealth Edison; and Philip K. Wrigley, chairman of the family gum empire.

32. While Daley would allow lesser talents but politically savvy architects, Louis R. Solomon and John D. Cordwell, to provide preliminary plans for the project, they were "not to be considered as being necessarily representative of an architectural and planning solution and should not be so construed" (from internal PBC document). When it came time to select the final team among nineteen submitting proposals that included Ludwig Mies van der Rohe, Harry Weese, Perkins and Will, and Holabird and Root, he went with a representative team of the best the city could offer.

33. The mayor used the PBC's condemnation of property for the Civic Center as a way to demonstrate to his new allies in the business community and his old ones back in the wards that he would do business his own way. No one would hold up condemnation proceedings to push up awards, and there would be no special deals downtown, as he had shown earlier when Frank Righeimer went to trial to condemn Congress Expressway (later renamed the Eisenhower Expressway) land. David Rockola, owner of the Peerless Weight and Vending Machine Company, owned three lots, all but fifty feet of the south part of the Civic Center site. He asked for more than the city offered for his land and hired a politically wired law firm to represent him. It was headed by Colonel Jacob

Arvey, who had been Daley's predecessor as Central Committee chairman and a power in the Twenty-fourth Ward. Arvey was credited with engineering the elections of Governor Adlai Stevenson and Senator Paul Douglas. The confrontation over these three lots had the look of a classic political deal. But Daley played it straight and had William H. Dillon, PBC legal counsel, take Arvey to trial. The jury awarded Rockola $3.9 million, a little more than half of what he sued for and less than the city offered in a negotiated settlement that he had earlier rejected. The city ended up paying $10,979,500 for the entire fourteen-lot parcel ($95.31 a square foot for the land). William Dillon of Cancannon, Dillon and Snook, who had been the attorney for the Chicago Land Clearance Commission and had drawn up the statute creating the Public Building Commission, was the special assistant corporation counsel who represented the city in the condemnations, completing the link between the early Fort Dearborn project and its apotheosis on the Civic Center site.

34. See Condit, *Chicago*, pp. 139–41, and Betty J. Blum, interviewer, *Oral History of William Hartmann* (Chicago: Art Institute of Chicago, Department of Architecture, 1991), pp. 218–52. See also Blum interviews with Larry Perkins and Norman Schlossman, also in the Department of Architecture, Art Institute of Chicago. Schlossman writes a letter from La Reserve, Beaulieu-Sur-Mer (May 22, 1963), to his partners detailing the meetings with Picasso.

35. SOM's Inland Steel Building (1957) on Dearborn Street, along with Naess and Murphy's Prudential Insurance Company's headquarters (1955), each customized for a single corporate client, were the first new buildings since the Depression.

36. The Brunswick Building is a good example of the way the scale of the money to be made from downtown land imitated the increased size of the buildings, on larger building lots. The site has a long real estate pedigree going back to William D. Kerfoot, who did business there in the ashes of the 1871 fire. Later, it was the site of the Chicago Title and Trust Company, until it was sold on July 3, 1946, for $2.65 million to Mr. Edward E. Glatt. The 241-foot-by-183-foot (including alley) Chicago Title and Trust Company lot included a sixteen-story fireproof building, four-story fireproof building, two-story taxpayer (modest new building built to pay expenses), and two old buildings (Winston and Company, *Record of Real Estate Sales* unpublished company archive). The price equaled $62.78 per square foot. Given a low inflation rate over the twenty years the property was held by Mr. Glatt, he would have been lucky to break even. The big return on the land came when Rubloff, anticipating the early benefits of the Central Area Plan, got his hands on the property. When it was resold on September 14, 1957, for $3 million, with Arthur Rubloff as broker, the price equaled $68.50 per square foot (44,103 square feet). In 1965, Rubloff's syndicate built a 650,000-square-foot building on the consolidated larger lot, multiplying the rentable property by sixteen times. At the end of 1991, the building was 94 percent occupied with a net square foot rental of $18 (*Metro-Chicago Office Guide* 6, no. 1 [First Quarter 1991]).

37. On March 14, 1961, the Public Building Commission signed a contract for architectural services with Naess and Murphy, supervising architects, and Skidmore, Owings and Merrill and Loebl, Schlossman and Bennett, associate architects (Minutes of the Public Building Commission of Chicago, Chicago Public Building Commission Mar. 2, 1961). The commission had received a $1.5 million advance from the federal Community Facilities Administration of the Housing and Home Financing Agency. For this fee, the architects agreed to provide, within 420 days, all the preliminary site and design work for the new Civic Center. Once the PBC bonds were successfully floated, the ar-

chitects would be paid 5 percent of construction costs. The architects' eagerness to do work under Daley is revealed by their willingness to accept tough city-negotiated terms and deliver on time. This arrangement had already been lucrative for Murphy in the massive construction of O'Hare and other public works commissions. The public work led, it seemed almost inevitably, to more lucrative private jobs, such as SOM's Brunswick Building, along the Dearborn corridor.

38. When the bank decided to build a new building it was significant that they used C. F. Murphy, already viewed as a firm politically connected to the Daley administration through its work on the Civic Center and a boyhood friendship between Charles Murphy Sr. and the mayor. The Perkins and Will Partnership, whose U.S. Gypsum Building (1961–63) had received considerable attention with its rotated prism form, opening four small triangular plazas at the corners of the lot, was favored by Gaylord Freeman and some other executives at the bank who admired its design skills.

39. Letter from Gilbert H. Scribner, Scribner and Co., to Homer J. Livingston, president, First National Bank of Chicago, Mar. 30, 1959 (company archive) p. 6.

40. Letter from Gilbert Scribner to Homer J. Livingston, chairman of the board, First National Bank of Chicago, Aug. 26, 1960. It is clear that the bank's decision is being influenced directly by downtown land values. On June 15, 1960, Scribner makes note of his $10.75 million estimate of "fair cash market value" for the buildings on the Civic Center site then slated for demolition and notes that it is his "understanding that you [Livingston] are not interested in a half block but only in obtaining a full block, within a very limited area of the downtown district." He also notes the PBC's advantage in having the powers of eminent domain to help set its price. On September 14, 1960, Scribner prepares a summary of values for Livingston, noting that earlier he had told him "that there were cases where properties in the past had sold or been leased at more than their present value." But it is still early in Daley's crusade to prop Loop values up, and Scribner doesn't want his client to be rash. He concludes with the caveat, "The point is not that downtown as a whole has slipped but the values of some of the properties have varied. In other words, It doesn't always go up in price."

41. See Homer Hoyt, *One Hundred Years of Chicago Land Values* (Chicago: University of Chicago Press, 1933), and Richard M. Hurd, *Principles of City Land Values* (New York: Real Estate Record Association, 1903).

42. Undated letter from the First National Bank to Otto H. Loser, acting city comptroller, confirming the bank's $77,500 offer to the city to vacate the alley. It needed this last piece to control the entire block (Interview with Robert Wilmouth, Oct. 22, 1991). Source on Daley's expediting of building of First National is interview with Thomas Foran, former U.S. attorney and at the time a private lawyer on contract with the mayor's office, May 12, 1992.

43. The architects at C. F. Murphy dominated the collaboration. On September 20, 1965, Gaylord Freeman wrote to Homer Livingston of his conviction that for the bank the architects should "use two materials of contrasting color (and possibly texture) to dramatize the structure." The vertical members would be white to "emphasize the dramatic vertical structure" and the spandrels darker. After Perkins and Will took up Freeman's cause, Carter Manny Jr. of C. F. Murphy led a successful public crusade, soliciting expert opinion, against the two-color scheme. The incident is revealing in that it shows how important architectural firms, for the time collaborators but about to compete for future work, took this building to be.

The earliest sketches for the bank included a transmitting tower, an honor reserved for the city's tallest building. The final spread-leg structure and castellated top, with the mechanicals and blowers differentiated, provided the building a strong image on the skyline. At street level, single-location banking required large-span bottom floors where all the tellers could be in the same space, accomplished by moving the elevator core out of the center and onto the building's "legs." The tapering from fifty-nine thousand square feet on the banking floors to twenty-nine thousand on the typical rental floors gave the building its "swoop" form, first used by I. M. Pei in an unexecuted design done earlier in the sixties for the New York Stock Exchange and refined by Bruce Graham in the John Hancock Center on North Michigan Avenue. The First National executives were well aware of both precedents for their own more utilitarian version. Theirs would be more "restrained," in acknowledgment of the neighboring public buildings, and not crowd every inch of the block.

44. The care the bank took in addressing its public role is evident in a series of meetings, the National Bank of Chicago Conference, June 25–28, 1964, which included planners, urban pundits, academics, and a journalist. William Brubaker, a principal at Perkins and Will, kept notes (now in the collections of the Department of Architecture, the Art Institute of Chicago, and the Chicago Historical Society). Throughout the proceedings, the bankers, who saw this as the first bank of the electronic age, and the architects stressed the building's importance for Chicago and the country. Professor Albert Bush-Brown of MIT reminded the group that "in spending $100 million the bank had a great moral and cultural responsibility to the city and country."

45. *Report of the National Advisory Commission on Civil Disorders* (New York: Bantam Books, 1968). In 1967, Chicago escaped riots on the order of Newark or Detroit. But on August 12, 1965, in the year of the Watts riot in Los Angeles, there was a violent incident in Lawndale a poor South Side Chicago neighborhood, after a fire department hook-and-ladder truck killed a twenty-three-year-old woman waiting at a bus stop. Eighty persons were injured and 169 were arrested in the demonstrations following the incident. Orlando Wilson's police department was a model of restraint. Daley praised the police chief as an "outstanding administrator." The following year, on July 12, 1966, there was a more serious riot, again in Lawndale. The violence lasted three days. Forty-two hundred National Guardsmen supplemented police units. Two died and sixteen civilians were wounded. The precipitating incident was the fire department's turning off of fire hydrants used by children to cool off in the hundred-degree heat.

46. Assured earlier by President Johnson that the convention was his, Daley had to wait until October 8, 1967, to receive formal acknowledgment from the Democratic Party's Site Committee. Chicago beat out Houston, in Johnson's home state. This indicates how much influence the mayor had going into 1968.

47. Completed only in 1960, the original McCormick Place—an immense 340-by-1,050-foot volume contained between unarticulated precast concrete walls—was an architectural white elephant, especially in Chicago, where Mies van der Rohe had created a graceful prototype of a clear-span convention hall in 1953. Mies's scheme was never built, but it became the model for such commissions. It had wide circulation in the architectural literature that gave it a reality it never had in fact.

48. On April 4, 1968, Martin Luther King was assassinated, and the West Side of the city was in flames. Established South Side black politicians had shared power with the white City Hall bosses since the Second World War, so compliant on the city council that they were called the Silent Five. In contrast, the West Side had no industry, no economic base, no indigenous leadership. The Twenty-fourth, Twenty-fifth, Twenty-sixth,

Twenty-seventh, Twenty-eighth, and Twenty-ninth Wards, and a piece of the First Ward, were all in flames. A two-day riot, requiring 16,000 police and the 101st Airborne to quiet down two miles of West Madison Street, had left 11 blacks dead, 48 people shot by police, 2,150 arrested.

49. Royko, Mike. *Boss: Richard J. Daley of Chicago* (New York: E. P. Dutton, 1971), p. 185.

50. With eight buildings and 5,026,783 square feet of new space, 1972 was the best postwar year. See Arthur Andersen and Company, *Downtown Chicago Building Survey,* 1986. For broader trends in the commercial real estate market in the 1960s, see Robert Moore Fisher, *The Boom in Office Buildings: An Economic Study of the Past Two Decades,* Technical Bulletin 58 (Washington, D.C.: Urban Land Institute, 1967).

51. In the period between 1970 and 1983, Chicago built 36 million to New York's 73 million square feet (Larry R. Ford, *Cities and Buildings: Skyscrapers, Skid Row, and Suburbs* [Baltimore: Johns Hopkins University Press, 1994], p. 51).

52. "No write-down basis" meant that the city would pay a certain price at market to condemn out land and sell it for the same price to private developers. Eventually, as property values rose, the city had to write down the price it charged developers for condemned land it bought at a premium price. Lewis Hill, interview by Miles Berger, on North Loop Redevelopment project, typed transcript from tape (Miles Berger's papers), 1990, p. 13.

53. While the city, in the 1960s, could condemn private property, taking it from the present owners and placing it in the hands of other parties, Chicago's police powers of condemnation had only been authorized for blighted residential areas or slums, never for the center of a still-prosperous downtown. It took until the early 1970s for the city to get proper authority from the state to declare commercial property blighted. It wasn't until May 8, 1975, that the Chicago city council passed the Commercial District Development Ordinance establishing the Commercial District Development Commission, which allowed the city to acquire and resell land in blighted areas. The city was, in fact, very much in tune with contemporary developments in land use, where eminent domain powers were increasingly broadened. See Charles M. Haar and Michael Allan Wolf, *Land-Use Planning: A Casebook on the Use, Misuse, and Re-use of Urban Land,* 4th ed. (Boston: Little, Brown and Co., 1989); and Charles M. Haar, ed., *Law and Land: Anglo-American Planning Practices* (Cambridge, Mass.: Joint Center for Urban Studies, 1964).

54. Back at the time of the fire, with $65 million in insurance, donations, loans, disaster relief, and investments from abroad, Chicago enjoyed its greatest period of growth between 1871 and 1900 (*Industrial Chicago: The Building Interests* [Chicago: Goodspeed Publishing Co., 1891], pp. 146–47). These were the city's own figures prepared by the mayor's office a year after the fire.

55. Haar, ed., *Law and Land,* xi. At the time Daley was first considering his assault on the Loop, Haar, a professor of law at Harvard, was creating the legal precedent required for the enabling legislation, passed in the midseventies by the Illinois state legislature.

56. David W. Craig, "Regulation and Purchase: Two Governmental Ways to Attain Planned Land Use," in *Law and Land,* ed. Haar, p. 195.

57. Interview with Earl Neal, Dec. 7, 1991.

58. Ibid.

59. In 1995, the problems for big-city mayors have just gotten worse. An increasingly

poor population requiring more expensive services is met by a shrinking tax base and the flight of jobs and middle-class taxpayers out of the city. At the same time these mandated programs amount to more than 90 percent of a city's budget. For an economic overview of the period see J. S. Duesenberry et al., eds., *The Brookings Quarterly Econometric Model of the United States* (Chicago: Rand McNally and Co., 1965). For a comparison with New York, see Edgar M. Hoover and Raymond Vernon, *Anatomy of a Metropolis: The Changing Distribution of People and Jobs Within the New York Metropolitan Region* (Cambridge: Harvard University Press, 1959). On the architectural effect of these changes, Percy Johnson Marshall, *Rebuilding Cities* (Chicago: Aldine Publishing Co., 1966).

60. Interview with James McDonough, Oct. 16, 1991.

61. R. Bruce Dold, quoting Earl Bush in *Chicago Tribune*, Apr. 16, 1989.

62. Interview with Arthur Rubloff, in Betsy Pegg, *Dreams, Money and Ambition: A History of Real Estate in Chicago* (Chicago: Chicago Real Estate Board, 1983), p. 147.

63. In a June 5, 1979, letter to Jane Byrne, then the new mayor of Chicago, Arthur Rubloff described his "official" dealings with the city during the Daley administration. "In 1973, Lewis Hill, who was then Head of the City of Chicago's Planning Department, asked me if I would be willing to undertake the redevelopment of the block between Washington/Randolph and State/Dearborn [Block 37] for the location of a new public library." He later recalled that "Mr. Hill procrastinated continually. We held many meetings and discussions with he [sic] and his two consultants, Miles Berger and Leonard Worsek." Worsek was Berger's partner at Mid-America Appraisal.

64. Interview with Robert Christiansen, Dec. 1, 1991, and with George J. Sax, Nov. 8, 1992. Christiansen was executive director from 1961 to 1974. George J. Sax is George B. Sax's youngest son. As late as the fall of 1973, Commissioner Hill suggested that the city was still considering the use of Public Building Commission funds for a new main library on State Street (Block 36, one block north of 37, rather than 37 itself). See interview with Paul Gapp, "North Loop Pins Hopes on Drastic Surgery," *Chicago Tribune*, Oct. 7, 1973. This was essentially Hill's bluff to give the impression of an active city involvement with a purely private initiative about to be announced by Arthur Rubloff.

65. Influential landowners on Block 37 besides those with ties to Rubloff included another PBC commissioner, William Gale, chairman of Commonwealth Edison, whose firm had a big substation on the Dearborn side of the block, was also opposed to a land taking through eminent domain. In addition, Miles Berger was not without complications of his own on Block 37. He had his offices at 30 West Washington in the Stop and Shop Building, and his wife, Sally, was on the city's library board. She would have a great deal to say about any plans to relocate the building from its Michigan Avenue site.

66. Daley kept his distance, using Lewis Hill to put Rubloff in position. Lewis Hill was Daley's most loyal ally, a key member of a tight circle of professional planners inside government. Lewis Hill was for thirty years the most durable professional member of the city planning establishment. He was there at the creation of the Department of Planning, which he would later head in 1967, when it was merged with the Department of Urban Renewal. Hill was there at the beginning of the city's urban renewal initiatives. He started his career back in 1951 when he joined the staff of the Land Clearance Commission (LCC), headed by executive director Ira Bach. He also worked briefly as a field superintendent for the University of Illinois Medical Center. In the late 1950s, he went back to the LCC, during its heady urban renewal days as the long line of highrise public housing projects was going up. Hill spent almost a year with the federal gov-

ernment, working on housing. When the Community Conservation Board (CCB) and LCC merged in 1962 to become the new Department of Urban Renewal, Hill was assistant commissioner until 1965, when he replaced John Duba as commissioner.

67. Susan S. Fainstein, *The City Builders: Property, Politics, and Planning in London and New York* (Cambridge: Blackwell, 1994). Fainstein's focus is on London and New York, primarily in the 1980s. Much of what she says applies to Chicago nearly two decades earlier, albeit in a highly embryonic form.

II: THE GREAT GAME

1. Sir Alexander Burnes (1841), quoted in G. Whitney Azoy, *Buzkashi: Game and Power in Afghanistan* (Philadelphia: University of Pennsylvania Press, 1982), p. 1.

2. Ira Rogers, quoted in Robert Cross, "The Loop: Love It or Leave It," *Chicago Tribune Magazine*, Feb. 20, 1972.

3. Caro, *Power Broker*, p. 12.

4. Donald Bogue, *Skid Row in American Cities* (Chicago: Community and Family Study Center, University of Chicago, 1963), table 1–1, p. 6.

5. Charles Hoch and Robert A. Slayton, *New Homeless and Old: Community and the Skid Row Hotel* (Philadelphia: Temple University Press, 1989), pp. 119–20.

6. Donald Bogue's comprehensive study of Skid Rows for the University of Chicago's Community and Family Study Center was conducted between 1960 and 1963. He concluded that while Skid Rows epitomized economic failure in the public imagination, they paradoxically were highly profitable operations. (Bogue, *Skid Row*, p. 484.) To work politically, urban renewal had to be made to appear at least as lucrative. Daley understood this unhappy fact.

7. Tishman Speyer Properties had earlier, in 1965, developed 10 South Riverside Plaza on Canal Street.

8. Guerdon Industries chairman F. L. Cappaert, quoted in *Business Week*, Aug. 30, 1969, p. 56. In another iteration of Madison-Canal, Swibel was involved in a $300 million private venture to "develop a six-square-block area in downtown Chicago with office and apartment buildings on land to be acquired from and cleared by the city" (p. 57). Swibel had a 15 percent share and Martin L. Bartling Jr. 10 percent, with Allied Mortgage and Development Company (Alodex Corporation) providing the remainder of the financing. Bartling, vice-president of government and trade relations for U.S. Gypsum Company, was Swibel's adviser in locating companies that could provide prefabricated housing when Swibel was on the board of the Chicago Dwellings Association (CDA). The CDA had promised to erect three thousand prefab townhouses to replace slum properties. Only ninety-five units were completed before the project stalled amid allegations of corruption and kickbacks by William Scott, Illinois attorney general. A competing contractor, Magnolia Homes Division of Guerdon Industries, withdrew from the project. By providing the Madison-Canal land at thirty dollars a foot, the city was offering it below cost. The Urban Renewal Board's own estimates of clearing the land alone was $18,497,000, or $25.98 a square foot (*Chicago Sun-Times*, Apr. 25, 1967). Nothing more was built on the land until the 1980s. The city essentially land-banked the property, at no cost to the developer, until Swibel could make the Presidential Towers deal. Presidential Towers was a four-tower, upscale condominium project that was completed in the mid-1980s. There was never any formal city plan, only a marketing brochure for this six-block land swap.

9. James Tuohy and Rob Warden, *Greylord: Justice, Chicago Style* (New York: G. P. Putnam's Sons, 1989), appendix 1, p. 259. Judge Holzer was originally convicted on one racketeering/bribery count, three extortion counts, and twenty-three mail fraud counts. All but the extortion convictions were reversed by the Seventh Court of Appeals on February 19, 1988, when he was resentenced to thirteen years in prison (prosecuting attorney Scott Turow quoted by Tuohy and Warden, p. 216).

10. Oscar Newman, study director, Institute for Community Design Analysis (contract number HC-5524, Oct. 27, 1981), for U.S. Department of Housing and Urban Development. The study is entitled *Review and Analysis of the Chicago Housing Authority and Implementation of Recommended Changes* (Mar. 31, 1982).

11. In February 1991 the Federal Housing Administration completed paying down the entire insured mortgage of $158 million, so $171 million in tax-exempt bonds for the project could be redeemed at par. The bonds never paid investors a cent in interest over six and a half years. The FHA payout on the bad mortgage was the largest in HUD's history and included an ill-considered additional $16 million bailout loan to the current developers to keep the project afloat until some refinancing scheme could be worked out. In 1994 HUD secretary Cisneros had homeless families living in 7 percent of the luxury units (*The Bond Buyer,* May 6, 1991).

12. " 'Not afraid of Loop,' says Daley," *Chicago Tribune,* Jan. 31, 1973. The North Loop was never unsafe. As part of the First Ward it has a greater police presence than any other area of the city. It has the lowest level of all categories of crime.

13. Tom Klutznick, a principal in Urban Investment, later owned by JMB, had an interest in the Plitt Theatres. From the beginning, Klutznick saw downtown theater ownership as a clever real estate ploy. In a July 1, 1993, interview, he explained, "In the late sixties, Henry Plitt came to me and he said he had an option to buy what was called the northern circuit of ABC theaters. And ABC, part of that time, had acquired Balaban and Katz theaters. So I go through this with Henry, and I know nothing about the exhibition business. But in this portfolio, I see the Chicago Theater, the UA Theater, the Roosevelt Theater, the State-Lake Theater, the northwest corner of State and Lake which was a garage, there was the old theater across from what today is the Civic Center." In addition, Klutznick discovered that Plitt had leases from the Michael Todd estate to run the Selwyn and Harris Theaters. A fifty-fifty partner with Plitt, by the early 1970s Tom Klutznick owned at least a piece of almost every block in the North Loop.

14. William Slayton, "Report on Urban Renewal," in *Urban Renewal: People, Planning and Politics,* ed. Jewel Bellush and Murray Hausknecht (Garden City, N.Y.: Doubleday, 1967), pp. 381–85.

15. Ed Zotti, ed., "Sandburg Village," unpublished memoirs of Ira Bach. Carl Sandburg Village created a mixed high-rise and townhouse residential wall between Cabrini Green, decaying public housing, and the depopulating white Gold Coast (north of Chestnut Street to Lincoln Park, from the lakefront to North State Parkway) on the Near North Side. Rubloff originally joined Robin and mortgage banker George Dovenmuehle after the project was already under way. He had a 25 percent financial stake and an agreement to provide management services. Rubloff got into deals as much for his perceived as for his actual influence. But Rubloff was never big on loyalty. He later sold off pieces of his stake without first offering them to his other partners. This was in direct conflict with the original agreement. See Steven R. Strahler's two-part series on Rubloff in *Crain's Chicago Business,* Oct. 29, 1990, and Nov. 5, 1990.

16. Arthur Rubloff's last interview, 1985. Videotape, Chicago Historical Society.

17. In 1955, he would receive his most prized honor when the American Schools and Colleges Association presented him its Horatio Alger Award.

18. Interview with Abel Berland, July 9, 1992.

19. Rubloff immediately returned the favor in 1939, soon after Murphy was out on his own, when he saw to it that Naess and Murphy was hired to build the New Capitol Building to replace Burnham and Root's Masonic Temple. Typical of Rubloff, he felt this one gesture discharged all his obligations to the architect. Subsequently, Rubloff continued to throw work in Murphy's direction whenever he needed him.

20. From "Document 10," Harvey W. Zorbaugh, *The Gold Coast and the Slum* (Chicago: University of Chicago Press, 1929), pp. 60–61. Zorbaugh, a colleague of Robert Park at the University of Chicago, did one of the pioneering sociological studies of Chicago's class and ethnic divisions.

21. Arthur Rubloff, April 13, 1962, letter to William Hartmann (collection of author).

22. Interview with Abel Berland, July 9, 1992.

23. Pegg, *Dreams, Money, and Ambition,* p. 143.

24. When Arthur Rubloff was first establishing himself in the city, the social register's "four hundred" WASP families controlled all the business activity downtown. "One extremely influential group, however, did live in the district and enjoyed city-wide ascendancy—the wealthy Anglo Saxon Chicagoans of the Gold Coast. These families owned, controlled, or worked as professionals with the leading economic units of the city" (Sam Bass Warner Jr., *The Urban Wilderness: A History of the American City* [New York: Harper and Row, 1972], p. 111. See also Zorbaugh, *Gold Coast,* pp. 46–68).

25. Rubloff had developed a relationship with Webb and Knapp, Zeckendorf's real estate firm, when he brought them into the development of North Michigan Avenue in the 1950s.

26. See Memorandum, Ira J. Bach, executive director, Chicago Land Clearance Commission, to Nathaniel A. Owings, principal partner of Skidmore, Owings and Merrill and recent chairman of the Chicago Plan Commission, Jan. 11, 1954 (Rubloff Papers, box 5, file 2, Chicago Historical Society).

27. Rubloff knew that federal capital grants were issued by the Housing and Home Finance Agency only if the redeveloped area was predominantly residential. Ira Bach, then executive director of Chicago's primary land clearance agency and administrator of any federal money the city received, clarified to Nat Owings, at the time Rubloff's principal architect, that "predominantly" defined in practice meant at least 50 percent residential. Of that, a certain large percentage would be lower income and not the sort of clientele that would support the kind of redevelopment projects Rubloff had in mind. Without some sort of commercial blight ordinance that permitted him to build on prime sites, Rubloff was not interested. Letter from Ira Bach to Nathaniel Owings, Skidmore, Owings and Merrill Jan. 8, 1954 (Rubloff Papers, box 5, file 2, Chicago Historical Society).

28. From a strict business point of view, Rubloff observed how poorly residential urban renewal had worked for his more socially active friend Ferd Kramer. Kramer developed Lake Meadows and Prairie Shores on the Near South Side. The first building in the hundred-acre, 2,033-residential-unit Lake Meadows complex was completed in 1953, with the last of the ten towers completed at the end of the decade. The five identical Prairie Shores apartment towers, built across from Michael Reese Hospital on Thirty-first Street, went up in the 1960s. Both proved to be modest financial successes for the New York Life Insurance Company and developer Kramer, a contemporary of Rubloff.

Unlike what happened with public housing, where the government after condemning the land took and kept title with Kramer's two projects, the city prepared the site and sold it written down to private developers, thereby ending its involvement in the project. Socially, it wasn't so successful. While it replaced a bad residential slum relatively close to the downtown, the former tenants were not able to afford to live in the new apartments. Ferd Kramer's desire to keep the apartments integrated also mostly failed. Sufficient numbers of whites never moved into Lake Meadows, but the record was better at Prairie Shores. Both together have managed to anchor a stable black middle-class neighborhood. See Harold M. Mayer and Richard C. Wade, *Chicago: Growth of a Metropolis* (Chicago: University of Chicago Press, 1969), pp. 382–86.

29. Arthur Rubloff, "The Central Business District Slum" address to the Building Managers Association, Chicago, May 28, 1959 (Arthur Rubloff Papers, Scrapbook, 4.351, Chicago Historical Society).

30. Arvey also had strong ties to the national Democrats, particularly during the Truman years. But in the early 1950s, Arvey was permanently crippled by the Kefauver committee's investigation of organized crime. Arvey had had the misfortune of slating one of the Kefauver targets—Daniel "Tubbo" Gilbert—for Cook County sheriff. Gilbert, whom the press celebrated as the "world's richest cop," was found to be active in several illegal gambling operations.

31. Rubloff's assumption of special favors from the mayor's office and Plan Commission became a part of city lore. Miles Berger, in a personal commentary at the end of his chapter on Rubloff in *They Built Chicago: Entrepreneurs Who Shaped a Great City's Architecture* (Chicago: Bonus Books, 1992), p. 279, writes, "Although I tried over the years of my relationship with Arthur Rubloff not to be surprised by anything he might do, I was in fact shocked and amazed when he appeared at a Chicago Plan Commission meeting that I was conducting in the mid-1970s to register his strenuous objection to the development of the 1100 North Lake Shore Drive apartment building. . . . The point Rubloff did not mention was the more obvious fact that he, himself, lived at the Carlyle apartments, 1040 North Lake Shore Drive. The proposed building was not so likely to create a hazardous traffic condition [the ostensible point of his testimony] as it was to affect to some extent Arthur's own scenic view of the lakefront and the Drive. Arthur Rubloff probably asked for more zoning variations and more special consideration from the City of Chicago than any other developer. . . . My candor produced a rift in our relationship that lasted until the time Arthur decided that he might need something more from me."

32. William Zeckendorf, quoted by E. J. Kahn Jr. in "Big Operator," *New Yorker,* Dec. 8, 1951, pp. 52–53.

33. Clipping from *Jewish Daily Forward,* Mar. 22, 1954 (Arthur Rubloff Papers, Scrapbook, Chicago Historical Society).

34. Rubloff knew how unreliable these private-public partnerships were. At the same time he first published his Fort Dearborn Plan in the privately circulated, subscription-only *Quadrennial Book of Valuations of the Central Business District of Chicago, 1951–1954.* If the bold urban renewal gambit failed, he would simply rejoin his friends on North Michigan Avenue. He claimed to be the father of the organization when only the Drake Hotel distinguished the street.

35. Letter from Arthur Rubloff to Mayor Richard J. Daley, Oct. 2, 1958 (Rubloff Papers, box 7, file 5, Chicago Historical Society).

36. Logan and Molotch, *Urban Fortunes,* p. 24.

37. Ibid., p. 25. The authors describe how underlying values are distorted by even a single aggressive investor like Rubloff. "Given the fixed supply of land and the monopolies over relational advantages, more money entering an area's real estate market not only results in more structures being built but also increases the price of land and, quite plausibly, the rents on previous existing 'comparable' buildings. Thus higher investment levels can push the entire price structure upward."

38. Frank A. Randall, *History of the Development of Building Construction in Chicago*, (Urbana: University of Illinois Press, 1949), p. 198, puts the original cost of the building, in 1893, at $3.5 million. It was sold by the Masons in 1922 for $3.1 million (J. Keith White, "Evolution on State Street: The Story of the Capitol Building," *Real Estate*, Feb. 24, 1940). See also "Successor to a Skyscraper," *Buildings and Building Management*, Oct. 1939, and "Old-Timers Shed Tears: Capitol Building Nears End, *Chicago Daily News*, Dec. 25, 1939.

39. The agent for the original Capitol Building was one of the city's ten mainline realty firms, Winston and Company. It prepared an appraisal on October 8, 1926, for Silas Strawn, one of the new owners, when ground values were one hundred dollars a square foot on its nineteen thousand square feet of land. Winston was unable to stop the slide into bankruptcy. The inactivity opened the door for Rubloff.

40. The New Capitol Building was 60,000 square feet, whereas the old had been 445,000. In its first year of operation the New Capitol Building generated a gross annual cash flow of $250,000, compared with $282,000 during the last year's operation of the old tower. Additional savings, adding to the overall profitability of the project, came from sharply reduced maintenance costs.

41. Language from Rubloff's 1939 prospectus for the New Capitol Building (Rubloff Papers, Chicago Historical Society, Architecture Department). Information on theaters from the 1939 Greyhound Bus Terminal prospectus (Chicago Historical Society, Architecture Department).

42. Gerald R. Larson, "Chicago's Loop, 1830–1890: A Tale of Two Grids," in *Fragments of Chicago's Past*, ed. Pauline Saliga (Chicago: Art Institute of Chicago, 1990), p. 71.

43. Rubloff simultaneously proposed to another group, including some of the same investors who had a piece of the New Capitol, a low-rise Greyhound Bus Terminal at Clark Street, in the middle of the entertainment strip.

44. After owning their supertaxpayer for only ten years, the company sold it for $3.1 million to the Prudential Insurance Company of America. At the time of the sale, rents per square foot had risen from $4.35 to $17.82, and the yearly income had gone from $250,000 gross to $360,526 net, after all taxes and operating expenses. These are the actual values as reported by Walter R. Kuehnle, *Valuation Study of Full and Assessed Land Values on Downtown State Street* (Chicago, 1951), p. 100. Kuehnle, a registered appraiser, was hired by the State Street Council in 1935 to provide a scientific statistical profile of land values for the one-mile-long State Street commercial corridor, from Van Buren to Lake Street. With the problem of blind land trusts hiding the actual amounts involved in real estate transactions, Kuehnle's State Street reports, which were continued up until the late 1970s, provide the best source of real values. Much of the information was provided confidentially for use exclusively in these narrowly circulated reports. The State Street elite cooperated with Kuehnle, one of their own, because the thrust of his reports was his on-the-scene reporting of the cyclical rise and fall in values of "traditional downtown retailing." The reports contained reliable data, employed to get the Cook County tax assessor to lower assessed valuation on downtown commercial

property that had been traditionally inflated by the Democrats to achieve a maximum return in real estate taxes.

45. But this nice riding up of the value was not the end of it; the property was to come full circle. In 1977, Prudential sold it to a German, George R. Dobbs, for only $2 million, or $104 per square foot of ground area, after all the value had shifted back again from the building to the land. The supertaxpayer, like the once-grand Masonic Temple, was now itself effectively worth nothing.

46. Lewis Hill, interview by Miles Berger, 1990.

47. Interview with Lewis Hill, Dec. 19, 1991.

48. Lewis Hill confirmed that Daley had $43.8 million in HUD funds, but was still holding back committing it to the North Loop (*Chicago Sun-Times*, Nov. 15, 1974). Under new federal guidelines—changes Nixon made in Great Society programs—cities like Chicago had more local authority over the allocation of HUD funds (*Business Week*, Mar. 15, 1974). Daley on his own authority was, in effect, withholding federal money from Rubloff until he saw what he produced.

49. As early as the planning of the Civic Center in the early 1960s, Daley considered using public funds from the Public Building Commission to build a public library. Directly to the west of Block 37, the Civic Center was the first post–Fort Dearborn redevelopment project initiated by the city. On some of the later working drawings for the Civic Center there are sketches for a library on Block 37. C. F. Murphy, the key designing firm for the Civic Center, has donated its working drawings to the Chicago Historical Society.

50. Taubman was quickly dropped from the North Loop after he established a strong contact with Hilton Hotels. Rubloff was using Taubman in the way that William Zeckendorf Sr. employed the Chicago developer in his early deals. Taubman was simply at the time on a lower rung in the food chain.

51. One of Rubloff's local competitors was Harry F. Chaddick, a trucking executive turned real estate developer. Chaddick developed what he called Ford City on the remains of a World War II aircraft-engine plant. Like Philip Klutznick's Park Forest (1949) and Rubloff's Evergreen Plaza (1952), Ford City, which opened on August 12, 1965, was a 242-acre mall/industrial park, provided a reasonable alternative to shopping downtown. Chaddick was a Daley confidant who supervised revision of Chicago's out-of-date zoning laws. His masterwork was the Comprehensive Zoning Ordinance of 1957, which organized 643,000 separate parcels of land into a workable code.

52. Rubloff's *grand projet* sputtered and stalled because he needed government as a partner. Philip and Thomas Klutznick at Urban Investment employed Rubloff's idea on a smaller scale. In 1976 they opened their successful Water Tower Place on North Michigan Avenue. A vertical mall containing two anchor department stores, eight levels of high-end retail shops, the Ritz-Carlton Hotel, luxury condos, and movie theaters, the development tapped the rich market for downtown shopping in a secure suburban milieu. See Bernard J. Frieden and Lynne B. Sagalyn, *Downtown, Inc.: How America Rebuilds Cities* (Cambridge: MIT Press, 1989), for a comprehensive discussion of recent private downtown development projects.

53. Persuasion rather than coercion was effectively the city's position as well since the city council voted 48–0 to establish the Chicago Commission on Architectural Landmarks, a purely advisory panel with limited professional staff. See Richard Cahan, *They All Fall Down: Richard Nickel's Struggle to Save America's Architecture* (Washington,

D.C.: Preservation Press, 1994), for a dramatic account of the struggle to preserve historic architecture.

54. Arthur Rubloff quoted in *Architectural Forum* 116, no. 5 (May 1962), p. 116.

55. On October 3, 1973, the Department of Urban Renewal appropriated a $100,000 study of the North Loop, almost a year after Rubloff had begun his plan with $75,000 from the State Street Council. The State Street Council was using Rubloff to protect its interests. The businessmen feared a successful new retail mall killing off their already diminished piece of the economic pie. Rubloff had so deftly positioned himself in the middle that, in the beginning at least, he was courted by both public and private sides.

56. Rubloff decided early in the game not to let Brubaker's firm design the final and soon was auditioning other architects. Years before he formally dismissed Perkins and Will and shifted all the architectural work to C. F. Murphy Associates, he was busy tantalizing established designers like Harry Weese with the promise of a North Loop block. He thought dangling business in front of hungry architects raised his prestige at no cost while at the same time it enhanced his Burnhamesque self-image. In early 1976, Rubloff engaged Jared Shlaes, a respected real estate consultant who had worked for him at one time, to contact Weese. Arthur wanted him to provide some "schemes"—really nothing more than rough sketches—for the Sherman House block. This was one of the North Loop blocks to the west of the three original State Street parcels. Specifically, Weese was asked to show how a new State of Illinois Building might fit the block directly north of City Hall.

57. David Farber, *Chicago '68* (Chicago: University of Chicago Press, 1988), provides a good description of how quickly, through a series of catastrophic missteps, Daley's power eroded. He would never fully retrieve it.

58. See Banfield and Wilson, *City Politics.* Banfield and Wilson anticipated some of the unexpected negative results of liberal municipal reform. "If any substitute at all is provided for the power of the boss, it is a partial one. La Guardia's reforms in New York, Clark and Dilworth's in Philadelphia and Daley's in Chicago, although strengthening administrative authority, nevertheless weakened the influence of the city government as a whole. Because of this weakening of the city government, the reform of the machine, although increasing efficiency in routine matters, may at the same time have decreased in those more important matters which call for the exercise of power" (p. 126).

59. The full force of the so-called Shakman decrees was felt in the early 1970s. A young attorney, Michael Shakman, challenged the city's patronage system when he chose to run for office without the machine's blessing. He won his suit, upheld in appeals, and encouraged a series of judicial decrees, effectively dismantling a venerable, century-old employment system presided over by the mayor and administered by the aldermen, commissioners, and committeemen of all fifty wards. Before Shakman as many as forty thousand workers owed their jobs, in one way or another, to the machine.

60. After an earlier negotiation with Cadillac Fairview, at that time a key part of the Seagram family real estate holdings, fell through, Rubloff then went immediately to Olympia and York in Toronto. Cadillac Fairview required too much cash on cash, or actual cash flow, from rent, to make the deal work. Rubloff, Paul Reichmann, head of development, Tibor Pivko, director of the mortgage division at O&Y, and Robert J. Coleman of Charles Allen and Company, a venture-capital firm, met in April of 1978 at the Ritz Carlton. This was followed shortly in May by another meeting in Chicago, at which Rubloff showed Olympia and York his new North Loop plan. In a June 1, 1978, letter to Paul Reichmann, Rubloff promised to bring Mayor Bilandic with him on their

July 24–25 meeting in Toronto. To save time he used Cadillac Fairview's own rejected estimates of a fifteen-dollar net rent to keep Reichmann interested. A year earlier he had put on the same show with Ephraim Diamond at Cadillac Fairview.

61. Rubloff's habit of trading confidential information was a critical part of the show he learned in the promotion of Michigan Avenue and during the Fort Dearborn days. It was a subtle way of implicating a confederate in a scheme without smearing him in the manner of a guy like Swibel. For example, while still representing the North Michigan Avenue merchants, he communicated their private report, dated August 6, 1954, to Earl Kribben at Marshall Field's, who was in direct competition with them and an ally of Rubloff's on Fort Dearborn. He wrote "Dear Earl" on August 10, 1954, and continued, "I hand you this report from The Greater North Michigan Avenue Association in absolute confidence, I don't know whether I am over-stepping my bounds in relaying this information to you. Whatever the case may be—I do so in the spirit of trusting that it will be in the best interests of those concerned." Just to be safe, he concluded, "After you read this will you please return it to me" (Rubloff Papers, box 5, file 5, Chicago Historical Society).

62. See Nelson Forrest's March 9, 1954, confidential letter (CHS, Rubloff Papers, box 5, file 2) cautioning Rubloff about the Forty-second Ward's disdain of large civic projects initiated by downtown businessmen. These machine stalwarts dismissed projects like Fort Dearborn or the North Loop as Republican improvements and could potentially stand in their way.

63. Rubloff bought some time, but the city did nothing to implement his plan. On August 7, 1976, he took the now-dusty model, putting it out in the sun in Daley Plaza across from his offices and invited the public. Paul Gapp, architecture critic for the *Chicago Tribune,* called it a "stunning architectural model." This was the beginning of the end for Brubaker and Perkins and Will. Arthur soon asked Helmut Jahn, design partner at C. F. Murphy, to try his hand at redesigning the entire North Loop for ten thousand dollars. Jahn accepted and began a fifteen-year involvement with the project. Rubloff never bothered paying the fee.

64. Daley, quoted in *Time,* July 2, 1973.

65. Leon M. Despres, "Corruption in Chicago," *Nation,* Mar. 12, 1960, p. 221.

66. Julian Levi, quoted in *Chicago Daily News Panorama,* Dec. 1–2, 1973.

67. On May 2, 1973, James Bade, head of the State Street Council, and Arthur Rubloff signed a contract. They agreed to invest ninety-six thousand dollars in a North Loop study of the three State Street blocks. The council invested seventy thousand dollars and Rubloff twenty-six thousand dollars. Point G of the agreement specifically stated that the development would not "enlarge" beyond three city blocks. Rubloff drew the ninety-six-thousand-dollar figure from Charles William Brubaker's cost analysis of the State Street project (letter from Brubaker to Edward Kenefick, vice-president, Rubloff Development, Feb. 6, 1973). The largest single item was twenty thousand dollars for an architectural model of the entire North Loop. Rubloff used the council funds as seed money for his assault on all twenty-seven acres. Even Brubaker's earliest drawing included blocks beyond State Street.

68. Miles Berger interceded directly with Mayor Bilandic in behalf of a Canadian developer. In a memo to the mayor, October 3, 1977 (with a copy to Lewis Hill), Miles informed him of a call from Ephraim Diamond, chairman and CEO of Cadillac Fairview. He identified Mr. Diamond as a friend of his brother, Ronald. Rubloff had called Berger over the weekend to confirm that he and Cadillac Fairview had already entered

into negotiations for the North Loop. Specifically, Miles was trying to arrange for the mayor to fly with him and Rubloff to Toronto to see Cadillac Fairview's T. Eaton Center. He had cleverly positioned himself right in the middle of the deal.

69. Mid-America Appraisal and Research Corporation internal memo, July 24, 1973.

70. Berger's appraisal firm was rewarded with a total of eleven consulting contracts, amounting to $394,000, in 1977 and 1978. Miles along with members of his firm contributed $4,000 to the Cook County Democrats' fund-raising dinner in May 1978. Specifics of this sort of insider dealing were made public February 2, 1979, in a rare display of openness by a disgruntled city purchasing agent, James P. Arnold (*Chicago Tribune*, Feb. 4, 1979, and *Chicago Sun-Times*, Feb. 4, 1979). The revelations came during Byrne's successful challenge of machine incumbent Michael Bilandic. Miles Berger and his wife, Sally, were especially close to Jane Byrne. At their own expense, Miles and Sally accompanied Mayor Byrne and her husband on a widely publicized European junket.

71. In 1994, the city was spending tens of millions in federal and state aid, along with contributions from the State Street Council and other civic groups, to tear out, or "de-mall," the work completed in 1980.

72. Letter from Fairview Cadillac to Rubloff Development, Dec. 29, 1977 (author's collection).

73. Berger's appraisal company released a report, prepared for the city, that strenuously argued the hotel chain's case. From Hilton's point of view, it had assurances both from Rubloff and a key mayoral adviser that its interpretation of the North Loop redevelopment plan was the same as the city's. Nowhere in the record is there a point where anyone from the mayor's office steps forward to contradict this impression.

74. On May 24, 1978, the Plan Commission was handed an eight-point laundry list of "major items which have to be resolved to the satisfaction of Hilton in order to give prime consideration to locate an 1800 room hotel in the North Loop project." Hilton by this time was actively calling the shots, including demand number 5 that the city make a commitment to "acquire all undesirable present uses along Wabash Avenue between Roosevelt and Congress" and (number 8) "block the proposed Section 8 development of Blackstone [Hotel]."

75. Official North Loop papers of the Department of Planning and Development. Recognizing in the summer of 1980 that the city cannot pull off the North Loop redevelopment themselves, Mrs. Byrne appoints Charles Shaw as coordinator of the North Loop.

76. Geoffrey Smith, "I Just Stopped," *Forbes*, Mar. 3, 1980, p. 78.

77. Interview with Abel Berland, July 9, 1992.

III: THE BOYS ON THE BLOCK

1. John W. Stamper, *Chicago's North Michigan Avenue: Planning and Development, 1900–1930* (Chicago: University of Chicago Press, 1991), pp. 206–16. The first Magnificent Mile building was a $1.5 million four-story Bonwit Teller store on the northwest corner of Pearson Street. Groundbreaking ceremonies were held on November 17, 1947. Rubloff said that this stretch of Michigan Avenue would be the "most modern mile in the world" (*Chicago Tribune*, Apr. 10, 1947).

2. According to 1960 census data, Chicago's total population was 3,550,404, and 1,740,865 (49.5 percent) were defined as living in poverty areas. Seven hundred thousand had annual family incomes of less than $3,000, or individual incomes of less than

$1,500. Figures were compiled by the Chicago Committee on Urban Opportunity (CCUO), the city's official agency to process War on Poverty funding from the federal government. See Seymour Z. Mann, *Chicago's War on Poverty*, (Chicago: Center for Research in Urban Government, Loyola University, 1966), p. 5.

3. Berry and Cutler, "Polarization of the Central City," pp. 47–83. See also Glenn W. Fisher, *Financing Government in the Chicago Area: An Overview* (Chicago: Center for Research in Urban Government, Loyola University, 1966).

4. Neil Harris, "The City That Shops: Chicago's Retailing Landscape," in *Chicago Architecture and Design, 1923–1993*, ed. John Zukowsky (Chicago: Art Institute of Chicago; Munich: Prestel-Verlag, 1993), p. 179. Harris got these figures from a study done by Mayor Richard J. Daley's Commission on Shopping in 1973. Private studies, commissioned by the downtown business community, done at the same time come to the same conclusion.

5. Marshall Field and Company, Mandel Brothers, Carson Pirie Scott and Company, Goldblatt Brothers (Davis Store), Boston Store, the Fair (later Montgomery Ward), and Sears, Roebuck and Company. Only Marshall Field and Carson Pirie Scott remained. The most comprehensive statistics on the economics of State Street appear in a series of quadrennial papers, "Report on the Indicated Level of Land Values on Downtown State Street Chicago" (timed to the Cook County reappraisal of downtown land). Prepared by Walter R. Kuehnle, MAI, a respected local appraiser, and circulated privately to the Committee on Taxation of the State Street Council, the papers confirm the precipitous fall in retail revenues, especially among the fine specialty shops and eventually the department stores, published in census data and other government reports. In chilling statistics, collected without interruption between 1935 and 1979, for the private use of the select real estate trade, Kuehnle soberly chronicles the steady deterioration of land values that by 1980 made the street ripe for development.

6. Cafferty and McCready, "Chicago Public-Private Partnership Experience," pp. 133–34.

7. Joel Warren Barna, *The See-Through Years: Creation and Destruction in Texas Architecture and Real Estate, 1981–1991* (Houston: Rice University Press, 1992), pp. 4–8. Barna's book is a fine review of ambition and excess during the Texas real estate boom. He documents the intimate relationship between high-priced architects and high-flying developers before the bottom fell out of Texas land. Occurring a few years before the national real estate collapse that started in 1990, the Texas example should have been read as a cautionary tale. It was not, even though many of the same individuals were active in places like Chicago and New York.

8. "Architecture as a Corporate Asset," *Business Week*, Oct. 4, 1982, p. 125.

9. All of the city's major planning efforts, beginning with the 1956 Central Area Plan and culminating in the Chicago 21 Plan of 1971, were done, in house, by Skidmore, Owings and Merrill. After the Second World War, one of the Skidmore partners always held a critical pro bono position with the city. For the early years Nathaniel Owings was chairman of the Chicago Plan Commission, the government advisory panel responsible for all decisions concerning the man-made environment. Skidmore was always prominently represented on the Central Area Committee.

10. Originally the marketing plan was for 183 living units priced to sell for $83 million. But working back from the $83 million figure, Levy calculated that even when he sold out one half the building he would not have enough money. He needed a bigger aggregate purchase price. So he abruptly raised the target to $94 million, inflating the price

of each unit $100,000. After the initial flurry of December sales, he didn't sell another one for more than two years.

11. In the end, with Levy using a powerful zoning attorney to plead his case, the building was only two floors short of its designed height. At an FAR of just under 30 and a height of about 660 feet, the building was nearly 1 million square feet. Barancik had squeezed out every inch of salable space. SOM's tube structure reduced the need for interior columns that got in the way of open floor plans. The more allowable square feet, the lower the developer's costs. All these savings, like cheap land, translated into a greater payoff up front. For example, Levy's $7 million land cost averaged out to seven dollars a square foot with an FAR of 30. If he had no variance, or legal exemption, he would have paid nearly thirteen dollars a square foot. This was a fixed expense that he had to deduct from every square foot of profit the building generates. Since the footprint of the building was 35,000 square feet, every additional point of FAR equals 35,000 square feet that can be built in the air. For example a zoning bonus of 2 FAR (70,000 square feet) is given for every street exposure or public alley. One and one-half FAR (52,500 square feet) are awarded for an atrium space inside a tower. Since a modern skyscraper, given the elevator technology and building costs, has an economy of scale that makes the upper floors increasingly cheap to produce (up to a limit of about sixty stories) and, given the economics of real estate, increasingly valuable to rent or sell, increased FAR is money in a developer's pocket.

12. Graham's civic influence continued to grow in the early eighties with his leadership of a group planning the world's fair, scheduled for Chicago in 1992–93. During Jane Byrne's administration (1979–83), Chicago won the international rights to host the 1993 world's fair (marking the centennial of the World's Columbian Exposition). Bruce Graham organized groups of architects to plan the downtown site along the lakefront. Community opposition during Harold Washington's first term (1983–87) threatened the project. A week before Washington died in office in late 1987, he was said to have supported the fair because of its promise of economic development, particularly for the black South Side. With Washington gone, it was impossible to get the work done in time. Chicago lost out to Seville, Spain. This was the second major setback for Bruce Graham, who had led the private initiative to support Mayor Richard J. Daley's ambitious Crosstown Expressway project, which eventually was defeated by organized community opposition after the mayor's death in 1976.

13. Memorandum, Nov. 26, 1980 (Department of Planning and Development files).

14. "North Loop Redevelopment Concept," Nov. 13, 1980 (City of Chicago Press Release).

15. Letter from Charles H. Shaw to Martin R. Murphy, chairman, Commercial District Development Commission, Apr. 9, 1981 (Department of Planning and Development files). On May 21, 1981, the bill was scaled down to $511,714.80 and sent to Commissioner Murphy by Shaw's new lawyer, Thomas T. Burke.

16. Levy had no idea that in the beginning of 1981 he was about to plan a multimillion-square-foot project in the face of an office glut. Nearly 12 million square feet of new space came on line from 1977 to 1981. This was more than 10 percent of the city's entire inventory of office space. See Karen Marie Mokate, "The Office Construction Boom and Slowdown," *Illinois Business Review* 40, no. 3 (June 1983), pp. 10–11. Added to this was a credit crunch that began early in 1981 when interest rates soared after the head of the Federal Reserve moved aggressively to control inflation. Playing with someone else's money, Levy simply ignored the increased risk and moved ahead. The office

and retail portion never made it economically, and he had trouble with the apartments.

17. The $15 million appropriated in 1978 were earmarked for planning and land acquisition for the new State of Illinois Center in Chicago. In 1980, an additional $12 million was appropriated as the actual costs of condemnation had risen after the original announcement. The state paid $13,200,014 for parcels 34-5, 34-7, 34-8 (Sherman House) and a total of $6.4 million for the remaining seven parcels, including a bank, three parking lots, and a small hotel. All the statistics, chronologies and financial details are drawn primarily from a comprehensive report by Robert G. Cronson, Illinois auditor general (Springfield, Ill., March 1986). The audit was mandated by Legislation Audit Commission resolution number 70, adopted December 18, 1984.

18. Letter from Thomas Coulter to James Thompson, Jan. 19, 1978.

19. *Energy User News,* July 21, 1986. This brain-frying heat registered in an interior office. Closer to the windows, temperatures reached as high as 122 degrees. Workers were often sent home early.

20. In 1987, the state sued Helmut Jahn and twelve other contractors for $20 million. Murphy/Jahn quickly countersued. Paul Lurie, lawyer for the architect, reaffirmed the obvious that "Mr. Jahn wants once and for all to have his name cleared on this thing" (*Chicago Tribune,* Apr. 7, 1987, national edition.) In its countersuit, Murphy/Jahn was effectively suing Lester B. Knight, their engineering partner in the joint venture, blaming it for the HVAC problems and formally disowning any design decisions, such as substituting single for double glazing that might have exacerbated the overheating quandary.

21. At $143 a net square foot (excluding planning and art- and site-acquisition costs), the building was expensive even when compared with comparable private developments in the 1980s. The highest comparable figure cited by the auditor general's office was $164. For that JMB and Metropolitan Structures built the complicated trading floor and first tower for the Mercantile Exchange with a much higher level of detailing. The State of Illinois Center's inflated costs included $7.4 million for 509 change orders and high retrofitting costs for the inadequate HVAC system. No one has ever managed to get a reliable energy audit, but the yearly energy consumption per square foot has been reported to be the highest in the city. Costs associated with sixty-story towers were dwarfed by this squat seventeen-story public building.

22. The Supreme Court began to tighten up again on land-use regulations after the 1990 real estate crash (*Dolan* v. *City of Tigard* [1994]). In a five-to-four decision the court shifted the burden of proof to the city of Tigard, Oregon, to justify taking a 10 percent easement of a private development (A-Boy Supply Company on Main Street).

23. Office-retail space and employment estimates (based on an 80 percent office-occupancy figure consistent with the blighted area) prepared on August 11, 1978, for Martin R. Murphy, deputy commissioner, Department of Planning, by Mid-America Appraisal and Research Corporation. MARC's estimates were based on Bureau of the Census and U.S. Department of Commerce statistics, supplemented by its own on-site appraisals. These figures were used again in the Byrne and Washington administrations and by default became the official statistical analysis of the North Loop.

24. Interview with Larry Levy, June 16, 1993.

25. Insurance companies had since the early 1970s been entering into profitable joint ventures with developers, trying to use the co-ownership of office buildings as well as their traditional role as mortgagees to hedge inflation. The Prudential and Equitable were pioneers in this move from the debt to the equity side of real estate investment.

Their radical change in investment strategy initially proved prophetic and extremely profitable. They were soon copied by other insurance companies and cash-rich pension funds. Interest rates that had been climbing steadily since the first Arab oil shock in 1973 began to peak after Halloween Saturday. Halloween arrived weeks early that year. On October 6, 1979, in a rare weekend press conference, Paul A. Volcker, chairman of the Federal Reserve Board, announced that he was implementing changes to reduce the nation's money supply. The following Monday, the discount rate—the cost of money to banks—went to a record 12 percent, from 11. Consumer credit rates moved up quickly, passing 20 percent at the height of the 1981 to 1983 recession.

26. In 1981, the Prudential was not only competing with also-ran insurance giants like Travelers or Aetna, but with cash-rich pension funds, which for the first time with the Reagan tax reforms of 1981 were permitted to invest in mortgaged property. This fierce new competition that made huge sums of money available to developers inevitably led to laxer underwriting standards. Pension managers were worried that they would be left behind. The Prudential, still relatively conservative in its underwriting standards, was one of the earliest companies to draw away from these investments in the 1980s.

27. At the time Bluhm joined the company, Malkin was already in business with Robert A. Judelson. Judelson left in 1973 to form Balcor with Jerry Reinsdorf, a successful tax lawyer who brought wealthy investors to JMB in exchange for a 15 percent stake in the company. Reinsdorf is now principal owner of the Chicago White Sox and Bulls. Even with Judelson gone the company retained the augmented name, Judelson, Malkin, Bluhm and Company (JMB).

28. Interview with Stuart Nathan, June 10, 1993. Nathan joined the company in 1973.

29. The first speculative building came relatively late in the game, more than seventy years after Chicago architect William Le Baron Jenney's invention of the steel-frame skyscraper. Not until 200 South Michigan in 1958 does the city have its first office building constructed in advance of any definite use.

30. Jonathan R. Laing, "On Shaky Ground: The Slump in Real Estate Hits JMB," *Barron's*, July 27, 1992, p. 10. After showing unusual resiliency, weathering the severe 1974–75 recession, JMB demonstrated incredible growth in the 1980s. Beginning the decade with $1 billion in property, JMB at the end (1990) controlled $23 billion—managing $10 billion for its institutional investors, primarily pension funds, and $13 billion for individuals and its own account (Marcia Berss, "Tale of Two Syndicators," *Forbes 400*, Oct. 22, 1990, p. 352). JMB's decision to stay clear of wild tax syndications (like three-to-one write-offs), doomed by the 1986 Tax Reform Act, kept it in business long after high-flying firms like Robert Van Kampen's VMS Realty went bankrupt.

31. Daniel Yergin, *The Prize: The Epic Quest for Oil, Money and Power* (New York: Simon and Schuster, 1991), and Stefan Kanfer, *The Last Empire: De Beers, Diamonds and the World* (New York: Farrar Straus Giroux, 1993), are two excellent contemporary accounts of how cartels manipulated perceived market scarcity for their own profit. After wildcatters overran the most productive fields, oil was literally flowing through the streets, its price driven down to pennies a barrel. Diamonds in many parts of the world, including Australia and the former Soviet Union, are as common as pebbles on a beach. Without the De Beers monopoly autocratically controlling supply, these most precious stones would have little exchange value. Peter Foster, *Towers of Debt: The Rise and Fall of the Reichmanns* (Toronto: Key Porter Books Limited, 1993), and Neil Barsky's excellent reporting in the *Wall Street Journal* uncover some of the structural limitations that make real estate less than a perfect commodity. In the end, as the

Reichmanns sadly discovered, all that advertised liquidity meant nothing when creditors started asking for their money back. Then it looked less like an empire than an inadvertent Ponzi scheme.

32. Charles P. Kindleberger's *Manias, Panics, and Crashes: A History of Financial Crises*, rev. ed. (New York: Basic Books, 1989), is the classic study on the subject of large economic enthusiasms, from tulips to land.

33. Ron Chernow, *The House of Morgan: An American Banking Dynasty and the Rise of Modern Finance* (New York: Simon and Schuster, 1991), p. 637.

34. See Michael Lewis, *Liar's Poker* (New York: W. W. Norton and Co., 1989), for the best account of the eighties mortgage feeding frenzy. Lewis worked at Salomon Brothers in New York, where between 1981 and 1986 he observed that "every home mortgage in America, one trillion dollars' worth of debt, seemed to be for sale" (p. 103).

35. Statistics prepared by Dale Anne Reiss, managing partner in the Chicago office of Kenneth Leventhal and Company, cited in *Realty & Building* 205, no. 26 (June 29, 1991), p. 10.

36. JMB refinanced 10–30 South Wacker (Merc Towers) in 1989 with a $575 million offering in bonds and $50 million in preferred stock. This was a stunning appreciation in value in less than ten years. JMB's original investment was $350 million. Neil Bluhm and Judd Malkin personally took millions out of the deal when Nomura Securities International (Japan) and a Netherlands financing consortium operating out of the Cayman Islands bought the real estate at the height of the market. JMB, made rich with the refinancing, had radically reduced its risk, yet remained on the fee side, managing and leasing the property.

37. All quotes are from interview with John Loeb, May 5, 1993.

38. Levy's development business, in fact, was stopped cold. In late 1980, he had priced the 183 units at Mag Mile to compete with Water Tower Place, a few blocks down on North Michigan Avenue. The units were carefully priced to raise a total of $83 million. But this was before he thought he could sell out in only a few months. Buying his own salesmanship, Levy raised the total to $94 million. On paper, this immediately added $11 million to what the Levy Organization could claim as pure profit, but added a crippling surcharge of $100,000 to each unit.

Furthermore, to widen the spread between the financing and his actual expenses, he cut back sharply on details that fatally undermined the building's attractiveness to the luxury market. He and his construction managers, Schal, consistently hammered at the cost of the building. Spiking national interest rates made moot his original financing projections; his debt climbed to between $110 and $120 million. In 1986, only two years after its completion, Larry would lose One Mag Mile, the very building that got him into the big-time development game in the first place. His equity partner, the Colburn family, owner of Consolidated Electrical Distributors (CED), had to put in an additional $55 million when financing from the teachers' pension fund went bad. When Levy refused to put in any of his own money, the Colburns took the building back.

39. The $1.7 million is calculated by taking $2.1 million (Levy's payment to Zell for the Lanski leasehold) plus a year's rent roll *minus* the $300,000 security deposit and $215,000 Zell had paid in twelve months of rent to the Lanskis.

40. Characteristically, Levy softened the blow by agreeing to put up as little cash as possible to buy more time to conclude a joint-venture agreement. He paid the Sterns and Loebs, who were equal partners in the business and owned more than 90 percent of the stock with a few key employees having tiny stakes, only 25 percent in cash and

wrote a note for the additional $1.50. On April 30, 1983, after no additional principal had been paid, Marla (for Mark and Larry Levy) bought back the $1.50 notes for 50 cents, discounting their own contractual obligations by 66 percent.

41. Interview with Larry Levy, June 16, 1993.

42. The negotiations with Harvey Walken occurred before Metropolitan Structures and Metropolitan Life completed their formal fifty-fifty partnership in 1982. But even in 1979, the large insurance company viewed Weissbourd's company as a reliable partner in the risky commercial real estate business. It was around this same time that Weissbourd entered into negotiations with JMB to form a permanent development partnership. The idea was dropped shortly before the MetLife agreement was signed.

43. The city's first RFPs appeared in newspapers June 20 to 22, 1982. On August 14, 12 developers replied with 16 proposals.

44. This was the dominant perspective used by Jules Guerin in rendering the Chicago Plan.

45. JMB and Metropolitan Structures, without the services of Larry Levy, had responded to an earlier city request for proposal (August 18, 1982) and expressed interest in developing Block 35.

46. Or this was the plan when they answered, along with only one other bidder, specifically for 37, the city's RFP on May 1, 1983, for the redevelopment of Block 37.

47. The northwest corner of Randolph and Dearborn (14,400 square feet of land, December 1987 deed), across the street from Block 37, sold at $608 per square foot; 134–190 South LaSalle Street (27,500 square feet of land, November 1982 deed) sold at $1,019 per square foot; 123 North Wacker (21,800 square feet of land, May 1984 deed) sold at $642 per square foot. These were some of the comparable values put into evidence by the city's appraiser (Kowalski transcript, pp. 675–80) at the time a traverse was filed in 1988 challenging FJV's exclusive right to redevelop the block. Both FJV and Sidcor hired appraisers that put the block's reuse value at no less than $500 a square foot at a time the city was still required to sell it back to private developers at $151.50.

48. Arthur Andersen report prepared by Noah Shlaes for the American Society of Real Estate Counselors workshop, "The Office Building Revolution," Chicago, Sept. 25, 1990, p. 9.

49. *Chicago Tribune*, Nov. 26, 1989.

50. Ibid.

IV: THE WAY THINGS WORK

1. "Staff Report: North Loop Study Area," Oct. 2, 1973 (Chicago: Department of Urban Renewal). When the initial North Loop legislation was proposed in 1973, the three State Street blocks plus the two between Dearborn and Clark produced only $3,453,826 in taxes. Rock-bottom assessments and low property tax yield were the heart of the city's case for defining the area as blighted. The city's gamble was to trade all its low-end retail sales for the promise of greater future yields when Nordstrom's and Lord and Taylor were coaxed back to the Loop.

2. Buck and Stein had also benefited from the fallout from the Shaw plan. In place of the two-block Hilton convention hotel, John Buck developed on discounted land a 1-million-square-foot tower for the Leo Burnett advertising agency, and Richard Stein traded his redevelopment contract to the Prime Group, retaining a small interest in the

project so the city would not suffer the embarrassment of having to rebid the land. Prime later built a tower for the Chicago printer R. R. Donnelley and Sons, on Wacker to the west of Leo Burnett. These skyscrapers, retaining the remnant of the generous Hilton subsidies, were indistinguishable from the unsubsidized towers built by these same developers throughout the rest of the expanding downtown.

3. As of 1989, the improved block was to include a new county office building, a high-class corporate tower, and a huge retail mall on State Street. In the place of an odd collection of decaying buildings, most empty above the first floor, FJV offered to erect 2.2 million square feet of rentable space. Given 1989 assessments the city could reasonably expect to collect ten times the current property and sales taxes once the new buildings were up and running.

4. Memorandum, Charles C. Sklavanitis to Lewis W. Hill, commissioner of Urban Renewal, Feb. 5, 1974 (Department of Planning and Development). Department of Planning Files.

5. *Redevelopment Plan for Blighted Commercial Area, Project North Loop* (Chicago: Commercial District Development Commission, Mar. 1979, rev. 1982).

6. In November 1982, Leslie Savage, a staff member in the Department of Planning, prepared a briefing paper, "North Loop Redevelopment Project," for Miles Berger. Savage reviewed all North Loop activities from their inception in 1973 as Arthur Rubloff's private initiative. This limited-edition white paper is a rare surviving record of the highly improvisational nature of North Loop planning.

7. Jane Byrne, *My Chicago* (New York: W. W. Norton and Co., 1992), p. 183.

8. See Gerald D. Suttles, *The Man-Made City: The Land-Use Confidence Game in Chicago* (Chicago: University of Chicago Press, 1990), p. 34. Suttles discusses Chicago's big-project mentality. The city had issued no fewer than four major city plans between 1966 and 1983 alone. Although, in the end, it was more development than planning that reshaped Chicago. In the period 1965 to 1972 office space more than doubled and five hundred miles of expressways were built.

9. *Chicago 21: A Plan for the Central Area Communities*, September 1973, was an outline of possible development masquerading as a real city document. Overgeneralized and broadly drawn, the plan presented between silver covers contained drawings from the abandoned Fort Dearborn initiative. A letter from Mayor Richard J. Daley reproduced on the first page made it look like an official city document rather than a privately financed development wish list.

10. All under Manilow's personal letterhead, from his office at IBM Plaza, Lewis Manilow wrote Mayor Byrne on September 15 and October 9, 1980. He wrote separately to Swibel and Berger on November 5, 1980.

11. At least one member of the Chicago Plan Commission was disturbed by its chairman's frequent references to the marketplace. Leon M. Despres, an independent from Hyde Park, found Berger's laissez-faire notions dangerous and felt he was putting the North Loop up for grabs. Despres felt that following the entrepreneurs' naked desires had produced the mess in the North Loop in the first place. On April 23, 1981, he wrote Miles Berger, trying to get him to postpone a vote on the revised North Loop Guidelines. He also pointed out he felt Berger might have a conflict of interest as an active member of the same real estate community he was supposed to be overseeing.

12. For years, Goldberg planned an even more ambitious version of the distinctive corncob-shaped Marina City for Wells Street called River City, east of the South Branch of the Chicago River. When the Plan Commission, led by Miles Berger, radi-

cally scaled down the project, originally planned with many high-rise towers, schools, medical facilities, the size of many a midsize city, Swibel offered to help Goldberg get his way. Goldberg declined Swibel's help and Berger prevailed. The version of River City that was finally built had little of the social planning aspects that Goldberg thought essential for the project's success.

13. Swibel did not have a dime of his own money at risk. The whole deal was leveraged with one thousand dollars in capital stock from the original Marina City Management Corporation (Bob Tamarkin, "Condomania in Chicago," *Forbes*, Nov. 13, 1978).

14. By the 1990s Marina Towers was merely a small part of the nation's $500 billion inventory of nonperforming real estate seized from insolvent S and Ls.

15. Steven Gittleson, "The Battle over Charles Swibel," *Chicago*, July 1982, p. 102. The article recounts Swibel's final days as head of the public-housing agency. Swibel received seventy-nine thousand dollars a year from Continental for managing only one piece of property.

16. *Downtown Development Chicago: 1989–1992,* fourth report in a series by the Department of Planning, Charles Thurow, acting commissioner (Chicago).

17. Local representatives of Greyhound had been pressing the city for a new facility, even suggesting at one time that they be given land on the old Madison-Canal property controlled by Charles Swibel. Greyhound's agent communicated this by letter to Lewis Hill, commissioner of planning, as early as June 9, 1978, during the last year of the Bilandic administration. In a second letter, written the same day, the agent warned Hill that unless the bus company got what it wanted, it would delay condemnation on its North Loop renewal block up to five years rather than the six months Commissioner Hill had mentioned. It costs money every month a condemnation is delayed and almost inevitably raises the eventual amount of the award. Greyhound's people predicted in 1978 exactly what happened in the North Loop. Delays, on average, raised land values five times. The city was left paying the inflated costs.

18. Colonel Arvey started with "the Jewish immigrant's idea that any property downtown is good." He received small pieces of Loop land in return for legal work and his considerable political contacts. (Interview with Howard Arvey, Feb. 4, 1992).

19. At its peak, in 1988, new Japanese investment in American real estate was $16.54 billion. From 1985 to the end of the decade, the Japanese had purchased $76 billion worth of individual buildings here and made close to $250 billion in real estate loans. Before this accelerated participation in overseas real estate markets, the Japanese owned less than $1 billion worth of property in the United States. This enthusiasm for prestige buildings far from home proved short-lived and very expensive. At the end of 1992, direct real estate investment by the Japanese was back again to under $1 billion (*Wall Street Journal*, Mar. 19, 1993).

20. Quoted by Steven Greenhouse, "Greenspan Sees Risks Globally," *New York Times*, Oct. 14, 1992.

21. This was a highly capitalized economic bubble. For example, when the national real estate crash came in early 1990, American banks and insurance companies alone had $350 billion invested in commercial property (Anthony Downs, "What Have We Learned from the 1980s Experience?" *Real Estate Investment* [Solomon Brothers Report], July 1991, p. 10). Add offshore investment, pension funds, S and Ls, and individuals, $1.009 trillion was invested in American office buildings and $1.115 in retail properties before everything fell apart. These figures come from a study, *Managing the Future: Real Estate in the 1990s*, prepared by the Arthur Andersen Real Estate Services

Group for the Institute of Real Estate Management Foundation in 1991, pp. 1–2. In 1993, when the real estate bubble burst, Goldman, Sachs & Company estimated that "problem real estate" held by government and private entities was about $250 billion.

22. Newton C. Farr, president of the Chicago Real Estate Board in 1930, later became president of Farr and Company Realty, the company his father founded in 1876.

23. St. Clair Drake and Horace R. Cayton, *Black Metropolis: A Study of Negro Life in a Northern City* (New York: Harcourt, Brace and Co., 1945), p. 208.

24. Ronald Chinnock, partner of Newton C. Farr, interviewed by phone by Neil J. King, certified appraiser and bank president, Feb. 28, 1993. King's father, Armand, was also in the real estate business and worked for Krenn and Dato. After the crash, Armand King was surprised to discover Mr. Farr and a subordinate as the new owners of Krenn and Dato foreclosed property.

25. Interview with Howard Arvey, February 4, 1992.

26. The city council passed the bond anticipation ordinance on April 1, 1981, and the full bond issue on September 16, 1982.

27. Public interest groups included professional coalitions like the American Institute of Architects (Chicago Chapter), Chicago Central Area Committee, Chicago Council of Lawyers, Civic Coalition Task Force on the North Loop, City Club of Chicago; preservation groups like Landmarks Preservation Council of Illinois, Metropolitan Housing and Planning Council, National Trust for Historic Preservation; tax protesters like South Austin Coalition Community Council, Property Conservation Council, Campaign Against the North Loop Tax Break; business groups like State Street Council; and cultural groups like those advocated by Lewis Manilow.

28. "North Loop Plan Saves 8 Buildings," *Chicago Sun-Times*, Mar. 14, 1981.

29. One of the fortunate eight was the Commonwealth Edison electrical substation on Block 37, which Berger advised Byrne was too costly to move anyway.

30. "Byrne to Identify N. Loop Owners, Calls for Funding," *Chicago Sun-Times*, March 7, 1981.

31. The fallout from the study would stall the development of Block 37 throughout the 1980s. Designation of the McCarthy Building as a city landmark became the source of litigation and nearly resulted in FJV's withdrawal from the redevelopment deal. The entire preservation issue was to become a major headache for the Washington administration (1983–87).

32. *North Loop Tax Increment Redevelopment Area: Redevelopment Plan and Project*, Jan. 1984, p. 26 (Report, City of Chicago). An African-American, Harold Washington had replaced Jane Byrne as mayor, but was still using Berger's calculations. Development had no color line.

33. Swibel had gotten $50 million to build Marina City in the 1960s and another $50 million in the 1970s to convert it into condominiums.

34. United Press International, Sept. 9, 1982. *United States* v. *Stephen T. Gorny*, 83–2118, (7th Circuit). On December 10, 1985, Robert Berger pleaded guilty to the indictment charging him and his company with paying county employees to lower tax assessments for Berger Company clients. He became a witness in the federal case. (Bureau of National Affairs, *United States Law Week*, Dec. 10, 1985.)

35. The formal name of the legislation is the Real Property Tax Increment Allocation Redevelopment Act. As for federal redevelopment programs, implementation depended upon the city's coming up with an approved redevelopment plan and project. The city plan, written in January 1984 and revised in April 1984 and September 1987,

defined the process: "The new tax revenue generated by the application of tax rates to the increase in assessed values due to redevelopment is described as tax increment revenue." TIF revenue was the spread between the preexisting tax revenues and the increase (higher assessed valuation/greater tax revenues) after redevelopment.

36. *Chicago Development Plan 1984* (Report, City of Chicago), p. 53.

37. In addition, the city proposed to extend the five dollars per one thousand dollar real estate transfer tax to formerly exempt ownership transfers between secret trusts. This was a formerly sacrosanct tax loophole in Illinois, one of only seven states to permit blind land trusts.

38. With a 6 percent lease tax, Stein figured the original land discount was no longer such a good deal. The city had bought the Stein property along with a piece for African-American developer Elzie Higginbottom and his partner, old-line real estate firm Baird and Warner, for $18 million and sold it for $13 million.

39. Mary K. Ludgin and Louis H. Masotti, quoted in the *Los Angeles Times*, May 21, 1986. A noted real estate economist, Masotti and his associate Mary Ludgin had written a study tracking the "central city renaissance."

40. Demolition under an Illinois statute passed in the late 1970s assured that municipalities would not have to await the outcome of often-lengthy court proceedings. If a jury later raised the compensation for an owner's land—as occurred in all the Block 37 litigations—the city was obligated to pay it.

41. The city in 1984 finally got around to submitting a semblance of a development plan. Not much detail, but a summary of renewal areas and projected financing appears in the Chicago Development Plan 1984. For all "North Loop Redevelopment Planning" the city projects $222 million (general obligation and tax increment financing), $341,000 (personnel), and $1 billion (private investment). The total topped one-quarter of a billion, as later condemnation awards dramatically inflated the cost of land acquisition.

42. *City of Chicago v. LaSalle National Bank, etc., et al.*, 87L50684, Cook County Circuit Court (filed Aug. 1, 1988); owners' memorandum *In Support of Traverse*, p. 41.

43. For example, among other decaying structures, the Oriental Theater Building (opened in 1927) stood on the burned foundations of the old Iroquois Theater. The Iroquois had burned down on December 30, 1903, killing 596 people, twice the official death count of the Great Chicago Fire.

V: THE PRICE OF PROGRESS

1. *Chicago Sun-Times*, Oct. 18, 1989.

2. Quoted in "A Loop Era Crumbling Down on Block 37," *Chicago Tribune*, Sept. 12, 1989.

3. Neil Smith, "Toward a Theory of Gentrification: A Back to the City Movement by Capital, Not People," *APA Journal*, Oct. 1979, p. 546. See also Neil Smith, Betsy Duncan, and Laura Reid, "From Disinvestment to Reinvestment: Tax Arrears and Turning Points in the East Village," *Housing Studies* 4, no. 4 (1989).

4. Otto A. Davis and Andrew B. Whinston, "The Economics of Urban Renewal," in *Urban Renewal: The Record and Controversy*, ed. James Q. Wilson (Cambridge: MIT Press, 1966), p. 54.

5. The ten-times multiple when real estate is transformed to a higher use is a conservative estimate deduced from studying the rent rolls of Arthur Rubloff and Company's

downtown properties near Block 37. See also Eric Clark, *The Rent Gap and Urban Change* (Lund, Sweden: Lund University Press, 1987); and Ralph A. Walker, "Urban Ground Rent: Building a New Conceptual Framework," *Antipode* 6, no. 1 (1974). Older buildings produce the majority of their revenue from the retail operations on the ground floor. As newer buildings get larger the multiple can be increased by another power of ten, figured as FAR. This was the value-added architecture FJV was after. The value-added FAR buildings were practical only after the ground rent had been exploited for all its economic potential during the first two decades after the Second World War.

6. "FAR" is specified within a city's zoning code, to describe the multiple available to a developer interested in acquiring a piece of property. FAR is given "as right," the maximum square footage allowed by the zoning code or negotiated on a block-by-block basis. For example, if a developer purchases 20,000 square feet of land with an FAR of 20, he can build a building with 400,000 square feet of rentable space. The inherent advantages of more FAR are financial, not aesthetic. The larger a building's area, the bigger the financing.

7. Stephen Zoll, "Superville: New York—Aspects of Very High Bulk," *Massachusetts Review*, 14, no. 3 (Summer 1973), p. 471.

8. Interview with Marshall Holleb, Oct. 29, 1991. Holleb is a prominent Chicago real estate lawyer responsible for, among other things, negotiating the air rights above the Illinois Central Railroad tracks to build Illinois Center. Holleb, now near eighty, knew Colonel Crown from his days as a young lawyer, often on the other side of deals.

9. A careful review of the land records held at the County Building and at the Chicago Title and Trust Company reveals a flurry of activity on Block 37 around the end of the Second World War. After that, there was an occasional sale, indicating that the new owners of land on the block were trying to assemble larger properties. But an equal number of entries indicate building violations of various sorts and few applications for building permits. Landlords saw value in the underlying ground, not in the buildings. These are classic signs that the land, after the war, was put to sleep.

10. Robert Heilbroner, "Reflections: Economic Predictions," *New Yorker,* July 8, 1991, pp. 73–74.

11. *Appraisal of Real Estate Located at 8–12 West Randolph Street and 160 North State Street Chicago, Illinois for the First National Bank of Chicago,* G. H. Scribner Jr., appraiser, May 29, 1952 (Scribner and Co. files, Chicago), p. 3.

12. Paul W. Gates, *History of Public Land Law Development* (Washington, D.C.: Public Land Law Review Commission, 1968).

13. These same secrecy laws also heightened the power of CT&T and other "trusts." Official land records held in the basement of the County Building are required only to provide the name of a designated officer of the bank, a straw man like Thomas Woelfle of LaSalle Trust, whose signature appears on nearly half the city's downtown land documents. "T. E. Woelfle, Bachelor," paid a sinecure to remain single so no disgruntled wife or child could put a lien on property, only his by a masterful fiction. A castrato Chicago style, this loyal, unattached, virtually unknown signer guarded the hoard of paper, the treasure maps to potential billions out on the street. Mr. Woelfle and others acted as efficient conduits so money could flow freely between trusts, making deals run smoothly with a minimum of scrutiny.

14. Chernow, in *House of Morgan,* remarks on a similar phenomenon accompanying the rise of Jewish trading houses in New York. Chernow describes the businesses as "dy-

nastic, with only blood or marriage securing partnerships. They worked in the interstices left by the big Christian houses" (p. 79).

15. The Court House block, present site of the City Hall and County Building, and school sections are a throwback to feudal law in Britain, where individual landownership was restricted to ancient royal concessions or a system of "fee tail that was the legacy of feudalism that still exists in muted form throughout the European world." See Vernon Carstensen, ed., *The Public Lands: Studies in the History of the Public Domain* (Madison: University of Wisconsin Press, 1962), pp. 4–5.

16. Hoyt, *One Hundred Years,* p. 445.

17. James Buckingham, quoted in John W. Reps, *The Making of Urban America: A History of City Planning in the United States* (Princeton, N.J.: Princeton University Press, 1965), p. 302.

18. From the days of the city's earliest real estate boom in the 1830s, when banks recklessly issued notes against wild unimproved land, Block 37 was in play. Under the United States Land Ordinance of 1785, land was made available to citizens at a minimum section of 640 acres for $1,280 to encourage settlement of the vast western territories. The Pre-Emption Act of 1841 relaxed these requirements to 160 acres or fewer, secured merely by occupying them and paying the government $1.25 an acre. See Peter Wolf, *Land in America: Its Value, Use and Control* (New York: Pantheon Books, 1981), pp. 41–43.

19. Hoyt, *One Hundred Years,* p. 24.

20. Bruce Lindeman, "Anatomy of Land Speculation," *Journal of the American Institute of Planners* 42 (Apr. 1976), p. 149.

21. William Cronon, *Nature's Metropolis: Chicago and the Great West* (New York: W. W. Norton and Co., 1991), pp. 29–30.

22. Warner, *Urban Wilderness,* p. 17.

23. James Grant, *Money of the Mind: Borrowing and Lending in America from the Civil War to Michael Milken* (New York: Farrar Straus Giroux, 1992), p. 296.

24. Exploiting property to raise large amounts of borrowed cash accelerated out of control in our time, beginning with the gradual deregulation of commercial banking during Richard Nixon's aborted second administration. Deregulation permitted bankers to participate more actively in the real estate markets at a time when land was purchased with the express intention of trading it fast. See Martin Mayer, *The Bankers* (New York: Ballantine Books, 1974); Elbert V. Bowden, *Revolution in Banking* (Richmond, Va.: Robert F. Dame, 1980); and Alan Rabinowitz, *The Real Estate Gamble* (New York: AMACOM, 1980).

25. Hoyt, *One Hundred Years,* p. 102. Unlike Manhattan, where people continued to live downtown, Chicago was never successful in resettling its core business district with apartments. Changes in scale from small retail-dependent buildings to tall office structures were the way architects allowed real estate investors to meet the escalating price of downtown land. See George B. Ford, *Building Height, Bulk, and Form: How Zoning Can Be Used as a Protection Against Uneconomic Types of Building on High-Cost Land* (Cambridge: Harvard University Press, 1931).

26. Hoyt, *One Hundred Years,* table 44, p. 345. Values on State Street between Washington and Randolph were higher because of the street's status as the city's primary retail district. They ranged from $1,750 in 1873 to a high of $35,000 in 1928. Hoyt reports the cyclical retreat of values after the economic panics in the 1830s, 1850s, 1870s, 1890s, and finally the Great Depression of the 1930s. Loop land valued at $1 billion in 1928 was worth $500 million in 1933 (table 45, p. 347).

27. Montgomery Schuyler, "A Critique of the Works of Adler and Sullivan," in *American Architecture and Other Writings*, ed. William Jordy and Ralph Coe (Cambridge: Harvard University Press, 1961), p. 382. Rem Koolhaas, in *Delirious New York* (New York: Moncaelli Press, 1994), called this uniquely American combination of land speculation and tall buildings "Manhattanism." First published in 1978, his "retroactive manifesto for Manhattan" has direct implications for Chicago's downtown—an exceedingly thin but dense version of Manhattan.

28. Colin Rowe, "Chicago Frame," in *The Mathematics of the Ideal Villa and Other Essays* (Cambridge: MIT Press, 1976), pp. 104–5.

29. *Industrial Chicago*, p. 129.

30. Information on Block 37, lots 3, 4, Original Town Section 9-39-14, drawn from land tracts held by Chicago Title and Trust Company and Cook County, Illinois.

31. Ibid., pp. 206, 218.

32. Emrys Jones, *Metropolis* (New York: Oxford University Press, 1990), p. 76. This was the period of Chicago's greatest economic rise, where "The concentration of buildings meant a rise in land values and this in turn prompted people to build higher to get greater returns."

33. Altgeld's huge Unity Building had settled unevenly and never leased up completely. The period between 1871 and 1893 was a significant real estate bubble. Old families like the McCormicks were safely out before the crash, leaving the newcomers holding the bag.

34. Interview with John Nelson, Sept. 20, 1990. Nelson was an elevator operator at the Unity Building for more than forty years, beginning as a young man on February 8, 1945. He was there to the last as the final tenants were evicted in 1989.

35. M and R Amusement Corporation, which held the lease for the 3,000-seat theater (the third-largest house in Chicago after the Uptown with 4,300 and the Chicago with 3,980), tried a two-week experiment in 1971 to bring live entertainment back to Randolph Street. In 1969, M and R aborted a plan to divide the huge auditorium into two smaller theaters to accommodate a changing audience (*Chicago Sun-Times*, Sept. 2, 1977).

36. Downtown Research Corp., *Upstairs Downtown: An Inventory of Upper Floor Shops and Services in the Heart of Chicago's Loop* (Chicago: Greater State Street Council, Jan. 1987).

37. Alex Polikoff, a brilliant corporate attorney who joined BPI in 1970, helped pursue the class-action Gautreaux case, originally filed in 1966, which successfully proved that there was a systematic pattern of segregation in the Chicago Housing Authority. The judgment was later affirmed and broadened in a 1976 United States Supreme Court decision. The Gautreaux litigation was followed by a decade of public defeats for Daley. This was reason enough, in his mind, for the city to single out Block 37 for demolition.

38. University of Illinois Chicago Center for Urban Economic Development, *The Displacement of Storefront Businesses in Downtown Chicago 1976–1981* (Urbana, Ill.: UICUED, Aug. 1982), p. 18. In this same five-year period, the authors note that sixty-seven of eighty-three displaced businesses were formerly on prime streets and were replaced by only fifteen new storefronts, resulting in a net loss of fifty-two "prime storefront locations" (p. 13).

39. *Crain's Chicago Business*, Aug. 21, 1989.

40. Interview with Michael Tobin, project manager, Metropolitan Structures, Oct. 4, 1990. Tobin, an architect, was responsible for negotiating with the city and handled the Designers Mart "problem." FJV sued him.

41. *Chicago Tribune,* Sept. 12, 1989.

42. Financing skyscrapers was traditionally tied to a developer's ability to rent space before construction began. This was to assure lenders that the project was going ahead before they started the cash flowing. But with pension fund managers and others with lots of cash to invest monthly, conservative performance criteria were relaxed. Before credit for speculative real estate investments was shut off in 1990, a developer could expect sometimes more than 100 percent financing with less than 25 percent of the tenants committed in advance to renting space.

43. At the time of the deal, *Forbes* listed Judd Malkin and Neil Bluhm, JMB's two general partners, as each having a personal fortune of more than $1 billion. Bernard Weissbourd, head of Metropolitan Structures, had amassed his own considerable nest egg building and holding large office buildings in Chicago for over thirty years.

44. Letter from Michael Tobin, representing FJV, to Rafael Rios-Rodriguez, deputy commissioner, Department of Planning, Aug. 22, 1990 (Department of Planning, North Loop files).

45. "BNA's Banking Report," *Bureau of National Affairs, Inc.* 54, no. 7 (Feb. 19, 1990), p. 281.

VI: FAULTY TOWERS

1. Stephen Roulac, quoted in the *Chicago Tribune,* Aug. 9, 1992.

2. Maggie Mahar, "The Great Collapse: Commercial Real Estate Is on the Skids across the Nation," *Barron's,* July 22, 1991, p. 10.

3. These are the industry's own statistics drawn from occupancy surveys conducted by the Building Owners and Managers Association (BOMA) of Chicago, spring 1993.

4. Steve Weiner, "Everything's Negotiable," *Forbes,* Mar. 19, 1990.

5. For an optimistic view of these developments, read Joel Garreau, *Edge City: Life on the New Frontier* (New York: Doubleday, 1991). On the refractory problems of the inner city, see two different views, William Julius Wilson, *The Truly Disadvantaged: The Inner City, the Underclass, and Public Policy* (Chicago: University of Chicago Press, 1987), and Richard J. Hernstein and Charles Murray, *The Bell Curve* (New York: Free Press, 1994).

6. *Chicago Tribune,* Feb. 26, 1993.

7. *Chicago Sun-Times,* Mar. 23, 1994.

8. *Crain's Chicago Business,* Apr. 8, 1991.

9. Since the condemnation was completed in 1990, in addition to debt relief and taxes, FJV has paid more than $6 million in penalties and forced contributions to the preservation of other historic buildings in the Loop.

10. These are the city's own projections prepared by the Department of Planning, October 1984.

11. Frederick Jackson Turner, "The Significance of the Frontier in American History" (paper read July 12, 1893, and first published in *Proceedings of the State Historical Society of Wisconsin,* Dec. 14, 1893) in *The Frontier in American History,* (Malabar, Fla.: Robert E. Krieger Publishing Co., 1985), p. 3.

12. Koolhaas, *Delirious New York,* p. 289.

SELECTED
BIBLIOGRAPHY

Algren, Nelson. *Chicago: City on the Make.* Garden City, N.Y.: Doubleday and Co., 1952.

Anderson, Alan B., and George W. Pickering. *Confronting the Color Line: The Broken Promise of the Civil Rights Movement in Chicago.* Athens: University of Georgia Press, 1968.

Andrews, Wayne. *Battle for Chicago.* New York: Harcourt, Brace and Co., 1946.

Azoy, G. Whitney. *Buzkashi: Game and Power in Afghanistan.* Philadelphia: University of Pennsylvania Press, 1982.

Banfield, Edward C. *Political Influence: A New Theory of Urban Politics.* New York: Free Press, 1961.

Banfield, Edward C., and James Q. Wilson. *City Politics.* Cambridge: Harvard University Press, 1965.

Barna, Joel Warren. *The See-Through Years: Creation and Destruction in Texas Architecture and Real Estate, 1981–1991.* Houston: Rice University Press, 1992.

Barrett, James R. *Work and Community in the Jungle: Chicago's Packinghouse Workers, 1894–1922.* Urbana: University of Illinois Press, 1987.

Bell, Daniel. *The Coming of Post-Industrial Society: A Venture in Social Forecasting.* New York: Basic Books, 1973.

Bellow, Saul. *It All Adds Up: From the Dim Past to the Uncertain Future.* New York: Viking Press, 1994.

Bensman, David, and Roberta Lynch. *Rusted Dreams: Hard Times in a Steel Community.* Berkeley: University of California Press, 1987.

Berger, Miles. *They Built Chicago: Entrepreneurs Who Shaped a Great City's Architecture.* Chicago: Bonus Books, 1992.

Berry, Brian J. L., and Irving Cutler, et al., eds. "Polarization of the Central City." *Chicago: Transformations of an Urban System.* Cambridge, Mass.: Ballinger Publishing Co., 1976.

Blair, Margaret M., ed. *The Deal Decade: What Takeovers and Leveraged Buyouts Mean for Corporate Governance.* Washington, D.C.: Brookings Institution, 1993.

Bogue, Donald. *Skid Row in American Cities.* Chicago: Community and Family Study Center, University of Chicago, 1963.

Bonbright, James C. *The Valuation of Property: A Treatise on the Appraisal of Property for Different Legal Purposes.* New York: McGraw Hill, 1937.

Bowden, Elbert V. *Revolution in Banking.* Richmond, Va.: Robert F. Dame, 1980.

Bradbury, Katharine L., Anthony Downs, and Kenneth Small. *Urban Decline and the Future of American Cities.* Washington, D.C.: Brookings Institution, 1982.

Burnham, Daniel H., and Edward H. Bennett. *Plan of Chicago,* ed. Charles Moore. Princeton, N.J.: Princeton Architectural Press, 1993.

Byrne, Jane. *My Chicago.* New York: W. W. Norton and Co., 1992.

Cahan, Richard. *They All Fall Down: Richard Nickel's Struggle to Save America's Architecture.* Washington D.C.: Preservation Press, 1994.

Caro, Robert. *The Power Broker: Robert Moses and the Fall of New York.* New York: Alfred A. Knopf, 1974.

Carstensen, Vernon, ed. *The Public Lands: Studies in the History of the Public Domain.* Madison: University of Wisconsin Press, 1962.

Chernow, Ron. *The House of Morgan: An American Banking Dynasty and the Rise of Modern Finance.* New York: Simon and Schuster, 1990.

Clark, Eric. *The Rent Gap and Urban Change.* Lund, Sweden: Lund University Press, 1987.

Cohen, Jean-Louis, and Andre Lortie. *Des Fortifs au Perif: Paris les Seuils de la Ville.* Paris: Picard Editeur, 1991.

Commons, John R. *Legal Foundations of Capitalism.* New York: Macmillan Co., 1924.

Condit, Carl. *Chicago 1930–70: Building, Planning, and Urban Technology.* Chicago: University of Chicago Press, 1974.

Cronon, William. *Nature's Metropolis: Chicago and the Great West.* New York: W. W. Norton and Co., 1991.

Cutler, Irving. *Chicago: Metropolis of the Mid-Continent.* Dubuque, Iowa: Kendall/Hunt Publishing Co., 1976.

Davis, Otto A., and Andrew B. Whinston. "The Economics of Urban Renewal." In *Urban Renewal: The Record and Controversy.* Ed. James Q. Wilson. Cambridge: MIT Press, 1966.

Downs, Anthony. *Urban Problems and Prospects.* Chicago: Markham Publishing Co., 1970.

Drake, St. Clair, and Horace R. Cayton. *Black Metropolis: A Study of Negro Life in a Northern City.* New York: Harcourt, Brace and Co., 1945.

Duesenberry, J. S., et al., eds. *The Brookings Quarterly Econometric Model of the United States.* Chicago: Rand McNally and Co., 1965.

Einhorn, Robin L. *Property Rules: Political Economy in Chicago, 1833–1872.* Chicago: University of Chicago Press, 1991.

Fainstein, Susan S. *The City Builders: Property, Politics, and Planning in London and New York.* Cambridge: Blackwell, 1994.

Farber, David. *Chicago '68.* Chicago: University of Chicago Press, 1988.

Feagin, John R., and Robert Parker. *Building American Cities: The Urban Real Estate Game.* Englewood Cliffs, N.J.: Prentice Hall, 1990.

Fisher, Glenn W. *Financing Government in the Chicago Area: An Overview.* Chicago: Center for Research in Urban Government, Loyola University, 1966.

Fisher, Robert Moore. *The Boom in Office Buildings: An Economic Study of the Past Two Decades, Technical Bulletin 58.* Washington, D.C.: Urban Land Institute, 1957.

Ford, George B. *Building Height, Bulk, and Form: How Zoning Can Be Used as a Protection Against Uneconomic Types of Buildings on High-Cost Land.* Cambridge: Harvard University Press, 1931.

Ford, Larry R. *Cities and Buildings: Skyscrapers, Skid Row, and Suburbs.* Baltimore: Johns Hopkins University Press, 1994.

Fosler, R. Scott, and Renee A. Berger. *Public-Private Partnership in American Cities: Seven Case Studies.* Lexington, Mass.: D. C. Heath and Co., 1982.

Foster, Peter. *Towers of Debt: The Rise and Fall of the Reichmanns.* Toronto: Key Porter Books Limited, 1993.

Fox, Kenneth. *Metropolitan America: Urban Life and Urban Policy in the United States, 1940–1980.* New Brunswick, N.J.: Rutgers University Press, 1990.

Frampton, Kenneth. *Modern Architecture: A Critical History.* New York: Oxford University Press, 1980.

Frieden, Bernard J., and Lynne B. Sagalyn. *Downtown, Inc.: How America Rebuilds Cities.* Cambridge: MIT Press, 1989.

Fuchs, Ester R. *Mayors and Money: Fiscal Policy in New York and Chicago.* Chicago: University of Chicago Press, 1992.

Garreau, Joel. *Edge City: Life on the New Frontier.* New York: Doubleday, 1991.

Gates, Paul W. *History of Public Land Law Development.* Washington, D.C.: Public Land Law Review Commission, 1968.

Gelfand, Mark I. *A Nation of Cities: The Federal Government and Urban America, 1933–1965.* New York: Oxford University Press, 1975.

Granger, Bill, and Lori Granger. *Fighting Jane: Mayor Jane Byrne and the Chicago Machine.* New York: Dial Press, 1980.

Grant, James. *Money of the Mind: Borrowing and Lending in America from the Civil War to Michael Milken.* New York: Farrar Straus Giroux, 1992.

Greer, Scott. *The Urbane View: Life and Politics in Metropolitan America.* New York: Oxford University Press, 1972.

Guterbock, Thomas M. *Machine Politics in Transition.* Chicago: University of Chicago Press, 1980.

Haar, Charles M., and Michael Allan Wolf. *Land-Use Planning: A Casebook on the Use, Misuse, and Re-use of Urban Land.* 4th ed. Boston: Little, Brown and Co., 1989.

Haar, Charles M., ed. *Law and Land: Anglo-American Planning Practices.* Cambridge: Harvard University Press, 1964.

Hall, Kermit L., ed. *United States Constitutional and Legal History.* New York: Garland Publishing, 1987.

Harris, Neil. "The City That Shops: Chicago's Retailing Landscape." In *Chicago Architecture and Design, 1923–1993.* Ed. John Zukowsky. Chicago: Art Institute of Chicago; Munich: Prestel-Verlag, 1993.

Harvey, David. *The Limits to Capital.* Chicago: University of Chicago Press, 1982.

———. *Social Justice and the City.* Baltimore: Johns Hopkins Press, 1973.

Hernstein, Richard J., and Charles Murray. *The Bell Curve.* New York: Free Press, 1994.

Hillman, Arthur, and Robert J. Casey. *Tomorrow's Chicago.* Chicago: University of Chicago Press, 1953.

Hirsch, Arnold R. *Making the Second Ghetto: Race and Housing in Chicago, 1940–60.* New York: Cambridge University Press, 1983.

Hoch, Charles, and Robert A. Slayton. *New Homeless and Old: Community and the Skid Row Hotel.* Philadelphia: Temple University Press, 1989.

Holland, Laurence B., ed. *Who Designs America?* Garden City, N.Y.: Doubleday and Company, 1966.

Holli, Melvin G., and Paul M. Green, eds. *The Making of the Mayor: Chicago 1983.* Grand Rapids, Mich.: William B. Eerdmans Publishing Co., 1984.

Hoover, Edgar M., and Raymond Vernon. *Anatomy of a Metropolis: The Changing*

Distribution of People and Jobs Within the New York Metropolitan Region. Cambridge: Harvard University Press, 1959.

Hoyt, Homer. *One Hundred Years of Land Values in Chicago: The Relationship of the Growth of Chicago to the Rise of Its Land Values, 1830–1933.* Chicago: University of Chicago Press, 1933.

Hurd, Richard M. *Principles of City Land Values.* New York: Real Estate Record Association, 1903.

Industrial Chicago: The Building Interests. Chicago: Goodspeed Publishing Co., 1891.

Jacobs, Jane. *The Economy of Cities.* New York: Random House, 1969.

Jahr, Alfred D. *Law of Eminent Domain: Valuation and Procedure.* New York: Clark Boardman Co., 1953.

Jones, Emrys. *Metropolis.* New York: Oxford University Press, 1990.

Kanfer, Stefan. *The Last Empire: De Beers, Diamonds and the World.* New York: Farrar, Straus and Giroux, 1993.

Kennedy, Eugene. *Himself: The Life and Times of Mayor Richard J. Daley.* New York: Viking Press, 1978.

Kindleberger, Charles P. *Manias, Panics, and Crashes: A History of Financial Crises.* Rev. ed. New York: Basic Books, 1989.

Kleppner, Paul. *Chicago Divided: The Making of a Black Mayor.* DeKalb: Northern Illinois University Press, 1985.

Koolhaas, Rem. *Delirious New York.* New York: Moncaelli Press, 1994.

Kotlowitz, Alex. *There Are No Children Here.* New York: Doubleday, 1991.

Kunstler, James Howard. *The Geography of Nowhere: The Rise and Decline of America's Man-Made Landscape.* New York: Simon and Schuster, 1993.

Larson, Gerald R. "Chicago's Loop, 1830–1890: A Tale of Two Grids." In *Fragments of Chicago's Past.* Ed. Pauline Saliga. Chicago: Art Institute of Chicago, 1990.

Lemann, Nicholas. *The Promised Land: The Great Black Migration and How It Changed America.* New York: Alfred A. Knopf, 1991.

Lewis, Michael. *Liar's Poker.* New York: W. W. Norton and Co., 1989.

Liebling, A. J. *Chicago: The Second City.* New York: Alfred A. Knopf, 1952.

Logan, John R., and Harvey L. Molotch. *Urban Fortunes: The Political Economy of Place.* Berkeley: University of California Press, 1987.

Lowe, Jeanne R. *Cities in a Race with Time: Progress and Poverty in America's Renewing Cities.* New York: Random House, 1967.

Mailer, Norman. *Miami and the Siege of Chicago.* New York: New American Library, 1968.

Mann, Seymour Z. *Chicago's War on Poverty.* Chicago: Center for Research in Urban Government. Loyola University, 1966.

Marciniak, Ed. *Reclaiming the Inner City.* Washington, D.C.: National Center for Urban Ethnic Affairs, 1986.

Marshall, Percy Johnson. *Rebuilding Cities.* Chicago: Aldine Publishing Co., 1966.

Mathewson, Joe. *Up Against Daley.* La Salle, Ill.: Open Court, 1974.

Mayer, Harold M., and Richard C. Wade. *Chicago: Growth of a Metropolis.* Chicago: University of Chicago Press, 1969.

Mayer, Martin. *The Bankers.* New York: Ballantine Books, 1974.

Meyerson, Martin, and Edward C. Banfield. *Politics, Planning, and the Public Interest.* New York: Free Press, 1955.

Mollenkopf, John H. *The Contested City.* Princeton, N.J.: Princeton University Press, 1983.

Moody, Walter D. *Wacker's Manual of the Plan of Chicago.* Chicago: Chicago Plan Commission, 1911.

Nelson, Richard L., and Frederick T. Aschman. *Real Estate and City Planning.* Englewood Cliffs, N.J.: Prentice Hall, 1957.

Pegg, Betsy. *Dreams, Money and Ambition: A History of Real Estate in Chicago.* Chicago: Chicago Real Estate Board, 1983.

Peterson, Paul E. *City Limits.* Chicago: University of Chicago Press, 1981.

Pierce, James L. *The Future of Banking.* New Haven, Conn.: Yale University Press, 1991.

Rabinowitz, Alan. *The Real Estate Gamble.* New York: AMACOM, 1980.

Rainwater, Lee. *Behind Ghetto Walls: Black Family Life in a Federal Slum.* Hawthorne, N.Y.: Aldine Publishing Co., 1970.

Rainwater, Lee, and William L. Yancey, eds. *The Moynihan Report and the Politics of Controversy.* Cambridge: MIT Press, 1967.

Rakove, Milton L. *Don't Make No Waves . . . Don't Back No Losers: An Insider's Analysis of the Daley Machine.* Bloomington: Indiana University Press, 1975.

———. *We Don't Want Nobody Nobody Sent: An Oral History of the Daley Years.* Bloomington: Indiana University Press, 1979.

Randall, Frank A. *History of the Development of Building Construction in Chicago.* Urbana: University of Illinois Press, 1949.

Relph, Edward. *The Modern Urban Landscape* Baltimore: Johns Hopkins University Press, 1987.

Report of the National Advisory Commission on Civil Disorders. New York: Bantam Books, 1968.

Reps, John W. *The Making of Urban America: A History of City Planning in the United States.* Princeton, N.J.: Princeton University Press, 1965.

Rivlin, Gary. *Fire on the Prairie: Chicago's Harold Washington and Politics of Race.* New York: Henry Holt and Co., 1992.

Rossi, Peter H., and Robert A. Dentler. *The Politics of Urban Renewal: The Chicago Findings.* New York: Free Press, 1961.

Rowe, Colin. *The Mathematics of the Ideal Villa and Other Essays.* Cambridge: MIT Press, 1976.

Royko, Mike. *Boss: Richard J. Daley of Chicago.* New York: E. P. Dutton, 1971.

Ruchelman, Leonard I., ed. *Big City Mayors: The Crisis in Urban Politics.* Bloomington: Indiana University Press, 1969.

St. John, Jeffrey. *Countdown to Chaos: Chicago, August 1968.* Los Angeles: Nash Publishing Corp., 1969.

Saliga, Pauline, and John Zukowsky. *The Sky's the Limit.* New York: Rizzoli, 1991.

Sassen, Saskia. *The Global City.* Princeton, N.J.: Princeton University Press, 1991.

Scargill, D. I. *The Form of Cities.* New York: St. Martin's Press, 1979.

Schultz, David A. *Property, Power, and American Democracy.* New Brunswick, N.J.: Transaction Publishers, 1992.

Schuyler, Montgomery. "A Critique of the Works of Adler and Sullivan." In *American Architecture and Other Writings.* Ed. William Jordy and Ralph Coe. Cambridge: Harvard University Press, 1961.

Sennett, Richard. *The Uses of Disorder: Personal Identity and City Life.* New York: Alfred A. Knopf, 1970.

Slayton, William. "Report on Urban Renewal." In *Urban Renewal: People, Planning and Politics.* Ed. Jewel Bellush and Murray Hausknecht. Garden City, N.Y.: Doubleday, 1967.

Smith, Neil. *Uneven Development: Nature, Capital and the Production of Space.* Oxford: Basil Blackwell, 1984.

Squires, Gregory D., et al. *Chicago: Race, Class, and the Response to Urban Decline.* Philadelphia: Temple University Press, 1987.

Stamper, John W. *Chicago's North Michigan Avenue: Planning and Development, 1900–1930.* Chicago: University of Chicago Press, 1991.

Stewart, Murray, ed. *The City: Problems of Planning.* Harmondsworth, Engl.: Penguin Books, 1972.

Suttles, Gerald D. *The Man-Made City: The Land-Use Confidence Game in Chicago.* Chicago: University of Chicago Press, 1990.

Trachtenberg, Alan. *The Incorporation of America: Culture and Society in the Gilded Age.* New York: Hill and Wang, 1982.

Tuohy, James, and Rob Warden. *Greylord: Justice, Chicago Style.* New York: G. P. Putnam's Sons, 1989.

Turner, Fredrick Jackson. *The Frontier in American History.* Malabar, Fla.: Robert E. Krieger Publishing Co., 1985.

Vance, James E., Jr. *The Continuing City: Urban Morphology in Western Civilization.* Baltimore: Johns Hopkins University Press, 1990.

Walsh, Annmarie Hauck. *The Public's Business: The Politics and Practices of Government Corporations.* Cambridge: MIT Press, 1978.

Warner, Sam Bass, Jr. *The Urban Wilderness: A History of the American City.* New York: Harper and Row, 1972.

Wendt, Lloyd, and Herman Kogan. *Lords of the Levee.* New York: Bobbs-Merrill, 1943.

Wilber, Charles K., ed. *The Political Economy of Development and Underdevelopment.* New York: Random House, 1973.

Wilson, James Q. *The Amateur Democrat: Club Politics in Three Cities.* Chicago: University of Chicago Press, 1962.

———, ed. *Urban Renewal: The Record and the Controversy.* Cambridge: MIT Press, 1966.

Wilson, William Julius. *The Truly Disadvantaged: The Inner City, the Underclass, and Public Policy.* Chicago: University of Chicago Press, 1987.

Wolf, Peter. *Land in America: Its Value, Use and Control.* New York: Pantheon Books, 1981.

Yergin, Daniel. *The Prize: The Epic Quest for Oil, Money and Power.* New York: Simon and Schuster, 1991.

Zorbaugh, Harvey W. *The Gold Coast and the Slum.* Chicago: University of Chicago Press, 1929.

SELECTED ARTICLES
AND DOCUMENTS

Berss, Marcia. "Tale of Two Syndicators." *Forbes 400,* Oct. 22, 1990.

Blumenfeld, H. "The Economic Base of the Metropolis." *Journal of the American Institute of Planners,* no. 21 (Fall 1955).

"BNA's Banking Report." *Bureau of Nation Affairs, Inc.* 54, no. 7 (Feb. 19, 1990).

Chicago 21: A Plan for the Central Area Communities, Sept. 1973.

Cohen, Michael. "The Urban Interest." *Historic Preservation and Public Policy: The Case of Chicago* (Fall 1980).

Copetas, A. Craig. "How the Barbarians Do Business." *Harper's*, Jan. 1984.

Cross, Robert. "The Loop: Love It or Leave It." *Chicago Tribune Magazine*, Feb. 20, 1972.

Crump, Joseph. "Less Is Skidmore." *Chicago*, Feb. 1991.

Despres, Leon M. "Corruption in Chicago." *The Nation*, Mar. 12, 1960.

Downs, Anthony. "What Have We Learned from the 1980s Experience?" *Real Estate Investment*. (Solomon Brothers report), July 1991.

Drucker, Peter F. "The Age of Social Transformation." *Atlantic Monthly* 274, no. 3 (Nov. 1994).

Du Bois, Peter C. "The International Trader." *Barron's*, Oct. 8, 1990.

Duggar, George S. *The New Renewal*. Berkeley, Calif.: Bureau of Public Administration, 1961.

Eastwood, Carolyn. *Chicago's Jewish Street Peddlers*. Chicago: Chicago Jewish Historical Society, 1991.

Gittleson, Steven. "The Battle over Charles Swibel." *Chicago*, July 1982.

Gottmann, Jean. "Why the Skyscraper?" *Geographical Review* 56 (1966).

Hauser, Philip M. *Integration of the Public Schools: Chicago 1964*. Chicago: Advisory Panel on Integration of the Public Schools, Mar. 31, 1964.

Hazard, Leland. "Are We Committing Urban Suicide?" *Harvard Business Review* 41 (May/June 1963).

Heilbroner, Robert. "Reflections: Economic Predictions." *New Yorker*, July 8, 1991.

Hill, Lewis W. *The People of Chicago: Who We Are and Who We Have Been*. Chicago: Department of Development and Planning, 1976.

Hoyt, Homer. "The Urban Real Estate Cycle Performances and Prospects." *Urban Land Institute Technical Bulletin*, no. 38 (June 1960).

Kahn, E. J., Jr. "Big Operator." *New Yorker*, Dec. 8, 1951, and Dec. 15, 1951.

Krohe, James, Jr. "Cityscape: The Rise and Fall of Michigan Ave." *Chicago Reader*, Sept. 27, 1991.

Laing, Jonathan R. "On Shaky Ground: The Slump in Real Estate Hits JMB." *Barron's*, July 27, 1992.

Lindeman, Bruce. "Anatomy of Land Speculation." *Journal of the American Institute of Planners* 42 (Apr. 1976).

Mahar, Maggie. "The Great Collapse: Commercial Real Estate Is on the Skids across the Nation." *Barron's*, July 22, 1991.

Manners, Gerald. "The Office in Metropolis: An Opportunity for Shaping Metropolitan America." *Economic Geography* 50, no. 2 (Apr. 1974).

Mokate, Karen Marie. "The Office Construction Boom and Slowdown." *Illinois Business Review* 40, no. 3 (June 1983).

Report of the Chicago Riot Study Committee to the Hon. Richard J. Daley, Chicago: Chicago Riot Study Committee, Aug. 1, 1968.

Schlereth, Thomas J. "Moody's Go-Getting Wacker Manual." *Inland Architect* 24, no. 3 (April 1980).

Shapiro, Beatrice Michaels. *Memories of Lawndale*. Chicago: Chicago Jewish Historical Society, 1991.

Smith, Neil. "Toward a Theory of Gentrification: A Back to the City Movement by Capital, Not People." *Journal of the American Planning Association* 45 (Oct. 1979).

Smith, Neil, Betsy Duncan, and Laura Reid. "From Disinvestment to Reinvestment: Tax Arrears and Turning Points in the East Village." *Housing Studies* 4, no. 4 (1989).

Tamarkin, Bob. "Condomania in Chicago." *Forbes,* Nov. 13, 1978.

Walker, Ralph A. "Urban Ground Rent: Building a New Conceptual Framework." *Antipode* 6, no. 1 (1974).

Ward, Richard C. "The Enduring Chicago Machine." *Chicago History* 15, no. 1 (Spring 1986).

Weimer, Arthur M. "Investors and Downtown Real Estate—Opinion and Comment." *Urban Land Institute Bulletin* 39 (Nov. 1960).

Weiner, Steve. "Everything's Negotiable." *Forbes,* Mar. 19, 1990.

Whalen, Richard J. "A City Destroying Itself." *Fortune,* Sept. 1964.

White, J. Keith. "Evolution on State Street: The Story of the Capitol Building." *Real Estate,* Feb. 24, 1940.

Zoll, Stephen. "Superville: New York—Aspects of Very High Bulk." *Massachusetts Review* 14, no. 3 (Summer 1973).

INDEX

ILLUSTRATION CREDITS